The Philadelphia Campaign

The Philadelphia Campaign

◆ VOLUME I ◆

Brandywine and the Fall of Philadelphia

THOMAS J. MCGUIRE

STACKPOLE
BOOKS

Published by
STACKPOLE BOOKS
5067 Ritter Road
Mechanicsburg, PA 17055
www.stackpolebooks.com

Printed in the United States of America

1 3 5 7 9 10 8 6 4 2

FIRST EDITION

Library of Congress Cataloging-in-Publication Data

McGuire, Thomas J.
    The Philadelphia Campaign / Thomas J. McGuire.
      p.   cm.
    Includes bibliographical references and index.
    ISBN-13: 978-0-8117-0178-5 (hardcover : alk. paper)
    ISBN-10: 0-8117-0178-6 (hardcover : alk. paper)
    1. Philadelphia (Pa.)–History–Revolution, 1775-1783. 2. Pennsylvania–
History–Revolution, 1775-1783–Campaigns. 3. Maryland–History–Revolution,
1775-1783–Campaigns. 4. Delaware–History–Revolution, 1775-1783–
Campaigns. 5. United States–History–Revolution, 1775-1783–British forces.
6. United States–History–Revolution, 1775-1783–Campaigns. I. Title.

E233.M3   2006
973.3'33–dc22

2006010732

For Mom
With love and thanks

CONTENTS

ACKNOWLEDGMENTS

I thank the following institutions and individuals for their assistance in this work: in the United Kingdom, the British National Archives (formerly the Public Record Office) at Kew; Capt. David Horn of the Guards Museum, London; Mr. and Mrs. Oliver Russell of Ballindalloch Castle for use of the Grant Papers; Lord Howick of Howick Hall for use of Lord Cantelupe's diary; Durham University Library; the King's Map Collection at Windsor Castle, especially Martin Clayton; Sir Richard Osborn, Bt., and Sarah Saunders-Davies, for their constant support, encouragement, and friendship; Col. Graeme Hazlewood of the Royal Logistics Corps; Andrew Cormack of the *Journal of Army Historical Research*, for opening many doors, especially at "the Castle"; Robert Winup, for his help with newspaper research; John Mackenzie of Britishbattles.com.

Back home, thanks are due to the Historical Society of Pennsylvania; the Chester County Historical Society and the Chester County Archives, especially Diane and Laurie Rofini; the Lancaster County Historical Society; the Manuscript Department and Map Department of the Library of Congress, especially Ed Redmond; Col. J. Craig Nannos (Ret., PNG/USA) and Bruce Baky, two great history colleagues; the Clements Library, especially John Dann; the New York Public Library; the Maryland Historical Society; the Historical Society of Delaware, especially Dr. Connie Cooper, for her constant help and endless good humor; Lee Boyle, former historian at the Valley Forge National Historical Park Library; and Joe Seymour of the First City Troop.

The David Library of the American Revolution at Washington's Crossing deserves special mention, not only as an extraordinary depository of primary materials on the Revolution, but also for its excellent staff, especially Kathy Ludwig and Greg Johnson, as well as former directors Dave Ludwig and Dave Fowler, who made working there a joy.

Thanks also to my good friend and mentor, David McCullough, for his enthusiasm, advice, and encouragement; Kyle Weaver, my editor and friend, for providing the opportunity to make this book a reality and a labor of love, and his team of professionals, particularly copyeditor Joyce Bond and production editor Amy Cooper, for their tireless work; and to my wife, Susan, who has kept me going through thick and thin—mostly thick!

"Remember what our Father oft has told us:
The Ways of Heav'n are dark and intricate;
Puzzled in Mazes, and perplex'd with Errors;
Our Understanding traces 'em in vain,
Lost and bewilder'd in the fruitless Search;
Nor sees with how much Art the Windings run,
Nor where the Regular Confusion ends."

—Joseph Addison, *Cato*, act I, scene I

PROLOGUE

On a warm September morning in a southeastern Pennsylvania school-room many years ago, a little girl named Sally Frazer couldn't concentrate on her lessons. The atmosphere was tense, the air thick and still as the sun burned off the early-morning haze, the type of weather that always makes students listless. It had been a terribly hot summer, especially in August, when the thunderstorms were memorable for their violence.

But there was something else, something ominous in the air, for through the open windows of the schoolroom, what at first sounded like occasional rumbles of thunder from a distant storm steadily grew louder and more unsettling, and nine-year-old Sally wondered what it could mean. Her little brother Robert, who had just turned six, and her sister Mary Anne, who was not quite four years old, were in school too, and she worried about them. She also wondered about her daddy and if he was all right.

The day was Thursday, September 11, about nine o'clock in the morning, and Sally's teacher went out of the room for some time, then came back in and said, "There is a battle not far off, children you may go home." The place was Thornbury Township, Chester County, Pennsylvania, the year 1777. The noise was the thunder of cannon from the Battle of Brandywine, less than ten miles away.

Sally and the others hurried home, and near their house on Chester Creek, the Frazer children met their mother on horseback. Mary "Polly" Worrall Frazer was thirty-two years old and the mother of four; her youngest was just over eighteen months. She was also now one month pregnant. Polly knew exactly what the noise meant, and she was coming to make sure that her children were safe. Once they were home, Polly galloped west toward her mother's house in the direction of Chads's Ford and the sound of battle. She knew that her husband Percy was going to be in the thick of it.[1]

Several miles away to the north, in another classroom, nine-year-old Tommy Cope couldn't concentrate on his schoolwork either, and for the same reason: the noise. He was in school near the Turk's Head Tavern in Goshen Township, learning the sums and letters that would serve him well later in life when he became one of Philadelphia's most prominent merchants and the head of a global shipping company, the Cope Packet Line. He, too, had a younger brother, seven-year-old Israel, with him at school. "We were within hearing of the battle, even to the small arms," Cope recalled. "Our teacher was sadly alarmed & the scholars but little at ease."[2] Tommy also may have wondered about his older friend John, who had played marbles with him the year before and had given him a watercolor picture as a present, for John, too, was in the battle.

Both Sally Frazer and Tommy Cope were children in Chester County, Pennsylvania, on September 11, 1777, the day of the Battle of Brandywine. Sally, whose real name was Sarah, lived for sixty-four more years and Thomas for more than seventy-five years after the battle. Neither Sarah nor Thomas played any part in the planning or the fighting, but both were directly affected by it and never forgot it. Their world was forever changed by the American Revolution, and Brandywine was one of the largest battles of that war.

They shared a common experience that remained with them for the rest of their lives, even though they were very different. Sarah lived with her parents in Thornbury Township, about eight miles east of Chads's Ford; Thomas was living with his aunt and uncle in East Bradford Township, about eight miles north of Chads's Ford. Sarah's family was of English and Scottish Presbyterian background and was fully committed to the Revolution; Thomas's family was English Quaker and pacifist. The Frazers owned three slaves; the Copes were appalled by slavery.

Sarah's father, a native of Chester County, was a farmer, ironmaster, businessman, and soldier: Lt. Col. Persifor Frazer of the 5th Pennsylvania Regiment, who at that moment was stationed several hundred yards behind Chads's Ford in the center of the Continental Army's line of defense. Thomas's father, Caleb Cope, was also born in Chester County but had since moved to the city of Lancaster and was a well-to-do craftsman, a plasterer who, along with the Quakers in general, was suspected of being a Loyalist.

Earlier in the war, the Cope family in Lancaster had hosted an artistic and very charming young British officer, Capt. John André of the 7th Royal Fusilier Regiment, who was a prisoner of war captured in Canada in November 1775. This was Tommy's friend John, who had played marbles with him and gave him the watercolor.[3] Of André, Cope later wrote, "I have always been accustomed to regard him with the affection of a brother." The officer had become so close to Tommy's older brother John that when André was exchanged, fourteen-year-old Johnny Cope ran away and tried to follow him to New York. Caleb went after his son, and "John suffered the mortification of being brought back & the bitter anguish of seeing his schemes of future greatness & happiness blighted by what he deemed a cruel interposition of parental authority."[4]

Since the beginning of the war, Lancaster, which was then the largest inland city in America, had been filled with militiamen, supplies, suppliers, politicians, and hundreds of British and Hessian prisoners of war. The city also drew prostitutes, thieves, and the usual assortment of less-than-honorable opportunists and profiteers, described at the time as "scoundrels, rogues, caitiffs, and rascals," words that have softened in meaning over the centuries but were by no means quaint or cute at the time. "It was the hotbed of dissipation," Thomas Cope recalled in his polished, nineteenth-century phraseology, "rendered more rank & offensive by the prevalence of the war & the pestiferous vices which grew out of it."[5] To get some of his sons away from the influence of the military, Caleb Cope sent young Thomas and Israel to live with Uncle Nathan at the Cope ancestral homestead in East Bradford Township, Chester County, a comfortable Quaker farming community in the Brandywine Valley about halfway between Philadelphia and Lancaster, a place so remote as to be thought safe from the bad influences brought on by the war.

But now a parent's worst nightmare was in the offing: children, sent to a safe place, ending up in a battle zone.

The Philadelphia Campaign is a story about people—soldiers and civilians, husbands and wives, mothers, fathers, and children—all of whom shared a common experience in the American War for Independence. It is a story of battles and politics, valor and cowardice, life and death, told largely by those who experienced it. It is a tale of when war came through America and the nation's future was in question.

Scholarship continues to open new windows into the past, and each window, however small, has a story to tell. Surprises, too, abound as new material comes to light from family letters, forgotten documents, and misplaced diaries. Research for this work uncovered two small watercolors in the diary of a British officer, Lord Cantelupe, which have significance far beyond their size and art quality. They are the only two known images done while the British Army was in the field, and the depiction of *A Rebel Battery on the Heights of Brandywine* is the only known contemporary image of the Battle of Brandywine rendered by a participant. The two paintings are also the earliest known images of the Chester County landscape, made nearly a century after the county was founded.

Working with eighteenth-century documents is a labor of love and a great challenge because of the orthography—grammar, spelling, and punctuation. Formal English writing of the period did have well-established rules of grammar and spelling, as is evident by documents written by university-trained clerks, but much of the common writing is archaic, with random spellings, sometimes written phonetically in dialect or accent; poor grammar; and abysmal punctuation, with dashes often serving as commas, colons, or periods. I have retained as much of the original form of the writings as possible to retain the flavor of the period, making changes only where needed to clarify meaning and adding or removing punctuation when necessary to avoid confusion. I have kept bracketed interpolations to a minimum, as they tend to be distracting; scholars are encouraged to seek the original sources listed in the notes.

As Sally Frazer and Tommy Cope learned that morning, the world beyond the schoolroom can be a stormy place.

CHAPTER I

"This unhappy Country, This Country, turned Topsy Turvy."

NORTHERN NEW JERSEY,
WINTER–SPRING 1777

The revelation from the British secretary of state was disturbing and most distressing, part of a growing trend: "I cannot guess by Sir Wm. Howe's letter when he will begin his operations, or where he proposes carrying them on," Lord George Germain confessed to Undersecretary William Knox in late June 1777. "I incline to hope that his preparations are in greater forwardness," he continued, in a letter filled with misgivings. Two weeks earlier, Germain had told the undersecretary "he hoped that Balfour"—Maj. Nisbet Balfour, one of General Howe's aides—"will have convinced Sir Wm. Howe that he distresses us by not communicating his ideas more frequently and more explicitly."

The American Revolution—"this unnatural rebellion," as the Tories called it—was dragging into its third summer, and the Tory minister in London most responsible for directing the war effort of His Majesty's government had no idea what the commander in chief of His Majesty's forces in America planned to do next to end it.

Lack of communication, lack of coordination, and reliance on wildly inaccurate information all played a part. "I hope the *New York Gazette* gives us in general true accounts," the secretary of state said of a Tory newspaper so filled with distortions and blatant propaganda that even he recognized its limitations. "I am sorry to see such falsehoods inserted with regard to the expected reinforcements. I wonder those who inspect the paper do not prevent such notorious blunders, as it must bring discredit upon the rest of the intelligence." With lame optimism, Germain concluded, "I shall be glad of an opportunity of applauding the General's conduct this campaign."[1]

The Philadelphia Campaign officially began in June 1777, six months after the Battles of Trenton and Princeton. Those battles, small as they were in military terms, had had a massive impact politically and psychologically on both sides. For the Americans, the two victories brought life back into the fight for independence after four months of defeat and near collapse. "Am happy in acquainting you that we have return'd from Trenton after defeating the Brass Caps," Capt. Thomas Forrest of the Philadelphia Artillery crowed, referring to the distinctive metal headgear of the captured Hessian grenadiers. "We have taken, exclusive of what were not able to march off, 946, with a Compleat band of Musick."[2]

For the Crown Forces, the defeats were demoralizing and divisive, with much finger-pointing and acrimony behind the scenes between British officers, who privately blamed the Hessians for incompetence, and Hessian commanders, who were embarrassed by the Trenton disaster and privately blamed the British for a badly run campaign. Gen. James Grant, the British commander in New Jersey at the time of Trenton, admitted that "the misbehaviour of the Hessian Brigade revived the drooping spirits of the Rebells and has rekindled the half extinguished Flame of Rebellion."[3] Of the British defeat at Princeton, a senior Hessian field commander, Col. Count Karl von Donop, wrote, "Mr. Washington, who always had certain warnings of our least movements . . . surprised the Princeton garrison, and we would have had une *Affaire Trentownienne* if this place had not been advantageously situated on a height."[4]

The one thing on which the British and German officers could agree was blaming the now-deceased commander of the Trenton outpost, Col. Johann Rall, for failure to follow orders. Sir George Osborn, captain of the Grenadier Company of the Brigade of Guards, who was also "Mustermaster-General and Inspector of the Foreign Troops, and a lieutenant-colonel in the army," told his fellow members of the House of Commons some time later "that he lived in a degree of friendship with Col. Donop, and very frequently after the misfortune at Trenton, Donop acquainted Sir George, that if Col. Rall had executed the orders Sir George delivered to him from Sir W. Howe, to erect redoubts at the post of Trenton, his opinion was, it would have been impossible to have forced [defeated] Col. Rall's brigade before he (Donop) could have come to his assistance."[5]

"It is the Damnd Hessians that has caused this," Nicholas Cresswell, an English civilian visiting America, wrote venomously in mid-January. "Curse the scoundrel that first thought of sending them here." Trapped in Virginia by the war and surrounded by enemies, Cresswell had to hold his tongue in public, for "Poor General Howe is ridiculed in all companies and all my countrymen abused. I am obliged to hear this daily and dare not speak a word in their favour." He noted with bitter sarcasm, "Now the scale is turned and Washington's name is extolled to the clouds. Alexander, Pompey and Hannibal were but pigmy generals, in comparison with the magnanimous Washington."[6]

His back to the wall, Washington had saved the Revolution with an army that had technically ceased to exist. *The Annual Register*, a British publication edited by Whig leader Edmund Burke and dedicated to recording the history of each year based on primary documents, concluded, "Thus by a few well concerted and spirited actions, was Philadelphia saved, Pennsylvania freed from danger, the Jerseys nearly recovered, and a victorious and far superior army reduced to act upon the defensive." Concerning the effect that the battles had on Washington's reputation, "These actions, and the sudden recovery from the lowest state of weakness and distress, to become a formidable enemy in the field, raised the character of General Washington, as a commander, very high both in Europe and America," the *Register* noted with some admiration, and "gives a sanction to that appellation, which is now pretty generally applied to him, of the American Fabius."[7]

Fabius (Quintus Fabius Maximus, ca. 275–203 B.C.) was a Roman general who fought against Hannibal by avoiding large battles, relying instead on attrition and "wasting" the enemy through harassment. Allusions to ancient history and classical figures like Fabius, Hannibal, Pompey, and Cato were common on both sides during the American Revolution. Roman history, in fact, was foremost among the literati in Britain in 1777 as a result of the publication of a monumental book by Edward Gibbon in 1776. "We do not remember any work published in our time, which has met with a more general approbation than Mr. Gibbon's *History of the Decline and Fall of the Roman Empire*," trumpeted *The Annual Register for 1776* when the first volume appeared. "We are happy in adding our suffrage to the public voice, which has so justly declared in its favour."[8] Gibbon himself commented, "My book was on every table, and almost on every toilette."[9] In the eighteenth-century world of great struggles for empire in Europe and elsewhere, comparisons with ancient Greece and Rome were not only fashionable, but inevitable.

"It was the Wisdom of Fabius to put himself in the State of Defence but by no means of Inactivity," Samuel Adams told Gen. Nathanael Greene, one of Washington's most reliable commanders, a few months after Princeton. Alluding to Fabian tactics, the Massachusetts congressman wrote, "By keeping a watchful Eye upon Hannibal and cutting off his forraging & other Parties by frequent Skirmishes he had the strongest Reason to promise himself the Ruin of his army without any Necessity of risqueing his own by a general Engagement."[10]

For the remainder of the winter of 1777, the two forces settled into winter quarters, and low-level Fabian tactics became routine. Popular histories of the war tend to gloss over the nine months after Princeton, for besides what at first glance appear to be inconclusive skirmishes and pointless maneuvers, nothing "major" happened—except the recovery and rebuilding of the American Revolution and the Continental Army after its near extinction in the 1776 campaign. Washington's true leadership abilities were often put to their fullest test during the obscure times of the war, holding the cause and the army together through the long periods of attrition, when they were neglected by the nation and Congress. After Princeton, "General Washington, with the little remnant of his army at Morristown, seemed left to scuffle for liberty, like another Cato at Utica," Capt. Alexander Graydon, a Pennsylvania officer, wrote of this period.[11]

The British Army's general headquarters was in New York City, but its main post in the field was New Brunswick, New Jersey, a provincial trading town on the Raritan River, with outposts between the Raritan and Perth Amboy, the capital of East Jersey. Capt. Johann Ewald of the Hessian Jäger Corps, an elite unit of German marksmen, wrote that New Brunswick "consisted of about four hundred houses, partly deserted and partly destroyed," and was occupied by "the two battalions of English grenadiers under Colonel Monckton, the four battalions of Hessian grenadiers under Colonel Donop, the two English brigades under General Grant, the artillery, and the 16th Regiment of Light Dragoons."[12]

Six months earlier, New Brunswick had been a thriving port, its handsome buildings a colorful mix of Dutch and English Colonial architecture. It became a rendezvous point for American forces arriving from

Pennsylvania and points farther south, volunteers who had streamed by the thousands toward New York City in the heady days after independence was declared. It was here in a crowded tavern on September 10, 1776, that John Adams and Benjamin Franklin, on their way to Staten Island for a peace conference with Admiral Lord Howe (the general's brother), provided a memorable scene when they shared a bed in a small, stuffy room and argued over the merits of fresh air, the two great leaders alternately opening and shutting the window.

But the fortunes of war turned rapidly, and within a matter of weeks New Brunswick suffered abandonment by the Americans, evacuation by many of its residents, and occupation by the Crown Forces, along with pilfering and plundering committed by troops from both sides and the lawless elements thrown up by war. Now, in early 1777, it became the main base for His Majesty's forces in New Jersey, an island of British control in a sea of uncertainty and danger.

In reaction to the Trenton debacle, which the British blamed on lax security by the Hessians, New Brunswick was guarded by fortifications and outposts of elite units. Lt. Gen. Charles Earl Cornwallis was placed in command. "Since this place lies in a valley surrounded by hills, several redoubts and flèches were erected to cover the approaches from South Amboy, Princetown, and Millstone," Captain Ewald explained. "The two light infantry battalions, under Lieutenant Colonel Abercromby, cantoned in the houses above Brunswick at the Raritan bridge and occupied the approaches from Hillsborough and Bound Brook. Lord Cornwallis's brigade, under Colonel Webster, cantoned in and around Bonhamtown." Across the Raritan:

> The 42nd Scottish Regiment had occupied Piscataway, adjoining the English brigade under General Leslie, which cantoned on the plantations up to Raritan Landing. The English Guards Brigade cantoned at the landing, and Chevalier [Sir George] Osborn with three hundred grenadiers occupied the outlying houses where the road runs to Quibbletown and Bound Brook. Captain Wreden and the Donop Jäger Company, and the twelve mounted Jägers under Captain Lorey, were stationed at a plantation on the road to Bound Brook in front of the English grenadiers."[13]

Superseding Grant as commander in New Jersey, Lord Cornwallis settled in for the winter. "But surely ye force you have now at Brunswick is full sufficient to drive Washington to ye devil if you could get at him," Howe had chided Grant from the comforts of New York on January 9. "An army you will know does not go into Cantonments to fight, but with an intention to be left quiet."[14]

Washington's situation was desperate, almost beyond belief. After Princeton, he took the remains of his forces into the Watchung Mountains of north-central New Jersey, with general headquarters at Morristown. Who was left? A handful of volunteers, mainly Associators from Pennsylvania, together with militia from parts of New Jersey and a few die-hard Continental regulars who stayed with the commander in chief beyond their term of enlistment. More than 90 percent of the force he had had in New York six months earlier—over 20,000 men—was gone: dead, sick, or in ghastly New York prisons, while thousands of others deserted or went home when their time was up.

The Continental Army had been authorized by Congress in 1776 for one year, and the soldiers' enlistments expired at midnight on December 31 of that year. Congress would have to authorize a new army and once more begin the endless task of finding the wherewithal to equip it. Additionally, the army's basic organizational structure had to be drastically altered, with enlistments extended to three years or "during the war," and a more professional arrangement was needed for the officer corps.

In the meantime, Washington became a master of illusion by moving his few available troops from place to place and ordering them into action: sniping, ambushes, alarming British outposts—anything to give the appearance of numbers and to keep the Crown Forces off balance and agitated. "The two Companies under Command of Col. Durkee, aided by the militia of that Quarter should be constantly harassing the Enemy about Bound Brook and the westroad side of Brunswick," he wrote to his adjutant general, Col. Joseph Reed of Pennsylvania, on January 17. "I have directed Genl. Sullivan to do the like on the quarter next him." Regarding Gen. William Winds of the New Jersey Militia, Washington wrote, "I recollect of my approving of Wind[s's] waylaying of the Roads between Brunswick and Amboy." He asked Reed, "Would it not be well for the Militia under Colo. Malcolm to unite with the Rangers for the purpose of keeping out constant scouts to annoy and harass the enemy in manner before mentioned?"[15]

Militiamen were not regular soldiers; they were citizen-soldiers called up for military service in times of emergency. Because of their general lack of training and discipline, the militia were frequently a problem, and yet they were indispensable. Too often they were the only forces available. In most states, they were drafted for home defense only and for short tours of duty, usually sixty days.

Some militia companies were well drilled, uniformed, and properly equipped, but most were not. Pennsylvania did not even have a government-sponsored militia system until early 1777, for the prewar government had refused to authorize one. Instead, units of volunteer Associators had provided defense for the province since the 1740s, and in 1776, hundreds of Associators had formed battalions to fight alongside the Continental regulars. Ironically, the three battalions of Philadelphia Associators, as well as the Philadelphia Artillery and the Philadelphia Troop of Light Horse, were among the few units on active duty in 1776 and 1777 that were properly uniformed, equipped, and fairly well drilled. However, they were not under the Pennsylvania government's jurisdiction in 1776, and they were not enlisted in the Continental Army.

Chaos resulted from this arcane arrangement as companies of volunteers came and went, sometimes without so much as a by-your-leave. "The misfortune of short enlistments, and an unhappy dependence upon militia, have shown their baneful influence at every period, and almost upon every occasion, throughout the whole course of this war," an exasperated Washington wrote in late January. "At no time, nor upon no occasion, were they ever more exemplified than since Christmas . . . all of our movements have been made with inferior numbers, and with a mixed, motley crew, who were here to-day, gone to-morrow." Continually frustrated by uncertain and undependable forces, he continued, "In a word, I believe I may with truth add, that I do not think that any officer since the creation ever had such a variety of difficulties and perplexities to encounter as I have. How we shall be able to rub along till the new army is raised, I know not. Providence has heretofore saved us in a remarkable manner, and on this we must principally rely."[16]

The British response to American harassment was lethargic, which puzzled the American commander. "The Enemy must be ignorant of our Numbers, or they have not Horses to move their Artillery," Washington told Congress in late January, "or they would not Suffer us to remain undisturbed."[17]

The British Army had its own command-and-control problems, in part a result of the employment of "the Foreign Troops." The British government had signed treaties with six German states to hire soldiers: Hesse-Cassel, Hesse-Hanau, Anhalt-Zerbst, Anspach-Brandenburg, Waldeck, and Braunschweig (Brunswick). The majority of German soldiers with Howe's forces were from Hesse-Cassel, so they are collectively referred to as Hessians, but there were also Waldeckers and Anspachers who arrived later in the spring, each of whom had to be dealt with separately. But the most serious problem here for British commanders was the fact that the foreign troops were not directly subject to British military discipline, and they not only ignored Howe's orders that forbade plundering or marauding, but also plundered indiscriminately—from rebels, Loyalists, and neutrals alike—thus infuriating the entire American population.

In February 1777, a New York Loyalist told a friend in England about the strange turn the war had taken. "For these two months, or nearly, have we been boxed about in *Jersey*," he wrote. Who in England could possibly imagine that "our cantonments have been beaten up; our foraging parties attacked, sometimes defeated, and the forage carried off from us; all traveling between the posts hazardous; and in short, the troops harassed beyond measure by continual duty"? Astonished and dismayed, the Loyalist added, "Yet the friends to government have been worse used by these troops than by the rebels. Plundering, and destroying property, without distinction, have been practiced."[18]

As muster master general of the foreign troops, thirty-five-year-old Sir George Osborn was required to keep track of the numbers and condition of the Germans and make frequent reports about them to Lord George Germain, who passed them on to the prime minister and the king. He did his job so well and so thoroughly that King George III, after reading some of the reports, wrote a terse note to the prime minister, saying, "Lord North—I return the letters received from Sir G. Osborn, who seems to write with his usual desire of giving every information that he can acquire."[19]

Sir George was the fourth Baronet Osborn, a title bestowed on the Osborn family by King Charles II more than 100 years earlier at the

Restoration. Born in 1745, George was the eldest son of Sir Danvers Osborn, who died tragically after becoming governor of New York in 1753.[20] A personal friend of George III, Groom of His Majesty's Bedchamber, Member of Parliament for Bedfordshire, grandson of the first Lord Halifax and nephew of the second, cousin of Lord North, and nephew of Sir John Burgoyne, Sir George was not only well connected, but also much respected in the army and at court.

The previous October, Osborn had told Lord Germain, "The Circumstance of Plunder is the only Thing I believe gives Trouble or Uneasiness to General Howe with respect to the foreign Troops." He continued, apprehensively, "It is that which I much fear No public Orders can ever reclaim, as the Hessian Troops even in their own Country could never be restrained from the Crime of Morauding More or less, and they were unfortunately led to believe before they Left the Province of Hesse Cassel, that they were to come to America to establish their private Fortunes, and hitherto they have certainly acted with that Principle."[21]

Part of the problem lay in the chain of command. The Hessian commander was sixty-nine-year-old Lt. Gen. Leopold Philip von Heister, who did not speak or understand English. Osborn did not speak or understand German; communication between British and Hessian officers was usually done in French, the international military language of Europe.[22] Not until November 1776 did Howe acquire a multilingual aide on his staff, Capt. Levin Friedrich Ernst von Münchhausen of the von Minnegerode Regiment, who revealed, "General Heister was very pleased with [my appointment] because he had often received oral and written English orders, which he did not understand."[23]

Despite this, Hessians on plundering parties could always plead ignorance to English verbal orders or printed protection papers issued to Loyalists from Howe's headquarters. Even Gen. James Grant, who repeatedly advocated draconian measures to crush the Americans, *all* Americans, was moved to comment, "Heisters Corps behaves well, but plunders a great deal too much, & it will not be Easy to put a stop to the Abuse."[24] According to another British officer, Lt. William Hale of the 45th Regiment, von Heister himself was largely to blame. His successor, "Gen. Knyphausen who is said to be one of the best Generals in Germany," Hale wrote in 1778, "has by the severity of his discipline in a great measure put a stop to the infamous practice of plundering, which was much encouraged by De Heister who shared in the profits of this lucrative occupation."[25]

Plundering caused numerous problems. It not only damaged relations with the local people, but also threatened discipline within the army itself. "There is not an officer in the world who is ignorant, that permitting the soldier to plunder, or maraud, must inevitably destroy him," wrote John Graves Simcoe, a British grenadier captain in 1777 who later commanded the Loyalist Queen's Rangers. Simcoe correctly observed "that, in a civil war, it must alienate the large body of people who, in such a contest, are desirous of neutrality, and sour their minds into dissatisfaction." That was easy enough to see; "but," Simcoe quickly added, "however obvious the necessity may be, there is nothing more difficult than for a commander in chief to prevent marauding."[26] Although General Howe had issued a number of orders and proclamations throughout the 1776 campaign forbidding his soldiers to plunder on pain of death, British troops saw Hessians plundering without restraint, and some followed suit.

Those British officers who were repelled by such practices often felt overwhelmed by the scale of the looting, and if they tried to interfere, they were sometimes were threatened by the men. Howe's deputy adjutant general, Lt. Col. Stephen Kemble, was a native of New Jersey and had important family connections in New York. He had served in the British Army in America with his brother-in-law Gen. Thomas Gage since 1757. Kemble noticed a disturbing and very dangerous reality associated with plundering while the army was near White Plains, New York, the previous November: "8 or 10 of our People taken [i.e., captured while] Marauding; Scandalous behaviour for British Troops; and the Hessians Outrageously Licentious, and Cruel to such a degree as to threaten with death all such as dare obstruct them in their depredations. Violence to Officers frequently used, and every Degree of Insolence offered." With trepidation for his home province, he added, "Shudder for Jersey, the Army being thought to move there Shortly."[27]

At the same time, there were some British officers who boasted of their plundering exploits. Lt. Martin Hunter of the 52nd Regiment was a young officer in the regiment's light infantry company, part of a unit that was always "on the point," assigned to outpost duty or on patrol. He and twelve of his fellow junior officers in the 2nd Light Infantry Battalion spent the winter of 1777 at New Brunswick crammed in a two-room house with a Loyalist family, the officers all sleeping on straw in one room while the men slept in barns. Perhaps it was his youth—Hunter was nineteen years old, and many of the junior officers in the British Army were about the same age, some considerably younger—or perhaps it was the bond of sharing in the sort of hard living and certainly the same dangers as the men that gave Hunter a more lighthearted view of marauding. "The 52nd Light Infantry were famous *providers*," he reminisced years later. "They were good hands at a Grab. Grab was a favourite expression among the Light Infantry, and meant any plunder taken by force; a Lob when you got it without any opposition, and I am very certain there never was a more expert set than the Light Infantry at either grab, lob, or gutting a house." With fondness he recalled, "The Grenadiers used to call us their *children*, and when we got more plunder than we wanted we always supplied *our fathers*."[28]

For civilians unlucky enough to have an army encamped in their neighborhood, quartering officers in one's home was often a better alternative than housing the rank and file. Wrote one distraught resident of the New Brunswick area:

> I suppose you would gladly hear how we have fared the winter past with the regular soldiers; which, in a word, is beyond my tongue or pen to express. I could not have thought there was such a set of blackguards in the world. I have said, and have no reason to recall it, "That if the Devil had a permission to send the worst crew from Tophet, these people, if they may be allowed the title, would outdo them in swearing, lying, stealing, and blackguarding." The last thing they do when they go to bed, and the first in the morning, is to remind God to damn their eyes, tongue, liver, pluck, heart and soul, and this they do more than a thousand times a day.[29]

By no means were British troops alone. Washington and others found the scale of profanity among American troops very disturbing. "It is much to be lamented, that the foolish and scandalous practice of *profane Swearing* is exceedingly prevalent in the American Army," he published in the General Orders for May 31, 1777. "Officers of every rank are bound to discourage it, first by their example, and then by punishing offenders."[30]

John Adams, too, was shocked and dismayed by the foul language and other vices common to armies. "The Prevalence of Dissipation, Debauchery, Gaming, Prophaneness, and Blasphemy, terrifies the best people upon the Continent from trusting their Sons and other Relations among so many dangerous snares and Temptations," he complained to Nathanael Greene. "Multitudes of People who would with chearfull Resignation Submit their Families to the Dangers of the sword shudder at the Thought of exposing them to what appears to them, the more destructive Effects of Vice and Impiety."[31] Greene replied, "I remember you lament the general corruption of manners and the increase of vicious habits that prevail in the Army. It is a serious truth and much to be lamented." He agreed and told Adams, "I am sensible of the force and justness of your remarks, that the vices of the Army prevents many from engaging in the service more than the hardships and dangers attending it."[32]

Washington also had great difficulty preventing some of his troops from plundering. The main culprits in this period were some of the New Jersey militia, who witnessed firsthand the devastation of their state by royal troops and were furious with their fellow Jerseyans who remained loyal to the king or stayed neutral. In late January, Washington told Gov. William Livingston, "The irregular and disjointed State of the Militia of this Province, makes it necessary for me to inform you, that, unless a Law is immediately passed by your Legislature, to reduce them to some order, and oblige them to turn out, in a different Manner from what they have hitherto done, we shall bring very few into the Field, and even those few will render little or no Service." Disgusted, he wrote, "Their Officers are generally of the lowest Class of People; and, instead of setting a good Example to their Men, are leading them into every Kind of Mischief, one species of which is, Plundering the Inhabitants, under the pretence of their being Tories." Further, Washington told Livingston, "A Law should, in my Opinion, be passed, to put a Stop to this kind of lawless Rapine; for, unless there is something done to prevent it, the People will throw themselves, of Choice, into the Hands of the British Troops. But your first object should be a well regulated Militia Law; the People, put under good Officers, would behave in quite another Manner; and not only render real Service as Soldiers, but would protect, instead of distressing, the Inhabitants."[33]

Support for independence was far from unanimous, and a vicious civil war was the result, particularly in New Jersey. Such conditions also provided a means to settle old scores between neighbors and within families;

for others, there were chances for social and political advancement and the acquisition of power, however petty. This was also a grand opportunity for lawless elements to take advantage of the power struggle and commit crimes in the name of one cause or another.

By mid-January, in cold, dreary weather, the war had degenerated into a desultory, monotonous round of foraging parties and inconclusive skirmishes that continued for the next five months. Commerce was at a standstill, prices skyrocketed, and many goods were unobtainable. In New York City, one Loyalist concluded a bittersweet letter to England by writing, "Well, my good friend, God Bless you and yours! It is now near one o'clock, Feb. 10, 1777. My fire is out, and wood is very scarce. It has been 5 *l.* the chord. *Beef* is from 12 to 18 pence, the pound; *mutton* the same; *veal* from 18 to 24 pence; a couple of *Fowls*, 10 shillings; trade entirely ruined, and my purse almost empty: And so, '*God save great George our King.*'"[34]

On the American side, the euphoria over Trenton and Princeton had dissipated, and Washington faced the greatest enemy of all: apathy, which meant lack of support, which in turn spawned desertion. "Our Army is shamefully reduced by desertion," he informed John Hancock on the last day of January, "and except the people in the Country can be forced to give Information, when Deserters return to their old Neighbourhoods, we shall be obliged to detach one half of the Army to bring back the other."[35]

The nasty, dirty little war of ambushes, sniping, and occasional atrocities in this era has come to be known as the Forage War. In more recent times, this sort of activity is called guerrilla war, a Spanish term derived from resistance to Napoleon's occupation of Spain in the early nineteenth century. In the eighteenth century, such warfare had a French name: *la petite guerre*, literally meaning "the little war," or skirmishing, and its tactics were referred to as partisan warfare. "There have been and almost daily are, some small skirmishes, but without much loss on either side," Washington told Gen. Philip Schuyler in late February. "I do not apprehend, however, that this Petit Guerre will be continued long. I think matters will be transacted upon a larger scale."[36]

Contrary to misconceptions ingrained in popular history, the British Army was well equipped to deal with this sort of warfare and conducted its own effective partisan operations, using light infantry, dragoons, German Jägers, Scottish Highlanders, and American Loyalists. "We have a pretty amusement known by the name of foraging or fighting for our daily bread," a British light infantry officer, Capt. Sir James Murray of the 57th, told his sister in Scotland. "As the rascals are skulking about the whole country, it is impossible to move with any degree of safety without a pretty large escort, and even then you are exposed to a dirty kind of *tiraillerie* [random gunfire], which is more noisy indeed than dangerous."[37]

Occasionally the skirmishes grew into large firefights, and casualties mounted. On February 23, a 2,000-strong British foraging party left Perth Amboy and headed toward Woodbridge. As the foragers fanned out, the Grenadier Company of the 42nd Royal Highlanders was attacked by Continental forces under Gen. William Maxwell of New Jersey. The Scots fought fiercely, as usual, but were heavily outnumbered and left unsupported. By the time the action ceased, the British had suffered over seventy casualties, while American losses were negligible. Visiting his wounded grenadiers the next day, Capt. Lt. John Peebles of the 42nd commented bitterly, "What pity it is to throw away such men as these on such shabby, ill managed occasions."[38]

Yet in the same fight, one of the British light infantry officers with the main force, Capt. William Dansey of the 33rd, had a wholly different experience. He boasted to his mother, Martha, the widow of a career military man, "as to War's Alarms they are now come so familiar that a Day's Yankie Hunting is no more minded than a Day's Fox Hunting, at both Diversions a broken Bone may be got." Like many of his fellow officers, on first arrival, Dansey was gravely concerned about American "frontier" tactics and rumored marksmanship, which had already become the stuff of legends. Stories abounded of how British officers were deliberately picked off, so their uniforms were adapted to make them appear less conspicuous. Gold and silver lace was reduced or removed entirely, cocked hats were cut down into "round hats," and many British officers opted to carry light muskets called fusils, or "fuzees," with them. But after several months of field experience, Dansey changed his views and stated, "I flatter myself with understanding fighting the Rebels so well now that I am not in half the danger I was in at first and mind a shooting match with them no more then a Days Cockshooting." He told his mother, "You know I was never a famous shot but I made a very good one in the Skirmish we had on the 23rd. A Fellow jump'd from behind a [fence?] near me, ran behind a Tree and presented [aimed at] me; I up with my Fuzee and knock'd him as quick as a Cockrooster wou'd a Cock." Dansey hastened to reassure her, "So don't fear for me, who never was cool enough at home to kill a Woodcock, yet now am got cool enough to shoot a Man," adding, "I think I shall make one of the coolest Shooters in the Country when I return."[39]

As February came to an end, Washington reached new limits of exasperation with the inaction of Congress and the state governments, whom he had to beg incessantly to send troops, clothing, food, weapons, and ammunition. On March 2, he wrote a remarkable private letter to Robert Morris, one of the most influential members of Congress, in which he frankly and honestly and, in many ways, at great risk laid out the facts of the situation: "General Howe cannot, by the best intelligence I have been able to get, have less than 10,000 Men in the Jerseys and on board of Transports at Amboy: Ours does not exceed 4,000: His are well disciplined, well Officered, and well appointed: Ours raw Militia, badly Officered, and under no Government. His numbers cannot, in any short time, be augmented: Ours must very considerably, and by such Troops as we can have some reliance on, or the Game is at an End."

The situation was truly desperate. "My Opinions upon these several matters are only known to those who have a right to be informed: As much as possible, I have endeavoured to conceal them from every one else," he confided to Morris. "To deceive Congress, or you, through whose hands my Letters to them are to pass, with false appearances and assurances, would, in my judgment, be criminal and make me responsible for consequences. I endeavour, in all those Letters, to state matters as they appear to my judgment, without adding to, or diminishing aught from the Picture: From others my sentiments are pretty much hid." Washington concluded, "In a Word, common prudence dictates the necessity of duly attending to the circumstances of both Armies, before the style of Conquerers is assumed by either; and sorry, I am to add, that this does not appear to be the case with us; Nor is it in my power to make Congress fully sensible of the real situation of our Affairs, and that it is with difficulty (if I may use the expression) that I can, by every means in my power, keep the Life and Soul of this Army together." Chiding the Congress, he wrote bitterly, "In a word, when they are at a distance, they think it is but to say Presto begone, and everything is done. They seem not to have any conception of the difficulty and perplexity attending those who are to execute."[40]

Notwithstanding the hazards of frontline duty and the provincial nature of their surroundings, the British and Hessian officers managed to make their routine a bit more bearable with social gatherings. One of the more curious features of the New Brunswick cantonment involved the van Horne family. Mr. Philip van Horne owned a country house called Convivial Hall, or "Phil's Hill," near Middlebrook, but his family spent much of the winter in New Brunswick. His daughters were favorites with officers on both sides. "There were five of the Miss Vanhornes, all handsome and well bred," wrote Alexander Graydon, an American officer whose mother visited the van Hornes on her way to New York that spring, but they were "avowed Whigs, notwithstanding their civility to the British officers."[41]

Convivial Hall was used as headquarters by Gen. Benjamin Lincoln, commander of the American outpost at nearby Bound Brook, even though van Horne was suspected of being a Loyalist; Phil managed to remain on good terms with the officers on both sides. In 1778, his daughter Mary, "the Belle of Middlebrook," married Col. Stephen Moylan, commander of the 4th Continental Dragoons and one of Washington's top intelligence officers. Three of his other daughters, Susan, Jeanette, and Anne, were very popular with the British and Hessian officers, including Capt. Johann Ewald of the Jägers.

Johann Ewald was a fascinating character. The son of a postal employee and a merchant's daughter, he was born in the Hessian city of Cassel in 1744. At sixteen, he entered the military during the Seven Years' War, which raged all through Germany; he even participated in the siege of Cassel, his hometown, in 1761 and was wounded in action while on campaign. After the war, during a drunken argument one night in 1770, Ewald fought a duel with a friend and lost his left eye. He since wore a glass eye and also used an eye patch to cover the injury. In 1774, he published his first book and was promoted captain of the Hessian Jäger Corps, a special unit of riflemen dressed in distinctive green uniforms. Ewald arrived in America during the late summer of 1776, and by 1777, he had established his fame as a good and dependable officer. He was also a thirty-three-year-old bachelor of medium height, very erect and slender, who fell in love with Jeanette van Horne. Ewald wrote a number of love letters, addressing her as "Mademoiselle Jeannette von Horen."[42]

Sir George Osborn of the Guards, a widower at this time in his life, was also charmed by the van Horne girls. A letter from the bishop of Worcester to Lord North, two of Osborn's cousins, provides a glimpse into the sort of socializing hosted by Sir George during the early spring of 1777. "We have had a chearful letter from Sir George in which he seems to consider the War as nearly at an end," the bishop wrote. "He had been giving a Fete to some rebel ladies which he calls a *fête champêtre* and thought it very lucky that his company were entertained by the enemy attacking his picquet Guard upon a distant hill during the Fete. The ladies were invited, said they would wait upon him but they had no shoes and he sent a Grenadier who had been a shoe maker to equip them."[43] The "rebel ladies" included the van Horne girls, and the fête was given on St. George's Day, April 23, according to Colonel von Donop, who was also much taken with the young ladies.[44]

Captain Graydon of Pennsylvania recalled that during his mother's visit to New Brunswick in late May, "There soon after came in two or three British officers, who, entering into conversation with the ease of men of fashion, gave her to understand that there had been a ball the preceding evening, at which had been the Miss Vanhornes, the ladies whom they now called to see. These gentlemen, one of whom was Sir John Wrottesley, were such frequent visitors at this house, that my mother, during her stay in it, became pretty well acquainted with them."[45] Sir John was a Guards officer, a bon vivant, and a very close friend of Osborn, who may well have been one of the other officers present.

But the *petite guerre* continued. In early April, to up the ante and help shake off the doldrums of a long winter cantonment, Lord Cornwallis decided to strike Lincoln's outpost at Boundbrook. On the night of April 12, a force of nearly 4,000 British and Hessian troops moved along both sides of the Raritan River toward Lincoln's position. "An outpost of the enemy . . . at Boundbrook . . . has harassed our Jägers not a little since we came here," noted General von Heister's official report.

> General Cornwallis, tired of this harassment, at last resolved to attack them unawares. The 13th April was fixed for it; the arrangements for it were made in three different detachments. Colonel v. Donop commanded the centre, which consisted of the two Grenadier Battalions von Linsing

and Minnegerode . . . the left flank consisted of two Light Infantry Battalions, the 1st English Grenadier Battalion and a detachment of Light Dragoons; the right flank of the Hessian Jägers, the Grenadier Company of the English Guards, commanded by Lt-Colonel Osborne, and also a detachment of Light Dragoons. Generals Cornwallis and Grant commanded the whole [3,000 to 4,000 troops].

The Hessian report complimented the British strategy:

The project was well planned; as Boundbrook lies at the foot of a range of hills, the two wings were to surround it from the side of the hills; but as the heat is usually too great on such enterprises the center did not let the wings come far enough round and made the attack too soon, with the result that the greater part of the rebels escaped, and only 70 men, including three officers, were taken prisoners, and three metal [brass] fieldpieces captured. Perhaps ten to twenty men were killed. On our side only three Jägers were wounded.[46]

Ewald commanded the Jägers in front of Grant's column. "As I set out with the advanced guard, General Grant said to me, 'Captain Ewald, you know the area. I say nothing further to you. You know everything else.'" The Jägers moved out enthusiastically, and as they engaged the American sentries, Ewald quickly discovered that he had advanced too far too soon: "The picket received us spiritedly and withdrew under steady fire. . . . The day dawned and I was exposed to a murderous fire." Outnumbered and pinned down, the captain recalled, "We had no choice but to lie down on the ground before the bridge, whereupon I ordered 'Forward!' sounded constantly" by the hornblower. "Luckily for us, Colonel Donop's column appeared after a lapse of eight or ten minutes, whereupon the Americans abandoned the redoubt. We arrived in the town with the garrison of the redoubt amidst a hard running fight."[47]

Lincoln's headquarters at "Phil's Hill" was quickly overrun. "General Linckoln must have retired *en Profond Négligé* ["profoundly undressed," i.e., in the buff], as he did not take time to dress himself," von Donop reported with a smirk. "His adjutant is among the Captured Officers."[48] Ewald observed, "Afterward the place was ransacked and plundered because all the inhabitants were rebellious-minded, and then the entire corps withdrew along the road from Bound Brook to Brunswick."[49]

Once back at New Brunswick, the camp scuttlebutt began to circulate. "I learned later that I was accused of attacking too rashly, for General Grant's attack had been a feint," Ewald ruefully noted. "But I had not heard a word about it. I should have been advised if this attack was to have been a feint, for then I would only have skirmished with the enemy picket."[50]

For all of the fuss and bother, planning, marching, skirmishing, and recriminating, Cornwallis's goal was only partially realized and of short duration. "In the morning of the 13th Instt Lord Cornwallis in person with Major Generals Grant & Skinner attempted to surprize our post at Bound Brook and to take off the Troops we had there," Washington wrote. "Happily his Enterprize was not attended with the Success he wished; however, before our little force could withdraw to the Mountains in their Rear the Enemy advanced and possessed themselves of two or three pieces of Field Artillery which we had there. We lost in prisoners & killed, by the best accounts I have obtained, from thirty five to forty men." But in a few hours, everything was back to where it had been before. "The enemy lost the post at Eleven O'Clock the same day, & our people took possession of it again. Fortunately, Our Stores there were trifling and not worth mentioning. It was considered as an out post, and nothing of consequence kept there."[51]

The American force that reoccupied Bound Brook included Maj. Gen. Nathanael Greene of Rhode Island. Referring to *Convivial Hall* and the flexibility of its occupants, "The British Generals breakfasted and I dind at the same house the same day," Greene told his wife Kitty, "this is the State of War."[52]

The day after Boundbrook, Washington predicted, "If I am to judge from the present appearance of things the Campaign will be opened by General Howe before we shall be in any condition to oppose him."[53] Time was working against the Americans, who were slow to respond to the call for troops. Howe had Washington significantly outclassed by every measure of military professionalism—troop numbers, weapons, training, support systems—and spring was well under way.

But nothing happened. Two weeks later, on April 27, Greene passed on to his wife some startling news: "We learn the Enemy are to take the field the first of June." It made no sense to him. "Their delay is un[ac]countable already. What has kept them in their Quarters we cant immagin." With

one eye on the need for time to raise an army and the other on the cor-
roding effects of attrition if things dragged on too long, he ruefully
observed, "Their foolish delays and Infernal disputes I fear will protract
the War."[54]

Washington didn't complain; every week brought new units to his
army, however slowly, and the months of badgering Congress and the
states finally started to pay off. "The rebels in Jersey have increased to the
number of 10,000 since the commencement of May," Maj. Carl Baurmeister, adjutant general of the Hessian headquarters staff, reported later
that month. "They have harassed all the quarters, and still they do not
remain quiet in spite of the losses they have sustained thereby. The losses
on our side have not been of any importance, but this kind of warfare
fatigues the troops very much."[55]

Supplies in the Continental camps were improving also, but they at
best remained basic by the standards of the day, even among the generals. A Hessian messenger sent by General von Heister to Washington on
May 8 to make arrangements for supplying the Hessian prisoners captured at Trenton was only allowed to go as far as Lord Stirling's quarters,
where, since "wine and everything else essential to good cheer being so
rare among the rebels, he could regale him with nothing better than *grogge*
and salt beef."[56] A few weeks later, another Hessian officer on a similar
mission, Lt. Matthaeus Müller, quartermaster of the Knyphausen regiment, dined with General Lincoln at Convivial Hall in Bound Brook. "At
the table during the meal the master of the house, Sir Van Horne, was
present with his wife and daughter, Gen. Greene, Col. Bland of the Light
Dragoons, with his wife." As for the food, Müller reported that "the dinner was very good, savory, and abundant. The drink, however, owing to a
lack of wine, was water mixed with brandy and sugar. I was treated very
well indeed."[57]

"We Make out to Live very Well here," Capt. James Moore of the 5th
Pennsylvania Regiment, posted at "Bonebrook," reported with a soldier's
humorous sarcasm. "With a great Deil of Care In the Eating and Drinking Way, all We Want [are] Tarts, Custard & floating Island!" But the business of war was still serious and deadly. The troops posted at Bound
Brook "are frequently Deprived of our Rest by the Bloody Backed Vil-
lians Who Very frequently Come and fire upon our Centries," Moore
continued. The "tit-for-tat" nature of the *petite guerre* was in full bloom

that spring. "We are frequently allarmed by them but Not so Much harrassed as they are. Not a Day But our Scouts & other Partys, Goes Down and fires Upon them, yesterday our Scout killed three or four of thier Guard, & Came off Without any Damage."[58] The desire for revenge smoldered and grew increasingly more dangerous with each incident.

Warmer weather and the resulting outbreak of "camp fevers" such as typhus, typhoid, dysentery, or cholera required the Crown Forces to shift from the cantonments in New Brunswick to fresh campgrounds on the outskirts of town in mid-May. Sickness had spread rapidly, especially among the Hessians in town. After five months of close, uncomfortable quartering of thousands of troops, the town itself was a stinking shambles. "The Hessian Grenadiers have lost within these two Months more than 300 Men by a Putrid fever which got among them at Brunswick," Sir George Osborn informed Lord Germain on May 15. "By some Care and Reform in their Hospital, I flatter myself they will be able to take the field in tolerable health." By contrast, "the Chasseurs [Jägers] have remained exceeding healthy notwithstanding they have maintained one of the alertest Posts in our Cantonement during the whole of the Winter Season."[59] Activity, discipline, and uncrowded conditions—the Jägers were far out of town—made the difference.

Still, there were no signs of serious campaign activity. "Nothing new in Jersey," Congressman Richard Henry Lee of Virginia quipped to Thomas Jefferson on May 20.[60] Day after day passed, with the king's troops growing more restless and Washington's forces ever increasing. The spring weather helped rouse spirits on both sides, and the *petite guerre* intensified.

In New York City, twenty-seven-year-old Nicholas Cresswell, having escaped from Virginia, was waiting to take a ship back to England after three years on his own in America. During his stay, this thoroughly loyal Englishman from Derbyshire had met George Washington and John Hancock, carried letters from Virginia to Thomas Jefferson in Philadelphia, lived freely with Indians and under close surveillance by Virginians, and traveled extensively. An intelligent, resourceful young man and a dogged adventurer, Cresswell kept a journal and made astute observations of events and people.

On Wednesday, May 21, on the outskirts of New York, he "saw three regiments of Hessians reviewed by Generals De Heister and

Knyphausen, Regiment De Donop, Regiment De Losberg, Regiment De Knyphausen." The young Englishman noted, "They are fine troops, but very slow in their motions when compared with the English. They fired several rounds with the greatest exactness." Cresswell was equally impressed by their artillery drill: "They had a train of Artillery consisting of ten fine brass Field pieces which they fired several rounds. Their Artillery men seem to be the only active men they have. When they have a piece of Artillery to draw they move very quick, at other times they seem half dead or quite stupid."

Military punishments were shocking for their brutality, even in an age of frequent hangings and public floggings. "One of their Corporals ran the Gauntlet eight times through the Regiment"—a punishment where the condemned passed through two ranks of his comrades, each of whom struck him hard across the back with a stick—"he had upwards of 2000 lashes which he bore with the greatest resolution and firmness, not a single muscle of his face discomposed all the time." Blank, expressionless faces were part of German military discipline, leaving Cresswell and others who encountered them with the impression that "they appear to be a set of cruel, unfeeling people."[61]

Over in New Jersey that same day, among the Hessian Jägers on outpost duty at Raritan Landing with Captain Ewald was Capt. Friedrich Heinrich Lorey (or Loray), who commanded a small squadron of mounted Jägers on the road between the landing and Bound Brook.[62] A rare old soldier who had begun his military career in Europe as a private during the Seven Years' War, he was one of the few who rose into the officer corps through merit rather than by birth. Clever and ruthless, Lorey distinguished himself by his daredevil tactics. "Captain Lorey the day before yesterday in the morning played a little joke on the enemy which did him credit," von Donop reported on May 21.

> 40 to 50 men came from the direction of Bound Brook and attacked Captain Ewald's outposts. Captain Lorey, who was camped behind the Jägers with his cavalry, at the first shot, together with 8 men, mounted his horse, he (secretly) had no more at that moment with him, and went around by Quibble-town, and came back by the woods, through the place where the Rebels usually make their Retreat. When the before-mentioned troops of Rebels retired as usual through the wood, Lorey came to meet them, and cooly took up such a position that no shot could touch any

one of them. By hastily jumping the fences many Rebels succeeded in saving themselves; 6 men were brought in prisoners, who begged pardon on their knees.[63]

Not content to leave the American outposts in peace, Lorey himself decided to rattle their cage with another daring exploit. "In the night just passed he played another game on those Rebels. At 10 at night he mounted his horse, he galloped to every Rebel post along the road, quite up to and into Bound Brook itself, and alarmed them in such a manner that they actually started firing in Platoons, when he got back again to his quarters as proof that he had really been in the place he broke several windows *en passant* as he went up the street of the town."[64]

Despite Lorey's hell-raising, the rebel outpost at Bound Brook continued to be a thorn in the side of the king's forces. Then on May 26, word reached New Brunswick that the Americans were evacuating the place. A small British force under General Grant headed north along the Raritan. "The 1st Battalion of Light Infantry with a party of the 16th Light Dragoons to march at two this Morning," Ens. Thomas Glyn of the Guards reported. "This Corps moved towards Boundbrook but finding the Enemy were still in force after some skirmishing took post on some rising ground, the Brigade of Guards (upon the firing being heard) were ordered to march, & formed in the Rear of the Light Infantry." The Guards, who functioned much like a light infantry unit in the American campaigns, used common-sense, flexible tactics when faced with heavy gunfire. "The Enemy advanced with two pieces of Cannon & began to cannonade us, when we were ordered to lay down," Glyn noted, "& being covered by the ground no loss ensued except Major General Grant having his Horse shot dead under him." Once the Guards had taken cover, "upon our returning the fire with our field Pieces, the Enemy moved to Boundbrook with great precipitation. We returned to Camp."[65]

The death of Grant's horse occasioned much comment, some of it less than flattering. "General Grant's horse was killed under him . . . as we were endeavouring to discover where the rebels entended going after striking their Tents at Bound Brooke," Lt. William Hale of the 45th told his parents. "I wish it had been the General instead of the horse," he added wistfully, "no man can be more detested."[66]

"I had a Horse killed the other Day with a Cannon Ball at the Head of the Brigade of Guards," Grant wrote. Making light of the fact that the horse's head was torn off by the shot, showering the pompous general with the results, Grant said, "He was dead & stiff before He fell to the Ground, but I got clear of Him, without being the least Hurt."[67] An arrogant, opinionated, self-interested Scottish laird with a taste for high living and hyperbole, Grant was not a popular commander, and he was loathed even more by the Americans for bragging in Parliament that he could easily march through the colonies with 5,000 men. On the American side, "We Offered Gen'l Grant Battle six times the Other day," a brash, newly arrived commander, Brig. Gen. Anthony Wayne of Pennsylvania, himself no stranger to bombast, commented. "[He] who was to March through America at the head of 5000 men had his Coat much Dirtied, his Horses head taken off, and himself badly Bruis'd for having the presumption at the head of 700 British Troops to face 500 Pennsylvanians."[68]

At general headquarters in New York City, Howe's Hessian aide, Capt. Friedrich von Münchhausen, noted the British Army's intelligence problem as it related to this small episode: "The fact that a sizeable enemy corps can march away and be gone for two hours before we learn of it, shows that we are in a bad way in not having good spies among them."[69] The failure of the British intelligence network during this six-month period was part of the reason why so little significant activity took place. Estimates of Washington's strength, as noted in British and Hessian sources, were consistently and significantly overinflated.

June began with a stark reminder of just how brutal war can be, especially on a small scale.

On June 2, a warm, listless day, a wagon pulled by four thin and worn horses slowly rattled its way down a dusty road along the Raritan River. Escorted by grim-faced Continental officers under a flag of truce, the creaking vehicle jostled over ruts and potholes on its journey to New Brunswick. Behind the teamster was a large box covered by a fly-blown blanket, protecting its precious cargo from dust. One of the officers carried a letter from His Excellency, General George Washington, Commander-in-Chief of the United States Army, to the Right Honourable Lieutenant General Charles Earl Cornwallis, commander of His Majesty's forces in New Jersey. The letter and cargo were being sent directly from Washington's headquarters at Middlebrook to Cornwallis's headquarters at Brunswick for His Lordship's personal inspection.

Ahead at Raritan Landing, directly across the river from New Brunswick, was an outpost manned by 1,000 elite troops of the Brigade of His Majesty's Foot Guards. The pickets on duty that day were from Sir George Osborn's Grenadier Company. When the Continental officers were stopped by the pickets, Sir George went out to see what they wanted.

Osborn, a thoroughly professional and combat-hardened soldier, possessed those self-assured manners and deportment that were the hallmarks of aristocratic good breeding. He examined the letter from Washington to Cornwallis but refused to accept the cargo or allow it to go any farther. The smell from the box must have been revolting, but Sir George apparently showed no visible reaction. A contemporary account of the incident states that Osborn, "with much admired *sang froid*, simply returned for an answer that *he was no coroner*."[70]

Inside the box were the mutilated remains of Lt. William Martin, a Virginian in Spencer's Additional Continental Regiment. Two days before, on the evening of May 31, somewhere between Raritan Landing and Bound Brook, not far from Osborn's outpost, a Hessian Jäger patrol ambushed an American patrol led by Martin. A Hessian report stated:

> Captain Lorey about 6 O'clock had a second little skirmish with the Rebels, Captain von Wreden with 50 foot Jägers and he with 8 mounted ones, were out making a patrol, but they kept themselves as much as possible under cover of the woods in order to bring the enemy's patrol into an ambuscade. An officer with 20 men came along and they being unsuspecting, were in between the fences and the bushes, when Lorey and his men cooly set upon them. At the very first encounter two of the mounted Jägers, Eisentrager and Nolte, were severely wounded, and a third and his horse men became so beside themselves with fury, that they hacked to death the Rebel officer and 6 men on the spot, and made seven prisoners, of whom the sergeant is severely wounded.

The narrative dispassionately mentioned the fact that "the Officer, who after he received his first wound, attempted to defend himself with his bayonet, had his head cut off by Lorey himself with his sword." The same Hessian report commented, "In the meantime I believe they have by this affair made for themselves a name among the Rebels which will be feared, for enough of the patrol got away as was necessary to carry a report of it to their Commander."[71]

Martin's body was recovered the next day and taken to Washington's headquarters at Middlebrook. There, "seventeen wounds were plain to be seen, most of which, it is said, were sufficient singly to prove mortal."[72] The body was in such ghastly condition that it was put on display in the open for the army to see. "I saw his corps[e] as did also every officer and soldier in camp that chose it," twenty-year-old Col. Alexander Hamilton, one of Washington's aides, told Congressman John Jay. Hamilton further reported that "his men 'tis said quitted him. But however other matters may be 'tis certain his dead body was found most horribly mangled. He had not a single bullet wound, but was hacked to pieces with the sword. He had several cuts in his head, each of which was sufficient to dispatch him, besides a number of more inconsiderable scars about his body and hands." Death in combat is an accepted risk of soldiering, but what infuriated the Americans was the fact that it was "evident, that the most wanton and unnecessary cruelty must have been used towards him; for the greater part of his wounds must have been given him when utterly out of a condition to resist. This may be relied on as a fact."[73]

Previous episodes of excessive brutality, such as the repeated bayoneting of Gen. Hugh Mercer at Princeton and the death and mutilation of another American officer in early February, had prompted letters to British commanders from Washington and other American generals protesting such treatment. But now, furious at this latest outrage, Washington fired off a letter to Cornwallis and sent it with Martin's body to New Brunswick:

> It is with infinite regret, I am again compelled, to remonstrate against that spirit of wanton cruelty, that has in several instances influenced the conduct of your soldiery. A recent exercise of it towards an unhappy officer of ours—Lieutenant Martin—convinces me, that my former representations on that subject, have been unavailing. That Gentleman, by the fortune of war, on Saturday last, was thrown into the hands of a party of your horse, and unnecessarily murdered with the most aggravated circumstances of barbarity.

With a cold sarcasm fueled by previous British denials that such things could actually happen, Washington added, "I wish not to wound your lordship's feelings by commenting on this event, but I think it my duty to send his mangled body, to your lines, as an undeniable testimony of the fact, should it be doubted, and as the best appeal to your humanity for the justice of our complaint."[74]

"The letter was taken from the flag and sent in," Hamilton wrote; "the flag and the body not permitted to pass their out posts."[75]

The officers escorting Martin's corpse were seething with rage. "2 officers of the enemy came with a flag of truce and a wagon, in which lay the body of the officer in a casket," General von Heister remarked. "The officers themselves have so strongly expressed themselves orally against it that their hitherto reserved manner and conduct will in the future be unknown." The Hessian general also noted, "This letter was taken from them, and they were sent back with their dead body."[76]

After the wagon departed, Lord Cornwallis composed a reply to Washington. "I understand that Lieut. Martin when surrounded by a Party of Hessian Cavalry did not ask quarter, but on the contrary wounded one of the Hessians, when they were close to him, which so exasperated the others that they immediately cut him down with their Sabres." Parrying Washington's cold anger with a patronizing explanation, Cornwallis wrote, "When a man is kill'd in that manner his body must of course be mangled: But the Hessians gave the strongest Proof that they were not actuated by a spirit of wanton cruelty, As they brought in a Serjeant and six men of the same party Prisoners, of whom only one was wounded."[77] Privately, among some British officers, Osborn's comment that he was no coroner "was a theme of considerable merriment, and the *bon mot* of Sir George not a little applauded."[78]

The *petite guerre* would continue to take its toll, and certain units gained notoriety for brutality. The Scottish Highlanders already had a long-established reputation as fierce fighters, and Gen. James Grant, himself a Scottish laird with a fabulous castle at Ballindalloch in the heart of the Highlands, wrote on June 7 that the rebels "made two Attempts upon Piscataway, the Quarters of the 42nd—but were repulsed both times & pursued with great spirit, even a little too much Zeal, but the eagerness of the Men who could not be brought off luckily was attended with no bad consequence & has had on the contrary a very good Effect, for the Yankies say in talking of the Highlanders 'I vow now it is a wicked Regiment, they would kill us all if they could.'"[79] Anthony Wayne wrote the same day, "they notwithstanding affect to hold us cheap and threaten to beat up our Quarters—*if we don't* beat up theirs first which is in Contemplation."[80]

The first week of June came and went, and still no campaign. "Monday, June 2, 1777. I have been here almost three weeks and I am as ignorant of the Motions or designs of our Army as if I had been in Virginia," Nicholas Cresswell wrote from New York. "Only this, the Soldiers, seem very healthy and long to be in action. The Commander in Chief is either inactive, has no orders to act, or thinks that he has not force sufficient to oppose the Rebels." Cresswell commented with not a little sarcasm about Howe's military inactivity and his activity on "other fronts," namely with his mistress, Mrs. Elizabeth Loring: "Which of these or whether any of them is the true reason I will not pretend to say, but this I am very certain of, if General Howe does nothing, the Rebels will avail themselves of his inactivity by collecting a very numerous Army to oppose him, whenever he shall think it proper to leave Mrs. Lorain [Loring] and face them."[81] A New York Loyalist commented in the same vein: "All this time General Howe was at *New-York* in the lap of Ease; or rather, amusing himself in the *lap* of a Mrs. L——g, who is the very *Cleopatra* to this *Anthony* of ours."[82]

Cresswell and the Loyalist were not the only ones puzzled by Howe's inaction. Germain's habit of allowing the senior generals to pursue their own campaign policies—while suggesting but not *requiring* cooperation or coordination between them—had allowed the British war effort to become hydra-headed. "I do not understand why Sir G. Carleton sends a part of his force to Crown Point so early as the beginning of May if Sir Wm. Howe's intelligence is right, that he does not propose being upon the Lakes himself till the beginning of June," Germain wrote. "I incline to hope that his preparations are in greater forwardness; if they are not, Burgoyne's arrival may cause him to change his dispositions and create a delay." In Parliament, the opposition, led by Charles James Fox, were mounting attack after attack on the Ministry, zeroing in on Germain. Not surprisingly, the minister wrote, "I shall be glad of an opportunity of applauding the General's conduct this campaign."[83]

Meanwhile, great changes were in progress with the royal forces, especially among the Hessians. As a result of the Trenton debacle and his inability to get along with General Howe, seventy-year-old General von Heister was to be replaced as Hessian commander by sixty-one-year-old Lt. Gen. Wilhelm von Knyphausen. In July, von Heister departed for home on board HMS *Niger.* Before the year was out, the old veteran would

be no more, for he died "of grief and mortification" shortly after returning to Hesse Cassel.[84]

Reinforcements from Europe arrived at New York in late May, among
them some German riflemen from the principality of Anspach-Brandenburg.[85] "A number of Hessian Chasseurs or Yaugers arrived in green uniforms and boots, all armed with rifles," Cresswell observed on June 4. "I
am told they are as expert with them as the Virginians, but they appear
to me to be too clumsy for the Woods and too heavily clothed." These
Jägers had been recruited from the hilly forests of central Germany and
were remarkable for their handsome appearance. They were supposed to
be mounted, but because of a transport mix-up, their tack and saddlery
had not arrived. "I can't conceive why they wear boots," Cresswell wondered, "they must be inconvenient and troublesome in this hot and
woody country."[86]

A contingent of officers from His Majesty's Foot Guards also arrived,
including Col. Charles O'Hara of the Coldstream Regiment.[87] There was
much clamor among the Guards officers in London to serve in the American war, for field service meant opportunities for glory and adventure as
well as promotion, and some of the Guards officers were now being
rotated back to England after a year of active field duty. Aristocrats in
Great Britain viewed service in the Guards as an important part of status, and it was tradition in many families.

The Brigade of Guards in America, commanded by Brig. Gen. Edward
Mathew, was a special composite force made up of 1,000 men chosen by
lottery from the three regiments of Foot Guards.[88] The unit was divided
into two battalions of 500 men each and, unlike the other British regiments, retained its own flank companies (grenadier and light infantry)
while on campaign. All of the Guards, officers and men alike, were
dressed in uniforms modified for campaign service: Their coats were
shortened into jackets, without lace or decoration; their hair was cropped;
and their hats were cut down into "round hats" for the regular companies and light infantry-style caps for the flank companies.

The Guards had played an active and distinguished part in the 1776
New York Campaign, and Howe was not at all pleased to be losing some
of his most dependable field officers. "I have the satisfaction to report
to your Lordships the safe arrival of the Transports and Store Ships on
the 24th May, having on board the Officers of the Guards to be relieved,"

he told Lord Barrington on June 1. "I sincerely wish that the [Guards officers] who had acquired a perfect knowledge of the Service best adapted to this Country, and whose Zeal and alacrity has been conspicuous during the last Campaign & Winter, when those Qualities were essentially necessary, had not been ordered Home; and I can assure your Lordship that Justice alone has a Right to demand this acknowledgement of their Service."[89]

After spending a week in New York City, the replacements sailed by sloop to New Brunswick, where they arrived on June 6. The service of those who were leaving did not go unnoticed. "The Guards Officers & Men have great Merit—they had hard Duty & bad Quarters during the Winter but put up with both cheerfully," Grant wrote on June 7. "Complaints & Grivances were out of the Question; every body was in good Health, good Humour and good Spirits." Echoing Howe's sentiments, he added, "I am sorry so many Officers of that Corps accustom'd to hardships, & broke into the service are to leave us."[90]

One of the new arrivals was a thirty-year-old captain-lieutenant, the Honorable Richard Fitzpatrick of the 1st Guards Regiment. Fitzpatrick was a member of Parliament, the brother of the Irish Earl of Upper Ossory, and lifelong best friend and confidant of Charles James Fox, head of the Whig faction in the House of Commons. Later, as secretary at war in 1783, Fitzpatrick was described by a contemporary as "more elegant than solid, more adapted to entertain and delight than fitted for the desk." Socially, Fox and Fitzpatrick were at the center of the most fashionable and outrageous circle of "fops and macaronis" in London, sharing bachelor quarters in Piccadilly and leading lives of drinking, gambling, classical scholarship, and brilliant conversation at Brookes's (Almack's), the most prominent club in the capital. "They had been brought up together from early life, remained inseparable to the last, and were strongly attached to each other. Fitzpatrick, like his friend, was a constant votary at Brookes's club."

Richard "Dickey" Fitzpatrick was the quintessential young man of late-eighteenth-century London society. "His person tall, manly, and extremely distinguished, set off by his manners, which, though lofty and assuming, were nevertheless elegant and prepossessing, these endowments added grace to the attractions of his conversation." He was quite popular. "No man's society was more eagerly courted among the highest orders by persons of both sexes." Like many of his social contemporaries, Fitzpatrick composed poetry, wrote in French and Italian, and was well versed in theater. "He possessed no mean poetic talents, peculiarly for compositions of wit, fancy, and satire, in all which he far exceeded Fox."[91] One of their newest friends, whom Fitzpatrick had just left in England, was a nineteen-year-old French nobleman who visited London in early 1777, the Marquis de Lafayette.

Assigned to the Grenadier Company of the Guards, Fitzpatrick was also a close friend of Sir George Osborn. Both Osborn and Fitzpatrick had attended Westminster School (though six years apart) before entering the army, both were career soldiers who later achieved the rank of general, and both were members of Parliament. Unlike Sir George, who was a staunch Tory, Fitzpatrick was a firm Whig and strongly opposed the Ministry, headed by Osborn's cousin Lord North. He was highly critical of the conduct of the war, and his first weeks in New Jersey confirmed his views, which were often at odds with the attitudes of many of the other officers. As the campaign progressed, his letters home grew more and more vehement about the outrageous conduct of the common soldiers and the overall prosecution of the war.

The same day that Fitzpatrick and the other Guards officers arrived in New Brunswick, a dramatic scene was unfolding a few miles away in British-held Perth Amboy. Abraham Patten, "a rebel captain who had lived in Brunswick for some time as a spy, and during that time passed himself off as a merchant, was hanged on a tree close to our camp," wrote Quartermaster Carl Bauer of the Hessian Platte Grenadier Battalion. "A letter, which he wrote to General Washington, and in which he promised to set fire to all the magazines in Brunswick on the King's birthday, 4 June, had been given for delivery to an English grenadier who had offered to desert for a promised amount of guineas. The grenadier, however, delivered it to Lord Cornwallis. The plan was exposed that General Washington was ready that same day, as soon as the fires were set, to attack us." Bauer was impressed by Patten's conduct at the end: "The enthusiasm of this spy was so great that as he came to the ladder and was about to climb it, he pulled the white hood over his eyes and said, 'I die for liberty.'"[92]

"The spy supposedly died in the most noble manner and his death has been celebrated as a sacrifice for freedom," another Hessian officer, Lt. Johann von Bardeleben of the Regiment von Donop, noted, also recording Patten's last words: "that is, at the gallows he said, 'I die for liberty, and do it gladly, because my cause is just.'"[93]

"The Spy Patoun was hang'd to day," Capt.-Lt. John Peebles of the 42nd Royal Highlanders stated. He also pointed out, "Deserters coming in as usual & some Rascals are deserting from us. The 2d. Battn. Gr[enadie]rs have lost 6 or 8 within this short time."[94]

On the American side, concern about spies in the guise of British deserters appeared in the General Orders. "It is Suppos'd that a number of Deserters now coming out are employ'd by the enemy as Spies, the Genl. Strictly orders that no officer or Soldier except those that have them immedietly in Charge, Shall attempt to Speak to or hold any Conversation with them," Capt. Robert Kirkwood of the Delaware Regiment wrote in his Orderly Book on June 10, while stationed at Princeton. "The parties having them in Charge Shall bring them immediately to Head Quarters," and "All officers are Requested Immedietly to Confine every non Commissioned officer, or Soldier who shall be Seen gathering Round or holding any Conversation with any Deserter."

But deserters were by no means the only source of suspected spies. On June 11, a general court-martial found "Mary Quan, try'd . . . for acting as an Enemy to her Country, no Evidence appearing the Genl. orders her to be Releas'd." Mary was fortunate; another woman was not so lucky. "Elizabeth Brewer try'd by the Same Court & found guilty of acting as A Spy in the Service of the enemy, do Sentence her to be Confin'd During the War, the Genl. Approves the Sentence & orders her to be sent to Morrow . . . to Philadelphia."[95]

Finally, after months of uncertainty and second-guessing, and despite traditional superstition, on Friday, the thirteenth of June, "the Body of the Army March'd from Brunswick at Night in two Divisions—The Campaign Opens," Peebles wrote in his diary.[96] Howe was making his first major maneuver with the bulk of the army—nearly 17,000 men—since the capture of Fort Lee the previous November.

Boats that could be carried on wagons had been built at great expense in New York City, strongly suggesting a plan to march across New Jersey and cross the Delaware River. "All the Long-Bottomed Boats were put into Waggons, and everything got in readiness; the Troops lay upon their Arms that Night," noted Sgt. Thomas Sullivan of the 49th Regiment.[97] Now, finally, it seemed that the king's army was moving to finish what had been called off nearly six months to the day before, on December 14, 1776: the advance on Philadelphia.

"An Expedition was made from Brunswick to Middlebush, the 1st Battalion of Guards went," wrote twenty-year-old Ens. William Lord Cantelupe, a recently arrived Coldstream Guards officer who remained behind with the 2nd Battalion to hold New Brunswick.[98] The Guards were in the column commanded by General von Heister, here on his last campaign, accompanied by Sir William Howe. Some other new faces were also present: Maj. Gen. Charles Grey, who would build an infamous reputation for brutality in America, had landed the previous week and was on the march, accompanied by his newly appointed aide-de-camp, Capt. John André, lately exchanged after a year of captivity in Pennsylvania.

The Guards Light Infantry Company, led by Capt. Thomas Twistleton, was accompanied by a small corps of about 100 British riflemen commanded by Capt. Patrick Ferguson, a Scottish officer on special assignment. This newly composed light unit was dressed in green jackets and equipped with the Ferguson rifle, an experimental breech-loading weapon developed by the captain, here on campaign for the first time.[99]

Capt. Archibald Robertson of the Corps of Engineers accompanied General Howe. "The 2nd Division under General Howe took up their Ground at Middle bush, about 5 miles from Brunswick and 3 from Hillsboro'," the engineer wrote. "General Washington with his Army suppos'd to be about 7 or 8000 Men Occupied a Strong Camp about 4 miles North of Bond Brook on the Road to Baskin Ridge amongst the Mountains," Robertson noted, and remarked, "He stood Firm."[100] Howe's Hessian aide, Capt. Friedrich von Münchhausen, speculated, "I believe that General Howe has planned a forced march at dawn in order to cut off and to throw back General Sullivan, who is at Princeton with 2000 men."[101]

From his camp at Middle Brook, Washington watched these movements very carefully and prepared for the worst: a full-scale push on Philadelphia. He, too, had newly raised units of light troops, including a corps of Rangers led by Col. Daniel Morgan of Virginia. "We have a partizan Regt.—Col. Morgan Commands—Chosen Marksmen from the Whole Army Composes it," Col. James Chambers of the 1st Pennsylvania Regiment wrote. "Capt. Parr, Lts. Lyon and Brady, & fifty men from my Regt. are amongst the number."[102] Morgan's Corps was made up of 500 frontiersmen, mostly from the mountains of Pennsylvania, Virginia, and Maryland, armed with Pennsylvania long rifles. "The Corps of Rangers newly formed, and under your Command, are to be considered as a body of light Infantry and are to Act as such," Washington told Morgan, "for which Reason they will be exempted from the common duties of the Line." Morgan had standing orders directly from the commander in chief: "In case of any Movement of the Enemy you are Instantly to fall upon their Flanks and gall them as much as possible, taking especial care not to be surrounded."

Though accurate up to 300 yards, the rifles were slow to reload and were not designed to hold bayonets, which meant that riflemen were vulnerable to swift attacks by light infantry or dragoons. Washington's instructions to Morgan included a desperate remedy for this deficiency: "I have sent for Spears, which I expect shortly to receive and deliver to you, as a defence against Horse; till you are furnished with these, take care not to be caught in such a Situation as to give them any advantage over you." To add a further element of surprise, Washington suggested an extraordinary tactic: "It occurs to me that if you were to dress a Company or two of true Woods Men in the right Indian Style and let them make the Attack accompanied with screaming and yelling as the Indians do, it would have very good consequences especially if as little as possible was said, or known of the matter beforehand."[103]

Concerning the use of rifles among regular troops, Anthony Wayne wrote to Richard Peters, chairman of the Pennsylvania Board of War, with a request for "two hundred Stand of Arms, i.e., Muskets & Bayonets, to be exchanged for an Equal number of Rifles—which his Excellency wishes to lay Entirely aside except those in the Hands of a Corps of that Marks men under Col. Morgan who were lately Draughted & are to be Armed with Spears in place of Bayonets—without which a Rifle would not be formidable."[104] Wayne, commanding a brigade of Pennsylvania regiments that included many frontiersmen armed with rifles, had little use for the weapons or frontier dress. He firmly believed that smartly uniformed and properly trained infantry armed with muskets and bayonets were a much more formidable opponent than scruffy, undisciplined frontiersmen with their slow-loading rifles and drab, shabby, homespun clothing. "Experience has taught us that they are not fit for the field," he told the Pennsylvania Board of War about the rifles. "I am Confident . . . that you will use every means in your power to expedite the Arming & Clothing of our People as Soldiers."[105]

The following day, June 14, the action was confined to skirmishing near Hillsborough on the Millstone River. Almost unbelievably, the Royal Army had halted and established camp. "Their conduct was perplexing," Gen. Henry Knox, chief of the Continental Artillery, commented incredulously. "It was unaccountable that people who the day before gave out in very gasconading terms that they would be in Philadelphia in six days should stop short when they had gone only nine miles." The purpose of the maneuver gradually became clear: "In the course of a day or two [we] discovered that they . . . had come out with an intention of drawing us into the plain."[106]

In the British Army, Maj. Charles Stuart of the 43rd Regiment was also astonished but not surprised by Howe's strange maneuver. To him, it seemed consistent with the inept pattern of command. The twenty-four-year-old son of the influential and much-hated Tory minister John Stuart Lord Bute, the major had been sent to Rhode Island several months earlier to command a grenadier battalion, only to have Howe recall his unit to New York without him. Humiliated by this public demotion, which he believed was done out of spite for political reasons, Stuart exchanged several sharp letters with Howe and asked permission to go to England, which was refused. The major returned to New York in the spring with no command and accompanied the army from New Brunswick as an observer.

Now, as the campaign was opening, Stuart told his father, "The report circulated by those in power is that it was thought necessary to march to Hilsborough to *offer Washington battle.*" He, too, was dumbfounded, believing that "the idea of offering these people battle is ridiculous; they have too much caution to risk everything on one action, or rather too much sense to engage an army double their numbers, superior in discipline, and who never make a show of fighting but upon the most advantageous ground. If we wish to conquer them we must attack him."[107]

News of Howe's advance to the Millstone River arrived in Philadelphia late on the fourteenth. "Yesterday We had an Alarm, and news that the Enemy were on their March, towards Philadelphia in two Divisions," John Adams told Abigail. "We feel pretty bold, here," he reassured her and quipped, "If they get Philadelphia, they will hang a Mill stone about their necks."[108]

As Howe's army set up camp in new territory, an old problem resurfaced. "Great symptoms of a disposition to plunder being perceived in the Troops," Grey's aide, Captain André, wrote on June 15. "The Commander-in-chief sent a message to General De Heister desiring him to warn the Hessians not to persist in such outrages, as they would be most severely punished." André also mentioned that "most of the Brigades received the same injunctions from the Officers commanding them."[109]

Some skirmishing involving the Jägers took place, but not much else. The following day, copious amounts of dirt flew as the British began to build entrenchments. Howe's chief engineer, Capt. John Montrésor, directed the construction of three sizable redoubts, or earthen forts— not the sort of activity conducive to a swift-moving campaign. Once again, criticism of Howe's lethargic leadership began to mount. "Many

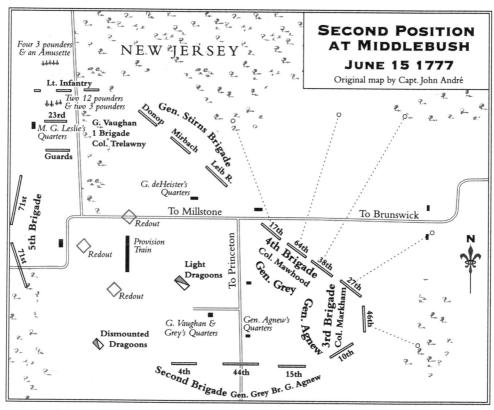

SECOND POSITION AT MIDDLEBUSH JUNE 15 1777

Original map by Capt. John André

The opening maneuvers of the campaign, June 13–18, 1777. The Crown Forces left New Brunswick on June 13 and marched ten miles west to Middlebush. There they build three redoubts, shown here on André's map, and skirmished with Washington's light troops. After five days of skirmishing and plundering, they returned to New Brunswick.

blame General Howe for not having followed Washington immediately," von Münchhausen wrote. Defending his commander, he emphasized, "Nobody in the world could be more careful than he is. This is absolutely necessary in this cursed hilly country."

The rebels were firmly ensconced in the Watchung Mountains. "Washington is a devil of a fellow, he is back again, right in his old position, in the high fortified hills," the Hessian aide remarked. "By retreating he supposedly intended to lure us into the hills and beat us there."[110] Von Münchhausen was correct. "When the Enemy first advanced, General Sullivan Retreated over [the] Delaware, in order to Draw the Enemy on towards Princetown, and then we would have fallen in their Rear," Colonel Chambers of the 1st Pennsylvania explained, "but they thought it not Safe to Leave so formidable an Enemy in their Rear, Least they should find Difficulty in case of a Retreat." The Pennsylvanian added, "It seems to me they see his Scheme, and Will not Go that Way, for if they do their Ruin, to all appearances, is inevitable."[111]

"Hints from head-quarters, that his Excellency, ever attentive to the *sparing* of his Gallant Troops, could not bear the idea of risking two or three thousand brave men to be sacrificed by '*base scum, and dunghill villains,*'" a New York Loyalist complained with bitter sarcasm. Frustrated, he scribbled to a friend in England, "Rebellion, which a twelvemonth ago was really a contemptible Pigmy, is now in appearance become a Giant."[112]

The mood of the people of New Jersey turned vengeful as plundering once more erupted unchecked. Volunteer militia appeared by the hundreds, eager for a chance to shoot British redcoats and Hessian "brass caps." "Nothing could exceed the spirit shown on this occasion by the much injured people of the Jerseys," Gen. Henry Knox wrote, cheering the turnout. "Not an atom of the lethargic spirit that possessed them last winter—all fire, all revenge."[113] Joseph Clark of New Jersey, the adjutant of Stephen's Division, commented in his diary that the British seemed headed for Philadelphia. "This rouz'd the militia of all the neighbouring Counties, & they turn'd out with such a Spirit as will do them honour to the latest ages. Never did the Jersies appear more universally unanimous to oppose the enemy," he noted with enthusiasm. "They turn'd out young & old great & small, Rich & poor Scarcely a man that cou'd cary a musket was left at home. . . . [The enemy] could scarcely stir from their camp but they were cut off."[114]

In the same vein, "The Jersey Militia have turned out, with great Spirit," John Adams proudly informed Abigail. "Magistrates and Subjects, Clergy and Laity, have all marched, like so many Yankees."[115]

Lt. Col. Persifor Frazer of the 5th Pennsylvania Regiment, part of Wayne's 1st Pennsylvania Brigade, watched the maneuvers from the camp at Mount Pleasant. "The intent of their movement was to procure forage and in case we should move to attack," he explained to his wife, Polly, "that they might take possession of the Ground we occupy, which is naturally very strong; a river on each wing of their army, and a large deep swamp in their Front; so that an attempt to attack them would be very imprudent." Frazer went on to say that "a number of Rifle Men and two or three regts. were Sent off and kept them employ'd Saturday and Sunday. The enemy fired a vast deal, and all the Execution they did was to kill One Man and wound another. We have taken several Prisoners, a great Number of deserters have come Over to Us lately." He reassured Polly, "In a very short time you may expect to hear of a General attack; as We shall be greatly reinforced."

"The General has the entire confidence of the army," Percy Frazer declared, "and if God will but smile upon us every thing within human foresight appears encouraging." Believing that this would be a decisive encounter, he was proud to say, "Our regiment with several others of our State have the Post of Honor in the Front at the Gap of the Hills; the remainder of the army are encamp'd behind us. I am clearly of Opinion a very Short time will decide the Controversy. . . . One grand exertion will certainly put a finishing stroke to the dispute, and then peace and Happiness will ensue if We have Virtue enough to accept the desirable guests."[116]

By June 18, day five of the Campaign, Howe's force had moved less than ten miles, skirmished, encamped, foraged, plundered, built three redoubts, plundered, skirmished, plundered some more, and was no closer to Philadelphia. "We are under no more Apprehensions here than if the British Army was in the Crimea," John Adams wrote from the city that day. Regarding Washington's leadership, he wryly commented, "Our Fabius will be slow, but sure."[117]

Also from Philadelphia on the eighteenth, Dr. Benjamin Rush told Anthony Wayne, "The Accounts we receive daily of the Strength, discipline, and Spirit of our Army give us great pleasure. I need not add, that we expect [to] hear that the Pensylvanians will show us the 'metal of their pasture' in the day of tryal." With some provincial pride, Rush added, "Let not Virginia bear away from us the palm of Military glory. I am sure our men are made of as good Stuff for soldiers and officers as any men on the continent." He concluded, "As for yourself my dear friend—may you be glutted with well earned fame," adding a friendly needle at Wayne's well-known vanity, "'for if it be a Sin to covet honor,' I am sure 'you are the most offending Man alive.' God bless you."[118]

Incredibly, this force of some of Europe's finest troops—part of the largest overseas expedition mounted by the British Empire up to that time—found itself surrounded and almost cut off from its main base by small, determined bands of militia, frontiersmen, and Continental regulars, few of whom were regarded as real soldiers by European standards. Here was the genesis of the new United States Army, conceived in desperation just before Princeton, born in conflict, now nurtured in vengeance. Within the year, it would be baptized by fire at Brandywine, grow through hard experience at Germantown, and come to maturity at Valley Forge. If Washington can be described as the army's father, Howe might aptly be described as its nanny.

In the midst of all the plundering, skirmishes, and ennui, an episode of "heroics" occurred that served to lighten the moment. Col. Timothy Pickering of Massachusetts, a thirty-two-year-old Harvard graduate, was Washington's newly appointed adjutant general and had just arrived at headquarters to take up his duties. On June 18, his first full day on the job, he noted that "two lieutenants of grenadiers, taken by the Jersey militia, were brought to head-quarters, and twelve privates were taken the same day."[119] The taking of prisoners was usually unremarkable, even the capture of low-ranking officers. But in this case, the plot was thicker than the mere capture of two British officers, as the trail of comments through both armies reveals. Howe's deputy adjutant general, Col. Stephen Kemble, wrote, "We lost about half a dozen men, and two Lieuts. of 55th Grenadiers, supposed Prisoners, as they were known to have had an Intrigue in that Quarter."[120] The details of the "intrigue" were revealed in Captain von Münchhausen's diary: "Something very unpleasant happened, which made General Howe very angry. . . . Two well-behaved young English grenadier lieutenants went about 50 paces beyond our pickets to see two sisters whom they knew during the last campaign, when we held most of Jersey. A third sister, supposedly because she was jealous, sneaked away and brought back a detachment of rebels, who made these two sons of Mars their prisoners."[121]

The episode was noteworthy as a warning to all officers; years later, in his *Treatise on Partisan Warfare*, Capt. Johann Ewald referred to the two hapless "sons of Mars" (on a mission to Venus!) in a chapter titled, aptly enough, "On Ambushes": "Officers will also fall into your hands now and then, among whom there are always some who, despite the strictest prohibition, will risk everything to look for a girl. . . . This way two English officers were caught in the . . . camp near Millstone."[122]

Then, without warning, after all the "gasconading" and maneuvering, "at daybreak on June 19 the English army marched back to the heights of New Brunswick," Ewald reported. "On this march all the plantations of the disloyal inhabitants, numbering perhaps some fifty persons, were sacrificed to fire and devastation."[123] Some minor skirmishing and much marauding took place on the return march. "General Howe decamped with the greatest precipitation from Millstone, and retired to Brunswick, his troops burning seven or eight houses on their way, and having plundered all the houses where they had been," Col. Timothy Pickering wrote. "Extreme caution marked the whole of Howe's conduct."[124] The royal forces marched "without beat of drum or sound of fife," General Knox noted. "When his army had gotten beyond the reach of pursuit, they began to burn, plunder and waste all before them. The desolation they committed was horrid, and served to show the malice which marks their conduct."[125]

"The Enemy notwithstanding their great Threats and preparations have return'd again to Brunswick," Colonel Frazer wrote home. "We have constant parties attacking them," he noted, observing, "They are very much afraid of Us, every Motion shews it, their Cannon are constantly brought up if but ten men attack them." In horror and disgust, he told Polly, "They have in many instances behav'd very cruel to the Inhabitants where they pass'd. A respectable woman they Hung by the Heels so long that when they took her down she liv'd but a few Minutes. Plunder and Cruelty Mark their steps where there is scarce a soul but Tories."[126]

This odd maneuver succeeded in baffling many people. "We traced out 4 redoubts at Middlebrook [Middlebush], and one to cover the Bridge at Hilsborough, most of which were nearly finish'd, when, to our astonishment, we received orders to retire to Brunswick," Major Stuart informed his father, Lord Bute. "I am convinced that, from the redoubts built . . . and the pontoon bridge we incumbered ourselves with, we intended to establish a magazine there, and pursue our way to the Delaware . . . [but did not] for the fear of our escorts being attacked bringing provisions from Brunswick." Stuart went on to point out, "The risk which all armies are liable to was our hindrance here, and has absolutely prevented us this whole war from going 15 miles from a navigable river."[127] Of Howe's tactics, "What reason he cou'd have for making this strange march into the Jersies I cannot conceive," the major told his father. "Indecision alone can be an excuse for it."[128]

It seems inconceivable that the purpose of the march was to move thousands of troops and tons of equipment ten miles, build three large forts, and then abandon them. It is harder to believe that Washington's force was so formidable that Howe felt his army to be in mortal danger. And it is incomprehensible that a commander would allow his supposedly disciplined forces to commit the sort of marauding guaranteed to do nothing but further infuriate the population, rouse armed opposition, and provide factual basis for enemy propaganda. Yet this is what occurred in mid-June 1777 in East Jersey.

It was all part of the campaign plan, according to Gen. James Grant, and there never was any British intention of marching to the Delaware. "As Washington had it still in his power to cross the Delawar at Easton or Alexandria, it became evident that moving to Flemington, Prince Town, Trenton or Penington would not have the desired Effect of drawing the Rebells from their fastnesses," he told General Harvey in England. "Remaining longer in the Jerseys could of course answer no good End, as we did not intend to pass the Delawar in Boats," even though boats were constructed in New York at great expense and brought along with much trouble. "It was therefore thought expedient to return the 19th to Brunswick & to proceed from thence on the more important operations of the Campaign."[129]

In Philadelphia, the news that Howe's forces had "skulked back to Brunswick" was devastating to the Loyalists. "The Tories in this Town seem to be in absolute Despair," John Adams gleefully reported. "Chop-fallen, in a most remarkable Manner," he added. "The Quakers begin to say they are not Tories—that their Principle of passive Obedience will not allow them to be Whiggs, but that they are as far from being Tories as the Presbyterians."[130]

What was next? On June 20, a bright, clear day, Nicholas Cresswell left New York City by sloop and headed for New Brunswick to see the British Army in the field. After passing through the Narrows at the mouth of New York Harbor and turning west into Princess Bay, "We were entertained with one of the most pleasing and delightful scenes I ever saw before. Four hundred sail of ships, brigs, schooners and sloops with five sail of the Line [large warships] all under-way and upon a Wind at once, in the compass of two miles." He was witnessing the beginning of the next phase of the campaign: "They are all bound to Perth Amboy, it is said, to take the Troops on board."[131]

Two days later, on June 22, the Crown Forces evacuated Brunswick and marched eastward to Amboy, where the transport ships awaited them. "The Retreat of our Troops from Jersey will give the Rebels great Encouragement, and strengthen their cause much," a puzzled and anxious Stephen Kemble wrote from headquarters in New York. He quickly added, on a hopeful note, "But [I] have that Confidence in our General as to think his measures right, for few can know his Reasons and judge of the propriety of the Steps he has taken."[132]

The king's men were not at all happy about the withdrawal. "The troops growled at the ignominy of something that looked very like a *retreat*; whilst other people were either stung with disappointment, or lost in silent wonder at what could be intended by so mysterious a conduct," wrote a New York Loyalist.[133] A Philadelphia Tory expressed similar thoughts about "which conduct appears to be a great mystery to us, or what intentions they can possibly have in thus leaving the Jersies & their friends in it wholly exposed to the ravages & insults of an incensed army, who will greatly exult & rejoice in this retreat of the English." Horrified at the prospect, Sarah Logan Fisher wrote, "How much to be pitied are those men who had fled to the English for protection."[134]

The British appeared to be hastily evacuating New Jersey. Rumors flew, and American light forces, composed of Morgan's Ranger Corps and part of Wayne's 1st Pennsylvania Brigade, pursued the Crown Forces, peppering the British rear guard at every opportunity. "The whole army quitted Brunswick in the morning & cross'd over by Moncrieffs bridge," a bridge over the Raritan designed by Capt. James Moncrieff of the British Engineers. "The Grenadiers & Light Infantry in the Rear, halted for a little on

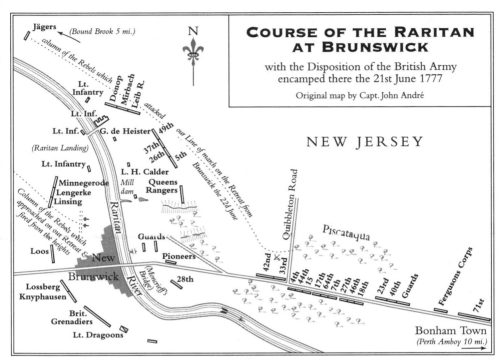

Jägers　(Bound Brook 5 mi.)

N

COURSE OF THE RARITAN AT BRUNSWICK

with the Disposition of the British Army encamped there the 21st June 1777

Original map by Capt. John André

column of the Rebels which

Lt. Infantry

Donop
Mirbach
Leib R.

attacked

Lt. Inf.

Lt. Inf.

G. de Heister

49th
37th
26th
5th

our Line of march on the Retreat from Brunswick the 22d June

(Raritan Landing)

Lt. Infantry

NEW JERSEY

Minnegerode
Lengerke
Linsing

L. H. Calder

Mill dam

Queens Rangers

Raritan

Quibbleton Road

Column of the Rebels which approached on our Retreat & fired from the heights

Loos

Guards

New

Brunswick

Pioneers

Piscataqua

Lossberg
Knyphausen

Moncrieff's Bridge

28th

42nd
33rd

4th
44th
15
17th
64th
7th
27th
46th
18th
23rd
40th

Guards

Fergusons Corps

Brit. Grenadiers

Lt. Dragoons

71st

Bonham Town
(Perth Amboy 10 mi.)

The Crown Forces evacuated New Brunswick on June 22 and moved east to Perth Amboy. Washington's forces pursued, and heavy skirmishing erupted near the Quibbletown Road and at Moncrieff's Bridge, where Wayne and Morgan "peppered severely" the British rearguard. Howe's maneuver succeeded in luring Washington's forces out of the hills behind Bound Brook and set them up for an attack.

the heights of Eastside ye River," Capt.-Lt. John Peebles of the Royal Highlanders wrote, "when a body of about 1000 of the Rebels appeared on the upper ground near the Landing with 3 pieces of Cannon which they play'd for some time."[135] Maj. Charles Stuart watched as Morgan's Corps arrived; "on our rear parties passing the Bridge about 500 of the rebels appear'd on the other side, and fired several cannon shot without doing any damage." He then saw the rest of Wayne's troops boldly march up, followed by Sullivan, "near 3000 with guns, Colours, and heaping every kind of insolence." Ever critical of Howe, Stuart told his father, "The General did not think proper to attack them, the consequence of which was that they threw 500 or 600 men into the wood upon our left, who warmly harassed our rear for 6 miles, and killed or wounded 30 men."[136]

Stuart was not entirely correct, for Howe himself was directing the British rear guard. "At the end of the bridge was a small height, where General Howe stopped with us and observed the passing troops, who looked quite sullen because of the march back," Captain von Münchhausen wrote. "Suddenly our side-patrols, marching at the left of our column in the woods, were so fiercely attacked by about 800 riflemen that they started to retreat toward our main column. General Howe hurriedly took the next two following regiments out of the column and personally led them toward the advancing riflemen."

Howe's fearlessness under fire was always an inspiration, especially to his favorite troops, the light infantry. "They skirmished with us for about half an hour and would probably have continued if General Howe had not brought up two cannon and fired several grape shot at the riflemen, whereupon they retreated. We lost about 30 men killed and wounded, the rebels, without doubt, lost many more." According to von Münchhausen, "General Howe . . . remained in this position for two more hours, showing the rebel gentlemen that he was waiting for them with this small corps. But since they showed no inclination to come and do battle, he proceeded with great caution and reached Amboy unmolested."[137] Sgt. Thomas Sullivan of the 49th wrote, "Before the Army reached Amboy, the Enemy made three different attacks upon the Rear, and were as often repulsed."[138]

One of Wayne's officers, Colonel Frazer, offered a considerably different version of the fight at Brunswick Bridge:

> Genl Wayne with part of his Brigade amounting to about 500 was sent off to intercept their march on the East side of the Rariton. About Sunrise our vigilant countryman began to fire on a very large Body across the Bridge at the Landing, they fled with the greatest Precipitation though at least 5 to one superior. . . . Wayne however with his little party about 500 Rifle kept on the attack from Hill to Hill where they had fortified themselves till he had put the whole to flight, he follow'd them while Sullivan and some others took possession of Brunswick. They had set fire to two small vessels with Stores and attempted to Burn a New Bridge they had built, but in vain.

Regarding casualties, Frazer reported, "The Best accounts We have, make their loss from the time they went to Somerset to the end of this Engagement 500 at least—they made the Best of their way to Amboy where they were strongly fortified. I saw from a Hill near our Camp the whole of the Engagement, Our Division being order'd to stand their ground till further Orders."[139]

From the east side of the Raritan, Nicholas Cresswell also witnessed the battle and the line of march close up, noting the behavior of the men in this "minor skirmish" and the deadly fire at close range:

> Some of the Rebels' Scouting parties fired upon our Sentinels, which brought on a sharp skirmish. I happened to see them in the bushes before they fired, but mistook them for some of our rangers. They were about 300 yards from me. When the engagement began I got upon a little hillock to see the better, but an honest Highlander advised me to retire behind a small breastwork just by. . . . I had a very good view of their proceedings. When they were about 100 yards from each other both parties fired, but I did not observe any fall. They still advanced to the distance of about 40 yards or less, and fired again, I then saw a good number fall on both sides. Our people then rushed upon them with their bayonets and the others took to their heels, I heard one of them call out "murder!" lustily. . . . A brisk fire then began from six field pieces the Rebels had secreted in the Woods, which did some mischief to our men, the engagement lasted about thirty-five minutes. Our people took the Field pieces about 40 prisoners and killed about 150 of the Scoundrels with the loss of 39 killed and 27 wounded.[140]

Washington told Congress that day, "Gen. Green desires me to make mention of the conduct and bravery of General Wayne and Col. Morgan, and of their officers and men upon this occasion, as they constantly advanced upon an enemy far superior to them in numbers."[141] The closeness of the action was further described by the commander in chief: "By some late Accounts I fancy the British Grenadiers got a pretty severe peppering yesterday by Morgan's Rifle Corps. They fought, it seems, a considerable time within the distance of, from twenty, to forty yards."[142]

Capt. David Harris of the 1st Pennsylvania noted an episode with one of his fellow officers:

> Coll. Butler, Captain Parr, with two subalterns, and about 50 privates, are detached in Morgan's Partizan Corps. Captain Parr has killed three or four men himself this Summer. His expressions at the Death of one I shall ever Remember. Major Miller had the Command of a Detachment, and had a skirmish at very close shot with a party of Highlanders. One of them being quite open, he motioned to Capt. Parr to kill him, which he did in a trice, and, as he was falling, Parr said: "I say, by God, Sawny, I am in you." I assure you Parr's bravery on every occasion does him great Honour.[143]

As soon as the shooting was over, "I went to the place where I saw the two parties fire upon each other first before the wounded were removed," Nicholas Cresswell wrote, "but I never before saw such a shocking scene, some dead others dying, death in different shapes." Horrified, he heard "some of the wounded making the most pitiful lamentations, others that were of different parties cursing each other as the author of their misfortunes. One old Veteran I observed (that was shot through both legs and not able to walk) very coolly and deliberately loading his piece and cleaning it from blood. I was surprised at the sight and asked him his reasons for it. He, with a look of contempt, said, 'To be ready in case any of the Yankees come that way again.'"

Cresswell also observed: "All the Country houses were in flames as far as we could see. The Soldiers are so much enraged they will set them on fire, in spite of all the Officers can do to prevent it. They seem to leave the Jerseys with reluctance, the train of Artillery and Waggons extends about nine miles and is upwards of 1000 in number."[144] A Hessian officer confirmed, "The entire army marched back to Amboy. All the houses along the road were set on fire."[145]

"The enemy evacuated Brunswick this morning, and retired to Amboy, burning many houses as they went along," Washington informed Congress. "Some of them, from the appearance of the flames, were considerable buildings."[146] A British soldier, Pvt. John Warrel of the 23rd Royal Welch Fusiliers, reported that "on the retreat from Brunswick his Regiment was one of the last that marched, that they were ordered to set fire to a large white house in the skirts of the town which had been used as a Storehouse (this probably was burned on account of some stores [the army] could not take away . . .)." Warrel further stated that "the general conversation amongst the men on the retreat was that they were intended to go up the North river."[147]

After more than six months of occupation, New Brunswick was left a shambles and the condition of the surrounding countryside was deplorable. Cresswell, who stayed in the British camp across the Raritan from the town the night before the evacuation, wrote in his diary, "Almost bit to death with Mosquitoes and poisoned with the stink of some Rebels, who have been buried about three weeks in such a slight manner that wagons have cut up parts of the half corrupted carcasses and made them stink most horribly."[148] The town itself was a disgusting wreck, not only from the usual wear and tear of soldiers, but also from deliberate vandalism and fouling of the houses with filth. "I was at Brunswick just after the enemy had left it," Lt. Col. William Palfrey of Massachusetts, the paymaster general of the Continental Army, wrote. "Never let the British troops upbraid the Americans with want of cleanliness, for such dog kennels as their huts were my eyes never beheld." He noted with disgust, "Mr. Burton's house, where Lord Cornwallis resided, stunk so I could not bear to enter it. The houses were torn to pieces, and the inhabitants as well as the soldiers have suffered greatly for want of provisions."[149]

Col. Percy Frazer of the 5th Pennsylvania confirmed both Cresswell's and Palfrey's observations. "They have been fam'd for cleanliness and but every account and every thing I have seen of them contradict that Character," he wrote. "Their Tents, etc., and Quarters exceed every thing for Nastiness," and numerous bodies were "found buried in the cellars of Brunswick . . . with a design to keep their Mortality a Secret. In places numbers have been dug up after the late engagements with them, that they have hall'd from the field."[150]

Artist Charles Willson Peale of Philadelphia went with Washington's army to observe, paint and sketch, and offer his services as a militia officer. "How solitary it looked to see so many Farms without a single animal—many Houses Burnt & others Rendered unfit for use," he wrote. "The Fences all distroyed and many fields the wheat Reaped while quite Green." New Brunswick itself "has some hundreds of Houses, but, judged at this time that it had only 30 familys Living [in] it. The Enemy having Terrifyed many of them by telling them we would hang them all. Here was much distruction of the Houses. The Presbeterian Meeting Torn to pieces. The English Church was in Tolerable order."[151]

Percy Frazer described the scene to Polly:

> On Monday I went down to take a view of Brunswic, but believe me the Worst Accounts you have heard of their rapine fall infinitely short of the reality, it passes all description, the greatest part of the Houses within their limits for 4 or 5 miles around Bunswic, Burnt, or Pull'd down or otherwise tore to pieces, not a sign of a Fence to be seen and a universal scene of savage Barbarity and Cruelty presented themselves to View and this to those who had taken protection from the mighty infamous Howe. I have had information from undoubted authority that while they Were

about Somerset they Violated many Women forcibly, two they hung by the Heels. One of whom an elderly Woman and of good family died immediately on her being taken down, they cut down many Orchards, destroy'd all the furniture that came in their Way, wounded many and kill'd some of the inhabitants and on their retreat from Somerset and Brunswick Burnt the greatest part of the Houses along the road.

Thinking of home and the Loyalists among his Chester County neighbors, Percy added, "I sincerely wish those stubborn advocates for British Tyranny in our neighborhood cou'd only make it their Business to take a small ride and see the Devastation and ruin the deluded inhabitants of the Jersey have been treated with."[152]

What at first appeared to be a humiliating and hurried British withdrawal from New Brunswick was actually part of a carefully crafted strategic maneuver to lure Washington out of the mountains and into the plains of East Jersey. Continental forces now occupied New Brunswick, and Maj. Gen. William Alexander, "Lord Stirling" of New Jersey, was positioned on Washington's left flank at Short Hills, several miles north of New Brunswick and east of Bound Brook. The Americans began to send more forces down toward Perth Amboy—just as Howe hoped.

Sir William shrewdly calculated that the appearance of evacuation to Staten Island and to the fleet would be enough temptation for Washington to risk an attack on the British rear guard. He was partially right— the Americans kept a close eye on the activities at Perth Amboy and Staten Island and steadily came closer. On Tuesday, June 24, "We were order'd to march to Quibble Town about 5 miles toward the Enemy," Colonel Frazer wrote. "Our Generals went to reconnoiter the Enemy but found they were so very strongly posted that it would be Madness to attack and run the risk of a Defeat." The British and Hessians "were posted on a Hill near Amboy, the Rariton cover'd their left Wing, their Right extended to the sound, a Battery of 32 pieces of Heavy Cannon cover'd their Front." With a brashness similar to that of his good friend and commander Anthony Wayne, Frazer commented, "Thus they were station'd, and the Mighty Conquerers of America amounting to near 15,000, were satisfied to have their partys, their Guards and Centry's insulted hourly by our Rifle men and scouts."[153]

Or so it seemed. "Everything concurred, along with the vanity natural to mankind, in inducing the Americans to believe, that this retreat was not only real, but that it proceeded from a knowledge of their superiority, and a dread of their power," *The Annual Register* reported. "Even Washington himself, with all his caution and penetration, was so far imposed upon by this feint, that he quitted his secure posts upon the Hills, and advanced."[154]

Then Howe made his move. In the middle of the night on June 25, Cornwallis quietly led a column rapidly toward Scotch Plains and Short Hills by way of Woodbridge, intending to cut Stirling's force off from the mountain passes. Another British column under Gen. John Vaughan, with Sir William Howe in attendance, moved toward New Brunswick and then turned north toward Scotch Plains.

The strategy was a replay of the Battle of Long Island, where Howe had masterfully outflanked and nearly annihilated Washington the previous year, capturing Lord Stirling and Gen. John Sullivan in the process. This time, as he once again went after Stirling, Howe hoped to coax Washington out of his strong position in the mountains and catch him in a pincer movement.

Near Ash Swamp, about sunrise, "Cornwallis's column came upon a picket of Lord Stirling's force at six o'clock," Captain von Münchhausen wrote.

> Stirling's picket ran off after a few shots. Both columns continued on their march till about eight o'clock in the morning, during which time there was a steady fire on us from out of the bushes, and from behind trees. Their fire was answered by the Hessian Jägers, the English light infantry and our side patrols. Then we met a corps of about 600 men with three cannon on a hill before a woods. They held their position until we approached them with some deployed battalions and cannon, whereupon they hurriedly withdrew into the woods behind them.

Not long after this first encounter with the advance guard, von Münchhausen said:

> On a bare hill before some woods, we came upon approximately 2500 men with six cannon. They started cannon fire early, at a distance of 1000 paces, and then began with small arms fire. We took two 12-pounders and several 6-pounders to our left flank, where we had some rising ground. From our right flank the Hessian grenadier battalion von Minnegerode ascending the slope in deployed formation, attacked their left flank. Our battalion had to move considerably to the right in order to outflank their left flank. The rebels continued a strong but not very effective fire upon us. They finally fired grape-shot at von Minnegerode's battalion, but after that, they ran away into the woods.[155]

The flank companies of the Guards launched a bayonet charge up a steep hill, and the Grenadier Company captured one of the guns. "The Light Infantry, a Battalion of Hessian Grenadiers, and the Grenadiers of the Guards, commanded by my friend Sir George Osborn, distinguished themselves very much upon this occasion," Lt. Col. William Harcourt of the 16th Queen's Light Dragoons wrote, "and took three pieces of Cannon, with some prisoners."[156] Captain André noted, "They were French guns."[157]

Sgt. Thomas Sullivan of the 49th Regiment caught the spirit and enthusiasm of the attack in his account:

> The Troops vying with each other upon this occasion attacked the Enemy so close, that, tho' they were inclined to resist, could not long maintain their ground against so much Impetuosity, but were soon dispersed on all sides, leaving behind three Pieces of Brass Cannon, 3 Captains and 60 men killed, and upwards of 200 Officers and men wounded and taken. Our Loss was 5 men killed, and 30 wounded. The ardour and merit of the engaged Troops on this occasion was highly commendable. One Piece of Cannon was taken by the Guards, the other two by Colonel Mingerode's Battallion of Hessian Grenadiers.[158]

A captain of the Guards Light Company, the Honorable John Finch, was mortally wounded while leading his men up the hill. Finch attempted to capture not only the guns, but also Lord Stirling himself. "The Light Company of the Guards . . . fell in with a considerable body of the enemy, and lost half the Company killed and wounded," according to Lt. Martin Hunter of the 52nd Light Company. "Captain Finch, a very fine young man, was killed."[159] An American officer wrote:

> I must not omit to mention a little affair, that happened in the late engagement. The fire growing hot, and our men beginning to retreat, a British officer singly rode up to a cannon that was playing on the enemy, and with his pistols and *hanger* [sword] forced every man from it, then seeing Lord Sterling he cried "Come here, you damned rebel, and I will do for you." Lord Sterling answered him, by directing the fire of four marksmen upon him, which presently silenced the hardy fool, by killing him upon the spot. Our men recovered the field piece which their want of small arms obliged them to abandon.[160]

Banastre Tarleton, at that time a cornet in the 16th Light Dragoons, confirmed that "in the attack of the Cannon fell the Honorable Capt.

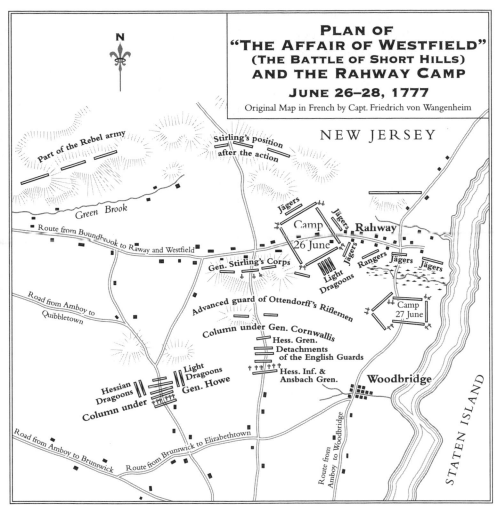

**PLAN OF
"THE AFFAIR OF WESTFIELD"
(THE BATTLE OF SHORT HILLS)
AND THE RAHWAY CAMP
JUNE 26–28, 1777**

Original Map in French by Capt. Friedrich von Wangenheim

N

NEW JERSEY

Part of the Rebel army

Stirling's position after the action

Green Brook

Jägers

Camp 26 June

Rahway

Route from Boundbrook to Raway and Westfield

Gen. Stirling's Corps

Jägers

Jägers

Rangers Jägers Jägers

Light Dragoons

Road from Amboy to Quibbletown

Advanced guard of Ottendorff's Riflemen

Camp 27 June

Column under Gen. Cornwallis

Hess. Gren.

Detachments of the English Guards

Hess. Inf. & Ansbach Gren.

Woodbridge

Light Dragoons Gen. Howe

Hessian Dragoons

Column under

STATEN ISLAND

Road from Amboy to Brunswick

Route from Brunswick to Elizabethtown

Route from Amboy to Woodbridge

Howe's night march in two columns on June 25 caught Washington by surprise on the morning of June 26, and Gen. Stirling's Corps at Short Hills was badly defeated by Cornwallis. The Continental forces withdrew back into the hills while the Crown Forces ravaged the area between Westfield and Amboy. Howe's effective use of light troops and his favorite tactic of dividing his forces would be used again at Brandywine.

Finch of the Light Infantry Guards," lamenting, as many others did, "a youth strongly attached to his Profession and ever to be regretted if amiable and manly Virtues claim Regard."[161]

The dashing young Guardsman was taken back to Perth Amboy, where, three agonizing days later, on Sunday, June 29, John Montrésor sadly recorded in his journal, "Captain Finch . . . died of his wounds and buried this day at Amboy."[162] News of his death was reported with much sorrow to the highest levels in the army and the British government. "Our loss not worth mentioning if poor Capt. Fynch of the Guards had not been mortally wounded," Grant informed General Harvey in London, adding, "He was a spirited Young Man, and is regretted by every body."[163] After reading the dispatch that reported the young officer's death, Lord George Germain replied to Howe, "I must always feel great Concern, when I recollect that the army, by the Death of Captain Finch, has been deprived of an officer who gave the strongest Proofs of military Genius, and promised to be an Ornament to the Profession of Arms."[164]

Washington's intelligence system failed miserably during this maneuver. "In fact Washingtons Spys if He had any were deceived," Grant scoffed.[165] A congressman fumed, "Was it not shameful to be surprised when the Enemy were within 8 Miles? Nothing but Severity will introduce Discipline into our Armies, and dear bought Experience only can convince our officers & Men of its Utility, nay of its absolute Necessity."[166]

Howe's march came as a complete surprise to Washington, according to Adj. Gen. Timothy Pickering:

> About seven in the morning a light-horseman brought word to the General, that the enemy were at hand, within two miles and a half. The General ordered the alarm guns to be fired. The men ran briskly to arms. Next, a light-horseman of the enemy was brought in prisoner. . . . This prisoner said he was taken not more than two and a half miles from headquarters at Quibbletown. It was surprising to the General, that of so many parties he had ordered out to watch the enemy, none gave him earlier notice of the enemy's advancing. . . . One body of the enemy having marched toward our left, to attack and pursue Lord Stirling, who was pretty far advanced, General Washington ordered the troops at Quibbletown to retire to the mountains.[167]

Howe had attempted to draw Washington out of the Watchung Mountains and onto the plains of New Jersey to offer battle to the new Continental Army on level ground. According to Grant, the British themselves were somewhat surprised by Washington's response. "We thought He might probably march small bodies from the Mountains to keep up an appearance of acting offensively," the Scottish general wrote incredulously, "but did not imagine, that He would wantonly run a Risk of disgracing his Army by exposing Himself to the possible Necessity of a precipitate Retreat, which must have a bad effect upon his Troops, & discourage the Continent at large."[168]

The British strategy almost worked; fortunately for Washington, he recognized Howe's intentions at the last minute and quickly pulled his forces back into the Watchungs. "It was judged prudent to return with the army to the mountains," Alexander Hamilton wrote, "lest it should be their intention to get into them and force us to fight them on their own terms."

But prudent moves for the long term do not allay the frustration of soldiers in the short term, as Hamilton was aware. "It is painful to leave a part of the inhabitants a prey to their depredations; and it is wounding to the feelings of a soldier, to see an enemy parading before him and daring him to a fight which he is obliged to decline," he said bristling. "But a part must be sacrificed to the whole, and passion must give way to reason." Washington's strategy was clear: "Our business then is to avoid a General engagement and waste the enemy away by constantly goading their sides, in a desultory way." The American Fabius would continue employing Fabian tactics.

The plain truth was that the Continental Army was not yet ready for a major battle with a professional European force. Numbers of troops did not matter nearly as much as quality, professionalism, and experience. But all of that was immaterial, for in each of these areas, the Crown Forces were superior by far.

Washington knew all too well that his survival since January was nothing short of astonishing, and it would have been foolish to waste his good fortune on a dare from Howe. "The liberties of America are an infinite stake," Hamilton pointed out. "We should not play a desperate game for it or put it upon the issue of the single cast of the die. The loss of one general engagement may effectually ruin us, and it would certainly be folly to hazard it."

Nonetheless, Hamilton anticipated that Washington would be severely criticized for his withdrawal. "I know the comments that some people will make on our Fabian conduct," he wrote. "It will be imputed either to cowardice or to weakness: But the more discerning, I trust, will not find it difficult to conceive that it proceeds from the truest policy."[169]

The young colonel was right. Of the June maneuvers, an increasingly impatient John Adams wrote on June 29, "The two Armies are now playing off their Arts. Each acts with great Caution. Howe is as much afraid of putting any Thing to Hazard as Washington."[170] Adams, the very member of Congress who had sponsored Washington as commander in chief in 1775, was becoming one of his critics.

The Battle of Short Hills took place on the morning of what proved to be a miserably hot summer day. As His Majesty's forces continued on the road to Westfield, heat exhaustion and sunstroke began to take a toll on the men. The sudden, sheer parapet of the Watchung Mountains reflected waves of intense heat into the flat, sandy plains of North Jersey, turning the area into a baking inferno blanketed with humidity. To make matters worse, little drinkable water could be found, for many of the creeks in that region were brackish. When water was found, the men drank it greedily, with disastrous results. "The day proving so intensly hot, that the men could with difficulty continue their march homeward," Sgt. Thomas Sullivan of the 49th wrote, "many of them dropping dead in the Ranks through the means of drinking too much water."[171] Captain Montrésor reported, "One man raved with a *coup de soleil* [sunstroke] and fired at our own flankers."[172] Major Stuart told his father of "20 men who dropp'd down dead from the heat or fatigue."[173]

The pattern of mindless destruction continued along the route, exacerbated by the sniping of American riflemen and the heat. "They marched up as far as Westfield, plundering and burning Houses and driving off what little stock remained," Washington told Congress.[174] Alexander Hamilton reported, "They remained at Westfield 'till the next day . . . plundering and burning as usual. . . . They got three field pieces from us, which will give them room for vapouring, and embellish their excursion, in the eyes of those, who make every trifle a matter of importance."[175] Ironically, Captain Fitzpatrick of the Guards wrote in a similar vein, "The advantage we gained was however in reality of no consequence though I suppose they will endeavour to magnify it prodigiously."[176]

The Crown Forces camped for the night at Westfield, reserving special treatment for the Westfield Presbyterian Meeting House. The Presbyterians and New England Congregationalists were Calvinist "Dissenter" churches, which were anti-Anglican and as such were regarded by many as the chief instigators of the Revolution, so their meetinghouses were often targeted by British forces. "Places of public worship seem everywhere marked as objects of their fury and bigoted rage," wrote Col. Timothy Pickering, who witnessed the results of an especially deliberate and disgusting act of desecration. "At Westfield the meeting-house was converted into a slaughter-house, and the entrails of the cattle thrown into the pulpit."[177] "The enemy even destroyed all the bibles and books of divinity they came across; this I assert as a fact," wrote an anonymous American officer in a letter published in *The Pennsylvania Gazette* to arouse public indignation.[178]

The following day, Howe's army continued on a wide sweeping circuit to Rahway, followed at a distance by American light troops. "The spirit of depredation was but too prevalent on these marches," Capt. John André admitted. "This day, however, it was much restrained in the Second Column (then in front). . . . The Army hutted this night along the banks of Rahway, six miles from Amboy."[179]

Among the American troops in pursuit was Maj. Samuel Hay of the 7th Pennsylvania Regiment in Wayne's Brigade. "About 800 turned out volunteers under Brig. Genl. Scott, of which your humble Servant was one & 80 men of the regiment," Hay wrote to his commander, Colonel Irvine. "We kept upon the rear until we convoyed them into Amboy; our intention was to harass them on their march, but they made their dispositions so well that we were not able to do them much damage, as we had no field pieces." As for plundering, "We prevented them from robbing the country, as they durst not send out any parties for that purpose; but along the road where they went, they stole sheep, cattle, and hogs, & robbed & plundered the houses as they went along, & committed such barbarities on the female sex as would make me blush to mention."[180]

Once again, the suffocating heat wrought havoc among the troops. "Several men died on this March from the Excessive Heat," Capt. Archibald Robertson of the British Engineers noted.[181] "The march was very strenuous again and the day unbearably hot, to which was added a shortage of beverages," Quartermaster Carl Bauer of the Hessian Platte Grenadier Battalion wrote. "Our regiment lost a man who was so worn out by the heat and march that he dropped dead."[182]

On June 28, "the army marched back in two columns to its former encampment at Amboy," Capt. Johann Ewald stated. "On this march an enemy party followed our rear guard, but it was constantly repelled by the jägers."[183] Washington commented the next day, "Whether, finding themselves a little disgrac'd by their former move, they wanted to flourish off a little at quitting the Jerseys, or, whether by this sudden eruption they meant to possess themselves of as much fresh Provision as they could, plunder the Inhabitants; and spread desolation . . . I know not; but certain it is they have left nothing which they could carry off, Robbing, Plundering, and burning Houses as they went. We followed them with light Troops to their Works at Amboy, but could not prevent the Desolation they committed."[184] Grant sneered, "We were much obliged to Washington & his Generals for putting it in our power to leave the Jerseys with Éclat."[185]

Grant was elated by the maneuvers: "I do not think they have been so much down since the affair of Trenton, but the Mercury in a Thermometre or the Tides are not more easily affected than the spirits of our American Sons of Liberty—they will avoid a General Action, but are averse to accommodation." He boasted to General Harvey, "We can go where we please & beat them where ever We find them, their Woods are no security to them, our Light Infantry & Chasseurs [Jägers] are infinitely superior to them." Yet despite these advantages, even Grant recognized the reality of the larger picture: "But how the business is to be brought to a Conclusion I know not, We have no Friends & Lenity will not make our Enemys good Subjects—I have never varied from that opinion since I landed at Boston."[186]

Captain Fitzpatrick of the Guards would have agreed with Grant about having no friends, but for widely different reasons. "The Army is disconcerted & Exasperated to the most violent degree, and seem to consider laying the whole country waste & extirpating the inhabitants as the only means of putting an end to the war," the increasingly pessimistic Whig officer told his brother Lord Ossory. "Declaring everywhere these sentiments, & permitting if not encouraging, all kinds of pillage, plunder, & barbarity, they are astonished to find they have not a single friend in the country." Horrified by the actions of some of the men, he told his brother in disgust, "The stories of cruelty related on both sides are dreadful, but I assure you since I have been in this country I have heard many more instances of it amongst ourselves than ever I heard in England; & I could send you a collection of horrible examples of it that would make your blood run cold to read."[187]

On Sunday, June 29, the Crown Forces rested, and the Guards buried John Finch in the Anglican churchyard at Perth Amboy. The following day, in the midst of wind and rain, they moved out. "This morning early began to call in our posts which were advanced . . . 1/2 past 3 this afternoon when the Province of New Jersey was entirely evacuated by the King's Troops," Captain Montrésor wrote of the historic moment. "The Rebels were so disconcerted by the secret and very unexpected movement of the army on the 26th Instant that not a shot has been fired by them since."[188]

After all of the maneuvering, destruction, and bloodshed, New Jersey was again in American hands. "We have abandoned the Jerseys, & left Genl. Washington to enjoy the satisfaction of having sent us *pour chercher fortune ailleurs* [to seek fortune elsewhere]," Richard Fitzpatrick told his brother. "He was a little too much elated with his first triumph in having obliged us to leave him behind us, & gave us an opportunity of giving him a little rap before we took our leaves by following us rather too close."[189] Major Stuart told Lord Bute, "The consequence of this last unlucky retreat is that we have more clearly united those who were disaffected; we have helped to increase and inspirit the rebel army, and we have begun a campaign, that well managed would settle the affairs of this country, with the stigma of a retreat."[190]

Thus on Monday, June 30, 1777, after a year of hard campaigning, the British Army was back where it started: Staten Island, where it had first landed on July 2, 1776, the same day that Congress had adopted the resolution on independence. New York City and its immediate environs were under British control, as was Newport, Rhode Island. In that same period, Washington had had his army all but destroyed, rallied the cause of independence, and in six months rebuilt the Continental Army and the American Revolution. "An angel from Heaven cou'd not have the confidence of the Troops equal to Genl Washington," Col. Percy Frazer told his wife, Polly, on July 2.[191]

"As an Officer, he is quite popular, almost idolized by the Southern Provinces, but I think he is not so great a favourite with the Northern ones," Nicholas Cresswell observed about Washington. "The ignorant and deluded part of the people look up to him as the Saviour and Protector of their Country, and have implicit confidence in everything he does. The artful and designing part of the people, that is, the Congress and those at the head of affairs, look upon him as a necessary tool to compass their diabolical purposes." With grudging admiration, this astute Englishman further commented, "Washington, my Enemy as he is, I should be sorry if he should be brought to an ignominious death."

As he sailed for England in July after three years in America, where he had maintained his English patriotism against many difficulties, a bitter and disillusioned Cresswell wrote, "General Howe, a man brought up to War from his youth, to be puzzled and plagued for two years together, with a Virginia Tobacco planter. O! Britain, how thy Laurels tarnish in the hands of such a Lubber!" He added that Washington "certainly deserves some merit as a General, that he with his Banditti, can keep General Howe dancing from one town to another for two years together, with such an Army as he has." Frustrated by Howe, he scribbled, "Confound the great Chucclehead, he will not unmuzzle the mastiffs, or they would eat him and his ragged crew in a little time were they properly conducted with a man of resolution and spirit."

Viewing the desolate Connecticut shoreline from Long Island Sound, Cresswell could not help but ruminate over the terrible changes that war had brought to America:

> If we have good luck, we shall not be long before we leave sight of this unhappy Country, this Country, turned Topsy Turvy, changed from an earthy paradise to a Hell upon terra firma. I have seen this a happy Country and I have seen it miserable in the short space of three years. The Villainous arts of a few and the obstinacy of many on this side of the Water, added to the complicated blunders, cowardice and knavery of some of our blind *guides* in England, have totally ruined the Country. I wish the Devil had them. These unhappy wretches have substituted tyranny, oppression and slavery for liberty and freedom.[192]

On Tuesday, July 1, at British general headquarters in New York City, Deputy Adj. Gen. Stephen Kemble wrote in his journal, "Gen. Sir William Howe came this Evening from Staten Island to New York; nothing extraordinary."[193]

CHAPTER 2

"Where the storm will turn now, no one knows as yet."

THE MIDDLE ATLANTIC STATES, JULY–AUGUST 1777

Tongues of fire and pillars of smoke spewed from the blackened mouths of naval cannons thundering in the Delaware River, "which was terrible to hear," as one unhappy citizen put it, shaking buildings and rattling windows all over Philadelphia.[1] Thick, billowing white clouds engulfed warships streaming with flags and pennants, blanketing the water with a choking, sulfurous haze. In Second Street, amidst the screams of children and shouts from civilians, soldiers who had seen years of service in the British Army stood in double ranks, took aim, and discharged their weapons one after another down the line in rapid sequence like a huge string of firecrackers, the deafening reports of the muskets amplified by the time-stained brick walls of the houses. Drums rumbled and fifes squealed as plumes of acrid smoke enveloped the troops and the rotten-egg stink of burned gunpowder hung in the air, layered over the usual stench of city streets in the heat of summer.

The city was not under attack; rather, "we have had a Day of Rejoycing here to Celebrate the Aniversary of our Independence," Col. David Grier of the 7th Pennsylvania Regiment reported to Gen. Anthony Wayne. "All the ships of war &c. were lined from Opposite to the Coffee House" at Market Street and "down the River."[2] The troops were from the 4th Georgia Battalion, "a corps of British deserters, taken into the service of the continent by the State of Georgia." At Smith's City Tavern on the corner of 2nd and Walnut, they were "drawn up before the door," where they "filled up the intervals with *feux de joie*," or "joyful firings."[3] This type of running gunfire was done by armies for celebrations and was quite impressive as it went from one end of the line to the other.

Describing Philadelphia's first Fourth of July festivities, John Adams wrote, "The wharves and shores, were lined with a vast concourse of people, all shouting and huzzaing, in a manner which gave great joy to every friend to this country, and the utmost terror and dismay to every lurking tory." The city commemorated independence in fine style, though almost as an afterthought, Adams told his daughter Nabby. "The thought of taking any notice of this day, was not conceived, until the second of this month," John noted, "and it was not mentioned until the third."[4]

Congress marked the occasion by adjourning early and attending a series of special events, beginning with a review of the armed schooners and row galleys that constituted the Pennsylvania Navy. Several of the ships were "beautifully dressed in the colours of all nations, displayed about upon the masts, yards, and rigging." At 1 P.M., the sailors "were all ordered aloft, and arranged upon the tops, yards, and shrowds, making a striking appearance—of companies of men drawn up in order, in the air."[5]

As chairman of the Marine Committee in Congress, Adams, together with President John Hancock and other dignitaries, went on board the largest ship, the new thirty-gun Continental frigate *Delaware*, where they were received with a salute of thirteen cannons. The other war vessels fired salutes in reply, and "a great Expenditure of Liquor, Powder &c. took up the Day."[6]

"It was too late to have a sermon, as everyone wished," according to Adams, "so this must be deferred another year."[7] Instead, at 3 P.M., the members of Congress, the Pennsylvania Supreme Executive Council, the general officers in town, and city officials assembled at City Tavern for a banquet and the drinking of toasts.

Dinner music for the U.S. government's first Independence Day celebration was provided by a professional band that included two sets of fathers and sons—the Hatteroths, Sam and Will, and the Saechtlings, John Sr. and John Jr.—along with Emmanuel Grau, John Nickell, Philip Pfeil, John Sondermann, and John George Wickhard. They were members of the latest and most popular musical group in the city, the Hessian Band, nine German oboists captured at Trenton the previous December.[8]

Adams described being "very agreeably entertained with excellent company, good cheer, fine music from the band of Hessians taken at Trenton, and continual volleys between every toast, from a company of soldiers drawn up in Second-street before the city tavern, where we dined."

There were thirteen toasts in all. "The toasts were in honour of our country, and the heroes who have fallen in their pious efforts to defend her."[9] The soft, harmonious droning of "hautboys," or oboes, wafted through the tavern rooms between the toasts and firings, and Congressman Thomas Burke of North Carolina noted that the Hessian musicians "performed very delightfully, the pleasure being not a little heightened by the reflection that they were hired by the British Court for purposes very different from those to which they were applied."[10]

After dinner, a parade was held on Second Street, consisting of two troops of Maryland Light Horse, a train of artillery, and about 1,000 North Carolina infantry who were en route to join Washington's army in New Jersey. With drums throbbing and fifes lilting, "the troops paraded thro' the streets with great pomp," Sarah Logan Fisher wrote, "tho' many of them were barefoot & looked very unhealthy."[11] The soldiers marched to their camp in "Governor Penn's Woods" near the Common, an open area on the western outskirts of town, where they went through maneuvers and fired volley after volley, thirteen in all.

It had been a splendid day, with temperatures in the mid-seventies, a relief from the usual summer steambath of July in Philadelphia. Earlier in the week, temperatures plunged to the low sixties as a Nor'easter pelted the area with rain and chilly winds.[12] "A long, cold, raw northeast Storm has chilled our Blood, for two days past," John Adams wrote on July 1. "It is unusual, to have a Storm from that Point, in June and July. It is an Omen no doubt." He asked Abigail, "Pray what can it mean? I have so little Ingenuity, at interpreting the Auspices, that I am unable to say whether it bodes Evil to Howe, or to Us."[13]

Unusual natural phenomena were frequent in 1777, some of them quite dramatic. One had occurred a few weeks earlier on June 9, when "Severe Thunder Struck the steeple of Christ Church," the tallest structure in the city. Gracing the point of the spire was a gilded crown, symbol of royal authority over this Anglican parish. The lightning bolt "carried away some part of the Ornaments of the Crown on the top of the rods."[14] Meteors, northern lights, and a series of massive Atlantic storms were among the unsettled weather conditions that year, along with several very rare earthquake tremors, interpreted by some as omens reflecting the state of the country.

The evening of the Fourth was spectacular, filled with ringing bells and pageantry. Thirteen rockets opened a fireworks show that played across a starry, moonless sky above the Common, while bonfires blazed in the streets and candles glowed from thousands of windows in a "Grand Illumination." Adams strolled through the city and was moved to write, "I think it was the most splendid illumination I ever saw; a few surly houses were dark; but the lights were very universal. Considering the lateness of the design and the suddenness of the execution, I was amazed at the universal joy and alacrity that was discovered, and at the brilliancy and splendour of every part of this joyful exhibition. I had forgot the ringing of bells all day and evening." He smugly concluded, "Had General Howe been here in disguise, or his master, this show would have given them the heart-ache."[15]

Not everyone was as happy with the occasion, even among the patriots. William Williams, a dour, humorless congressman from Connecticut who earlier in life had trained for the ministry as a Congregationalist pastor, was appalled by the conspicuous consumption of liquor and hundreds of pounds of gunpowder. His wife, Mary, was the daughter of Connecticut governor Jonathan Trumbull and sister of artist John Trumbull. "Yesterday was in my opinion poorly spent in celebrating the anniversary of the Declaration of Independence," Williams told his father-in-law on July 5, "but to avoid singularity & Reflection upon my dear Colony, I thot it my Duty to attend the public Entertainment." The congressman's joyless disposition was not improved by a painful rheumatic swelling in his right arm. He noted peevishly, "Candles thro the City, good part of the night, I suppose."[16]

Rev. Henry Muhlenberg, father of Brig. Gen. Peter Muhlenberg of Virginia and the senior Lutheran churchman in America, was also outraged by the festivities. "The Philadelphians observed the day with special solemnity according to the advanced taste and sensuous magnificence," he commented sourly several weeks later. "The air was filled and shaken by artificial fireworks and thunderclaps. Empty skins were bloated with food and drinks of health. Houses with their artificial *illumination* outshone the moon and stars," a slight hyperbole, for a new moon began on the evening of the Fourth. No matter; like Williams, Muhlenberg was disturbed by the giddy, triumphant tone of the celebration and the lavish waste, which in the view of both tempted divine retribution. "In connection with all this it occurred to me," Muhlenberg wrote, along more secular lines, "in the words of the common saying, 'The birds that sing early are easily caught by the cats.'"[17]

Political neutrals made up a large portion of the city's population, as did Loyalists. Outspoken Tories had been few but were silenced or gone; most others kept a low profile and bided their time. Nicholas Cresswell, who had met several local Loyalists as he passed through Philadelphia the previous September, wrote in his journal, "Great numbers—I believe half the people in town—are *Sgnik Sdneirf* ["King's Friends" spelled backward]."[18] Active Whigs were a loud minority, as were "the violent men," the overzealous who sometimes took matters into their own hands and used violence or threats or committed vandalism in the name of liberty, more often than not for the sheer thrill of hell-raising.

Concerns about violence prompted the Pennsylvania Supreme Executive Council to advise the city magistrates "to exert themselves in preventing any kind of Riot happening in the City this Evening." The town major, Lewis Nicola, was to parade guards of militiamen during the Illumination from 8 until 11 P.M. to prevent disturbances, and "a Bellman be sent round to give notice to the inhabitants, that the Council do expressly order all the lights . . . be extinguished at Eleven O'Clock." Further, "the Wardens are requested to order the Watchmen to attend at their Stands at 8 O'Clock this Evening, in order to assist in preventing any riots which may otherwise happen."[19]

Despite these precautions, the crash and tinkle of shattering glass punctuated the night's festivities as darkened windows all over town were smashed, highlighting the unpleasant side of the political situation. "In the Evening the whole City (Except Torry Houses whose Windows Paid for their Obstenacy) were Iluminated with Lights at every Window," Colonel Grier told General Wayne.[20] Congressman Williams said dryly, "I conclude much Tory unilluminated Glass will want replacing."[21]

Quakers in that era did not participate in such public celebrations as a matter of religious scruple against ceremonies and outward show, but their unlighted windows were targeted anyway, since they were generally suspected of being Loyalists. On Front Street between Arch and Race, Elizabeth Drinker, wife of prominent merchant and Quaker leader

Henry Drinker, wrote in her diary, "July 4—the Town Illuminated and a great number of Windows Broke on the Anniversary of Independence and Freedom."[22] Sarah Logan Fisher, a Loyalist who lived on Second Street below Walnut, a few doors from the City Tavern, and whose husband, Thomas, was also a wealthy Quaker merchant, enumerated: "We had 15 broken, N[icholas] Waln 14, T[homas] Wharton a good many more, and Uncle [James] Logan had 50 cracked & broken, & all this for joy of having gained our liberty."[23]

At his hilltop parsonage in Trappe, twenty-five miles to the northwest, Reverend Muhlenberg wrote in his diary on July 4, "News that the British troops have left Amboy, too, and are assembling on Staaten Island, near New York, where they have their sea power at hand." The German pastor mused with some apprehension, "Where the storm will turn now, no one knows as yet." Quoting from the Book of Revelation, he added prophetically, "Woe to the inhabitants over whom the vials of wrath are poured out!"[24]

At "Camp in Staten Island" that same day, Sir George Osborn fulfilled his duty as muster master general of the foreign troops by writing a report to Lord George Germain, updating him on the status of the Hessian forces and command structure. Two thousand German reinforcements had recently arrived, and major changes occurred in Hessian leadership. In addition to the imminent departure of General von Heister, several other high-ranking officers were going home, mainly for health reasons. "Lt. General de Heister proposes returning to Europe by the first Kings Ship," Osborn reported. "He carrys with him Colonel Block, & I believe Major General Mirbach, Who are both so ill that they are totally unfit for his Majesty's Service."[25]

Word of this reached Congress via Col. Samuel Miles, a Pennsylvania officer taken prisoner at the Battle of Long Island a year before and who, together with Capt. Alexander Graydon, was sent home on parole. "Mr. Howes Projects are all deranged," a delighted John Adams told Abigail. "His Army has gone round the Circle and is now encamped on the very spot where he was a Year ago." He crowed, "The Spirits of the Tories are sunk to a great Degree, and those of the Army, too. The Hessians are disgusted, and their General De Heister gone home, in a Miff."[26]

Capt. Richard Fitzpatrick of the Guards was also disgusted—thoroughly disgusted—with the state of affairs. On July 5, he told his brother about the general mood of the British officers and noted that even his optimistic messmates, Sir George Osborn and Sir John Wrottesley, were somewhat discouraged by the recent maneuvers. "We are fast preparing to Embark from this place, after a very inauspicious opening of the campaign," Fitzpatrick grumbled. "[Lord] Chewton had a horse wounded under him; & got a fall, but he was not much hurt; he is most thoroughly sick of this War, as indeed is almost every body else, of which all people now acknowledge the impracticability, except Sr. G. Osborne & our wise Cousin Sr. John, & even they begin to despond since our retreat from the Jerseys."[27]

Not so, according to Osborn. "You will hear from all who return from America that no one can be in better health and spirits than I am," Sir George told his brother John, the British minister to Saxony, stationed in Dresden. "No person can be more zealous in the cause, few have been more sanguine, and that keeps my thoughts and spirits always at work; Capt. Fitzpatrick, who is one of my Lieutenants, Sir John Wrottesley and I live together."[28]

Fitzpatrick's gloomy outlook no doubt provided a great source of merriment and needling from such bon vivants as Osborn and Wrottesley, for, jaundiced as he was over the general state of affairs, the Whig captain found himself somewhat amused by the antics of his friends. "The absurdity of these two Gentlemen is really not unentertaining, they are so credulous that they bite at every report that is raised, though I believe they themselves are the authors of many of them. But this country is fruitful to an astonishing degree in the producing of Lies, which they both swallow with the greatest Eagerness." His pessimism, however, was unabated as he wrote bitterly, "I need not tell you how much I wish to quit a scene like this, knowing my sentiments, as you do, upon these matters, can you conceive a situation more unpleasant or more disgusting."[29]

Col. Stephen Kemble, Howe's deputy adjutant general, wrote in his journal on July 4, "Find from the general tenor of Officers Conversation that they are not well pleased with Affairs, but they often speak without thought." Defending his commander, he added, "The General is the best judge of his own Actions."[30]

Preparations for a major voyage were well under way, though its destination was anybody's guess: the Delaware River; up the Hudson, also called the North River; or perhaps somewhere in New England. "The

Preparations which have been made will answer either for the North River or the Delawar," General Grant had written to London nearly a month earlier. "Washington I believe has not been able to discover, with any degree of certainty which Move is to be made, but suspects Philedelphia as the greater Object." He explained to General Harvey, "Possession of that place would please the Merchants at Home, cure Lord North's Fever, turn the doubtfull Scale of Foreign Politicks, & probably influence the Councils of other European Powers—for every Body has heard of Philedelphia and no body ever thought of North River—High Lands—Esopus—Kinderhook & Albany."[31]

Opposite the mouth of New York Harbor, Gen. David Forman of the New Jersey Militia was stationed at the Highlands of Navesink (or Neversink) near Sandy Hook, a spit of land on the south side of Raritan Bay, with a full view of the Staten Island shore from the Narrows west to Perth Amboy. Perched at the tip of the Hook a mile or so from the Highlands was a magnificent stone lighthouse, octagonal in shape and nearly 100 feet tall, topped by a seven-foot iron beacon with a copper roof. Built a dozen years earlier by New York merchants and illuminated by "48 oil blazes," brass whale-oil lamps, the beacon had had some of its lamps removed by patriot militia in 1776 to confuse British shipping.[32] It was now occupied by "provincials," Loyalist militia posted there to keep the light functioning and who also sent raiding parties into Monmouth County. Forman was stationed in this vicinity to curb the raids and send Washington intelligence on ship movements.

From a hill near the Hook, Forman could see the comings and goings of British ships, well over 200 of them, in and out of the Narrows and the Raritan River. He reported to Washington on July 6, "The Ships from Amboy and Prince's Bay are gone up to New York. Yet from Some Circumstances I am led to believe they meditate an Expedition to the westward by Water—They have a Number of Brigs, Schooners, and Sloops, prepared for taking Horses on board." The details of the preparations alerted Forman to their possible destination: "Their Stalls are all Cover'd and the Sides lined with Sheepskins with the Wool on to prevent the Horses Chafing—they would not make Use of Such precautions if they Intended up the North or East River."

The militia general also included the written testimony of two deserters: Bertrand Detchevery, of the British hospital ship *Dutton*, and George

West, a Loyalist. From Detchevery, Forman learned, "The Hospital Ships are filled with Sick, that the present reigning Disease amongst them is the Bloody Flux [dysentery]—That the Troops in General appear much dejected." The deserter also relayed, "The Common report Amongst the Sailors and Soldiers is that the Fleet is a going to [the] Delaware." George West revealed to Forman, "There was for Several Nights a very hot Press in the City of New York for Seamen, to man the British Fleet . . . that the press Gangs [were] not being Able to Collect a Sufficient Number of Men to Answer their purpose." He, too, noticed, "A General Gloom Appears on the Faces of all the Inhabitants."[33]

On July 8, the king's troops began boarding the ships for a long voyage; "three weeks we were told to lay in for," according to one officer.[34] Lord Cantelupe of the Guards wrote, "In the Morning March'd to Coles Ferry, & embark'd on board the transports laying in the Bay near the Narrows."[35] Cole's Ferry, the main ferry between Staten Island and New York City, was located on the eastern shore of the island just above the Narrows and was largely out of view from Sandy Hook.

The army was about 18,000 strong, but that counted only enlisted personnel; officers, servants, staff, and camp followers, including women and children, added another 5,000 or so to be transported. The fleet numbered just over 260 vessels of all types. In his journal, Capt. John André made a record of the troop numbers and to which ships they were assigned, the ship tonnages, and pennant distinctions. For the two battalions of the Guards Brigade, André noted: "Distribution of Transports: Foot Guards: 945 [men] on the following transport ships: *Aolus* [414 tons], *Selina* [350 tons], *Gr[and] D[utchess] of Russia* [308 tons], *Amity's Admonition* [410 tons]. Total 1482 tons, Distinguishing Vanes: Red & blue (Main)."[36]

Sir George Osborn wanted first-class accommodations for his men. Writing from the *Aolus*, he told his brother, "My last letter . . . will have informed you that I was to embark and had got one of the best and the very prettiest ships in our fleet for the Grenadiers and Light Company of the Guards." Sir George was pleased: "The ship in every respect has answered my expectations."[37] The *Aolus* carried 119 grenadiers and 87 light infantrymen, with 10 officers, 8 sergeants, 2 drummers, 2 fifers, 14 servants, 13 women, and 1 child, for a grand total of 256 passengers from the 1st Guards Battalion.

Lord Cantelupe was on board *Amity's Admonition* with three companies—Stephen's, Murray's, and O'Hara's—from the 2nd Guards Battalion, with 241 rank and file, 11 officers, 10 sergeants, 6 drummers and fifers, 5 servants, 19 women, and 1 child, for a total of 293. In his diary, Cantelupe drew a diagram of the fleet's arrangement as it deployed for the voyage.[38]

The heat was back with a vengeance, and the radical variations of climate were distressing to those not used to an American summer. "I have never experienced more unpleasant changes of weather than last night," Chaplain Johann Philipp Waldeck of the 3rd Waldeck Regiment, one of the German regiments stationed on Staten Island, complained on July 6. "Yesterday evening it was still astonishingly hot. At twelve o'clock the wind blew so cold through the tent that it was necessary to use an overcoat as a blanket. By midday it was again hot enough to cause a stroke."[39] Pvt. Johann Conrad Döhla of the Bayreuth Regiment commented, "A day in the summer in the months of June and July is not as long as at home, because the sun rises after five o'clock and sets before seven o'clock, so that by eight o'clock it is already pitch black. In the day, the great heat causes suffocation and death. On the other hand, at night it is as cold as if it were fall." Staten Island's geography presented other variations: "Above all, the air, because of the frequent fog from the nearby ocean and the foul fumes on Staten Island, is highly unhealthy. Therefore, sicknesses such as putrid fever, diarrhea, and dysentery, often spread through our regiment, and half the men were ill."[40] On land, it was unbearable; on crowded transport ships, bobbing up and down at anchor, it was almost indescribable.

The orderly book of the British 49th Regiment contained special orders for modifying the men's uniforms to cope with the heat on the voyage and also to preserve them for land campaigning. "Regimental Orders 9th July 1777: Sir Henry Calder desires A Return may be given in of the Number of Caps wanting in each Company—The Men are not to wear their Hatts or Coats on any Account; they are to put Sleeves to their Waistcoats [vests] out of Old Stockings, or Such other Stuf they can procure."[41]

But just when the fleet was going to sail or where it was headed remained anybody's guess. Capt. William Dansey of the 33rd Regiment took the time to write to his mother from "On Board *the Earl of Oxford*,

July 10th, 1777: My dear Madam, Yesterday we embark'd but where we are going to Lord knows."[42] Howe's aide Capt. Friedrich von Münchhausen confided in his diary the same day, "It is said that General Howe will go aboard on Sunday . . . then we shall see where we will go, which is not known to anyone." He remarked, "Everyone surmises that we are going to Philadelphia."[43]

"Sir Billy" confided in no one except his swarthy brother "Black Dick," the admiral, that he planned not only to go to Philadelphia, but also to take an unexpected and roundabout route: up the Chesapeake Bay rather than the Delaware River. Joseph Galloway, leader of the Pennsylvania Loyalists, learned of the general's plan quite by accident and later told the House of Commons how he figured it out. "After my return from Hillsborough to New York" during the June maneuvers, "I met on the road accidentally Lord Howe. From a conversation which passed between us, I suspected that Sir William was going with his fleet and army round to the Chesapeak." Galloway explained to the Commons that he took it upon himself to write down the problems he foresaw—distance, heat, terrain—and showed them to Capt. John Montrésor, the chief engineer, "through whom I often communicated with the General." According to Galloway, Montrésor read the list of concerns, agreed with them, and said "he would chearfully deliver them to the General." Howe sent for Galloway several days later. "[He] asked me, how I knew he was going to the Chesapeak? I answered, I did not positively know it. He said, I did, from the paper in front of him. I replied, the paper was not positive, but conditional, supposing he intended to go there."

Next, Howe put a curious question to Galloway. "He then asked, whether my objections rested on the difficulties of the navigation of the Chesapeak? I replied, they did not."[44] The general's confidence in his fifty-one-year-old brother's abilities "through a most intricate and dangerous navigation for such a multitude of vessels" was unshakable. As events played out, *The Annual Register* reported that "the Admiral performed the different parts of a commander, inferior officer, and pilot, with his usual ability and perseverance."[45]

Along with the expedition was James Parker of Virginia, a forty-eight-year-old Scottish-born tobacco merchant from Norfolk who accompanied the army as a volunteer guide. Parker had suffered the loss of his valuable business and many properties and was imprisoned for months in Alexandria. He and several companions escaped, partially through the efforts of Nicholas Cresswell, who later said, "None of them (Goodrich excepted) have had the good manners to thank us for the risk we ran in assisting them," and "They are a set of ungrateful scoundrels."[46] For his part, Parker was determined to make himself as useful to General Howe as possible but was in the dark about the fleet's destination. "Formerly I had a very good spy of knowing things," he told his friend Charles Steuart in Edinburgh, "'tis not so now, every thing is Secret & misterious. I hope it is all for the best." Regarding the military situation, Parker wrote, "We hear the Rebels in the south have been singing Te deum on the evacuation of the Jerseys, after which our Troops encamped on Statten Island. They were all embarked the 11th," and added, "everything has the appearance of a Southern Expidition, & I am this day [July 16] ordered on board the *Fanny* transport to attend it," together with Lord Howe's secretary Ambrose Serle and Capt. Archibald Robertson of the Engineers.

Having lived in southern Virginia since 1750, Parker knew the climate all too well. "I do not wish to See them in Virginia before the beginning of September," he declared. "The Army is in high health & Spirits now, I fear that will not long be the Case—if they go South in the dog days."[47]

Everyone dreaded the dog days of summer, and with good reason: They were marked by excessive heat and humidity, swarms of irritating insects, and "the agues"—fevers and sickness. Also called the canicular days, the dog days, which "begin towards the end of July, and end the beginning of September," are "a certain number of days preceding and ensuing the helical raising of canicula, or the dog-star, in the morning," according to the 1771 *Encyclopaedia Brittanica.* "The Romans supposed it to be the cause of the sultry weather usually felt in the dog-days; and therefore sacrificed a brown dog every year at its rising, to appease its wrath."[48] Col. Karl von Donop told the crown prince of Prussia on July 14, "God knows whether we shall go south or north, but the heat which is beginning to make itself felt with the approach of the dog-days makes one wish that the general would choose the north rather than the south."[49]

Gen. James Grant was also familiar with summer on the East Coast, having spent years in America during the French and Indian War and seven years afterward as governor of East Florida at St. Augustine. "Our

Officers have no Idea where they are going," he smugly informed General Harvey. "The most intelligent are wide of the mark from a mistaken Idea of climate, which is the same all over America in the Months of July & August. During that time the Heats are as great at Boston as at St. Augustine." He confidently assured his friend, "The Secret of our Destination has been well kept—Washington must be at a Loss. He has moved to Morris [County] to have it in his power to direct his course South or North."[50]

The guessing game was widespread. In Philadelphia, John Adams told James Warren, "What Mr. Howes present Plan is, no Conjurer can discover. He is moving and maneuvering with his Fleet and Army, as if he had some Design, or other, but what it may be no Astrologer can divine." Fed up with all the second-guessing around town, Adams fumed, "Some conjecture he is bound to the West Indies, others to Europe, one Party to Hallifax, another to Rhode Island. This set sends him up the North River, that down the East River, and the other up the Delaware. I am weary of Conjectures—Time will solve them."[51] He informed Abigail, "I am much in doubt whether he knows his own Intentions," and concluded, "It is impossible to discover the Designs of an Enemy who has no Design at all. An Intention that has no Existence, a Plan that is not laid, cannot be divined."[52]

Nor was the mystery confined to North America. In Great Britain and Ireland, the lack of news from the seat of war, and Lord Germain's inability to fathom Howe's intentions, caused great concern in the government and ridicule in the press. The dearth of reliable information lasted well into the autumn, provoking much speculation and derision in the newspapers. Throughout the summer, the following advertisement appeared in several publications:

> *LOST, this SUMMER,*
> in the enclosures about New-York, in North America,
> *The* BRITISH ARMY.
> Whoever can give an account of it to his Majesty's
> Secretary at War, shall not only receive a large premium,
> but have the high honour of kissing his Majesty's hand.
> A part of it is said to have been seen, in the Spring,
> near Danbury; but its stay was so short,
> that its tracks were not deep enough to be traced.[53]

In America, optimistic reports from the mother country further exasperated Captain Fitzpatrick. "I have just received a large packet of letters from England from Lord Rawdon who arrived the day before yesterday," he told his brother on July 8. "Nothing can appear more ridiculous to every body here than the letters they receive from England, talking of the miserable situation of the Rebels, & of the war being certain of coming to a conclusion immediately."[54]

Twenty-three-year-old Lord Rawdon was an aide-de-camp of Gen. Sir Henry Clinton. Earlier in the spring, Clinton had gone home disgusted, planning to resign, for he and Howe did not get along at all. Howe had repeatedly shuffled him off since 1775, first to Charleston, then to Rhode Island, and Sir Henry had had enough. Upon arriving in England, he was met with a knighthood and a promotion to lieutenant general for his services. He was also prevailed upon to return to America. Now, back in New York, where he had grown up while his father was royal governor (1741–51), Clinton again found himself in the familiar disagreeable situation of fruitlessly arguing with Howe, this time against a voyage to Philadelphia.

Sir William was waiting to hear from Sir John Burgoyne, who was advancing south on Lake Champlain toward Fort Ticonderoga. Once more shuffling him out of the way, Sir William planned to leave Sir Henry in command at New York City with a very small force, while the main army went off to Philadelphia. Besides the annoyance at being pigeonholed yet again, Clinton feared that sending the army south would expose New York to an attack by Washington, leave Burgoyne unsupported, and render the army vulnerable to sickness in the southern climate.

As the generals bickered and waited for news of Burgoyne, the days dragged on. Von Münchhausen wrote on July 13, "No one seems to be able to figure out why we are waiting here so long, considering the fact that everyone, except Howe and a few officers, are aboard ship. Some malcontents have given some rather unfounded and unworthy reason for the delay," probably an allusion to Howe's dallying with Mrs. Loring.

Privately, the Hessian captain also expressed doubts about the overall quality of the British High Command. "General Leslie who commands the Highland Scots, has broken his leg," von Münchhausen noted. "It is a pity that we have to leave behind this very able and upright general, the like of which the English have only a few." A day later, he commented,

"General Howe is in a difficult situation because he has but few capable generals under his command here."

Five more days of waiting lay ahead, during which von Münchhausen speculated, "I wonder what kind of maneuver Washington will carry out once he is convinced that we are going to his capital, Philadelphia, which, I have no doubt, is now our objective. I fear that he will make some forced marches and attack Burgoyne who is believed not to be very strong, and, from what I hear, is eager to do battle." He fretfully concluded, "It would have been better if we had not stayed here so long, but had gone to Philadelphia four weeks ago—these are my ideas. We could then be returning by land to support Burgoyne."[55]

Washington was indeed maneuvering, trying to position himself to block Howe's move up either the Hudson or the Delaware, while keeping an eye on Burgoyne's progress on Lake Champlain. After the British evacuated New Jersey, Washington shifted most of his army northward, first to Morristown, then to Pompton Plains, then up to "the Clove," a long, craggy valley that leads from North Jersey into the Hudson Highlands near West Point. "We are now properly an army of observation as the Movements of the Enemy will determine our Rout[e]," Col. Percy Frazer wrote his wife from "Camp at the Cloves" on July 18. "The place we are now at is about 25 miles from the North River and 35 from Morris Town, where it is likely we shall halt until We have certain Accounts of their destination."[56]

At general headquarters in the Clove, Washington and his staff had to "rough it" in very tight, rustic quarters for a few nights. "Sunday, July 20 . . . Headquarters at Galloway's, an old log house," Col. Timothy Pickering, the adjutant general, wrote. It was a far cry from the genteel spaciousness of the elegant Ford Mansion in Morristown; now "the General lodged in a bed, and his family on the floor about him." They ate suppawn or sappaen, a type of porridge or hasty pudding of boiled Indian cornmeal that was standard supper fare among the Dutch farmers in the Hudson Valley area. Traditionally served cold in a large common dish, with individual "milk ponds" scooped out around the edges, each diner would eat the mush and milk with a spoon while enlarging his pond until the mess was gone. "We had plenty of sepawn and milk," Pickering commented with satisfaction, "and all were contented."[57]

From Frazer's description of the Continentals at the Clove, it would appear that Washington's efforts at rebuilding the army had come to fruition. "Our Army is in very fine health and Spirits," he told Polly. "It wou'd surprise you to see the vast number of soldiers, Horses, Waggons, Drivers, Cattle and Provision, tents, etc., that are here; yet everything goes smoothly on."[58]

Over on the Hudson, by contrast, things were not going so smoothly for the Marylanders of Sullivan's Division in the "Camp at Crumb Pond below Peeks Kills." "We have many of the Maryland troops without Blankets or Tents," Col. John Stone of the 1st Maryland Regiment informed Gov. Thomas Johnson on July 24, "they must undoubtedly be lost. We are promised these necessary articles immediately." Further, he told Johnson, "We have also suffered much for shoes, and I am afraid will suffer much more for that article this fall." Having been through the hardships of the 1776 campaign, Stone warned, "We shall also be very bare of all kinds of Cloathing by the winter and unless we are furnished, more than probable shall be in the same disagreeable situation we were last year. Much will depend upon having an army fit for the field this fall." In the Maryland Line, composed of Smallwood's 1st Brigade and DeBorre's 2nd Brigade, Stone was mortified to admit, "We have now in the field fit for duty only about 1100 men from Maryland, so that we make but a trifling figure with respect to numbers when compared with other States."[59]

The overall condition of the army had drastically improved in six months—from dire to barely adequate—with more troops and supplies arriving every week. In the command structure, on the other hand, problems were rapidly multiplying, and from many different angles.

First and foremost was the issue of seniority among the officers, especially the generals. After the disasters of 1776, a more professional organization of army leadership was required, and the new army of 1777 offered the perfect opportunity to straighten things out. To no great surprise, however, the endless challenge of choosing officers based on competence and practical experience versus seniority and politics consumed an inordinate amount of time and correspondence. It also proved to be a constant, drawn-out source of contention and annoyance for Washington, Congress, and the officer corps, resulting in much ill will and sour tempers.

"I am wearied to Death with the Wrangles between military officers, high and low," John Adams fumed in May. "They Quarrell like Cats and

Dogs. They worry one another like Mastiffs. Scrambling for Rank and Pay like Apes for Nutts." As chairman of the War Committee in Congress, Adams had to continually deal with the stream of complaints about slights to honor and demands for justice. "I have seen it among Boys and Girls at school, among Lads at Colledge," he scribbled furiously, telling Abigail of the jealousies, "among Practicers at the Bar, among Clergy in their Associations, among Clubbs of Friends, among the People in their Town Meetings," and in representative houses, councils, judges on the bench, and "that awfully August Body the Congress, and on many of its Committees—and among Ladies everywhere. But I never saw it operate with such Keenness, Ferocity and Fury, as among military Officers. They will go terrible Lengths," Adams noted with disgust, "in their Emulations, their Envy and Revenge, in Consequence of it."[60]

The friction between Continental officers from different states and the internal power politics was only one facet of the problem. Another involved those who were of British or Irish origin, not due to their place of birth but to their previous experience in European service. The Continental Army had an abundance of British- and Irish-born men in all levels of command, as well as in the ranks. Striking a balance between promoting English speakers with professional experience in regular armies and native-born Americans who had served as volunteers for a year or more was no easy matter, especially on a political level.

Then there were the Europeans—"shoals" of Frenchmen, as Washington described the onslaught, but Germans too, and a few Poles, many with recommendations from Silas Deane, one of the American diplomats in Paris. A number of these officers were offering assistance in specialized areas such as artillery, engineering, or cavalry. Their credentials and expertise, both real and alleged, together with the political pull of their assignments caused no end of tension in Congress and among the native-born American officers. "The congress and I do not agree in politics," Nathanael Greene told his brother Jacob in early June, "they are introducing a great many foreigners. I think it dangerous to trust so large a part of the American army to the command of strangers." He feared that "British gold is of a poisonous quality, and the human heart treacherous to the last degree. There are no less than four general officers of the [French] nation now in the American service." Alarmed and annoyed, Greene wrote apprehensively, "Wisdom and prudence sometimes forsake the wisest bodies. I am exceedingly distressed at the state of things in the great national council."[61]

When rumors reached camp that Congress was considering placing the Chevalier de Coudray in charge of the Continental Artillery, frustration among some of the generals boiled over. Gen. Henry Knox, the chief of artillery, supported by Greene and Sullivan, all New Englanders, wrote directly to Congress in early July and threatened to resign. John Adams was outraged; in a long, painful letter, he told Greene that the letters had placed the Congress in an impossible position. Already upset by Deane's free hand in promising high positions to the foreign officers, Congress now appeared to be threatened by its own generals. "I must be careful my Friend in Saying, that if you or the other Generals Sullivan and Knox, had seriously considered . . . the Necessity of preserving the Authority of the Civil Powers above the military, you would never have written such Letters." Furious, especially with Greene, Adams recommended that the only honorable course of action for the generals would be to write a public letter of apology to Congress; "if not I think you ought to leave the service."[62] Though stung, the generals apologized.

Sectionalism and provincialism were rife in Colonial America. The country—and the army—was divided into three general geographic sections: New England, the Middle States, and the South, representing a cultural, ethnic, and religious diversity reflected in the pattern of Colonial settlement. New England, composed of New Hampshire, Massachusetts, Rhode Island, Connecticut, and a disputed, renegade area of contention called Vermont, was referred to as "eastern"; New Englanders referred to anyone from south of Connecticut as "southern." Its inhabitants were mostly of English Calvinist stock and were called Yankees, a term of pride among New Englanders but often one of contempt and derision by others.

The Middle States—New York, New Jersey, Pennsylvania, and Delaware—were originally the Dutch colony of New Netherland and represented a great diversity in ethnicity, language, religion, and culture. New York City, founded as New Amsterdam, reflected old Amsterdam not so much in its Dutch Colonial architecture as in its international makeup and all-consuming dedication to commerce. Despite more than a century of English rule, the cultural influence of the New Netherland colony remained prevalent, and thousands of New Yorkers and New Jerseyans still spoke "Jersey Dutch" as their local language. Pennsylvania was only about half English speaking, and several *plattedeutsche* or Low German dialects mixed with English to create Pennsylvania Dutch, a Germanic Colonial language described by Dr. Johann Schoepf, a surgeon with the Anspach troops, as "a miserable, broken, fustian salmagundy of English and German."[63] There were also large areas of Welsh and Swiss, a few Swedes and Finns, and numerous Scots-Irish found in Philadelphia and along the frontier. Africans, both slave and free, were scattered throughout New England and the Middle States in small numbers.

The South, on the other hand—Maryland, Virginia, the Carolinas, and Georgia—was dominated by large plantations with tens of thousands of African slaves. The culture was mainly English, but large numbers of Scottish Highlanders and Scots-Irish from Northern Ireland settled in the backcountry and mountains as dirt farmers and frontiersmen, adding a distinct cultural component of ornery self-reliance and fierce, rugged independence. In the Chesapeake ports such as Norfolk and Alexandria, many of the wealthy tobacco merchants were Scottish Lowlanders from Edinburgh and Glasgow. The plantation owners—the Tidewater aristocracy—dominated the political, economic, and social scene with a genteel, ruthless firmness.

On his return voyage to England, Nicholas Cresswell made some interesting observations about the American language. Having spent three years in northern Virginia, with trips through Maryland, Pennsylvania, New Jersey, and New York and an extended stay in the Ohio Valley frontier, he had had the opportunity to meet more Americans from more areas than most Americans ever had. "Though the inhabitants of this Country are composed of different Nations and different languages," he astutely noted, "yet it is very remarkable that they in general speak better English than the English do. No County or Colonial dialect is to be distinguished here, except it be the New Englanders, who have a sort of whining cadence that I cannot describe."[64]

The sectional differences between them came through time and again, even regarding Howe's destination. Gen. Jedediah Huntington of Connecticut, stationed on the Hudson River near West Point, told his father in late July, "Genl. Washington has gone back to Pompton with Persuasion that the Enemy intend southward (you will note the General Officers about him are chiefly southern Men); at this Post (perhaps from like

Partiality), We think they intend Eastward."[65] John Adams took a more cynical view a few weeks later when he wrote that among the generals, "Sullivan Thinks the Fleet is gone to Portsmouth [New Hampshire]— Greene to Newport [Rhode Island]—Parsons, up the North River [New York]—Mifflin to Philadelphia. Thus each one secures his Reputation among his Townsmen for Penetration and Foresight, in Case the Enemy should go against his Town."[66]

News from Burgoyne finally came to Howe in New York Harbor on July 15: Fort Ticonderoga was in British hands. The post's commander, Gen. Arthur St. Clair of Pennsylvania, had evacuated the fort on the night of July 5 without firing a shot, after Burgoyne placed artillery on Mount Independence. Although it was later seen as a wise move, the news shocked many in the Continental Army, and Congress recalled both St. Clair and Gen. Philip Schuyler of New York, commander of the Northern Army, pending an investigation. "The British richly harvested what they had not sowed," Lutheran minister Henry Muhlenberg commented. "Luther had already said, in his time, that no fortress is invincible if asses can reach it with golden bullets."[67]

The easy recapture of Fort Ticonderoga further bolstered British confidence, and Howe later explained that he felt that Burgoyne had sufficient force to continue on toward Albany independently. Others would accuse Howe of abandoning Burgoyne, thus unhinging the overall British strategy.

American opinion, too, was divided. The New Englanders were furious with the "southern" generals for abandoning the fort, and recriminations were loud and long. Referring to the infamous fate of Adm. John Byng, who was shot by a firing squad during the Seven Years' War for failure in command, a Connecticut man wrote, "Col. [Samuel] Webb Writes from Camp . . . that the Army in general very much Resent the Conduct of the Northern Army, and that the Officers all say that America must have a *Byng*. Plain English I think!"[68] John Adams seconded the idea when he wrote in disgust, "I think we shall never defend a post until we shoot a General."[69]

As chairman of the Board of War in Congress, Adams was beside himself with fury at the loss of tons of equipment that he had spent months working to acquire. "The Papers inclosed will inform you, of the Loss of Ticonderoga, with all its Circumstances of Incapacity and Pusillanimity," he told Abigail in mid-July, adding sardonically, "Dont you pity me to be wasting away my Life, in laborious Exertions, to pro-cure Cannon, Ammunition, Stores, Baggage, Cloathing &c. &c. &c. &c., for Armies, who give them all away to the Enemy, without firing a Gun."[70]

On the other hand, "Some of our Leaders think it a happy event that that place has been left, as the Enemy may be tempted to penetrate into New England or York State," Col. Percy Frazer of the 5th Pennsylvania observed, "and as there is a very good body of men ready to oppose them," he hastened to add, "there is a good probability Burgoyne will not get so easily back, or join Genl. Howe as he may have imagined; and indeed I think he will repent this maneuver should he attempt to march into the Country."[71]

"We continue in Amazement & Chagrin at the Loss of Ticonderoga," Gen. Jed I Iuntington lamented to his father. "At present, the command-ing Officer stands in a very dishonorable Point of Light; however, an Opportunity of Vindication may clear him of the Disgrace that is so lib-erally cast upon him."[72] Even John Adams was eventually able to find a silver lining: "These vile Panicks that seize People and Soldiers too, are very difficult to get over. But at last they turn to Vigour, Fury and Des-peration, as they did in the Jerseys."[73]

Concerning Howe's apparent dithering, "I agree with you in Opinion that Genl. Howe is in some Degree of Perplexity," Huntington told another family member on July 20. Writing from Peekskill on the Hud-son, he commented, "As to this Post & the Situation of our Troops in the several Camps we think ourselves so well prepared to receive him that we are less fearfull of his Advances this Way than of his Incursions into the defenceless Parts of the Country. Should he go to New England I doubt not the Militia will meet him with the Zeal & Spirit which appeared in ye Militia of New Jersey when Genl. Howe moved from Brunswick."[74]

Finally, the deadlock broke. After twelve hot and tiresome days of waiting in New York Harbor, the British fleet began to move on Sunday, July 20. "Sailed this morning from Staten Island, with all the Transports, to Sandy Hook, where we came to Anchor," wrote a relieved Ambrose Serle, Lord Howe's secretary. "So many Ships at one Time under Sail, with the Wind for the most part ahead, which obliged them to transverse, rendered the Scene very grand & picturesque."[75]

From the Highlands near Sandy Hook that morning, Gen. David For-man witnessed the awesome spectacle of the main British fleet coming out of New York Harbor in full force, tacking back and forth through the Narrows. He told Congress that by sundown, "there was under the point of the hook and coming down 160 sail as near as we can count; it is beyond doubt that some of them have Troops on board, but to what amount cannot pretend to say."[76] The following day, Forman observed "fifteen transports & men of war joined them, & about 10 o'clock 80 small brigs, schooners & sloops came out of the Narrows & joined the grand fleet."[77]

Foul, rainy weather caused yet more delay, and with some disgust, Serle wrote on the twenty-second, "Rowed about the Fleet, & landed upon Sandy Hook, which is a dismal barren Spot, guarding the Entrance of the Harbor." Serle was not impressed by the lighthouse, nor by the Loyalists guarding it, for he commented, "Viewed the Light-House, a stinking Edifice, by means of the oil and the Provincials stationed in it."[78]

The same storm caught the fleet that sailed with Nicholas Cresswell and Gen. Philip von Heister at the eastern end of Long Island near Montauk Point as they headed for open sea from Long Island Sound. After his last glimpse of America, a "confoundedly sick" Cresswell wrote a memorable description of the chaos on board caused by the storm: "The sea a roaring, the ship a rolling, the rigging breaking, the masts a bending, the sails a rattling, the Captain swearing, the Sailors grumbling, the boys crying, the hogs grunting, the dogs barking, the pots and glasses breaking, the Colonel ill of the Clap in bed," he scribbled. "All from the Top Gallant truck to the keel, from the jibb boom to the taffrail in the utmost confusion."[79] It was better for Howe's fleet to wait until the storm passed.

At long last, a fortnight after boarding the ships and more than three weeks after leaving New Jersey, Howe's army put to sea. At 6:30 A.M. on Wednesday, July 23, General Forman reported to Congress, "The signal gun for sailing was fired. The wind north-west, at seven they began to get under way, & stood for sea; after they got clear of the hook, they steered a south-east course, under a very easy sail, in three divisions."[80] On board the transport Whitby, Lt. Gilbert Purdy of the British Corps of Guides and Pioneers wrote in his own inimitable way, "The 23th the Wind Being fair We Began to wey our onkers [weigh our anchors] Abought foor o'clock In the Morning and By Nine oclock was all under way Standing Out of the hook in five Devisions Consisting Of Abought three hundred

Sale with our Men of Wares & frigets to Every Devision Which was A Delightfull Site to See."[81]

The fleet proceeded slowly down the New Jersey coast, and much of it went out of sight over the horizon. Almost immediately, it became clear that the voyage was going to be long and tedious because of the summer weather cycle, the winds being generally from the south and southwest. There were also days of calm, such as July 24: "We have but little wind, the Weather is fair & very agreeable. The Whole fleet in View which exhibits a very agreeable prospect along the Jersey Shore."[82] Other days saw scorching heat and stifling humidity, often followed by terrific thunderstorms, which intensified as the summer lengthened. Each time a storm approached, the ships had to scatter to avoid collisions.

Fog also hampered the fleet for a few days. The weather was so uncooperative that it took seven days to sail from Sandy Hook to Cape May, a distance of less than 150 miles. "Happy it is for me that I do not sail in the Navy, where I remember to have heard of a custom of throwing those passengers overboard whose sins and transgressions occasion contrary winds," quipped Lt. William Hale of the 45th. "I am certainly one of those unlucky beings. . . . [This] voyage would sufficiently point me out as a proper sacrifice."[83]

News of the fleet's sailing and unknown destination caused great consternation in Philadelphia and in the American camp. Guessing that Howe was heading for the Delaware, Washington ordered Gen. Anthony Wayne to leave his brigade in camp on July 24 and head for Chester, Pennsylvania, fifteen miles south of Philadelphia, to arrange the militia gathering there in his home county. Gen. Thomas Mifflin, a wealthy Quaker merchant in Philadelphia before the war, also left the camp at Ramapo in the Clove and headed south to take charge of the city's defense.

That same day, the Pennsylvania Supreme Executive Council entrusted John Hunn, a thirty-one-year-old Philadelphia sea captain, with a difficult secret mission: "Make the best of your way to the Sea shore and observe what course the Enemys ships stear, & their numbers, and if they have Troops on Board." The Council placed a great responsibility on Hunn, saying, "As soon as you are convinced beyond a doubt where they mean to attack, send off a person in whom all confidence can be put, to Gen. Washington. . . . Repeat to the General your intelligence by another Express or two, and as much oftener as you may think proper, lest by any

accident the first should miscarry." They also requested that express riders be sent to the Council with the news and concluded with a warning to
"keep the business you are going upon as much a secret as possible as you
pass thro' New Jersey."[84]

Under clear skies and a waning full moon, Captain Hunn and several
companions crossed the Delaware River to Cooper's Ferry in Gloucester
County to begin the long ride overland to the Jersey coast. They proceeded
to Haddonfield, a large village where the New Jersey legislature had been
meeting and where several important roads came together. There they
picked up the Egg Harbor Road and continued east through a hamlet
called Long-a-Coming, beyond which lay a sparsely inhabited flat landscape, dark and foreboding. This sixty-mile ride to the shore passed
through the Pine Barrens of West Jersey (now South Jersey), a strange,
primeval wilderness of gloomy forests, tangled cedar swamps, and mossy
bogs interspersed with sandy plains of oddly dwarfed pines. "The Pines,"
as they were known to the locals, were a naturalist's delight and a traveler's
nightmare. Wolves, bears, and panthers still prowled the dense stands of
towering white Atlantic cedars and pitch pines that loomed over stunted
scrub oaks and thickets of laurel and holly, where rattlesnakes lay hidden
among ferns in the thorny underbrush. The cedars were so tall and thick
in places that to enter them was to enter a midnight darkness, even at noon.

On the road in broad daylight, the view was limited and monotonous,
a gray-green infinity with a disorienting sameness, occasionally broken
by swaths of blackened tree trunks where fires had raged until checked
by "cripples" and "spongs," sloughy creeks of tea-colored cedar water
oozing through impenetrable foliage, edged by marshy clearings that
swarmed with mosquitoes.[85] A contemporary traveler on the Egg Harbor Road described "Shoals of Musquetoes all the way who attacked us
on every quarter with great Venom" and "musquetoes in Clouds, Enough
to eat up a Horse."[86]

All of these features made the Pine Barrens an eerie and sometimes
dangerous place, a favorite hideout for smugglers and other outlaws.
Inland were "Swamp Angels," loners who lived by poaching, "many
straggling, impertinent, vociferous Swamp Men."[87] And yet, "there is
something grand, charming and desirable in this vulgarly despised Egg
Harbour," wrote Rev. Philip Vickers Fithian, a Presbyterian minister riding the circuit through the area in 1775. "I love the simplicity which I

see in the manner of the inhabitants, the country, the sand, the Pines
. . . it is Nature stark naked."[88]

This lonely route passed the ironworks of Atsion and Batsto, where
bog iron, noted for its peculiar resistance to rust, was made into a variety of superb iron products, but other than these and the occasional tavern, there were few signs of habitation. The road, used mainly by heavy
wagons transporting tons of smuggled cargoes, salt, timber, and iron
goods, including cannonballs from Batsto, was little more than two sandy
ruts that were deep in places, so travel was a tedious and exhausting chore,
especially in the stifling humidity of late July.

The speed with which Hunn and the other riders fulfilled their assignment is a tribute to their bravery and commitment, for Hunn himself
commented, "There is but few that Nowes the way through the Jerseys."[89]
And for the next week, the actions of Washington's army and Congress
would be determined by his observations.

"July 25—Dog-days begin," announced the *New-England Almanack* for
1777.[90] By early afternoon, Hunn and the others arrived near Little Egg
Harbor—"that nest of rebel pirates," in the words of Sir Henry Clinton—where there was a saltworks and a haven for American privateers.
Hunn sent a message back to Philadelphia that from his vantage point,
no British ships were visible.

Portions of the fleet were within sight of the shore from time to time.
Captain Montrésor observed from the schooner *Alert* on July 25, "Latitude at 12 this day 39.48″," about sixteen miles north of Little Egg Harbor. That afternoon, he "saw the Jersey Shore . . . supposed to be Great
Egg Harbour," twenty miles south of Little Egg Harbor.[91]

Captain Hunn and his companions rode down to Great Egg Harbor
that same afternoon, where they crossed from Somers's Point to Beesley's
Point in Cape May County, but again saw nothing of the fleet. They continued on to the house of Capt. Nicholas Stillwell, a fellow sea captain
and colonel of the Cape May County Militia, where they met five newly
captured British naval prisoners from the brig *Stanley* who had been
turned in by two deserters from HMS *Roebuck*, a forty-four-gun frigate.
Among the captives were Thomas Slater, the ships master, and Roland
Edwards, the chief pilot.

Earlier that day, the British seamen had taken an armed whaleboat
from the frigate and came into Corson's Inlet at the southern end of

Peck's Beach, an uninhabited barrier island on the southeast side of Great Egg Harbor. Rimmed with shimmering white sandy beaches and infested with mosquitoes and bloodthirsty greenhead flies from the nearby salt marshes, the island was covered with prickly cedar thickets and grassy savannas used for grazing cattle.[92] This small, heavily armed British expedition landed on Peck's Beach, looking for a cargo of rum from a schooner they had chased the previous day and possibly for cattle. Heat and fatigue built up a thirst, which induced the group to take a midday nap. While their companions were snoozing, the two sailors assigned to sentry duty took the opportunity to desert by stealing the whaleboat and rowing to shore. Upon reaching the mainland, they informed Stillwell of their situation; he promptly dispatched militiamen, who captured the rest of the crew. The spoils included all of their firearms, ships armaments, ammunition, and the source of their predicament, "I Bottle Rum, & Two empty ones."[93]

But at that moment, the *Roebuck* was not part of Howe's fleet. It was a well-known British presence at the Delaware Capes, having been assigned to patrol duty there from time to time since 1775, chasing smugglers, interrupting Continental commerce, and gathering information from Loyalists. The wait for fleet sightings continued.

Up at Little Egg Harbor the next morning, Saturday, July 26, Dr. John McGinnis sent an urgent message to Col. William Bradford "at the L Caffee house Philadelphia," the Old London Coffee House at Front Street and Market Street, the commercial hub of town: "This morning halfe after Eight I Discovered Seventy Saile Beating to windard the wind at South making Short Tackes and keeping the Shore Close aboard[.] Six hevy Ships just off the mouth of Little Egg harber."[94]

By Sunday morning, the note had arrived at the coffee house. This famous establishment, operated by Bradford since the 1750s, was the old Merchants' Exchange, the main spot downtown for news and gossip and a center of Whig political activity. It was also where the Pennsylvania Board of War office was located. At 9 A.M., Gen. Thomas Mifflin, newly arrived in town, wrote to Washington, "A Gentleman well known in this City is this Minute come to Town from little Egg Harbour—he declares he saw Seventy Sail of Vessels at 4 Oclock Yesterday afternoon pass by little Egg Harbour toward Cape May. I enclos'd to you a Letter from Doctor McGinnis to Colonel Bradford on the same Subject." With an authoritative air of certainty, Mifflin added, "The Destination of General Howe cannot now be mistaken, as Egg Harbour is but a few Hours Sailing from our Capes."[95]

A rumor flew through the city that the British had actually entered the Delaware Capes. It appears that Mifflin was the rumor's main source, for McGinnis's note says nothing about the fleet being anywhere but near Little Egg Harbor, about fifty miles above Cape May. Jacob Hiltzheimer, a prominent Philadelphia horse dealer, militia official, and very close friend of Mifflin, wrote in his diary that day that he "went to Mr. Joseph Morrises to see General Mifflin who came from our Army Last Night, and says that the Enemy are coming around to our Cape, where 70 Sail made their appearance all ready."[96]

The distorted news spread quickly and grew in the telling. Rev. Henry Muhlenberg, twenty-five miles out in the country, heard it that afternoon from a visitor, who "brought the terrible news that the British fleet of 160 transports which recently sailed from New York had made its way to and had already reached the capes of the Delaware." With foreboding, he wrote, "At last the two storm clouds are approaching each other over Philadelphia, and it appears that a vial of wrath will be poured out upon Philadelphia and Pennsylvania. Woe unto those who live upon the earth!"[97]

That night in town, Elizabeth Drinker witnessed a celestial phenomenon that would have sent Muhlenberg into further apocalyptic frenzy: "Evening between 9 & 10 o'clock, was seen by many, a Strange appearance in the Sky of Streamers, moveing in regular order, from the East to Westward."[98]

Washington's reply to Mifflin's letter was cautionary. "The appearance of the enemy's fleet off Little Egg Harbour, if it does not amount to a certain proof that their design is against Philadelphia, is at least a very strong argument of it," he wrote from Flemington, New Jersey, about sixty miles north of the city. Washington went on to say that he would issue new orders "as soon as the movement of the enemy makes it more evident that Philadelphia is their object." He told the Pennsylvania general, "It is far from impossible the enemy may still turn about and make a stroke" up the Hudson.[99]

Several days passed, and although reports of as many as 190 ships passing Egg Harbor continued to circulate, no word came to Philadelphia from Cape May. This is not surprising; John Hunn had nothing to report, for out in the Atlantic, on foaming, gray seas swelling with gale-force winds, Montrésor noted on the twenty-seventh, "The fleet very much scattered." The next day saw "a very wet and thick fog . . . wind Easterly and very squally with several continued showers of heavy rain. . . . Weather too thick for an observation."[100] Lord Cantelupe wrote in his diary, "28th: a fog till twelve at noon. The wind at N. E. by E. Thunder Lightening & rain." The visibility was so poor that to keep in touch and prevent collisions between ships, "the Admiral fired Guns every half hour. In the Evening much Thunder & Lightning. Sounded twenty one Fathom water, black Sand."[101]

With only a few reliable men and horses, and well over 120 difficult miles to travel between Philadelphia and Cape May, John Hunn could not afford to waste his resources on useless daily rides to report nothing. "The Reasons you have had No Express Since [the twenty-sixth] is the weather have Been So thick this three days past that it has Been Impossible to Discover Wheather thear was a fleet off or Not," he told the Council on July 29. "But the wind is Now at N.W. & the weather Verry Cleare & No fleet in sight." Years of experience as a sea captain allowed him to say, "if the fleet is Bound to Delaware By the accounts of the wind & Weather, they have had No Chance to arrive hear yet." Hunn reassured them, "I have sent No Express to General Washington as it is hard to get horses for so Long a Journey, But if theare should Be a fleet in sight Mr. Jones will go Express Immediately to head quarters."[102]

On the thirtieth, John Adams expressed his growing frustration with all the rumors. "Howes Fleet has been at Sea, these 8 days," he scribbled impatiently. "We know not where he is gone. We are puzzling ourselves in vain, to conjecture his Intention. Some guess he is gone to Chesapeak, to land near Susquehanna and cross overland to Albany to meet Burgoine." He added sardonically, "They may as well imagine them gone round Cape Horn into the South Seas to land at California, and march across the Continent to attack our back settlements."[103]

But through the mists off Cape May that morning, John Hunn's watchfulness was finally rewarded. He hurriedly wrote to Thomas Wharton, president of Pennsylvania's Supreme Executive Council, at 11 A.M. and sent Abraham Bennett with this news: "The fleet to the Number of 30 sail is Now in Sight, upon which I have sent off Mr. Bennet Express, as it is Not Seven Miles farther to head quarters By Philadelphia." Pru-

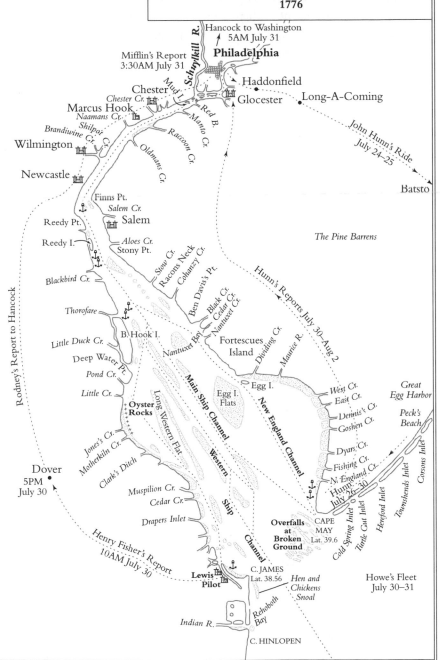

A CHART OF DELAWARE BAY AND RIVER

based on the original
by Mr. Fisher of Philadelphia
1776

N

Fisher's report reaches camp
10AM July 31
24 hours/160 miles

Hancock to Washington
5AM July 31

Mifflin's Report
3:30AM July 31

Philadelphia

Schuylkill R.

Chester

Chester Cr.

Mud I.

Haddonfield

Red B.

Glocester

Long-A-Coming

Marcus Hook

Naamans Cr.

Shilpoi

Manto Cr.

Brandiwine Cr.

Raccoon Cr.

Cr.

Wilmington

Oldmans Cr.

John Hunn's Ride
July 24–25

Newcastle

Batsto

Finns Pt.

Salem Cr.

Reedy Pt.

Salem

The Pine Barrens

Reedy I.

Aloes Cr.
Stony Pt.

Stow Cr.

Racons Neck

Cohanzy Cr.

Blackbird Cr.

Hunn's Reports July 30–Aug 2

Thorofare

Black Cr.
Cedar Cr.
Nantuxet Cr.

Little Duck Cr.

B. Hook I.

Ben Davis's Pt.

Deep Water Pt.

Nantuxet Bay

Fortescues
Island

Dividing Cr.

Maurice R.

Pond Cr.

Little Cr.

Egg I.

Egg I.
Flats

West Cr.

Great
Egg Harbor

East Cr.

Rodney's Report to Hancock

**Oyster
Rocks**

Long Western Flat

Main Ship Channel

New England Channel

Dennis's Cr.

Peck's
Beach

Goshen Cr.

Dover

5PM
July 30

Jones's Cr.

Motherkiln Cr.

Clark's Ditch

Western

Dyars Cr.

Fishing Cr.

N. England Cr.

Corsons Inlet

Muspilion Cr.

Cedar Cr.

Ship

Hunn's
July 26–30

Drapers Inlet

Henry Fisher's Report
10AM July 30

Channel

**Overfalls
at
Broken
Ground**

**CAPE
MAY** Lat. 39.6

Cold Spring Inlet

Turtle Gut Inlet

Hereford Inlet

Townshends Inlet

**Lewis
Pilot**

C. JAMES
Lat. 38.56

*Hen and
Chickens
Snoal*

Howe's Fleet
July 30–31

Indian R.

*Rehoboth
Bay*

C. HINLOPEN

dently sizing up the situation, he told Wharton, "I've not sent Mr. Jones off yet, but as soon as I am convinst they are bound up the Bay, I shall send the Express, but as there is but few that Nowes the way through the Jerseys, the Intilligence will go By Philadelphia as quick any way. The wind is E.S.E., & the Ships is now standing off."[104] Keeping Benjamin Jones in reserve, at 5 P.M. he sent another express rider, James Wilson, and reported to the Council, "45 sail in sight, & more of Cors will be in Sight . . . it appears to me they are bound up our Bay, but I may be deceived."

Loyalist activity was strong in parts of New Jersey, and Hunn was very concerned about the message getting safely through to Washington, whose headquarters was, to his knowledge, still up on the New York–New Jersey border at the Clove. He told President Wharton, "Mr. Jones comes off to Morrow Morning by way of Philadelphia, as going through Menmouth [Monmouth County in North Jersey] is attended with Dainger of being Stoped, as the people heare inform me."[105]

Unbeknownst to Hunn, Washington was well on his way to Philadelphia, with the army strung out for miles on the march from the Clove to Coryell's Ferry on the Delaware, thirty miles above the city.

Farther south, on board *Amity's Admonition* off the Delaware and Maryland coast, Lord Cantelupe wrote in his diary, "30th: The wind at N. E. fine weather. This Morning saw land which was Mary land."[106] Curiously, Lord Cantelupe, whose proper name was William Augustus West, made no remark about his first view of the Delaware Bay, which was named after his ancestor Thomas West, Baron de la Warr, the governor of Virginia who succeeded Capt. John Smith in 1610. Cantelupe's father, Lt. Gen. John West, Baron and Earl de la Warr, was colonel of the 1st Troop of Horse Guards, one of the most prestigious positions in the British Army. Lord de la Warr died in November 1777 while his son was in Philadelphia; thus, ironically, while stationed in the Delaware Valley, young Lord Cantelupe inherited the title from which the river, bay, and state had received their name.

Montrésor, whose schooner was farther up the coast, sighted the lighthouse at Cape Henlopen, the southern cape of the Delaware Bay: "Latitude at 12 o'clock 38.39″ . . . at which time the light-house bore N. W. 1/2 north about 5 1/2 leagues." This lighthouse, erected ten years earlier by Philadelphia merchants, was a octagonal structure seventy feet tall, built solidly of Brandywine River granite and perched on top of "the

Great Dune" nearly fifty feet above sea level. "Discovered the Pennsylvania [Delaware] Shore at 7 to the Southward Cape Henlopen," the engineer wrote. "Sea pretty smooth. Could discover Cape May only from the masthead."[107]

Cape Henlopen Light was the tallest structure around the flat coastal plains and was visible for miles.[108] From the lantern, forty-two-year-old Henry Fisher, Esq., of Lewes, a top-notch Delaware Bay ship pilot, and Col. David Hall, commander of the Delaware Continental Regiment, spotted the bulk of the British fleet that morning. Hall wrote to Gen. Caesar Rodney, a signer of the Declaration of Independence and commander of the Delaware Militia, "On Wednesday we first discovered them & in a little time we could make out 23 Sail from the Light-House; they had every Appearance of coming into our Bay." To guide the fleet away from a treacherous shoal called the Hen and Chickens, just east of the cape, Hall reported that "one of the small Vessels was placed in the Tail of the Hen & Chickens with a large flag as a Beacon for them & a Ship anchored in the Channel."[109]

Fisher, who kept a tireless watch for British activity in the bay all during the war, fired off a letter at 10 A.M. to Philadelphia, 130 miles away by land. "The Fleet is in sight, and at this time about 4 leagues from the Light House," he told the State Navy Board. "There is 228 (two hundred and twenty eight) sail. . . . They to all appearance will not be in till this afternoon."[110]

The express rider moved as quickly as possible up Delaware's sandy roads through Sussex County, another hotbed of Loyalist activity. "From the best information I have been able to Collect, & from my Own Observations, it appears that a large Majority of the Inhabitants of this County are disaffected," Col. William Richardson of the Maryland Militia wrote from Sussex County a few days later, "and would I believe afford the Enemy every Aid in their Power, except Personal Service in the Field, which the greater part of them want Spirit to do." With fatuous contempt, he added, "They are a set of Poor Ignorant Illetorate People, yet they are Artful and Cunning as Foxes, 'tis hardly possible to detect the most Open Offenders, yet they are almost every Day Offending."[111]

The report was delivered to General Rodney in Dover, fifty miles from Lewes, at 5 P.M. "Just now by Express from Lewis I am informed that two hundred and Twenty Eight of the Enemy's ships have appeared in the offing," Rodney told John Hancock. "I have Sent a fresh man and Horse that this Inteligence may be the sooner with you."[112] The "fresh man" was Thomas North, to whom Rodney gave a note stating that he "must be furnished with a Horse wherever he stands in need."[113]

Heading northeast toward New Castle, North galloped over the sandy coastal plains through terrain similar to the Jersey Pine Barrens: flat, heavily wooded territory, with many creeks and swamps. He continued on to Wilmington, where the land gets hilly. Illumination, if any, was provided by starlight, the moon being near the end of its last quarter.

A little over ten hours later, in the predawn darkness of July 31, the message arrived in Chester, Pennsylvania, sixty-five miles north of Dover, where it was received by General Mifflin at "10 Minutes after 3 O Clock at Chester and forwarded at 30 Minutes after Three."[114] John Hancock received it in Philadelphia at 5 A.M. and immediately sent an express to Washington at Coryell's Ferry on the Delaware, thirty miles farther north, where it arrived between 9 and 10 A.M., twenty-four hours and an astounding 160 miles after it was sent from Lewes.

Washington ordered the troops in motion, and later that day, he set out for the city.[115] In Philadelphia, "about 6 this morning the alarm guns fired, & an express came in which says that 280 sail appeared at the Capes standing in for our bay," noted Sarah Logan Fisher. "About 11 today another express arrived which says that two divisions have got in the bay & the third was coming in, but whether to believe the account or not we cannot tell, as we have been so frequently disappointed with so many false reports."[116] Out in the country at Trappe, Pastor Muhlenberg commented, "Nothing is said or heard now except war and rumors of war."[117]

In response to the impending invasion, a resolution was passed in Congress recommending to the Pennsylvania Supreme Executive Council that it immediately "make prisoners such of the late crown & proprietary officers and other persons in and near this city as are disaffected or may be dangerous to the publick liberty & send them back into the country." Heading the list of those to be arrested was Gov. John Penn, the founder's grandson, and Chief Justice Benjamin Chew, one of Philadelphia's most prominent lawyers. It was also resolved "that the militia of the states of New Jersey, Pennsylvania, Delaware and Maryland be immediately called out to repel any invasion of the enemy in the said states."[118] The Council replied to Congress that day, pleading, "The approach of the Enemy and the necessity of making every possible exertion, calls for large sums of money. . . . The Council, therefore, in these Circumstances, pray Congress to consider the business that presses on Council, and to order 100,000 Dollars to be furnished for public purposes."[119]

Washington arrived in town around 10 P.M., escorted by 200 light dragoons, and took up lodgings at the City Tavern.[120] He was well ahead of the main army. The previous week had been brutal for the troops as they maneuvered through the rugged hills of northwest Jersey in summer heat and torrential rain. "My Dear Polly, I am once more in Penna. after a very fatiguing March," Col. Percy Frazer wrote from Howell's Ferry on July 29. "We have March'd 2 Divisions consisting of 16 Regiments 90 Miles in four days, under several disadvantages. We cross'd the Delaware this morning with our Brigade. Orders arriv'd just then for the others to stand fast and for us to halt." He added, "General Washington with the other divisions of the Army are now at Corryells Ferry about 4 or 5 Miles below this place[;] it seems uncertain whether We shall go further to the southward," and reassured her, "I am still in good health tho a good deal fatigu'd."[121]

Meanwhile, in the Delaware Bay, the fleet met up with HMS *Roebuck*, the forty-four-gun frigate that had been patrolling the bay and gathering intelligence. Capt. Andrew Snape Hamond, the ship's thirty-nine-year-old commander, went to Lord Howe's flagship, HMS *Eagle*, at 10 A.M. on July 30 and was mortified to discover that General Howe was still in bed.[122] When finally called into the admiral's cabin, Hamond described the meeting as "a consultation between the Admiral & the General." The general wanted to know where Washington's army was; Hamond told him that Washington had crossed the Delaware and was marching to Wilmington. Where the captain acquired this information is unclear, but he may have surmised it based on sketchy reports. While the Continentals were in fact heading south, most of them were in New Jersey at that moment, and Washington, who was still at Coryell's Ferry that day, nearly seventy miles from Wilmington and almost twice that distance from the *Roebuck*, did not arrive in Philadelphia until the evening of July 31, more than thirty hours later.

From intelligence gathered by the *Roebuck*, the Howe brothers were updated on the state of the Delaware River defenses just below Philadelphia. Obstructions called *chevaux-de-frise* ("Frisian horses"), great squared timbers tipped with large iron spikes and mounted in stone-filled log cribs, were built by the rebels and sunk in the riverbed, pointing down-stream. They were covered by the guns of Mud Fort, or Fort Mifflin, on the Pennsylvania side of the Delaware, and Red Bank Fort, now called Fort Mercer, on the New Jersey side. Additionally, another earthwork was under construction downstream at Billingsport, New Jersey. Numer-ous fire ships and fire rafts had been prepared, and the small warships of the Pennsylvania Navy cruised the river.

Hamond later asserted that he had argued in favor of moving the fleet up the river and landing somewhere below New Castle, using the men-of-war as a screen against attacks by the smaller American vessels. He was incredulous that General Howe was strongly in favor of sailing to the Chesapeake, confirming Galloway's report to the House of Commons that the general had planned to go that way all along. Hamond revealed that Lord Howe "in confidence told me 'that the General's wishe and intention were first to destroy the magazines at York & Carlisle before he attacked the Rebel Army or looked towards Philadelphia; and therefore it was of course a great object to get to the westward of the Enemy.'" Hamond claimed that "in vain he pleaded against 'the great length of time it would take to make such a detour with so large a fleet, contrasted with the immediate opportunity of getting the whole army ashore in 24 hours,'" but his arguments went unheeded; "the General seemed resolved, and the Admiral would not oppose him." Thus on the morning of July 31, "to the astonishment of both Fleet and Army, the signal was made to turn away, and steer for the Capes of Virginia."[123]

Lord Howe's secretary, Ambrose Serle, was flabbergasted. "The Hearts of all Men were struck with this Business, every one apprehending the worst," he wrote with dismay. "*O quantâ, de spe!* is the universal Cry; and without the Loss or Risque of a Battel." Agonized, he confided to his diary, "What will my dear Country think & say too, when this News is carried Home? *Horreo.*"[124] Lt. Heinrich von Feilitzsch of the Anspach Jägers groaned, "No one any longer knew where we were bound. Every-one said something different and everyone had to leave the decision to General Howe."[125] From the *Aolus*, Sir George Osborn told his brother John, "When we came off the mouth of the Delaware we made a move-ment of the fleet as if we intended sailing up the river, but at night (*mais pour quelle raison j'ignore*) ["but for what reason I am ignorant"] we made off from land and are now destined for the Chesapeakes."[126]

Unaware of Howe's new move, Washington the next day went down to Chester, sixteen miles below Philadelphia, where he "had proceeded thus far in order to look out for a proper place to arrange the Army."[127] With the headquarters staff was a newly appointed major general with important connections in Europe, whose professional career would help shape significant events on two continents over the next sixty years. Nineteen-year-old Marie-Joseph Paul Roche Yves, Gilbert du Motier, Marquis de Lafayette, was here on his very first day of active service, August 1, 1777.

He was not supposed to have left France. "La Fayette's project surprized me very much," Captain Fitzpatrick of the Guards had written on July 8. "I should have not been at all so, if his Cousin the Vicomte de Noailles had done it." The young British Whig had become close friends with Lafayette, first in Paris several months earlier while on a visit there with Charles James Fox, then in London in the spring of 1777, when Lafayette visited the British capital right before Fitzpatrick left for active service. He was under the impression that Lafayette had been stopped from coming to America; "for his own sake I am not sorry he was prevented, for I think he would not have found it the kind of Army or the kind of service that he probably expected," Fitzpatrick mused, "though I suppose Washington would have treated him with the greatest distinction."[128]

After a long, difficult trip and a chilly reception by Congress, the young French aristocrat was presented with a purple shoulder sash signifying the rank of major general, "in consideration of his name, his great connections, and the sacrifices he had made through his love for liberty," with the understanding that he would not command a division of troops or receive pay. He was first introduced to Washington at the City Tavern, "who paid him a thousand compliments, and persuaded him to establish his headquarters in his household and dine at his table for the whole campaign," according to the Chevalier Dubuysson, one of several French officers who had accompanied Lafayette. All of Lafayette's companions had hoped to receive commissions but were disappointed. "In short, he was so dazzled that he forgot us for a moment," Dubuysson added bitterly. "But I must do him justice, he has too good a heart to allow his forgetfulness to last very long. He did his utmost to obtain positions for us, but in vain, as he has no influence."[129] The following morning, Lafayette found himself inspecting the river defenses with the commander in chief, while the others had to shift for themselves.

Washington consulted several of his top commanders, especially those who were from the local area, including Mifflin, Wayne, and Joseph Reed of Pennsylvania, his former adjutant general, who knew the area well. He asked their opinions on where to place the army to defend the city. Suggestions were put forth to entrench the heights between Ridley and Crum Creeks or fortify Darby Creek, all above Chester.

Then, around 7 P.M., John Hunn's fifth message arrived in Philadelphia from Cape May with the startling news that the previous morning, "the fleet stood off, steering E.N.E. & are now out of sight, and have been so these three hours." In landmen's terms, the British fleet had turned around and appeared headed back in the direction from which it had come. "This morning I was with many others of opinion they were bound up the Delaware," Hunn informed them, "but as they could have got in this morning and did not, I am now of opinion they are making a feint." His sea captain's expertise added a deduction that electrified the president of Congress and the commander in chief of the U.S. Army: "If so, they have a fresh wind at S. S. W which will carry them to the Eastward [New York or New England] very fast. . . . I believe their whole fleet was in sight, tho' I could count only one hundred & ninety sail." He concluded with the pledge, "I shall send off an Express if the fleet appears, if not I shall come up myself in a few days."[130]

Hancock quickly forwarded the message to Chester, where it arrived about 9 P.M. Washington had spent an exhausting day reconnoitering both sides of the river, having left Philadelphia early in the morning and proceeding as far south as Wilmington.[131] Now, candles would burn late into the night to deal with this new crisis.

With his army spread out nearly 200 miles from the Schuylkill to the Peekskill, Washington immediately dashed off a flurry of instructions to his commanders, ordering them to halt or reverse their marches. At 9:30 P.M., he wrote to Sullivan; at 10, he wrote to Gen. Alexander McDougall, whose New Englanders had been ordered to march south from Peekskill: "By an Express this Moment arrived from Cape May, The Enemy's fleet left the Capes Yesterday Morning at Eight Oclock—put to Sea and were out of sight Three Hours when the Express came away." Similar letters to other commanders were dispatched immediately.

Washington feared the worst—that Howe had lured him away from the Hudson and was now sailing north—so he now ordered McDougall to take all available troops to that area "to prevent the Enemy from effecting a Coup de Main against that post."[132] He told Nathanael Greene, "This unexpected event makes it necessary to reverse our disposition and I have accordingly sent orders to Sullivan's division and the two other brigades on the other side the Delaware to return and recross the North River."[133]

Because of contrary winds and tides rather than any deliberate maneuver on the part of the Howes, the fleet reappeared in the bay and just as quickly disappeared for good. "Today, no less than yesterday, the Admiral changed our course several times," von Münchhausen commented on August 2, "and it was difficult to tell where we were heading."[134]

The news only added to the tension and confusion in Philadelphia. Henry Fisher wrote from Lewes at 8 A.M. on August 2, "Just before sun set [on the thirty-first] we were alarmed from the light house that the fleet was standing in again; however on the 1st of August they were entirely out of sight." Puzzled, he stated, "Whether they are gone to the Southward or the Northward is not in my power to tell. When they disappeared the wind was about South." The Delaware pilot added, apologetically, "I should have sent off this express before, but delayed it from reports being often brought that they were standing in again. The *Roebuck* went off with the fleet, and has not been seen since."[135]

Yet again, Howe's conduct left many people scratching their heads. "All parties were disappointed," Congressman Henry Laurens of South Carolina wrote, "the cursed Tories who abound in and about this City, because they expected their Friends; the Friends of freedom, because they had wished to give a decisive Blow to those British Buccaniers."[136] Sarah Logan Fisher put it as succinctly as anyone could, regardless of political views, by quoting a line from Joseph Addison's play *Cato*, "But indeed the conduct of Howe may I think be justly said, in the words of the poet, 'to be dark & intricate, puzzled with mazes & perplexed with errors.' Strangely unaccountable is some of his conduct; perhaps time may unravel the mystery & justify his delays."[137] John Adams was, as usual, more acerbic: "What this Man is after, no Wisdom can discover."[138]

"All are baulked much, both Whigs and Tories," wrote Congressman James Lovell of Massachusetts, worried that if the British fleet headed east, "they will kill our army by a march to New England in this cruel hot season."[139] Continental forces were already arriving in the Philadelphia area, and Washington, "being fearful that if the Troops enter this City it will only tend to debauch them," directed Greene's Division and Morgan's Rifle Corps to halt at Germantown, a substantial village five miles to the north.[140] "Genl. W., with a considerable force is at German Town; for the mischiefs of actual war are very severe and grievous," President Thomas Wharton wrote. "But as a retreat out of sight may be only a new wile of Genl. Howe, the Genl. relaxes nothing till he find him elsewhere."[141]

The troops had a long and tiring march to Germantown during what proved to be the beginning of a brutal heat wave. Sunrise was at precisely 5 that morning; by 7, near Philadelphia, the temperature in the shade was already in the seventies, and by afternoon, it was in the mid-eighties; in the sun, it was a good 10 to 15 degrees hotter.[142] Lt. James McMichael of the Pennsylvania State Regiment, part of Weedon's Brigade in Greene's Division, briefly described his regiment's day, which began at the Cross Roads in Warwick Township, Bucks County, some twenty-five miles away: "At 3 A.M. the General [a drum signal to break camp] beat; tents were struck and at 6 A.M. we marched, proceeding thro' the Crooked Billet, reached Germantown at 6 P.M., on the plains of which we encamped. Our encampment was very beautiful."[143]

"A very disagreeable account came from Germantown this evening that 2,000 soldiers are there," Sarah Logan Fisher fretted, "some of them encamped on Shippen's common & some billeted on the inhabitants, & many of them we hear are at Stenton," the Logan family country seat.[144] At over 500 acres, with many rare plants and trees and much experimental cultivation, the Logan estate was one of the largest and most valuable properties in the Philadelphia area. Stenton was a handsome brick mansion built about 1730 at the southern end of Germantown by Sarah's grandfather James Logan, an outstanding scholar and scientist who had been the provincial secretary and a close friend of William Penn. Sarah's father, William, had died the previous October, and her oldest brother, George, who inherited the property, was in Edinburgh studying medicine, so the mansion was unoccupied at the moment. The estate was maintained by tenants.

Thomas Fisher, Sarah's husband and a Loyalist, went up to Stenton the next morning to "see what situation things are in there." He found

Morgan's Rifle Corps stationed on the property. "About a dozen officers have taken possession of the house & the men lie in the barn & about the lane," Sarah wrote, "about 90 of them at the tenant's & behave to him with great insolence, tho' treated my Tommy with great civility." Morgan, she said, "made many fair promises that no damage should be done by his men to the garden, orange trees, &c.," but Sarah had her doubts; the other troops in general "commit many outrages on the people's gardens, taking their apples, turning their horses into their mowing grounds & every other act of violence that a lawless banditti think fit to show."

Over the next few days, she was surprised to find that at Stenton, "things are in a better situation than we could expect considering the number of dirty creatures that are there."[145] It couldn't be helped; Morgan's men were a rugged crew, to be sure, but they were in the midst of a hard campaign, having moved well over 100 miles the previous week in the heat of summer. The campgrounds would have been terribly muddy, for five out of the six days saw showers and thunderstorms in a regular summer cycle.[146] Interestingly, the discipline in this corps showed in her description, for she wrote, "They do but little damage to the garden, & not any to the house except making it extremely dirty. One company dine in the large back room, & another company upstairs in the large empty room that is there. They find their own provisions & have their own cook but make use of all our kitchen furniture & cook in the kitchen as well as have many fires out of doors."[147]

The same could not be said for the army at large. Discipline regarding camp sanitation was a constant problem, as the General Orders repeatedly bear out all through 1777. Greene's Division Orders for August 6 commanded fatigue parties of forty men each from Muhlenberg's and Weedon's Virginia Brigades "to be employ'd in burying all the filth in and round about the Encampment." The "camp colors men," those soldiers responsible for preparing the layout of the encampments and seeing to the unpleasant task of digging "vaults," or latrines, were ordered "to be immediately set to work in filling up the old Vaults and digging new ones," for "there is such a stench arises on every side of it now as threatens the passengers with immediate Pestilence."[148] They were also ordered to properly place the vaults a distance behind the campgrounds and erect coverings of boughs for the sake of decency. Pine limbs were favored as a way to try to keep the stench in check.

Camping several thousand men in one spot for just a few days during the scorching heat and torrential downpours of the dog days could be more deadly than battle if basic sanitation rules were not observed. Washington repeatedly admonished the troops about their lack of discipline in this regard and chided the officers for failure to enforce the orders.

Despite the stench and the heat, the army had visitors—hundreds of them. "The largest collection of young ladies I almost ever beheld came to camp," Lieutenant McMichael said enthusiastically on August 3. "They marched in three columns. The field officers paraded the rest of the officers and detached scouting parties to prevent being surrounded by them."[149]

McMichael belonged to the Pennsylvania State Regiment (PSR), a unit of state regulars that was not militia but was not yet fully integrated into the Continental Army, though it was attached to Weedon's Virginia Brigade for most of this campaign. Numbering about 600 personnel, it was raised from the remnants of several Pennsylvania battalions that had seen hard service in New York the previous year, and many of the young ladies had friends or relatives among them. The regiment was handsomely uniformed in blue coats faced with red, complete with pewter buttons marked, "P.S.R."

Spine-tingling field music was provided by a full complement of twenty-two fifers and drummers who were enlisted in the army, collectively called the "field music," as distinguished from "bandsmen," who were privately hired civilians playing other instruments. The field music was the army's communication system; drummers and fifers in each regiment played signals in camp and in battle and provided cadences and lively tunes on the march. Following the British Army custom of wearing reversed regimental coat colors so as to be easily spotted by their officers, the PSR field musicians were dressed in red coats faced with blue.

The PSR was what a proper regiment should be in terms of numbers, appearance, and ability. But it wasn't only the fine music and handsome uniforms that drew the crowds; besides the pageantry, the young ladies had one other motive for visiting in such numbers. The regiment's Irish-born commander, twenty-one-year-old Col. Walter Stewart, had the reputation of being "the handsomest man in the army," for which "the Philadelphia ladies styled him *the Irish beauty.*"[150] Being thronged with so many breathless guests was gallantly taken in stride. "For my part being sent on scout, I at last sighted the ladies and gave them to know that they must repair to headquarters, upon which they accompanied me as prisoners," McMichael proclaimed unabashedly. "But on parading them at the Colonels marquee, they were dismissed after we treated them with a double bowl of Sangaree."[151]

The enthusiasm of the visits began to wilt as the days blazed on. After a week of no further news of the British fleet, Howe "may now be in the Moon for aught we know," Congressman Henry Laurens speculated, "but he is probably gone to New England & will Strive to join General Burgoine."[152] John Adams quipped in sporting fashion, "The Hounds are all still at a Fault. Where the game is gone, is the Question. The Scent is quite lost."[153]

Washington decided to move the army from Germantown back toward Coryell's Ferry. On August 8, the troops were ordered to pass in review before moving out; here, Lafayette saw the main Continental Army parade for the first time. "About eleven thousand men, poorly armed and even more poorly clothed, offered a singular spectacle," he recalled. "The best garments were *hunting shirts*, large jackets of gray linen commonly worn in Carolina." As for maneuvers, they were clumsy at best. For parade or for battle, "they were always formed in two ranks, with the small men in front"; unlike European armies with grenadiers, "no other distinction as to height was ever observed." Nonetheless, "they were fine soldiers, led by zealous officers, and each day added to their experience and their discipline."[154]

"The army was reviewed, and in the afternoon marched about nine or ten miles back from Germantown," Col. Timothy Pickering wrote in his journal on August 8. "But it was a hot day; the troops fatigued by being under arms from six o'clock in the morning till one or two in the afternoon; and the march afterwards hurt many of them, especially as some did not arrive at their ground till late in the evening."

Part of the army had marched to Whitemarsh, about eight miles north, and encamped along Sandy Run. "But the General did not intend they should have moved so far by four or five miles," Pickering noted. It was a mistake, a needless blunder so common in army operations as to fuel timeless jokes about "military intelligence." "The Deputy Quartermaster-General miscalculated the distance; and, besides, did not take the route which led most directly to Coryell's Ferry, so that the army marched ... five or six miles for nothing."[155]

Washington had remained near Germantown and departed on the tenth for Coryell's Ferry. "The soldiers went away about 5 this morning" from Stenton and "left it in a dreadful dirty condition, but have done no very material damage to us," a relieved Sarah Logan Fisher wrote in her diary. "Engaged two women to come & assist in cleaning the house & yard tomorrow." The tenant lost his apples, however, and his meadow was ruined by the army horses. Sarah also noted, "The weather is extremely hot."[156]

No sooner had Washington left Germantown than word arrived in Philadelphia that the British fleet had been spotted off southern Maryland near the Virginia border three days earlier. "We have found Howe again," Congressman Lovell crowed sarcastically. "I thought he was lost in the Gulph stream."[157]

"Where the Scourge of God, and the Plague of Mankind is gone, no one can guess," his irascible colleague John Adams told Abigail. "An Express from Sinnepuxtent, a Place between the Capes of Delaware and the Capes of Chesapeak, informs that a fleet of 100 sail was seen off that Place last Thursday." John, though, had his doubts; "whether this is Fishermens News like that of Cape Ann, I know not."[158]

John Hancock forwarded the report to Washington, who had just arrived at camp that evening at "the Crossroads" near Neshaminy Creek in Bucks County, about twenty-five miles northeast of the city. Concerned about the effect that all the marching and countermarching in the heat was having on the health of the troops, Washington decided to stay put until more firm intelligence could be obtained.

Eleven days of sailing from the Delaware Bay had brought the fleet less than 100 miles closer to the capes of the Chesapeake, and strong tides delayed entry for a few more days. "I am now entering my fifth week at sea in a passage of only fourscore leagues," Sir George Osborn told his brother on August 10. Vacillating between his own optimism and the frustration of a drawn-out voyage, Sir George tried to rationalize his feelings: "I am philosopher enough in great operations of the nature of that I am now engaged in to think that providence or chance directs us better than our own wisdoms and foresight can suggest." Ever optimistic, Osborn tried to look for a bright spot in the strategy: "The delay therefore of five weeks in a voyage, which in the common course of calculation might be laid at ten days, in the one light may be thought a calamity, but if we consider that we should have arrived just in the heat of the Dog Days in a climate under the latitude of 37, the length of our voyage may prove beneficial to our future operations."

But even Sir George could not help but face reality. "Indeed I dread the next six weeks for our troops," he admitted. "We shall probably land in three or four days and with the excessive heats of this month and the rains of September we must expect many agues and fevers." Still, he managed to find a bright spot, adding, "At present the army is pretty healthy. I have three hundred on board this ship and not one sick man: I never have my own health better than at sea."[159]

The unexpected length of the voyage was taking a serious toll on the food supplies and the army's horses. Captain Hamond of the *Roebuck* had noted at the end of July that even though Howe's decision to go to the Chesapeake was predetermined, it was "not untill the Quarter Master General was consulted as to the State of the Forage who reported, that sufficient remained for 14 days."[160] The estimate was somewhat optimistic; as early as August 7, Captain von Münchhausen commented, "Since it was not foreseen that we would be aboard ship so long, the horses were given very little space; this is the reason they are beginning to die."[161] From the *Alert*, Captain Montrésor wrote the same day, "Master of the horse Sloop came on board to signifie the distress for want of forage. Gave him a note to the Commissary General." Three days later, he reported, "The Horse Vessels in general lying too for Food from the forage vessel, they being much distressed."[162]

Fresh food ran out, so the troops and many of the officers were put on salt rations. "Three weeks we were told to lay in for," grumbled Lt. Loftus Cliffe. "Use brought us to relish our Salt Pork." He blamed the situation on the long wait "from my taking Shipping at Staten Island the 9th July or rather from the 23d July that we sailed, for that interval was taken up only in consuming our fresh Stock, very scantily laid in indeed."[163]

"The Officers were upon Salt Provisions for some Weeks before they came ashore, some of our Generals observed the same Regimen," General Grant commented imperiously from the comfort of the *Isis*, commanded by Capt. William Cornwallis. "Lord Cornwallis & I lived well on Board the *Isis* with his Brother, who neither eats or drinks himself— but takes good care of his Friends."[164]

"Col. [Henry] Monckton and Major Gardiner (the Genl's Aid de Camp, now acting as Major to our Battalion) and a set of pleasing officers, made us bare the horrors of a ship with resignation," Lt. William Hale told his parents. "Our fresh provisions were indeed exhausted for more than three weeks before our landing." As far as beverages were concerned, he wrote, "We drank claret [red Bordeaux wine] all the way, every officer contributing so many days' pay made the expense very easy to the subalterns, and Col. Monckton supplied us with his own claret when ours was out."[165]

The drinking water turned foul, adding to the overall misery. Montrésor observed on August 11, "The officers put to great shifts for want of fresh provisions, rowing about from ship to ship for relief. . . . Our fresh water on board became very offensive."[166] On board the *Martha*, Lieutenant von Feilitzsch bemoaned his situation in early August: "Anyone who has a desire to experience misery and misfortune should go aboard ship. . . . 1) There is no bread except zwieback [hard biscuits] which is spoiled or full of worms. 2) Stinking water with all possible impurities mixed in. . . . 3) The meat is miserable and frightfully salted so that it can hardly be eaten, and then one nearly dies of thirst. 4) The entire ship is full of lice; and when it storms, no one can think of anything else."[167]

Despite the lack of fresh food, Osborn and his companions, Fitzpatrick and Wrottesley, lived well on the *Aolus*, what with a French cook and a foppish touch of decadent opulence in the form of a German musician providing background music on a harp. "I have an Harper on board, one of the Musick of the Regiment de Ditforth," Sir George informed his brother John. "We have a Frenchman, one of the best campaign cooks I ever met with and at times we live *tres honnetement* ["very properly"], at present indeed *malheureusemen nous n'avons querre de provisions* ["unfortunately, we cannot fetch fresh provisions"]."

Still, even with these perks, Osborn yearned for some home cooking from Mrs. Blackford, the cook at the family estate in Bedfordshire, Chicksands Priory. He told his brother, "If Mrs. Blackford [only] knew how acceptable some of her good poultry and kitchen garden productions would be. You may tell her I am confident she would run out and gather them herself and be happy to send them to me." Sir George knew her temperament well: He should be home looking after the estate, not gallivanting around America with his friends, listening to harp music! "She would say probably that if she were me, she would eat them at Chicksands," he gibed, tongue-in-cheek. On a more serious note, he remarked to John, "You may likewise tell her that her Master is really and truly of a very different opinion; he feels himself one stake, though but a small one, in one of the most important struggles his or any other country was ever engaged in, and the period he trusts not very far off when he shall be eyewitness whether the finest Empire upon the globe shall be attached or wrested from Great Britain."[168]

The voyage had its share of hair-raising episodes, involving collisions, near misses, and spectacular electrical storms. Most frightening and fascinating of all were the lightning strikes. Fueled by the intense heat, the thunderstorms, memorable for their violence, left a vivid impression on these northern Europeans. Captain von Münchhausen described the effect of a lightning bolt hitting the *Brittania* on August 6: "Our foremast was shattered down to the keel, damaging the decks and knocking down the sails and yards. The whole forepart of the ship, which was set afire, was sunk into the sea by the force of the blow. Thus, the fire was extinguished and we were saved." But the danger was far from over: "We worked pumps hard and constantly to keep our ship from sinking. . . . There was no ship in the vicinity, because during the storm, ships always spread out to avoid collision. . . . Soon after we had been hit, the storm ended. A complete calm followed. . . . The Admiral ordered the nearest ships of the line to send their carpenters to us, who at once began to repair our damage by putting up a new mast etc. . . . With the exception of a sailor, who is not expected to recover, no one was injured."[169]

John Adams expressed little sympathy for the "Scourge of God" and "Plague of Mankind." "I wish this Wiseacre may continue to coast about until an equinoctial Storm shall overtake him," he wrote spitefully. "Such a Thing would make fine Sport for his Fleet."[170]

The voyage continued in the same desultory manner, and several more days passed before the fleet was able to clear the Chesapeake capes. To make matters worse, the dog days were in their full fury, and the mid-Atlantic region was in the grips of the hottest stretch in memory. "The winds were so contrary in this part of the voyage, that the middle of August was turned before they entered Chesapeak Bay," *The Annual Register* reported, commenting with elegant understatement, "a circumstance highly inconvenient and irksome in that hot season of the year, with so great a number of men and horses crowded and cooped up in the vessels."[171]

Up in the Pennsylvania countryside, "the heat is almost unbearable. Here and there people suddenly collapse and die when they are not careful in drinking cold water," Rev. Henry Muhlenberg entered in his diary on August 11. "Several officers stopped in and refreshed themselves with milk and water, which is the only drink that really slakes thirst."[172]

Out in the Atlantic on August 12, Captain Montrésor commented, "The heat of the Sun here feels more like an artificial than a genial heat, and the heat of this night Insupportable. The wind this night from S. W. to W. S. West," the classic regional summer "heat pump," which bore out Grant's earlier comments about the climate being the same all over the East Coast in summer.[173]

From his home west of Baltimore, Congressman Charles Carroll of Carrollton wrote to Benjamin Franklin in Paris that same day and told him, "The 1st [of August] the weather set in very hot, and has continued so ever since; yesterday was the hottest day I ever felt; this is almost as bad—I have not a thermometer or I would let you know the exact degree of heat."[174]

"We have been sweltering here, for a great Number of days together, under the scalding wrath of the Dog Star," a wilting John Adams wrote from Philadelphia on August 13. "So severe a Spell of Heat has scarcely been known these twenty Years. The Air of the City has been like the fierce Breath of an hot Oven." In a timeless summer ritual, "Every Body has been running to the Pumps all day long." John told Abigail that it made him feeble and irritable, so much so that "the Fatigue of even holding a Pen to write a Letter, is distressing."[175] The following day, August 14, he wrote, "The Day before Yesterday, Dr. Ewing . . . told me, the Spirit in his Glass [thermometer fluid], was at 91 in his Cool Room. . . . Yesterday, it was at 94, abroad in the Shade . . . against a Post which had been heated by the Sun, and the Spirit arose to 100."

Adams's thoughts turned again to the British expedition, whose whereabouts were any landsman's guess: "If Howes Army is at Sea, his Men between Decks will suffer, beyond Expression. Persons, here, who have been at Sea, upon this Coast, at this Season of the Year, say, the Heat is more intolerable, on Shipboard than on Land. There is no Comfort to be had any where, and the Reflection of the Suns Rays from the Deck, are insufferable."[176] Congressman Richard Henry Lee of Virginia commented, "Our accounts from France say that [King] George depends much on the 'desperate efforts that Howe & Cornwallis must make to redeem their bankrupt honor.' His present Manoeuvre seems the effort of a *despairing* Bankrupt. For what good can result from having multitudes of Men & Horses confined on board Ships at this season of the year, exposed to the torrid hell that beams upon their heads?"[177]

Earlier, after discovering that they were actually heading for the Chesapeake, Ambrose Serle had written, "May GOD defend us from the Fatality of the worst Climate in America at this worst Season of the Year to experience it!" Now, on August 14, he recorded, "The Thermometer in the Shade and at Sea stood frequently at 84° and 86°. What must it have been upon Shore?"[178] On the *Alert*, after a restless night with "the intense heat and closeness horrid," Captain Montrésor gasped that they were "obliged now to lay on deck. The heat of this day (if possible) more insupportable than yesterday, the pitch melting off the seams of the vessel."[179] His assistant, Capt. Archibald Robertson, noted, "Thermometer at 88°"[180]

That same day, August 14, the British fleet entered the Chesapeake Bay. Seeing the Virginia shoreline, not far from where his home had been in Norfolk, Loyalist James Parker wrote, "The View of the fleet in this place I make no doubt will incline the patriots to try the speed of their blooded Colts."[181]

Despite the heat, the change of scenery inspired much spontaneous commentary from the British officers. "The sailing up Chesapeak Bay was the Grandest Sight, sure that cou'd be seen," Lt. William Dansey wrote home to Ireland.[182] Lt. Loftus Cliffe told his brother, "We were ten Days sailing up the most beautifull Bay perhaps in the World."[183]

"It is the boldest Bay in the whole world," exclaimed Sir George Osborn, "twenty miles broad in many places." Barely containing his enthusiasm, he told brother John, "Nothing can be more beautiful than our sailing up the Bay of Chesapeak, the Rhine which I sailed through in the year '75 is really a plaything to it. The boldness of a coast of near 200 miles, which I shall have passed when I arrive at the Elk River (the place of our destination) coasting the length of Virginia and the two shores of Maryland are scenes which I probably may never see again and which falls to the lot of few to behold."[184]

The British public's first glimpse of this voyage came through the eyes of an anonymous British officer by way of a letter published in The *London Chronicle* a few months later. "After we got into Chesapeak, we came to anchor every night, and I assure you, this part of our voyage was very agreeable; the country on each side of us delightful; the well cultivated fields wore a beautiful aspect and afforded the finest rural prospect. In our way we passed Annapolis which I thought a handsome place, and pleasantly situated."[185] Ambrose Serle proclaimed, "Nothing could be more beautiful than the View of this immense Fleet passing round some of the Headlands. The Bay, the higher it is ascended, becomes more beautiful."[186]

The Chesapeake's natural bounty was not only a feast for the eyes. "It's remarkable in this Bay the multitude of crabs that swim nearly to the surface of the water," Captain Montrésor noticed just below Annapolis, "The Fleet caught thousands." A delightful change of diet, to be sure, from day after wretched day of boiled salt pork.

But the dog days blazed on. August 16 was a particularly oppressive day, sultry and still. "No wearing coats or waistcoats with any satisfaction," Montrésor stated. "This if possible the hottest day."[187] That evening, the fleet dropped anchor at dusk as a storm rose, and von Münchhausen reported that "by midnight we experienced the heaviest rain and thunderstorm I have ever seen." Lt. Heinrich von Feilitzsch confirmed that "during the night there was a thunderstorm such as has never been seen in Europe."[188] Sgt. Thomas Sullivan of the 49th wrote, "A Woman's shift being burnt upon her body, lying in a Birth [berth] on a Transport, and she aSleep, by a Flash of Lightning, without the least damage to her skin or Flesh, Also a Man's Coat and Shirt was burnt likewise on his Back, without his knowing of it till next morning: And the Arms of three Companies of men were japanned [blackened] on Board the same ship by the same Flash." The same storm "killed seven horses in a horse ship."[189]

The horses were in pitiful condition, lacking both forage and fresh water. Each day saw more pathetic carcasses heaved into the bay. "This day we spared a Horse Sloop in Quarter Master Genl's Department, one But[t] of Water or they must have thrown their horses overboard," Montrésor reported on the sixteenth. Three days later, he observed, "The fleet and army much distressed for the want of fresh water . . . but not so much so as the horse vessels, having been obliged to throw numbers of their horses overboard."[190]

The fleet left a grisly trail up the Chesapeake, as Congress later found out. "In a Letter from good Authority, Mr. [William] Paca," John Adams wrote to Abigail, "we are informed that many dead Horses have been driven on the Eastern shore of Maryland.—Horses thrown overboard, from the fleet, no doubt."[191] Maj. Charles Stuart of the 43rd told his father, "The Voyage had destroyed more than a hundred."[192]

The heat wave slowly began to relent. "Tuesday 19th . . . The Weather was this Day more moderate in Heat, than any we have felt for these 3 Weeks," Ambrose Serle wrote as the *Fanny* left the mouth of the Potomac River, where "the Bay begins to contract itself, and the Shores become distinctly visible on both Sides." Gasping in near disbelief at the torrid conditions, he noted, "Several of our People, who have been on the Coast of Guinea & in the West Indies, assured me, they never felt in either of those Countries such an intense suffocating heat, which we have experienced for several Days and Nights together." He added, "If possible, the Nights were more disagreeable than the days."[193]

Early on August 21, Howe's flotilla passed Annapolis, the capital of Maryland, located on the western shore of the bay at the mouth of the Severn River. Here the militia "formed a Battery from Mr. Walter Dulany's Lot round the Water's Edge to the Granary. . . . The Cannon are mostly 18 Pounders, and the Works appear strong. . . . They have another Fortification on Hill's Point, & a Third on Mr. Ker's Land, on the North Side of Severn, on a high cliff called Beaumont's Point."[194] As His Majesty's ships sailed by, Sir George Osborn noticed that two forts guarding the harbor "had the impudence to hoist rebel colours in the sight of our fleet," a defiant display that provoked much commentary.[195] "In the city and on the fort are flown big rebel flags (Union flags, as they call them)," Captain von Münchhausen explained. "They are white with purple stripes."[196] A British officer was quoted in the *London Chronicle* as saying, "Notwithstanding we could have battered it to pieces in half an hour, they had the impudence to display the thirteen stripes upon the two forts; but it was an object of little importance, it was looked at with contempt, and passed by without firing a shot."[197]

The display of flags was sheer bravado; the government of Maryland was fully prepared to evacuate the capital. "The British Fleet having this morning passed Annapolis and consisting of upwards of two hundred and Sixty sail," the Council minutes recorded, "The Governor and Council were unanimously of opinion that Annapolis cannot be defended by any force which may probably be collected against the force the Enemy may at any Time bring against it and that therefore the Town and Forts ought to be evacuated."[198] Rev. Francis Asbury, a tireless English Methodist missionary who "rode the circuit" that year in Maryland, wrote, "A report that a British fleet was sailing up the Chesapeake Bay, has induced many people to quit Annapolis. Lord, give thy people faith and patience sufficient for their day of trial!"[199]

Farther up the bay on the Patapsco River, Baltimore braced for an attack. A rapidly growing town of 600 houses and several thousand citizens, it was defended by a small, unnamed fort on Whetstone Point, commanded by Col. Nathaniel Smith of the Baltimore Artillery. The river was partially blocked by a boom of three large, floating chains. Colonel Smith told Governor Johnson the following day, "The Fleet Appeard off the mouth of this River . . . cant yet tell what their intentions is. the headmost Ship, which from her Carrying a Flagg at her maintopmast head, Supposed to be the Admiral, has come too in the mouth of the Channel." He went on to say that "Capt. Nicholson is down here with all his men which has nearly man'd Our Lower Battery."

The "Fort at Whetstone" defenses were pathetic. "I am very week as to guns[,] having only six 18-pounders," the militia colonel wrote. "[I] think if the Gallies had their Guns & I had Ten 18 pounders more with the Assistance of the Frigate & Defence we cou'd prevent them from taking this place by water." Smith bravely reassured the governor, "I am not so well prepared as I coud wish but shant give up the Fort, without giving them some trouble."[200] (During another British invasion in 1814, the defense of this post, enlarged and named Fort McHenry in the 1790s, was immortalized in "The Star-Spangled Banner.")

Gen. Andrew Buchanan was the field commander of the Maryland Militia. "General Buchanan is doing all he can to git the Militia togeather, hope they will turn out well," Smith told the governor. In the town itself, the "mechanicks," as artisans and skilled laborers were called, had formed the "Mechanical Melitia Company" of the Baltimore Town Battalion and turned out to a man. Their commander was thirty-eight-year-old Capt.

James Cox, "the most fashionable tailor in Baltimore town."[201] Father of five children, "three Sons & two Daughters, all Promising Children," ranging in age from two to ten years old, Cox was "the best of husbands," according to his wife, Mary.[202] Governor Johnson directed General Buchanan to issue a commendation to the company on August 24. "The Commander-in-Chief desires Capt. Cox at the Head of his Company to return them his sincere thanks for the readiness and Zeal which they have manifested on the present Important Occasion, in turning out unanimously as Volunteers to reinforce Genl. Washington. The noble Example he hopes will animate every Battallion cheerfully to turn out in defence of all that is dear and Valuable to Man."[203]

Cox's company was singled out as a "noble example" because it was the exception; the overall situation of the Maryland Militia was chaotic almost beyond belief. Col. Benjamin Rumsey wrote to the governor from the old port of Joppa, north of Baltimore, that one of the two companies there "had not above five Guns among forty men." He wryly commented, "Your Excellency will no Doubt conclude that Men unarmed can be of no Service to repel an Enemy. . . . They march with great Alacrity without Arms in full Confidence you will supply them at least to do all they can." In the face of the British invasion, "a little Fort is throwing up at this Place and We have got four 4-pounders and We hope to be able for a Tender if She comes but we have got but 13 Musketts[;] if your Excellency can spare a few for this Place it will contribute more to our Safety[:] We could arm 20 men more."[204]

Out in the fleet, Maj. Charles Stuart noted how the Chesapeake divided Maryland politically as well as physically. Off the starboard was the Eastern Shore of the Delmarva Peninsula, an area of strong Loyalist activity. "Our movements to the Chesapeake seem to indicate that Gen. Howe has hopes, or assurances, that Maryland will return to obedience," Stuart told his father. "It is probable that that part of Maryland, Virginia, and the lower Delaware Counties [the state of Delaware] situated on the peninsula form'd by the Delaware and Chesapeake, may answer these expectations." Across the bay, the large Continental flags of thirteen stripes flying over the forts told a different story: "The Western Coast of this Bay, from all I can learn, are very averse to a reconciliation. They have hoisted the rebel Colours, and the arm'd vessels we have observed are too strong proofs of this unreasonable enmity."[205]

The higher up the bay the fleet moved, the shallower and more dangerous the waters became for the larger ships. Just above Baltimore, the flagship *Eagle* came to anchor, as did the largest ships of the line, so the frigate *Roebuck* took the lead to the Elk River at the head of the Bay.

Lord Howe's seamanship achieved new levels of respect and high esteem as he personally took soundings ahead of the warships near the Elk River. No ships of this size had ever been known to have come so far up the Chesapeake, and the admiral showed that it could be done. "Lord Howe has great credit in the Care of this fleet, not one Vessel missing since we left New York; tho the Passage was unavoidably longer than common," wrote James Parker. He noted that "Capt. Hammond led the Van of the fleet in the *Roebuck* Marking out the chanel which was of Outmost Concequence. I am told by some of the Country people that there never was any very large Merchant ship above Swan point before this."[206] Montrésor observed with admiration that "the Shoalness of the Elk convinced the Rebels that our fleet would never navigate it, but through the great abilities of our Naval officers it was happily effected as the bottom was muddy and the ships on it were cutting chanels through it for each other."[207]

Gen. James Grant, by no means easy to please, paid His Lordship a very high compliment, noting that "as the Navigation is extremely difficult, the Chanel in many places narrow and intricate—Lord Howe has great Merit in conducting the Fleet which he certainly did with Ability. The Dispositions he made with his Sloops Boats & Tenders prevented any Accident happening to the Transports, to the great Astonishment of us Land Men." Momentarily humble, he told General Harvey, "I am no Judge but I look up to His Lordship exceedingly as I think few officers would have risked such a Navigation & I said at the time that Fleet & Army must be united under the Command of two Brothers to bring 64 Gun Ships into an American Forrest."[208]

On August 23, the Howe brothers together explored the upper reaches of the Chesapeake near the Susquehanna River and scouted about for landing places. Their personal bravery and leadership skills shone brilliantly in this expedition as they maneuvered around Spesutie Island in the waters near the mouth of one of the widest and shallowest rivers in America. Captain Montrésor accompanied them: "At 7 this morning I attended Sir Wm. Howe and Lord Howe with my armed Schooner, an armed Sloop and a Galley to the mouths of the Rivers Rappahannock [*sic*; Susquehanna] and the Elk and Turkey Point, the different vessels and Boats attending, sounding the Channel."[209]

The local patriot militia was desperately trying to remove livestock with the few available men, and they came under fire from the Howe expedition. Col. Aquila Hall, commander of the Harford County Militia, reported, "Captn. Francis Holland with two of my sons, Two of the Paca's and two or three more passed over to Spesuti Island with intent to drive off what Stock they could, but before they return'd with a Parcel of Cattle there came a Sloop and Schooner two Armed Vessels and Anchored." He told Governor Johnson, "as soon as the Enimy saw Captn. Holland enter the beach they sent off a boat with men to head him, and at the same [time] began to play on him & men with Cannon ball & Grape shott which drove the Cattle back and then Captn. Holland was Obliged to retreat down the island where I sent Canoes to take them off. . . . There is a fine Parcel of Stock on the Island and it's a Pity it should fall into their hands."[210] Montrésor noted, "The whole returned in the afternoon to the fleet. George Ford, principal tenant of Pasoosy [Spesutie] Island came off to offer his Services to supply the Troops and Fleet with Stock &c."[211]

Yet another violent thunderstorm struck the fleet on the night of the twenty-fourth. This time, the *Isis* was hit while Lord Cornwallis and General Grant were still on board. The ship was anchored on the south side of the Sassafras River, along with the *Nonsuch*, *Augusta*, and *Somerset*, all sixty-four-gun ships-of-the-line. The flagship *Eagle*, with Lord Howe and General Howe, was four miles ahead near Turkey Point. "The *Isis* was struck with Lightning, the night before we left her—the Main Mast damaged, & on Fire for a time," Grant wrote. "Lord Cornwallis & I were reading in the Cabin when it happened, which was filled in a Moment, with a Sulphureous Smell."[212] In the logbook of the fifty-gun frigate is recorded:

From 7 to 11 thunder lightning & heavy rain. at 1/2 after 8 a flash of lightning struck the mn. T. G. Mt. [main topgallant mast] shiverd it to pices, rent the Mn. topmt. [main topmast] from head to heel, split several pieces of the mainmast, & burnt one of the Mn. topmt. shrowds in two. . . . At 11 [the next morning] the Right Hon. Charles Earl Cornwallis Lieut. Genl., Major Genl. Grant & their aid de camps went on board the *Charming Nelly* transport.[213]

Thus, amidst thunder and lightning, phase two of the British campaign to Philadelphia, the voyage to the Chesapeake, came to a conclusion. Phase three, the march to Philadelphia, was about to begin.

CHAPTER 3

"*But is this conquering America?*"

PHILADELPHIA AND POINTS SOUTH,
LATE AUGUST–EARLY SEPTEMBER 1777

"An express came in today, which brings an account that the fleet are in Chesapeake Bay, nearly as high as the Head of the Elk, & it supposed they will soon attempt to land," Sarah Logan Fisher wrote on August 21, "but where their intention is to march to we are greatly at a loss to guess." Sarah's Loyalist sympathies compelled her to confide in her diary, "In consequence of this news we hear General Washington is to march with his army to oppose them, & prevent if possible their penetrating into the country, but vain will be his expectations & fruitless his attempts of that kind."[1]

It was the first reliable news of the fleet to arrive in Philadelphia for nearly two weeks, and the waiting had worn heavily on the army and on Congress. "Not a Word, yet, from Hows Fleet," John Adams had written to Abigail at 5 P.M. the previous day. "The most general Suspicion, now, is that it is gone to Charlestown S. C. But it is a wild Supposition. It may be right however, for Howe is a wild General."[2]

Washington's army was preparing to move on August 21—somewhere. Since leaving Germantown on August 10, the main camp was along Neshaminy Creek in Bucks County, with headquarters in Warwick Township. The camp was growing more foul each day and had to be moved before major epidemics broke out.

Much of the force was far-flung: Nash's Carolina Brigade was across the Delaware at Trenton, Sullivan's two Maryland brigades and half of Maxwell's New Jersey Brigade were in North Jersey at Chatham, and Putnam was still holding the Hudson Highlands with Connecticut troops at Peekskill. In Pennsylvania, Maj. Gen. Benjamin Lincoln's Division of two Pennsylvania brigades was at Graeme Park, ten miles west of the Neshaminy Camp. Lincoln was sent to the Northern Army along with General Gates, so the division was now commanded by Anthony Wayne.

Down in Philadelphia, one troublesome regiment, the 4th Georgia Battalion, the same troops who had fired volleys for Congress on the Fourth of July, were moved out of the city after one of their number was murdered in early August. This unit, composed of British deserters, left a trail of destruction everywhere it went. No sooner did the 4th Georgia relocate than some of its men began to terrorize farmers along the Lancaster Road six miles west of town. "The Petition of divers Inhabitants of the Townships of Lower Merrion & Blockley" was sent to President Wharton on August 15.[3] "That the repeated injuries, insults & abuses daily received & increasing, so as to render it a matter of the most alarming nature, to our lives and properties, from the Battalion of the State of Georgia, Commanded by Coll'l John White, now incamped in said Township, renders it our indispensable duty, & constrains us (tho' with reluctance) to lay our distressed situation before your Excellency." Thirty-six leading property holders, mostly farmers from the two townships, had signed the petition telling Wharton:

> It is notorious that from the first day of their incamping they began to shew their aversion for all Law, Divine or Human, abusing travellers, Robbing the neighbourhood of everything they could lay their hands on, pillaging their dwelling Houses, Spring Houses and Barns, Burning their Fence rails, Cutting down their Timber, Robbing Orchards and Gardens, Stealing their Piggs, Poultry & Lambs, and sometimes killing them through wantonness or bravado, & when complaints were made, they, with the most unparalleled impudence, would threaten the lives of the Complainants or their Houses with fire, frequently damning the Congress, and Swearing they will never fight against King George, &c., &c.[4]

The 4th Georgia was moved shortly thereafter to Lancaster, where by the end of the month, not even the commander was safe. "A great stir this morning in Town Occasioned by some of Col. White of the Georgia Regiment Robing of him Last night," Christopher Marshall wrote. "They were pursued & taken; part of the cash was recoverd but his trunk with all his papers, more money, his Commission &c. not to be found." The perpetrators were sentenced to death but reprieved by Mrs. White's intercession; instead, they were given 300 lashes each.[5] Though this desperate bunch was an extreme case, discipline in the Continental Army continued to be a problem, especially when it came to camp sanitation and property damage. It also did not help win support for the American cause.

The strain of so much marching in the blaze of the dog days had also taken its toll on the men. "I arrived here in good health yesterday morning," Percy Frazer told Polly on August 13, "but never endur'd more with the heat."[6] The same day, Col. Walter Stewart of the Pennsylvania State Regiment wrote to his friend and former commander, Gen. Horatio Gates, who had left Philadelphia the previous week to take command of the Northern Army, "After you left us, we were Order'd to March to, & Cross the Delaware, and I believe should have Continued our Rout[e] to the Eastward, but luckily for us, an Express Overtook the General at this place, Informing him of the Fleets being again seen off Sinepuxent, forty Miles to the Southward of the Capes of Delaware; it then consisted of two hundred and fifty sail, but where they have since gone is yet a secret here." Of the army's constant shifting, he speculated, "We expect however to change our situation very shortly, as it appears against the decrees of Fate our staying more than three or Four days at one place." He then remarked to Gates, "For my part, I must say, I would not wish to move until we know with a certainty where the Enemy Intend operating, as we have Certainly for some time past been Marching and Counter Marching to very little purpose."

The political tension between the army and Congress continued to simmer beneath the surface. Walter Stewart had served as Gates's aide-de-camp for more than a year in the Northern Department. Gates was superseded by General Schuyler in early 1777, and Stewart was appalled by Congress's treatment of his former commander. Now Schuyler was in disgrace and Gates was back in charge. "You can't Imagine my Dear Sir, the Satisfaction it gives me your being sent back to your proper Command," Stewart told his friend. "It is so great a thing, to get the better so Nobly of that petty party, for I can call them by no other Name." Disgusted by the political manipulation that seemed to dominate every decision, the "Irish beauty" wrote venomously, "Some of the Caitiffs, as our friend Wayne calls them, I have since seen," alluding to political enemies in Congress. "They dislike the Subject, and do not by any means wish to enter upon it." Referring to Schuyler, the young colonel commented, "[I] hope your Eastern friends will support you in a very different manner from what they did your predecessor, but what is to be expected, when a General has not the Confidence of the people he has under his Command?"[7]

Shortly after Gates left for the Northern Department, Washington dispatched Morgan's Corps of Rangers and a few other units to reinforce the army facing Burgoyne's invasion. Reports of Indian massacres had reached Congress, along with the horrific news that Burgoyne was offering bounties for American scalps. In late July, Jane McCrea, the fiancée of a Loyalist, was killed by Indians serving with Burgoyne's forces. News of her brutal murder helped rouse the New England Militia, but regulars were needed too, and Morgan's riflemen fit the bill perfectly: disciplined frontiersmen to take on British regulars, Tories, and Indians in a wilderness setting.

Burgoyne was "the abandoned servant of an abandoned Master," Richard Henry Lee of Virginia wrote vehemently. "Men, women, children, whig, Tory, and Protectiontaker, all promiscuously feel the keen scalping knife and the murdering Tomahawk." The congressman commented with disgust, "This Burgoyne is the true Type of the Court he comes from; Howe & Carlton have *some* humanity." Regarding the change in command of the Northern Army, Lee added, with some satisfaction, "Gates is able, and he is beloved in the Eastern Countries [New England]. The Men will now turn out. Morgans Corps, with some other Troops are sent up to check and chastise the inhuman butchers of bloody Burgoyne."

Closer to Philadelphia, "I went the other day to see the Army, the main body of which is about 20 miles from this City," Lee continued. "I think the Army is a gallant one, well disciplined, clothed, armed (for they all have bayonets now) and sound in every respect—The Soldiers in good health and spirits, and every thing looks *tout en Militaire.*" While in "French mode," he remarked, "Among other curiosities there, I saw the young Marquis de la Fayette, a Nobleman of the first fortune and family in France, the favorite of the Court and Country." That Lafayette left behind his wife and fortune "in a polished Country" to come and "fight in American wilderness for American Liberty" impressed Lee greatly. "After this can there be a Tory in the World?" Lee exclaimed. "How this example ought to gall the worthless Nobility & Gentry of England, who meanly creap into the Tyrants service to destroy that liberty which a generous Frenchman quits every delight to defend thro every difficulty!"[8]

Rumor and speculation about the British fleet continued to circulate as the molten days oozed on, and patience wore thin. "Where can Howe be gone?" Congressman Benjamin Harrison of Virginia wrote to Washington on August 20. "We begin to be under great apprehensions for South Carolina." Compounding the worry was the situation in upstate New York: "Can not a blow be given Burgoyne in his absence? If something can not be done in that quarter soon, N. York will certainly be lost." The waiting was agonizing. "Where the Devil is Gates," Harrison fumed, "why dos he loiter so on the Road? The weather has been hot it is true, and so is the Service he is going to."[9]

"It is like a great hunting expedition in which hunters and farmers form a large circle and drive the wild animals from every side into a central net, whereupon the noble connoisseurs of the hunt can amuse themselves," Rev. Henry Muhlenberg commented in his diary on August 20, astutely describing the overall British strategy, with Washington caught in the circle. "The barbarous Indians towards the north are already breaking loose," the pastor wrote. "The Christian British general is giving the inhuman heathens ten dollars for each scalp of an American settler." Believing that it was all "the plan and providence of the supreme Ruler," Muhlenberg observed, "We have surely deserved punishment and are in dire need of chastisement, yet the Lord also remembers his mercy." Bitter as he sounded, the elderly German preacher was by no means in favor of the British. "It is the same, if not worse, on the other side, for they are not angels but thoroughgoing, coarse Pelagians," he remarked acidly. "They think they can do everything without God, with their own might and strength."[10]

On August 21, Washington's general officers gathered for a council of war in headquarters at Neshaminy Camp. They unanimously agreed that since there was no news of Howe after all this time, the army should march northward to stop Burgoyne, or possibly even attack New York City. The General Orders instructed the men to strike camp at 3:30 the next morning and be on the road by 5 A.M. "As we understand, General Howe and his Myrmidons are gone toward South Carolina," Col. Percy Frazer wrote to his wife on the twenty-first. "We are now under orders to march tomorrow Morning, I think towards New York."[11]

That was the day when news arrived in Philadelphia that the fleet was in the Chesapeake. "This Method of coasting along the shore, and standing off, and on, is very curious," John Adams remarked to Abigail. "First seen off Egg Harbour, then several Times off the Capes of Delaware, standing in and out, then off Sinepuxtent, then off the Eastern shore of Virginia to steal Tobacco, to N. Carolina to pilfer Pitch and Tar, or to South to plunder Rice and Indigo, who can tell? He will seduce a few Negroes from their Masters let him go where he will. But is this conquering America?"[12]

Late in the day, the news arrived at Neshaminy Camp from Congress that the fleet had been spotted a week earlier, standing in the Capes of the Chesapeake; Washington decided to wait for further reports. As the Continentals were preparing to strike camp at dawn on the twenty-second, confirmation was received from Philadelphia that the fleet had entered the Chesapeake—news that was seven days old.

As the fleet came closer, reports began to fly into the city from northern Maryland. At Rock Hall on the Eastern Shore near Chestertown, William Bordley wrote to Congressman Samuel Chase at 4 P.M. on the twenty-first, notifying him of the fleet's position.[13] Chase received the news at noon on the twenty-second and passed it on to John Hancock, who hurriedly wrote to Washington at 1:30 P.M. that the fleet had come some distance up the Chesapeake. At sunset, the commander in chief notified Gen. Francis Nash at Trenton, "I have this minute received advice by express, that General Howe's fleet is high up in the North East part of Chesapeak Bay." He wrote to General Putnam, up at Peekskill, "the Enemy's Fleet have at length fairly entered Chesapeak Bay; Swan point being at least 200 Miles up."[14] Washington ordered all available forces to pull together and head southward.

Congress passed a resolution that same day, stating "that it be earnestly recommended to the state of Maryland immediately to call out not less than two thousand select militia to repel the expected invasion by the enemy of the state of Pennsylvania, Delaware, and Maryland." It also resolved "that the State of Pennsylvania be requested to keep up 4000 of their militia to assist in repelling the threatened attack of the enemy by way of Chesapeake and Delaware bays" by having the militia report to Lancaster, Downingtown, and Chester, and "that they be subject to the orders of General Washington," placing them under Continental jurisdiction. Delaware was requested to provide 1,000 militia to rendezvous at Christiana Bridge, and Virginia was also asked for some of its militia to gather at Frederick, Maryland.[15]

"A soldiers situation is a very uncertain one," Percy Frazer told Polly on the night of the twenty-second. "Last evening We had orders to march this Morning which was countermanded before night," he wrote from Graeme Park. "This afternoon We have orders to march tomorrow morning for Albany."[16] By morning, the orders had changed yet again; Wayne's Pennsylvania Division was staying close to home.

On the twenty-third, the Continentals broke camp at Neshaminy and marched sixteen miles south to Germantown. Washington established headquarters at Stenton, the Logan family plantation. "Went to Stenton in the morning, & on the road heard the disagreeable news that Washington's army is to march that way," Sarah Logan Fisher groaned. The house had just been cleaned up after Morgan's Corps had occupied it two weeks before. Now, after making her way up toward Germantown on roads clogged with army wagons and dragoons, Sarah was surprised to discover on reaching Stenton that "General Washington's bodyguard had taken possession there." She was informed by an aide that "General Washington would lodge there that night, with many of his principal officers." The general arrived at noon, with twenty officers and a number of servants. About 3 P.M., dining on fresh mutton, "they behaved civil, were very quiet." Sarah noted that "Washington appeared extremely grave & thoughtful."[17]

George Washington had much to consider at that moment. Between the waiting and the decisions that had had to be made during the previous three weeks—where to march and when—only having to countermand the orders once issued, compounded with the unbearable heat, his every nerve was strained. Now Howe was coming from an unexpected route—overland from the southwest, which placed Lancaster, America's largest inland city, in jeopardy.

Sixty miles west of Philadelphia, surrounded by rich farmland and dozens of mills, ironworks, and rifle shops, Lancaster, with a population of 5,000, was a large supply depot and crucial staging area for troops and supplies passing between New York State, Virginia, and the western frontier at Fort Pitt. It also housed hundreds of British and Hessian prisoners of war. Ringing Lancaster were other Pennsylvania settlements—

York, Carlisle, Lebanon, Downingtown, and Reading—which also had strategic importance for similar reasons. Reading, thirty miles north of Lancaster and sixty miles northwest of Philadelphia, was the Continental Army's main supply depot in the Middle States, and both Lancaster and Reading contained army general hospitals.

None of these places had any defenses to speak of. Philadelphia, though protected by the Delaware River forts and the Pennsylvania Navy against a water assault from the south, had nothing to protect it from a land attack. The Schuylkill River and the Brandywine River and Creek were the only formidable natural barriers to the west, but they could be forded. Incredibly, not a fortification or earthwork of any kind had been built to defend the largest and most important North American city from an overland invasion in 1777.

The Continental Army prepared to march through Philadelphia early on August 24, a Sunday morning. This city, founded ninety-five years earlier as the main settlement of "Pensilvania," William Penn's "Holy Experiment," had grown more rapidly than Boston or New York, both of which were older and much closer to the sea. Toleration of all faiths by the pacifist Society of Friends, also known as Quakers, was the major reason for this growth, together with lucrative land deals, and immigrants from the British Isles and central Europe flooded into the province. Germans came in such numbers that they were able to establish Germantown, their own inland settlement, in 1683, only a year after Philadelphia's founding. "Germanopolis," as it was sometimes called in the early days, grew so quickly that it had its own newspaper, printed in German, by 1685—before Philadelphia. Printing, milling, and stocking weaving became mainstays of the town's economy.

Washington's army once again occupied Germantown, but for only one night. The troops were ordered to march five miles down the Germantown Road at dawn on August 24 and enter the city by way of Front Street, where most of the major shipping merchants had their businesses and warehouses. The troops were to continue south on Front and cross High Street, also called Market Street, the main business thoroughfare running east-west. One block below Market, they were to swing right and march up Chesnut Street five blocks to the State House (today known as Independence Hall), where Congress would review them.

Philadelphia was laid out in a simple grid plan. Its north-south streets, running parallel with the Delaware River, were mostly numbered; its east-west streets were mostly named after trees or plants, such as Vine, Walnut, and Chesnut, to name a few. The main streets were 50 feet wide, mostly paved with cobblestone and lined with sidewalks of brick or slate flagstones. High Street (now Market Street) was 100 feet wide, with market sheds running down the middle for three blocks from the old courthouse at Second Street.

The city was built in a plain but handsome style, with buildings no higher than four stories. The skyline was pierced by a handful of steeples and spires and a few scattered cupolas. By 1777, Philadelphia had more than 5,000 dwellings and 3,000 other buildings—warehouses, stores, tanneries, and hundreds of small workshops—mostly built of red brick and found within less than one square mile. The population numbered between 30,000 and 40,000. Before the war, the waterfront was busy with dozens of ships daily, bringing a vast array of goods from Europe, Asia, and the Caribbean—all filtered through British ports and customs houses. Now, with independence declared, foreign goods mostly came through the West Indies, and much of the trade involved booty captured by privateers—legalized piracy.

Philadelphia and Pennsylvania had become wealthy largely on exports of flour and lumber from the surrounding counties to the West Indies and Europe. Flour alone demanded thousands of barrels annually; their manufacture required sawmills and lumber to make barrel staves, forges to make iron straps for hoops, and hundreds of coopers to fabricate the finished products. Barrel staves were shipped by the tens of thousands to the West Indies to make hogsheads for sugar, molasses, and rum. The lumber and iron businesses were also capable of producing all sorts of war materials.

Though Quakers had founded the city, they were a minority by 1777, but their presence and influence in the wealthy merchant class remained very powerful. John Penn, the founder's grandson, was the proprietor until independence was declared, but he was not a Quaker; he was Anglican and a member of Christ Church, located on Second Street above Market, the city's largest and most fashionable house of worship, its tall, spectacular white spire dominating the city's skyline.

Penn and the Provincial Assembly were replaced in 1776 by the Supreme Executive Council, a twelve-member board headed by a president, Thomas Wharton. John Penn was being watched closely by Whig authorities and was soon to be arrested, along with numerous other Pennsylvania officials and leading merchants who refused to "take the test" and swear allegiance to the United States.

The politics in the streets of Philadelphia were contentious and sometimes violent. Being the largest port in British North America, it had a large, rough, working-class population of dockworkers and laborers, as well and hundreds of small, independent craftsmen such as leatherworkers and shoemakers, printers, carpenters, and smiths of all types. Transportation of goods into and out of the city required porters, carters, draymen, and teamsters—tough, able-bodied characters who slaked their thirst at some of the more than 150 licensed taverns in the city. Others patronized illegal "tippling houses" or taprooms in the back alleys and waterfront areas, where "persons of evil name and fame and dishonest conversation" were known to congregate, according to city court records.

There was a large Scots-Irish presence in the city, contentious Presbyterians driven from Northern Ireland by crippling taxes and militantly in favor of independence. The Anglicans, by contrast, were sharply divided into Loyalists and patriots. The Germans, called "Dutch" by their "English" neighbors, made up nearly half of the city's population. They generally stayed neutral for religious reasons or supported independence. Most of the Quakers also stayed neutral but remained passively loyal to the crown, thus earning them the label of Tories. The city's small Jewish population kept a low profile, as did the Irish and German Catholics, also small in number and conditionally tolerated.

To complicate matters, the new Pennsylvania constitution was so radical in form that it sharply divided the Whigs. "I need not point out to *you* the danger and folly of the Constitution," Dr. Benjamin Rush told Anthony Wayne in May 1777. "It has substituted a Mob Government for one of the happiest governments in the world." Rush went on to say, "A *single legislature* is big with tyranny. I had rather live under the government of one man than of 72. They will soon become like the 30 tyrants of Athens. Absolute authority should belong only to God." Further, religious factions were strongly at work. "A majority of the Presbyterians are in favor of the constitution, and in no part of the State do they discover more Zeal for it than in Chester County," Wayne's home territory west of the city. "Add your Weight to the Scale of opposition," Rush encouraged Wayne, "especially in your native County. The most respectable Whig characters in the State are with us." He concluded optimistically: "Let us unite our efforts once more and perhaps we may recover Pennsylvania from her delirium—At present, she has lifted a knife to her own throat. Your timely prescriptions may yet save her life."[18]

Philadelphia was also a major center for the production and distribution of war materials. Iron products of all types—cannonballs, grapeshot, entrenching tools, assorted hardware, and recently, heavy cannons—were sent into the city from the many forges and furnaces around the Pennsylvania and New Jersey countryside. Large quantities of French weapons and gunpowder were smuggled up from the Caribbean and found their way to the city warehouses. Supplies of rice and other foodstuffs for the army, liquors, tobacco, and the blue dye indigo came up the Chesapeake to Head of Elk, Maryland, and overland to the metropolis. Salt, a crucial component in food preservation, especially in the heat of summer, was in critically short supply. The several saltworks established along the Jersey shore were unable to fill the gap in time, and prices skyrocketed to upward of twenty times the prewar price.

The city's shipyards turned out small war vessels of many types for the Pennsylvania Navy and the Continental service, including the thirty-gun frigate *Delaware*, launched in the spring of 1777. The State House Yard (now Independence Square) had became an artillery park—a dusty, rutted mud hole. Near the waterfront, a foundry to produce brass cannon opened in March 1777. John Adams told his seven-year-old son, Charles, that after visiting the new frigate *Delaware*, he "then went to the Foundery of brass Cannon. It is in Front street in Southwark, nearly opposite to the Sweeds Church." Adams described the process to the boy: "Here is an Air furnace, in which they melt the Metal. There is a great deep Cavern dugg in the Ground in which they place the Mould into which they pour the melted Metal, and thus they cast the Gun in a perpendicular Position. Several brass six-pounders newly cast, were lying there, and several old ones, to be cast over." Nor was this the only casting operation, for "there is another Man, one King, who lives in Front street, at the Corner of Norris's Alley, who casts Patterara's [Pedrero, a type of mortar] and Howitzers."[19] Several of these guns were now with the Continental Artillery, about to be paraded through town.

Wartime conditions had spawned major economic changes, not the least of which was profiteering from the demand for war materials and the resulting shortages, both real and contrived. Precious metals—gold, silver, and copper—were in such short supply that Congress issued paper currency. Its value was measured in Spanish silver dollars, not British sterling, for the dollars were the most common coins in circulation. The cannon cast at the brass foundry used whatever copper and tin could be had to make gunmetal, a specific type of bronze. This was similar to bell metal, another bronze that contained more tin. "Will not the Churches furnish their bells to make 24 pounders for the *Randolph* & the *Delaware* when they are to be employed against an enemy who mean to exterpate religion and every thing else valuable here?" Richard Henry Lee asked Robert Morris. "Should the enemy get possession of Philadelphia, they will surely strip the churches of their bells, as a perquisite for their chief Engineer, whereas, if they are lent to us, we shall repay in kind. I hope you will not suffer the enemy to have the honor of getting Philadelphia."[20]

Lead was in very short supply. Before the war, most finished lead came from England in the form of bars or of sheets for roofing and fabrication into rain gutters, flashing, and downspouts. It was also used for clock weights and had been widely used for casement windows earlier in the century. The army desperately needed the metal for musket ammunition and buttons; proper regimental coats alone sported forty or so buttons made of pewter, which often contained a high proportion of lead. With an invasion under way and battle in the offing, the Supreme Executive Council announced in late August 1777, "The Congress by a Resolve of yesterday, having recommended to this Council that 'the leaden Spouts in Philadelphia be taken down for the use of the Laboratory,'" the place where ammunition was fabricated, "it appearing to this Council to be a Salutary & necessary measure; therefore *Resolved*, That Evan Evans, Robert Allison & James Worrell, be appointed to take down all such Spouts accordingly, & make a just valuation thereof."[21]

By early 1777, prices were skyrocketing as the value of paper Continental currency dropped. Officers on active service in the Continental Army found themselves in an economically ruinous situation. "The Expenses We are unavoidably put to, every Necessary bearing so exorbitant a price, makes our pay far short of what it ought to be," Col. Percy

Frazer told Polly in nearby Chester County that summer, "and I am determin'd not to hurt my Family by the Service, whilst Robbers, plunderers and Villains in Philada. and other places, are accumulating immense Fortunes in ease and safety."[22]

The spirit of independence was flagging badly in the city. Capt. Alexander Graydon, a Philadelphian who had been taken prisoner at Long Island the year before, had returned home on parole in July. "I soon discovered that a material change had taken place during my absence from Pennsylvania," he noted with much disgust, "and that the pulses of many that, at the time of my leaving it, had beaten high in the cause of Whiggism and liberty, were considerably lowered." Alarmed by the shift, he wrote that "power, to use a language which had already ceased to be orthodox, and could therefore only be whispered, had fallen into low hands. The better sort were disgusted and weary of the war," and Graydon astutely recognized the fact that "the instigators of revolutions are rarely those who are destined to conclude them, or profit by them."

When fighting erupted in 1775, many Pennsylvanians responded to the call for defense. As the war to assert American rights as Englishmen turned into a war for independence, a large number withdrew their support, seeing the change as treasonous. Some, such as the Allen brothers— William, Andrew, and John, sons of William Allen Sr., one of the most prosperous and influential merchants in the city—became active Tories. William had led a Pennsylvania battalion in 1775 and early 1776 alongside Anthony Wayne; Andrew had been a delegate to Congress. Now both were with the British forces. "The great cause of schism among the Whigs had been the declaration of independence," Graydon wrote. "Its adoption had, of course, rendered numbers malcontent; and thence, by a very natural transition, consigned them to the Tory ranks." He lamented the rise of the "violent men" to positions of authority. "As to the Whigs, the very cause for which they contended was essentially that of freedom; and yet all the freedom it granted was, at the peril of tar and feathers, to think and act like themselves."

The social effects of the Revolution were by no means universally applauded by the patriots of the "respectable" classes. "As Whiggism declined among the higher classes, it increased in the inferior; because they who composed them thereby obtained power and consequence," Graydon continued. He noted with dismay that "uniforms and epaulets, with militia titles and paper money, making numbers of persons gentle-men who had never been so before, kept up every where throughout the country the spirit of opposition; and, if these were not real patriotism, they were very good substitutes for it."

The regular Pennsylvania Line regiments were feeling it all too well; their ranks were barely one-third full. "Could there, in fact, be any com-parison between the condition of a daily drudge in agricultural and mechanical labour, and that of a spruce militia-man living without work, and, at the same time, having plenty of continental dollars in his pocket!" Graydon exclaimed. "How could he be otherwise than well affected to such a cause!"[23]

As the army prepared to march, Washington ordered the four divi-sions with him—Greene's; Stephen's; Lincoln's, now commanded by Wayne; and Stirling's—to space the regiments properly and have their field artillery placed with them. The main artillery, or artillery park, was to march in between. The light dragoons were also to spread out, with orders specifically directing a spacing of 100, 150, or 200 yards between the various units. "I am induced to do this," the commander in chief told John Hancock, "from the opinion of Several of my Officers and many Friends in Philadelphia, that it may have some influence on the minds of the disaffected there and those who are Dupes to their arti-fices and opinions."[24] Graydon commented, "As it had been given out, by the disaffected, that we were much weaker than, in truth, we were, the General thought it best to show both Whigs and Tories the real strength he possessed."[25]

With the spacing, the line of march stretched for almost ten miles. "I like this Movement of the General, through the City," John Adams com-mented. "[It] will make a good Impression upon the Minds of the tim-orous Whiggs for their Confirmation, upon the cunning Quakers for their Restraint and upon the rascally Tories for their Confusion."[26]

There was a feeling among some that an invasion might be the best thing to clear the air in the city and its surrounding counties. "I really think that Providence has ordered this Country to be the Theatre of this Summers Campaign, in Favour of Us, for many Reasons," John had told Abigail in early August. "1. It will make a final and entire Seperation of the Wheat from the Chaff, the Ore from the Dross, the Whiggs from the Tories. 2. It will give a little Breath to you in N. England." And most interesting, "3. If they should fail in their Attempt upon Philadelphia, it will give Lustre to our Arms and Disgrace to theirs," something that could only benefit the cause. But Adams saw something deeper, a double silver lining: "If they succeed, it will cutt off this corrupted City, from the Body of the Country, and it will take all their Force to maintain it."[27]

After a violent thunderstorm during the night and an early-morning shower, "which will spoil our Show, and wett the Army," John Adams feared, the parade began. "Four regiments of Light Horse," he wrote, "Four Grand Divisions of the Army—and the Artillery with the Mat-trosses. They Marched Twelve deep, and yet took up above two Hours in passing by." John went on to say, "Our soldiers have not yet, quite the Air of Soldiers. They dont hold up their Heads, quite erect, nor turn out their Toes, so exactly as they ought. They dont all of them cock their Hats—and such as do, dont all wear them the same Way."[28]

The fifers and drummers had been instructed to mass in the center of each brigade; about 400 field musicians belonged to this force of just over 8,000 men. They were ordered to play a quick step, "but with such moderation that the men may step to it with ease; and without *dancing* along, or totally disregarding the music, as too often has been the case."[29] Viewing the parade from the State House, on Chesnut between Fifth Street and Sixth Street, Congressman Henry Marchant wrote that they "were upwards of two Hours in passing with a lively smart Step."[30]

"I happened to be there at the time," Captain Graydon recalled, "and, from the coffeehouse corner," referring to Bradford's Old London Cof-fee House on the southwest corner of Front Street and Market Street, "saw our army, with the commander-in-chief at its head, pass down Front Street." Lining the streets were thousands of spectators from all walks of life—Quaker merchants; Irish craftsmen and laborers; African "pepper-pot" women, who sold soup on the street corners; English cab-inetmakers; German bakers; Welsh milkmaids. "The sight was highly interesting to persons of all descriptions," Graydon continued, "and, among the many who, perhaps, equally disclaimed the epithet of Whig or Tory, Mr. Chew, from an upper window in the house of Mr. Turner, appeared a very anxious spectator."[31]

Benjamin Chew had been the chief justice of Pennsylvania under the Proprietary Government. A native of Maryland, he had read law at the Middle Temple in London and was one of Philadelphia's most successful lawyers. His house on Third Street was one of the city's most elegant, and the Chews lived and entertained well. John Adams had attended a dinner there during the First Continental Congress and wrote a glowing description of the repast. With ten daughters and one son, the Chews were one of Philadelphia's leading families. Their stone country house, Cliveden, custom built ten years earlier at the upper end of Germantown, was one of the finest examples of mid-eighteenth-century architecture in America and boasted classical statuary on the grounds.

Like John Penn, Benjamin Chew had refused to take a stand on independence. The two men did not actively oppose the Whigs, but passively allowed events to take their course. Joseph Galloway, the former speaker of the Pennsylvania Assembly, had also tried to stay out of the fray the previous year by retiring to his country estate, Trevose, in Bucks County, but after receiving numerous threats and a box containing a noose and a bogus life-insurance policy, Galloway fled and joined the British forces. Chew and Penn continued to sit on the fence and were under surveillance as the theater of war approached the city. Soon they would be arrested without charge and detained at a remote location in New Jersey.

Many civilians had already left the city to get away from the epidemics of camp fever that had killed hundreds of soldiers in town the previous winter and threatened the inhabitants. One such refugee was Christopher Marshall, an elderly apothecary whose shop on Chesnut Street near Second had supplied medical kits to the Pennsylvania regiments. Marshall was on the Pennsylvania Board of War but moved to Lancaster in the spring of 1777 to get away from the disease and constant tension in Philadelphia. Lancaster, though also busy, was thought to be far enough inland so as not to be in any immediate danger.

Now, with word of the British fleet in the Chesapeake, Lancaster was in a panic. "The Waggons are all engaged here in order to Carry our Stores and Some to take the Baggage of the Prisoners from this place to Reading &c.," Marshall wrote to his children on August 25, "as we were alarmed by Express the 23d of Hows fleet having Come up Chesepack bay and intend to land about 35 miles from here & to pay us a Visit." He told them, "The English, Scotch & Irish prisoners being 2 or 300 were sent off yesterday afternoon under a Strong guard for Reading. the Hessing [Hessian] Prisoners are Mustering for the same purpose and its said will be sent off this day, so that our place is in a great fermentation." As a precaution, "messengers are sent down to the Susquehania or to the Bay to keep a good look out in Order to give us timely Notice. Some of the Troops that had post here going down and recalled, the Militia are training So that God only knows how our Scituation may be." He closed by telling them, "[I] shall be Exceeding glad when I shall have something more Agreeable to Communicate."[32]

Forty miles southeast of Lancaster, the same morning that Marshall wrote to his children, Capt. John Henry of His Majesty's Armed Ship *Vigilant* entered in the ship's log, "At 6 the Admiral came on board & hoisted his flag at the Foretopmast head."[33] With the *Vigilant* and *Roebuck* in the lead, followed by flat-bottomed troop transports, the British sailed out of the Chesapeake Bay into the Elk River, heading for the landing at Elk Ferry on Turkey Point. Phase three of the campaign for Philadelphia had begun.

The Hessian Jägers, the British light infantry, and the British grenadiers formed the vanguard, commanded by Lord Cornwallis. They were personally led by the Howe brothers. From the *Vigilant*, "at 10 the Admiral and General went on Shore with the Army," Captain Henry noted in the log.[34] Admiral Howe, his brother, and the headquarters staff "went aboard the battery ship [*Vigilant*], which was in the lead," von Münchhausen wrote, "where we landed at 10 o'clock in the morning without the slightest interference."[35]

The Crown Forces began landing at Elk Ferry on Turkey Point, a rugged, thinly inhabited peninsula on the west side of the mouth of the Elk River. "Our landing here considering all things will surely throw the Senators of Carpenters Hall into some consternation," James Parker wryly speculated about Congress's reaction to the news. "Their whole preparation was in the Delaware, where they surely must have done a great deal of injury to the fleet with fire rafts, floating batteries &c."[36]

Captain Ewald remembered that the Jägers landed "amid boisterous shouts of joy and in the best order." Von Münchhausen observed, "My General advanced with the jägers and light infantry for three miles, and then made a halt."[37] The Jägers immediately fanned out in the countryside to screen the landing and to scout. "The whole peninsula, or headland, was a real wilderness," Ewald declared. "Just as we found the uncultivated vine, the sassafras tree, and wild melon in this region, so also was it full of different kinds of vermin. The woods, especially, were filled with snakes and toads." Adding to the general discomfort, the crescendo of noise from crickets, cicadas, and katydids swelled to deafening as darkness fell, their choruses intensified by the August heat. "Each tree was full of big chafers," the Jäger captain grumbled, "which made such a noise during the night that two men could not speak to each other and understand what was said."[38]

"The Troops are healthy tho' they were on Board Nine & forty days, the Passage tedious," General Grant told General Harvey. "You may believe every Body on Board was most heartily tired of their Situation, we have hardly recovered the Use of our Legs & the Horses are not very firm upon theirs."[39] Though happy to get off the ship, Capt. Sir James Murray of the 57th was less than enthusiastic about the area. "Every place where one can walk fifty yards in a strait line, and without the necessity of waiting for a fair wind, must appear you would think an earthly paradise after a six week voyage," he wrote scathingly, "but so very detestable is this part of the country that I was robbed of half the satisfaction I otherwise would have had in feeling myself upon *terra firma*."[40] Lt. Heinrich von Feilitzsch of the Anspach Jägers echoed the sentiment. "Here I must say that this region of Maryland does not appeal to me," he remarked. "Compared with other provinces where we have been, this region is not well developed. A bare woods, here and there a small place with a house and a field, but where not a soul is to be seen. How desolate it is I will let another describe."[41]

Capt.-Lt. John Peebles of the 42nd felt otherwise. "We land'd about 9 o'clock a little above the ferry & march'd about 3 miles up the west side of the River. The inhabitants almost all gone off & carried everything with them they could, a pretty Country & plentifull Crops."[42] Even the disgruntled Capt. Richard Fitzpatrick of the Guards found something to admire: "we do not live luxuriously, though in a country that has every appearance of plenty, and is more beautiful than can be conceived, wherever the woods are at all cleared."[43]

Few civilians were to be seen. "The people (Irish presbiterians) are Chiefly [rebe]ls, who left their houses on the fleets Appearence," James Parker observed. "Surprised no [doub]t to see such ships as the *Roebuck*, *Apollo*, *Vigilant*, sloops of [war &] large transports up Elk River."[44] Major Baurmeister of the Hessian staff commented, "Most of the inhabitants had fled from their homes, taking with them the best of their belongings; but they had also destroyed a great deal and driven their cattle into the woods."[45]

"The country was desolate of inhabitants," Lt. William Hale told his parents, "the men called to strengthen Washington, the women fled to avoid barbarities, which they imagined must be the natural attendants of a British Army."[46] Ensign Rüffer of the Hessian Regiment von Mirbach similarly noted, "In this stretch of land we have not seen any females because they were told by the rebels that the Hessians would have mis-used them in an unpleasant manner, so they have all fled."[47]

After the vanguard landed and the area was secured, the rest of the army followed in four debarkations. Upon arriving at designated camp-grounds, the men immediately began to build shelters. "The troops hut-ted with Rails and Indian Corn Stocks, no Baggage or Camp Equipage admitted," Montrésor said.[48] The huts, commonly called "wigwams" or "wigwarms" by the British and "booths" by American forces, were lean-to shelters that were easily and quickly constructed out of tree branches, fence rails, saplings, cornstalks, straw, sod, and other such materials. They served well in lieu of tents to shelter the men from the blazing sun and light rain, but did little in the case of heavy downpours. "We passed three most uncomfortable nights in Wigwams," Lieutenant Hale complained, "drenched to the skin by those torrents of rain common in this South-ern climate."[49]

According to Montrésor, the wigwams were barely finished when "came on about 10 this night a heavy storm of Rain Lightning and Thunder."[50] Down the bay near Baltimore, "we had an awful storm this evening at nine o'clock," Rev. Francis Asbury wrote in his diary. "The thunder, lightning, and sweeping winds were all in commotion," the fiery Methodist preacher observed, adding with pious enthusiasm, "Such a scene as this was enough to strike the boldest sinner with terror, and make him even shudder."[51]

The haste of the camp construction and the severity of the weather over the next few days caused many difficulties for the army and delayed its march. Most critical was the shortage of horses, for those that had sur-vived the voyage were in sorry condition. "The Horses look miserably emaciated by this long Voyage," Ambrose Serle commented on the twenty-sixth, "many of them will be but of little use for some Time."[52] Montrésor stated the next morning, "The roads heavy and the horses mere Carrion, the soldiery not sufficiently refreshed, and great part of their ammunition damaged. . . . The Guards only had Sixteen thousand Cartridges damaged by the storm," about one-quarter of their issued ammunition.[53]

Many of the horses died shortly after landing. "During our passage twenty-seven men and one hundred and seventy horses died," Baurmeister reported, "and about one hundred and fifty were disembarked totally unfit for duty."[54] Von Münchhausen wrote in early September, several days after landing, "The 120 horses that the Knyphausen Corps had gathered on its march cannot compensate for the 400 horses that perished on our unfortunately long voyage, or after landing here. I was more lucky than most officers since I did not lose a single horse at sea, but two of mine have died since we landed."[55]

The camp was no sooner established than widespread plundering began and quickly reached crisis proportions. In addition to horses, the army badly needed fresh provisions and water, so thousands of soldiers went into the countryside on authorized foraging parties to round up food and livestock. But after having been pent up on ships since early July, all the while enduring scorching heat, high humidity, and terrifying storms, and living on miserable rations of salted meat and foul water for the last three weeks, the troops were ready for release, and many of them went on plundering rampages.

This time, however, General Howe immediately responded with severe penalties. "Two men were hanged, and 5 severely whipped, for plundering," Ambrose Serle noted on the twenty-fifth, adding, "If this had been done a Year ago, we should have found its Advantages."[56] Major Baurmeister wrote that same day, "In spite of the strictest orders, marauding could not at first be entirely prevented. Several men in the most advanced English troops were caught by General Howe. One of these marauders was hanged and six others were flogged within an inch of their lives."[57]

"There was a good deal of plunder committed by the Troops, notwithstanding the strictest prohibitions," General Grey's aide, Capt. John André, admitted on the twenty-sixth. "No method was as yet fixed upon for supplying the Troops with fresh provisions in a regular manner. The soldiers slaughtered a great deal of cattle clandestinely."[58] Lt. Loftus Cliffe told his brother, "Fortunately the Enemy had no Idea of our reaching up by Water so far and left this Country well Stocked for us; had we had the precaution of reserving our Salt we should have lived like Nabobs on this March; we have thrown away many a good piece of Beef for want of that."[59]

Headquarters appeared determined not to repeat the situation of North Jersey, where plundering had done so much damage to the king's cause. The General Orders on August 26 stated that "Commanding Officers are to have the Rolls of their respective Corps immediately called, to examine the Men's Knapsacks and Haversacks, and Report to head Quarters every Man in possession of Plunder of any kind."[60]

The following day, August 27, Howe published a declaration to all of the "peaceable Inhabitants" of Pennsylvania, Delaware, and the Eastern Shore counties of Maryland, "regretting the Calamities to which many of His Majesty's faithful Subjects are still exposed by the Continuance of the Rebellion." He offered a general pardon to anyone taking part in the rebellion, either with arms or politically, provided they surrendered before an unspecified date. He also told the general population that, "to remove any groundless Apprehension which may be raised by their suffering by Depredations of the army under His Command," he promised that "the most exemplary Punishment shall be inflicted" on any member of his army who plunders "or molest the Persons of any of His Majesty's well-disposed Subjects."[61] Printed copies were distributed as part of the campaign to gain public confidence in the king's men.

The Hessians, not being directly subject to British military discipline, continued with their own foraging parties. "In the afternoon the Jäger Corps conducted a patrol into the country toward the North East River," Ewald wrote on the twenty-sixth. "We found waist-high grass, oxen, sheep, turkeys, and all kinds of wild fowl. Since we did not find any of the enemy, we skirmished with these animals, of which so many were killed that the entire Corps was provided with fresh provisions." But not all of his men were able to partake of the bounty, for "the heat was so great that several jägers fell down dead."[62]

"The country is quite deserted. Cattle and other things have been met with and found very acceptable," Capt. Lt. Francis Downman of the Royal Artillery commented. With so many troops landed, "General Howe has given strict orders against any kind of marauding, but it is not in anyone's power to prevent this where there is so large an army and such a

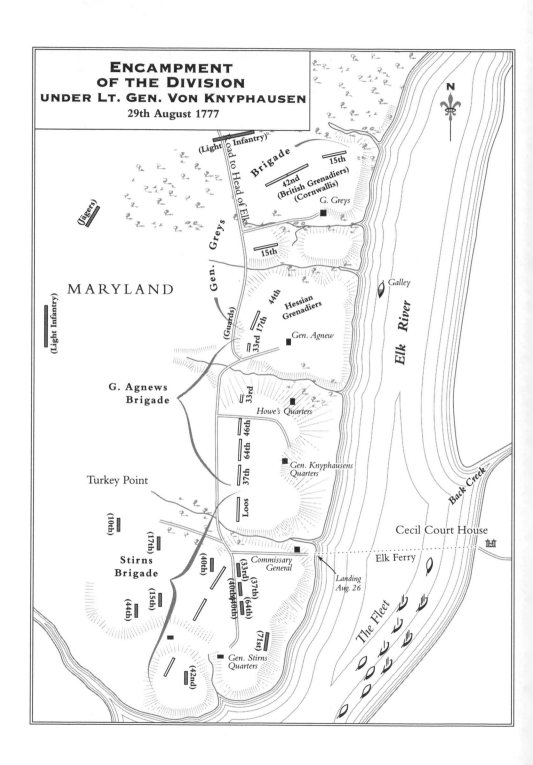

ENCAMPMENT OF THE DIVISION UNDER LT. GEN. VON KNYPHAUSEN
29th August 1777

N

(Light Infantry)

Road to Head of Elk

Brigade

42nd
(British Grenadiers)
(Cornwallis)

15th

G. Greys

15th

(Jägers)

Gen. Greys

(Guards)

MARYLAND

(Light Infantry)

44th

Hessian
Grenadiers

33rd 17th

Gen. Agnew

Galley

Elk River

G. Agnews
Brigade

33rd

Howe's Quarters

46th

64th

37th

Gen. Knyphausens
Quarters

Turkey Point

Loos

Back Creek

Cecil Court House

(10th)

(17th)

(40th)

(33rd)

Commissary
General

Elk Ferry

Landing
Aug. 26

Stirns
Brigade

(15th)

(44th)

(37th)

(40th)(40th)

(64th)

The Fleet

(71st)

Gen. Stirns
Quarters

(42nd)

mixture of troops." He commented, as did many other British officers, "The Hessians are famous and infamous for their plundering."[63]

But even the Hessian officers tried to reign in some of the worst offenders. Colonel von Donop and the commander of the Jäger Corps, Colonel von Wurmb, took drastic steps to restore order among the Germans. Howe applauded their efforts in the General Orders: "The Commander in Chief thinks himself much obliged to Col. Donop and Lieut-Col. Wurmb for their Zeal and Diligence in endeavouring to discover a disobedience of Orders in the Articles of plundering and Marauding."[64] Major Baurmeister explained that "Colonel von Donop and Lieutenant Colonel von Wurmb were praised in the orders of the 27th of August for maintaining the best discipline among their troops. General von Knyphausen made ten men of Stirn's brigade run the gauntlet for some excesses. The best order and discipline have now been almost entirely restored."[65]

On August 28, the Crown Forces divided, and Knyphausen took about a third of the army across the Elk River to Cecil Court House to forage the area for cattle and horses. The rest of the army, led by Ewald and a Jäger patrol, proceeded northeast to Head of Elk, a village where the Hollingsworth family dominated the local shipping enterprises between Philadelphia and the Chesapeake region.

Just outside the village, some local militia posted at a bridge opened fire on the British advance guard. Jesse Hollingsworth told Governor Johnson, "My Brother Henry had a small Skirmish at Gilpins Bridge," where he "was slightly wounded in the Cheek." Jesse also informed the governor, "We have several Deserters & near 100 Prisoners taken by our light Horse in Scouting Parties."[66]

"We found an enemy post stationed behind a creek about half an hour," or just over a mile, "this side of Elktown," Ewald wrote. The rebel militia "withdrew after an hour's skirmish."[67] Before falling back, "the rebels broke up the bridge at the End of the Town which we soon repaired," Montrésor, the chief engineer, reported. "In the mean time great part of the Army forded the Creek in about 3 feet water on a gravelly bottom."[68]

After crossing the creek, the Jägers fanned out to the right, south of the village, where Ewald spotted a number of ships' masts in the distance at Elk Landing, a small but very important port. Here was one of the key intermediary points of Chesapeake commerce, where goods traveling between Philadelphia and the Chesapeake region were transferred from land to water. "This is the great thorough Fare from the Southern Provinces tho' but a later Settlement," Grant wrote, describing Head of Elk and Elk Landing. "According to Custom most of the Inhabitants have left their Houses & drove away their Cattle. The Militia in Arms, to pop at Stragglers, & pick up Marauders in which they are too successful."[69]

Ewald noticed "some twenty ships lying at anchor," and he, "fired several shots at the people standing on the decks, who immediately made signs for peace with their hats and white handkerchiefs." The ships were filled with valuable cargoes, including "much indigo, tobacco, sugar, and wine." He reported the find to General Howe, "who accompanied the Jäger Corps." Unfortunately for the rifle captain, his "honesty was carried too far," for "the jäger detachment was replaced by Englishmen, and that was the end." The booty quickly disappeared; "they laughed at me," Ewald ruefully noted, "and I learned from my mistake."[70]

At the front of the army's line march was another special unit, the Corps of Guides and Pioneers, troops who moved ahead of the army to clear obstructions. Maj. Samuel Holland commanded this special corps, which consisted of 172 men equipped with axes, saws, and shovels, in addition to their muskets.[71] Heavy leather aprons and gloves were part of the unit's gear, along with peculiar leather caps. The Pioneers were also distinct in that the men were permitted to grow beards, and enlisted Africans made up a significant portion of the troops. Lt. Gilbert Purdy of this corps wrote, "The 28th Marched to the town of Elk which was About 6 Miles without the Loss of A man." He described it as "A Small Town Consisting [of] About 50 Houses. At the head of Elk [Landing] the Rebels Run off from this town in the Gratest Confusion Imaganable and Left A considerable [number] of Stores behind them of pork flour Tobaco & Molases About one Dozen of Sloops and Sconeers [schooners]."[72]

The line of march was more than ten miles long. "We continued our march [from 4 A.M.] till about 1 o'clock, when we came to the Head of Elk, about 12 miles," Captain Lieutenant Downman of the Artillery wrote, after the misery of "a most fatiguing march, the roads exceeding bad, horses very bad, and the sun intensely hot, with nothing to eat or drink but apples and water."[73] Curiously, Montrésor commented, "Large quantities of apples green and Indian Corn which are in moderation great refreshments to the Soldiery." The chief engineer, who was in charge of directing the train of artillery on the march, also noted that the weather was "extremely fine, which dried the roads, which would have been otherwise impassible, the medium 12 Pounders proved to be most difficult to pass through the Sloughs."[74]

"This is the county town," Downman noted, "and there are several very good brick houses, but the inhabitants are all fled except a Mr. Alexander at whose house our General resides." The Continental Army was very close, as he and many British officers quickly found out. "I was informed by a sick man who ventured to stay in his house, that General Washington dined here the day before yesterday, and had with him 500 light horse, and that this morning a party of rebels left the town just before we entered it."[75]

Washington was, in fact, still in the area. After his army marched through Philadelphia on the twenty-fourth, it camped at Darby, about ten miles below the city. At this camp, "the Commander in Chief possitively forbids the straggling of soldiers" from Stirling's and Wayne's Divisions—the New Jersey and Pennsylvania troops, here in their home area. He also ordered guards placed on the road back to the city "to prevent an inundation of bad women from Philadelphia."[76]

Sullivan's Division was not yet with the main army. On August 22, seeing an opportunity, Sullivan landed his Marylanders and several New Jersey regiments on Staten Island to attack the Loyalist regiments stationed there. Sir Henry Clinton, fearing that it was part of a major attack on New York while Howe's army and fleet were gone, wrote that Sullivan "effected an almost total surprise of two provincial battalions belonging to Skinner's Brigade, and after setting fire to the magazines at Decker's Ferry were on their march to Richmond."[77] Another force landed on the western part of the island near the Old Blazing Star Ferry and engaged three more Loyalist units. The British 52nd Regiment and some German Waldecker troops arrived and drove the Americans away, turning what at first appeared to be a successful surprise attack into a hurried withdrawal by Sullivan, who lost nearly 200 men captured. "In this Expedition we Landed on an Island possessed by the Enemy, put to Rout Six Regiments, Killed, wounded & made prisoners of at Least four or five hundred of the Enemy, vanquished every party that Collected against us," Sullivan told John Hancock. "In the whole Course of the

Day Lost not more than a hundred & fifty men, most of which were Lost by the imprudence of themselves & officers."[78] Small as it was, the Staten Island expedition was yet another military failure, coming on the heels of the loss of Fort Ticonderoga. Sullivan's name was linked with yet another disaster, and after receiving complaints from some of his subordinate officers, Congress demanded an inquiry into Sullivan's conduct.

The inquiry would have to wait. On August 25, the day that Howe's force landed, Washington arrived in Wilmington, Delaware, with Greene's and Stephen's divisions, nearly all Virginians. "Gen. Washington has none but Southern Troops with him," John Adams told Abigail on the twenty-sixth, including the Pennsylvanians and New Jersey forces. "The New England Troops and N. York Troops are every Man of them at Peeks Kill and with Gates. The Massachusetts Regiments are all with Gates." With the Northern Campaign in full cry, "if My Countrymen do not now turn out and do something, I shall be disappointed indeed," he wrote, referring to Burgoyne's invasion. "New Englandmen! Strike home."[79]

The American commander in chief was determined to make a stand with the force he had so painstakingly assembled over the spring and summer. On the twenty-sixth, "the General went with all the Horse save Sheldon's, to reconnoitre."[80] Accompanied by Greene and others, Washington was out to observe Howe's movements. Near Head of Elk, he was caught in a torrential thunderstorm. Lafayette, who was also there, wrote that "General Washington imprudently exposed himself to danger. After a long reconnaissance, he was overtaken by a storm, on a very dark night." The young French nobleman relayed the remarkable story that Washington's stubbornness put them all at risk. "He took shelter in a farmhouse, very close to the enemy, and, because of his unwillingness to change his mind, he remained there with General Greene and M. de Lafayette. But when he departed at dawn, he admitted that a single traitor could have betrayed him."[81]

Washington returned to Wilmington on the twenty-seventh, where the army prepared for Howe's advance on Philadelphia by digging entrenchments. He also sent part of his army to White Clay Creek, about four miles west of Wilmington, with advance posts farther west on Iron Hill. More Continentals continued to arrive in camp: Nash's 1,500 Carolinians, as well as Sullivan's 1,500 Maryland and Jersey troops after the "flash-in-the-pan" Staten Island expedition. Gen. William Smallwood, commander of the 1st Maryland Brigade, was sent into Maryland with Col. Mordecai Gist on a challenging assignment to arrange the Maryland Militia.

On the twenty-eighth, the day that the British Army moved into Head of Elk, Washington was again out reconnoitering. From Iron Hill, he watched the British troops march into town and take up positions on Gray's Hill, less than a mile away.

Howe, too, was out on reconnaissance. From Gray's Hill, "we observed some officers on a wooded hill opposite us, all of them either in blue and white or blue and red, though one was dressed unobtrusively in a plain gray coat," von Münchhausen noted. "These gentlemen observed us with their glasses as carefully as we observed them. Those of our officers who know Washington well, maintained that the man in the plain coat was Washington."[82]

As Washington and Howe eyed one other, Greene's Division moved from its position on Brandywine River behind Wilmington toward the British force. "We marched from our encampment at 4 A.M.," Lt. James McMichael of the Pennsylvania State Regiment wrote, "and proceeded thro' Wilmington, Newport and the Rising Sun," a crossroads hamlet one mile west of Newport, and "encamped in White Clay Creek Hundred, where we learned the enemy were near Newark and had driven in the Militia." The Pennsylvania officer noted, "Here we lay under arms, without tents or blankets, as the wagons were left in the rear. A detachment of 150 men were sent out from Gen. Weedon's brigade to observe the movements of the enemy. We expect a general attack to-morrow."[83]

No sooner did Greene's troops establish camp at White Clay Creek than the following order went out:

> Genl. Muhlenburgs and Genl Weedens Brigades each to furnish 100 men that are good marksmen to form a Light corps for the Division. As this is meant only for a temporary establishment & as the utility will depend on the goodness of the men and Officers for such a Service, the Genl desires the Commanding Officers of Regts to send none but such as may be depended on. Lt Col. Parker is to take the Command, Genl Muhlenburg will furnish a Major, two field Officers being necessary.[84]

In the absence of Morgan's Rangers Corps, Washington authorized the formation of a corps of light infantry that day, made up of 700 chosen marksmen, 100 each from the Continental brigades, and supplemented with more than 1,000 militia from Delaware and Pennsylvania. The army's senior brigadier general, William Maxwell of New Jersey, accepted command of this force, which took up positions on Iron Hill, blocking the road to Wilmington via Cooch's Mill and Christiana.

The following day, some twenty miles away in Chester, Pennsylvania, sixty-year-old Gen. John Armstrong, commander of the Pennsylvania Militia as well as a Continental brigadier general, wrote to President Thomas Wharton about his attempts to organize the state militia. "Gladly wou'd I have wrote sooner to council had not the only subject to be touched with propriety been that of a Chaos, a situation more easy to conceive than describe, however, I have got at least eighteen hundred men sent forward." Because of the army's needs, Armstrong, an old French and Indian War comrade of Washington's, offered to help with light troops. "In concert with Genl. Potter I have formed a Rifle Regt, and put a Coll. Dunlap at the head of it." He described Col. James Dunlap as "a prudent man, and not unacquainted with the business of a Partizan." In the same letter, he mentioned "a Rifle Battn of 300 privates" that would augment Maxwell's corps. "This Battalion marches to morrow morning from Hooke," referring to Marcus Hook, a small village on the Delaware River just below Chester.[85]

Pvt. James Patten, a twenty-six-year-old militia draftee, described the forming of Dunlap's "Partizan Regiment." Patten was called up in July 1777.

> [He] rendezvoused with the troops at Carlisle and was marched to Marcus Hook a little town below Philadelphia on the deleware River. At this point there was a call for men to volunteer from the ranks of the infantry as Rifle-men & he volunteered and Joined a rifle company commanded by Capt. Crawford. Dunlap was the Colonel of this Rifle Reigt. He was then Marched in this Rifle Reigt. to Wilmington in Delaware and was then stationed in the Brandywine Mills about one mile from Wilmington. Genl. Maxwell had the command of this corpse [Corps] of the militia. That while the troops to which he belonged were so quartered in the mills parties were continually kept out upon the Scout watching the movements of the British & prevented them as far as possible from foraging in the country. The troops to which this applicant belonged had frequent skirmishes with the British.[86]

The advance troops of the Continental Army positioned themselves around Iron Hill. "The hills from which they were viewing us seemed to be alive with troops," von Münchhausen commented. "My General deployed 3000 men and marched forward. As soon as they observed our advance, they retreated; we caught only two dragoons. These dragoons and some Negro slaves confirmed that it was Washington with his suite and a strong escort that was looking us over. Most of our troops halted on or around this height."

The ironies of war were not lost on the participants. "General Washington spent several days in the same house where we are now lodging," Howe's headquarters at Mr. Alexander's house, "and did not leave it until yesterday morning. So, he must have known, or at least suspected, that we intended to come here yesterday," von Münchhausen noted. Intelligence, too, was passed on: "From talk said to have been from the lips of Washington and some of his officers, we learn that Washington believes our objective to be Lancaster rather than Philadelphia."[87]

Howe took up positions around Head of Elk for a few days, with the grenadier and light infantry battalions posted on Gray's Hill, a mile east of the town. "We are now encamped, or more properly speaking enwigwamed, on the other side of the Town, though our tents are now come up which is all we are allowed to carry," Lieutenant Hale of the 2nd Grenadier Battalion wrote. The lack of proper camp equipment was irksome to Hale, who lamented, "For this past week we have lived like beasts, no plates, no dishes, no table cloth, biscuits supply the place of the first but for the others no substitute can be found; my clothes have not been off since we landed." But after spending the three previous nights in drenching, steamy rain, he realized that it could be worse: "Clean straw is as good a bed as I desire, and if it does not rain am happy." The food, though not the best, was tolerable. "I have had only two fresh meals since quitting the ship, but the Pork is so good as well for breakfast as dinner, that I feel no want of beef or mutton and was never in better health or spirits in my life. So much for household affairs." Despite the abysmal lack of amenities, Hale and other officers still had a few gentlemanly perks: "I write this under a tree, while my black is making a fire to boil my pork, and my white servant pitching my tent."[88]

Capt. William Dansey of the 33rd, part of the 1st Light Infantry Battalion camped "in a Wood near Head of Elk," told his mother, "We landed in this Country five Days ago with no other Conveniencies than what we cou'd carry on our Backs." He scribbled apologetically, "I hope you will excuse as also my present stile of Writing, as I am in an intire State of Ill conveniency, seated on the Ground at the Foot of a Tree, What a Savage Life ours is, I don't expect to have my Cloths off or see the inside of a House on this side Christmas but thank God I keep my Health well."[89]

Despite the optimistic reports on the twenty-seventh, the plundering continued unabated, even with dire threats and drastic punishments. Montrésor noted on the twenty-eighth, "Two houses got on Fire after quitting the Quarters but appeared to me to have been done on purpose. . . . Several of our men very irregular in pursuit of fresh provisions, so as to fall into the Enemy's hands. . . . 23 of our Troops, 3 of which Hessians missing, supposed to be taken by the Enemy plundering."[90]

On August 29, John Ballard, William Jackson, and Alexander Kerr, three grenadiers from Sir George Osborn's company of the Guards, were captured, "taken near Elk Head."[91] In the General Orders that morning, Howe authorized the provost martial "to execute upon the Spot all Soldiers and followers of the Army, Straggling beyond the outposts, or detected in Plundering or devastation of any kind." Later in the day, orders went out saying, "The Commanding Officers of Corps are immediately to send out Strong Patrols along their front and beyond their advance Sentries, to take up all Stragglers." The officers were told, "The present Irregularity of the Men makes it absolutely necessary for no Officer to leave Camp without permission of his Commanding Officer."[92]

"A want of firmness in not enforcing orders, and a total relaxation of discipline has been the cause of our beginning the Campaign by plundering and irregularity of every kind," Major Stuart told his father in disgust. "Most of the people either through disaffection or fear had left their houses, and those that remained had the melancholy prospect of seeing everything taken from them and the regret left of not having followed the stream." Worse yet was the breakdown in control and discipline, with ruinous consequences. "We have lost near 100 men," he noted, confirming Jesse Hollingsworth's statement to the governor, "not from the sword of the enemy (for enemy we have not seen), but who have been picked up by stragglers maurading, or desertion."[93]

The situation was out of hand and had to be stopped. "Went on Shore, and mortified with the accounts of Plunder, &c., committed on the poor Inhabitants by the Army and Navy," Ambrose Serle recorded with shame. Aghast at the chaos and lack of discipline, as well as the stragglers lost while plundering, the admiral's secretary wrote "[I] prevented several Depredations myself, being dressed somewhat like a Sea-officer, with a Cockade in my Hat & Hangar by my Side. Forty seven Grenadiers, and several other parties straggling for Plunder, were surprized by the Rebels." Like other British officers, he commented bitterly, "The Hessians are more infamous & cruel than any." Crossed out in this passage was "It is a misfortune, we ever had such a dirty, cowardly set of contemptible miscreants."[94]

There were British soldiers, too, whose actions horrified some of their officers. "A soldier of ours was yesterday taken by the enemy beyond our lines, who had chopped off an unfortunate woman's fingers in order to plunder her of her rings," Captain Fitzpatrick told his sister-in-law, the Countess of Ossory, on September 1. "I really think the return of this army to England is to be dreaded by the peaceable inhabitants, and will occasion a prodigious increase of business for Sir J. Fielding and Jack Ketch." (Fielding was a founder of the London police and Ketch a notorious executioner.) "I am sure the office of the latter can never find more deserving objects for its exercise."[95] It may have been small comfort for Fitzpatrick to learn that some Americans decided to save Jack Ketch the trouble, as Capt.-Lt. John Peebles of the Highlanders starkly recorded in his diary on August 31, "2 men of the 71st. [Fraser's Highlanders] found in the wood with their throats cut, & 2 Grenadiers hang'd by the Rebels with their plunder on their backs."[96]

"A Party of my Battalion took 3 prisoners This morning. We have them here," Col. John Thompson of the Maryland Militia reported. "Their Treatment to the Women here are brutal. Ravishment, plunder &ca. marcks Their steps," he told William Paca. He also apologized for his writing: "Excuse this scrall. I am in no situation to write."[97]

Overall disgust with the immediate situation and state of the war was evident in a letter written from "Head of Elke" by Capt. Sir James Murray of the 57th on September 1. "I cannot help beeng still of opinion that the Cause of Liberty is in a very delicate situation: and I sincerely wish that it was over," the Scottish light infantry officer told his sister

Betty. "It is a barbarous business and in a barbarous country. The novelty is worn off and I see no advantages to be reaped from it."[98]

The Continental forces were by no means free of abuses. "I have a complaint lodged against your Corps by a number of the reputable Inhabitants in the Neighbourhood of Elk," an outraged Washington wrote from Wilmington on September 2 to Col. Charles Armand Tuffin, a French nobleman who commanded a corps of dragoons made up mostly of European volunteers. "As I find that your men cannot be restrained from committing Violences while in the Country, I desire you will immediately march them to this Town," the commander in chief ordered. He wrote to General Maxwell the same day, "In consequence of the remonstrance from the inhabitants near Elk, I have commanded Armand's Corps to repair immediately to this place." Washington was determined to punish the offenders. "If any of the people who have been injured can point out the particular Persons, either Officers or Soldiers, they shall be made examples of."[99]

"Inhabitants drove in by the oppression of the rebels," Captain Montrésor noted in his diary on September 4.[100] The situation had become so bad that Washington launched a fierce tirade in the General Orders on that same day, lambasting both men and officers:

> Notwithstanding all the cautions, the earnest requests, and the positive orders of the Commander in Chief, to prevent *our own army* from plundering *our own friends* and *fellow citizens*, yet to his astonishment and grief, fresh complaints are made to him, that so wicked, infamous and cruel a practice is still continued, and that too in circumstances most distressing; where the wretched inhabitants, dreading the enemy's vengeance for their adherence to our cause, have left all, and fled to us for refuge! We complain of the cruelty and barbarity of our enemies; but does it equal ours? They sometimes spare the property of their *friends*: But some amongst us, beyond expression barbarous, rob even *them!* Why did we assemble in arms? Was it not, in one capital point, to protect the property of our countrymen? And shall we to our eternal reproach, be the first to pillage and destroy? Will no motives of humanity, of zeal, interest and honor, restrain the violence of the soldiers, or induce officers to keep so strict a watch over the ill-disposed, as effectually to prevent the execution of their evil designs, and the gratification of their savage inclinations? Or, if these powerful motives are too weak, will they pay no regard to their own safety? How many noble designs have miscarried, how many victories been lost,

how many armies ruined, by an indulgence of soldiers in plundering? If officers in the least connive at such practices, the licentiousness of some soldiers will soon be without bounds: In the most critical moments, instead of attending to their duty, they will be scattered abroad, indiscriminately plundering *friends* and *foes*; and if no worse consequence ensue, many of them must infallibly fall a prey to the enemy. For these reasons, the Commander in Chief requires, that these orders be distinctly read to all the troops; and that officers of every rank, take particular pains, to convince the men, of the baseness, and fatal tendency of the practices complained of; and that their own safety depends on a contrary conduct, and an exact observance of order and discipline; at the same time the Commander in Chief most solemnly assures all, that he will have no mercy on offenders against these orders; their lives shall pay the forfeit of their crimes. Pity, under such circumstances, would be the height of cruelty.[101]

"We are doubtless a wicked generation, and our army too much abounds in profaneness and debauchery," Col. Timothy Pickering had confessed to his wife on August 29, a blunt edge of Puritanical disgust plainly evident in this man from Salem, Massachusetts. "Nevertheless, our enemies do not fall behind us in vice, but rather, I believe, exceed us, and have besides none but the worst motives—the motives of tyrants— to steel their hearts against us." With fervent idealism and patriotic zeal, he told Rebecca, "Whereas we have a just cause, on which the happiness, not of innocent Americans only, but of the thousands of poor, oppressed people in every kingdom in Europe, depends, to point our weapons and brace our arms, to urge them against the mercenary foe." He hoped to return to her "if not 'crowned with the laurels of victory,' as you express it, at least without disgrace."[102]

Inconclusive skirmishing continued for a few days at the end of August and the beginning of September in the vicinity of Gray's Hill and Iron Hill. At White Clay Creek, "Genl. Washington has pushed down a light corps, consisting of about three thousand men mostly with rifles, together with the Malitia and Light Horse, to a post about a mile from them, called Iron Hill," Col. Walter Stewart of the Pennsylvania State Regiment wrote to Gen. Horatio Gates on September 2. "Here the country is, one would imagine, formed by Nature for defence, having a great quantity of woods, large morasses they must pass through, and many commanding hills, which the Malitia may take post upon."[103]

While the armies poked and prodded each other and the new Continental Corps of Light Infantry attempted to coalesce, Anthony Wayne and most of the Pennsylvania Line were left to the rear, along with some militia, to dig entrenchments around Wilmington. "Our company were then ordered to work on a hill in the rear of the town in the construction of a fascine battery," Pvt. William Hutchinson of the 2nd Battalion of Chester County Militia recalled. Lafayette, without a command of his own and attached to Washington's staff, moved among the troops, "and by him we had the honor of being reviewed on Quaker Hill at Wilmington, Delaware, while we were at work erecting the battery," Hutchinson noted with awe, "and were there addressed by him. He was with us both on horseback and on foot."[104]

Wayne was not awed; not only was it less than glorious work, but it also was contrary to his aggressive nature. The Pennsylvanian was furious; some of the disorganized, raw recruits of the Pennsylvania Militia, like Dunlap's "Partizans," were seeing more action than he and his regulars. With Morgan's riflemen gone, Wayne seemed to be the likely candidate to lead a new light corps, since the two of them had done so well at Brunswick Bridge back in June. He had recently suggested as much to Washington. But General Lincoln was also gone, and his division, composed of Wayne's 1st Pennsylvania Brigade and the 2nd Pennsylvania Brigade, whose brigadier general, John Philip DeHaas, never took command because of poor health, was now commanded by Wayne only; the division had no other generals. "I am peremptorily forbid by His Excellency to leave the Army," was Wayne's excuse to his wife, Polly, for not visiting home when the army arrived in Chester County in late August. "My case is hard—I am obliged to do the duty of three General Officers."[105]

Now, with the Corps of Light Infantry placed under Maxwell's command because of seniority and a battle in the offing, Wayne found himself posted in the rear at Wilmington, four miles behind the front lines, with orders to dig. The hotheaded Pennsylvanian was beside himself. "We are throwing up a few works at Wilmington, where Wayne is like a mad bear, it falling to his brigade," Colonel Stewart told General Gates. Knowing Wayne's temperament, Stewart could not help but add, "I believe he heartily wishes all engineers at the devil."[106]

Attempting to channel his fury and frustration, Wayne wrote Washington an astonishing letter that day in which he reminded His Excellency that it had been Wayne's suggestion to create a special corps "to make a Regular and Vigorous Assault on their Right or Left flank." He had the temerity to tell the commander in chief, "This, Sir, I am well Convinced would Surprise them much—from a persuasion that you dare not leave your Works." Salving the blow by carefully choosing his words, Wayne told Washington that "the Enemy would have no Other Alternative than to Retreat—for they dare not hazard any new manoeuvre in the face of your Army which would be cool & ready to take every Advantage of either their Confusion, Disorder or Retreat."

"This Sir is no new Idea," Wayne lectured the American Fabius, citing Caesar at Amiens under siege by the Gauls and quoting Marshal Saxe. He went on to say that the militia "will at all events be sufficient to guard against any bad Consequences in case of a *Military Check* by throwing themselves into the works and Strong Ground in your Rear," a backhanded reminder to Washington of Wayne's present position. He concluded the military history tongue-lashing by bluntly stating, "Should I be happy enough to meet your Excellency in Opinion—I wish to be of the number Assigned for this business," and ended his letter with a classic finish: "I know you have goodness enough to excuse a freedom—which proceeds from a Desire to render every service in the power of your Excellency's Most Obedient and very Humble Servant, Ant'y Wayne."[107]

Maxwell remained in command of the Corps of Light Infantry; Wayne remained at Wilmington.

Howe's army stayed at Head of Elk until the following day, September 3, when before daylight it began moving around Iron Hill to the right, swinging south and east toward Aikin's Tavern in Pencader. The king's troops crossed the Mason-Dixon line into the state of Delaware, formerly the three lower counties of Pennsylvania, as Capt. Lt. Francis Downman referred to it when he reported, "We entered Pennsylvania this day, having passed a large stone that is the boundary mark."[108] This was one of the crown stones, carved with the arms of Maryland and Pennsylvania, that had been set by the English surveyors Charles Mason and Jeremiah Dixon ten years earlier. By this move, Howe avoided a direct march on the American position at Iron Hill and outflanked Maxwell on the left. It also allowed von Knyphausen's column, which had been sent to the east side of the Elk River near Cecil Court House on foraging duty, to rejoin the main army with horses, cattle, and other livestock.

"This spot is the Welsh tract we called Penn-Cadder," Montrésor commented, noting one of the first Welsh settlements in America.[109] From Aikin's Tavern, which became Howe's headquarters, Sir William Erskine, the British quartermaster general, ordered Captain Ewald and six mounted Jägers to "march at once to the left, where I should follow for five to six hundred paces a road which led to Iron Hill and Christiana Bridge." As the sky lightened, the intrepid captain and the six horsemen started up the road, followed by the foot Jägers, who swung northward from the tavern and began marching toward Iron Hill and Newark.

A sudden sheet of gunfire at point-blank range from behind a hedge annihilated the mounted Hessians; all six were either killed or wounded instantly. Ewald's horse, "which normally was well used to fire, reared so high several times" that he expected to be thrown. It was no wonder; his horse was grievously wounded in the belly. "*Vorwärts, Jäger zu fuss!*" Ewald shouted. "Foot Jägers forward!"

Skirmishing erupted immediately, and the 400 Jägers fought a running battle between Pencader and Cooch's Mill near a bridge over the Christina Creek. Maxwell's Light Corps set up a series of small ambushes along the road and grudgingly fell back toward Iron Hill. "By this time it was broad daylight and we saw the mountain," Ewald wrote of Iron Hill, which rises abruptly more than 200 feet above the sandy coastal plain. The startling, blood red soil on the hill reveals the origin of its name. It was "overgrown with woods, rising up like an amphitheater and occupied by enemy troops."

General Howe himself rode up to the action and ordered Lieutenant Colonel von Wurmb to drive Maxwell off the hill. "The charge was sounded, and the enemy was attacked so severely that we became masters of the mountain after a seven-hour engagement."[110]

The battle was a classic Ranger-type affair, with troops on both sides taking cover and moving through the woods in skirmish order. "We Jägers approach the enemy just like on the hunt," Lt. Friedrich von Wangenheim had told his brother a few weeks earlier. "We crawl through the bushes on our bellies; upon sighting one, we stalk and shoot."[111] There was also fighting on open ground, where the light troops could mass into formation and charge with bayonets or hunting swords.

"Then we saw the enemy, consisting of about one thousand men, as they marched into a thin woods," the Jäger Corps journal recorded. "The

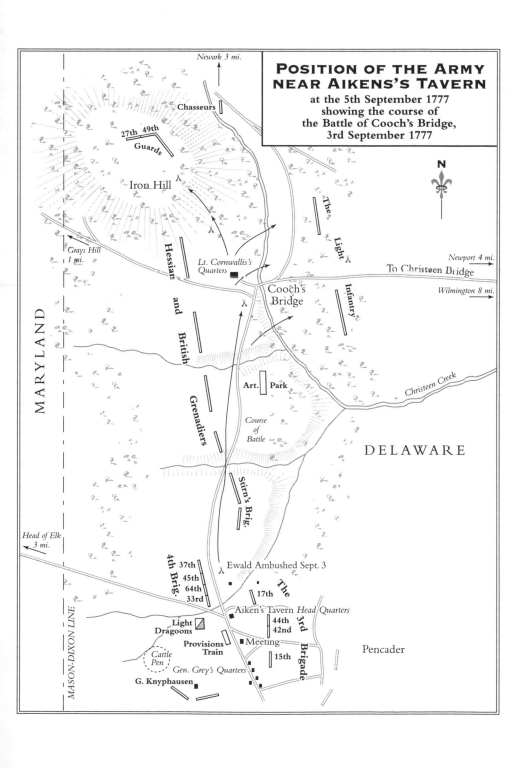

POSITION OF THE ARMY NEAR AIKENS'S TAVERN at the 5th September 1777 showing the course of the Battle of Cooch's Bridge, 3rd September 1777

Newark 3 mi.

Chasseurs

27th 49th

Guards

Iron Hill

Grays Hill 1 mi.

Hessian

and

British

Grenadiers

Lt. Cornwallis's Quarters

The

Light

Infantry

Cooch's Bridge

To Christeen Bridge

Newport 4 mi.

Wilmington 8 mi.

N

MARYLAND

Art. Park

Course of Battle

Christeen Creek

DELAWARE

Stirn's Brig.

Head of Elk 3 mi.

4th Brig.

37th
45th
64th
33rd

Ewald Ambushed Sept. 3

17th

The

3rd Brigade

Aiken's Tavern Head Quarters

44th
42nd

Light Dragoons

Provisions Train

Meeting

15th

Pencader

Cattle Pen

Gen. Grey's Quarters

G. Knyphausen

MASON-DIXON LINE

Jäger Corps deployed from the middle, to right and left, and formed so that the Anspachers were in the middle, the point which the enemy attacked." This was no easy fight; Maxwell's men made a spirited attack, and the report went on to say, "They were driven back into another woods with considerable effort. Here they defended themselves obstinately, which brought our right wing, under Captain Wreden, with the hangar [hunting sword] to the attack." Some of the Continentals fell back to the far side of Cooch's Bridge, while others remained on Iron Hill. "Now, and only after the enemy retreated," claimed the Jäger account, "a battalion of light infantry joined us for the first time, which General Howe had detached from the right to support us."[112]

The 1st Light Infantry Battalion attempted to come around on the left but was detained by swampy ground. The 2nd Light Infantry came up on the right of the Jägers, with the British grenadiers following behind. "The Yaugers received a heavy fire from them, & made some difficulty in passing the Bridge, but the 2d Batt Light Infantry coming up dash'd over and drove the Rebels, with the loss of 1 kill'd & 10 wounded," Captain-Lieutenant Peebles of the grenadiers noted. "The Yaugers suffer'd about the same. The skirmishing continued in different parts of the wood first & last about an hour. The Rebels must have lost a good many, as five officers were found dead in the field."[113]

"The Hessian foot Jägers under Lieutenant Colonel von Wurmb . . . encountered the enemy outposts at Cooch's Bridge and attacked them," Major Baurmeister reported. "Captain von Wreden gained a patch of woods on the enemy's left flank, from which he made a spirited attack." The Jägers were equipped with a form of light artillery called "amusettes," large, heavy muskets capable of firing a 1-inch ball several hundred yards. "When his jägers cannonaded their front with some amusettes and charged with bayonets [actually, hunting swords], the enemy withdrew in the direction of Christiana Bridge, leaving behind thirty killed—among them five officers—but taking their wounded with them."[114]

"Fell In With the Rebels at Seven [or] Eight in the Morning," Lt. Gilbert Purdy of Major Holland's Guides and Pioneers wrote, "but They had not forgt their old Costoms: Stood A few Shot and Made the best of their way off. We Pursued them about and Killed 24 which we found the same Day and Some wonded." Among the many difficult and dirty tasks of the Pioneers was the burial of the dead. "But the Loss of Rebels

Could not Be none [known] for they Carried them off," Purdy continued. "The Lose of our Army Was 2 men Killed and the number Wonded
unnone [unknown.] We inCamped that Day at Couches Bridg."[115]

"The rebels left about 20 dead among which was a Captain of Lord
Stirling's Reg't," Montrésor noted. "The Rebel Deserters since Come in,
say they lost 5 Captains." The next morning, the chief engineer added,
"Pioneers employed in burying the Rebels, more being found in the
woods. Two of them Captains Dallas and Cumming lay just beyond the
Bridge at Cooch's Mill."[116]

Capt. Archibald Dallas of New Jersey was from Spencer's Additional
Continental Regiment, a unit attached to the Jersey Line and often
referred to as the 5th New Jersey. His regimental commander, Col. Oliver
Spencer, said he "served as a good and brave officer untill he fell which
was in a skirmish with the enemy near Christian bridge in Delaware State
in Sept. 1777." Dallas's wife, Rachel, whom he had married five years earlier, was nine months pregnant and delivered a son, Archibald Dallas Jr.,
three weeks after her husband's death.[117]

"In the morning of the 3rd Cornwallis & Knyphausen having formed
a junction near Pencader or Atkin's tavern attacked Maxwell, who after a
short resistance retired over White Clay Creek towards the main army
with the loss of about forty killed," Trooper John Donnaldson of the 1st
Troop of Philadelphia Light Horse recalled. "Two of our Troopers fell
in with a party of militia near Cooches mill from whence they had been
driven by the enemy, & brought the intelligence to camp. The whole of
the American army except the light infantry which remained on the lines,
now took a position behind Red Clay Creek, having its left at Newport
on the Christiana & on the road leading directly from the British camp
to Phila."[118]

Howe was delighted. "Ye light Infantry & Yagers gave ye Rebel
Corps at this place & Iron hill a complete trimming—they went on in
ye most covered country you ever saw with more (I think) than their
usual spirit," he wrote to Grant in his barely legible scrawl. "Their per-
fidity was so great that ye Granadiers who were as willing to have had
their share in ye business as could be wisht, could hardly keep up to
support them in a run, their Guns galloping to get a shot." His praise
for the light troops—his favorite troops—was enthusiastic. "Worm
[von Wurmb] behaved amazingly, as did our 2nd L. Infantry; ye first

[1st Light Infantry] to their great disappointment being shut off by an abominable Creek, that had it been fordable, Abercrombie would have cut off ye whole Party consisting of about 200 Men." In the postscript, he emphasized, "Ewald, Freden [Wreden] & indeed all ye Officers of ye Yagers behaved charmingly."[119]

Based on reports filtering back to headquarters, Washington tried to put as good a face on the loss as possible. "This morning the Enemy came out with considerable force and three pieces of Artillery, against our Light advanced Corps," he told Congress, "and after some pretty smart skirmishing obliged them to retreat, being far inferior to them in number and without Cannon." As far as casualties were concerned, "ours, though not exactly known is not very considerable," he prevaricated. "Theirs, we have reason to believe, was much greater, as some of our parties composed of expert Marksmen, had opportunities of giving them several close, well-directed Fires, more particularly in once instance, when a body of Riflemen formed a kind of Ambuscade," most likely a reference to the opening volley where Ewald was ambushed.[120]

Exactly what went wrong is difficult to say, but it likely was due to the new corps, a lack of coordination, a lack of experience, and a commander who was coming under increasing criticism. "After advancing as far as Wilmington," Lafayette commented, "the general detached a thousand men under Maxwell, the senior but also the most inept brigadier general in the army. At the first advance of the English, he was beaten by their advance guard near Christiana Bridge."[121] Congressman Henry Laurens, soon to become the president of Congress, wrote on September 5 that he had spoken with Lt. Col. Louis Casimir, Baron de Holtzendorff, a Franco-German soldier of fortune who had served on the staff of Frederick the Great and was author of the book *Elements of Tactics.* "Baron Holzendorff this minute from Camp tells me one of our Generals misbehaved," he said, referring to Maxwell. "The Baron whispers—'Your Soldiers my Dear Colonel are very good Mans, so good as any brave Mans in the World, but your Officers my Dear Colonel your Officers'— & then bursts his soft Laugh. I understand him and & believe he is pretty just in his meaning."[122] Another critic of Maxwell was Lt. Col. T. Will Heth of the 3rd Virginia, who was one of the light infantry officers and a good friend of Daniel Morgan. "You have been greatly wishd for since the Enemies Landing at the head of Elk," Heth told Morgan. "Maxwell's

Corps 'Twas expected would do great things—we had opportunities—
and any body but an old-woman, would have availd themselves of
them."[123] Despite the criticisms and the defeat, Maxwell retained command, and the Light Corps was to continue in its duties of scouting
and screening.

Howe established camp on the battlefield. "Part of the army with the
first Battalion of Guards marched at 4 in the Morning to Iron Hill & fell
in with a party of the Rebels commanded by Col. Maxwell," Lord Cantelupe wrote in his diary. "They killed & wounded about an hundred chosen Rebels. In the Evening [we] Encamped on Iron hill."[124] The Guards
did not actually engage in this fight, as Sir George Osborn indicated to his
brother: "I have nothing material to say of my own particular situation to
interest you more than that the Brigade of Guards have always been with
the advanced part of the army. At Cristina Creek we came up just upon
the Corps under the rebel General Maxwell giving way."[125]

The British placed their left flank on Iron Hill, with their right
beyond Howe's headquarters at Aikin's Tavern. From this position, they
were within sight of both the Delaware and the Chesapeake. Captain-
Lieutenant Peebles was camped with the British Grenadiers on the low
ground west of Cooch's Bridge. "About 1/2 a mile in our Rear the
Guards are Encamp'd on a high ground call'd Iron Hill from which there
is a very extensive prospect of the Country all round," the Highland officer wrote. "You see the Delaware below New Castle about 7 miles distant, about East, a long view of the Eastern Shore & Lower Counties,
flat & woody. The Ground about Head of Elk & Chesapeake, & on the
Wilmington road, you see the Village of Newark & the Ground about
Christeen &ca."[126]

For the next five days, Howe camped at Cooch's Bridge and Iron Hill,
while Washington's army pulled back from White Clay Creek and began
to build entrenchments along Red Clay Creek near Newport, a small village on the road to Wilmington. "Now then is the time for our most
strenuous exertions," Washington harangued the army in the General
Orders on September 5. "One bold stroke will free the land from rapine, devastations and burnings, and female innocence from brutal lust
and violence." He reminded the men, "Two years we have maintained the
war and struggled with difficulties innumerable. But the prospect has
brightened, and our affairs put on a better face." Calling them to duty, he

told the troops, "If we behave like men, this third Campaign will be our last. Ours is the main army; to us our Country looks for protection. . . . Animated by motives like these, soldiers fighting in the cause of innocence, humanity and justice, will never give way, but, with undaunted resolution, press on to conquest."[127]

Despite Washington's tirade in the General Orders about damaging the local area, problems persisted. "Notwithstanding the repeated orders against plundering & burning fences, that abominable practice is still continued to the Shame & disgrace of the brigade," Weedon's Brigade Orders stated on September 6. "Complaints are made that Corn fields are pillaged without restraint, the fence rails burn'd up & many other outrages committed by the soldiery, to prevent which in future, the Officers are once more requested to attend particularly to the behaviour of their men & to punish Such as they see with green corn unless they can make it appear they bought it & any fence rails they may see burning, the Mess to which the fire belongs is to be made answerable." Further, camp sanitation was still a disgrace and a danger, not to mention obnoxious. "The QM [Quartermaster] Serjeants will immediately parade the C C [Camp Colors] Men of their Regts. & cover up all filth & nastiness in their respective fronts, and any Soldier daring to ease himself in any other place but the proper necessaries provided for that purpose shall receive Ten lashes on his bare back for every Offence."[128]

On September 6, "the whole Army moved nigher to the Enemy, head Quarters was moved from Willmington to new Port," Joseph Clark of Stephen's Division wrote. That night, "all the heavy Baggage was sent off to Brandewine expecting next morning to make the attack, but the Enemy did not come on, so nothing was done this day but fortifying. Parapet walls were thrown up to a great extent, trees fell to secure the flanks & important passes."[129]

The Continentals prepared for a major showdown. "As the Approach of the Enemy gave reason to apprehend an Attack, the whole of the troops were ordered to throw up Breast Works in front of their respective Camps," Lt. William Beatty of the 7th Maryland noted in his diary. "We began this work to day and Compleated it on Monday the 8th about 10 o'Clock."[130] Trees were felled and their branches sharpened into *abatis*, tangled obstructions, to block roads. From Wilmington, Private Hutchinson remembered that his fellow militiamen "were then ordered to the banks of Red Clay Creek and were employed in cutting timber to create all possible obstructions in the public roads and highways for the purpose of preventing the passage of the enemy in their march to Philadelphia."[131] Gun emplacements were constructed; according to Ewald, General Sullivan "had stationed himself behind the Christiana Bridge. He had interspersed the marshy bank with thirty cannon, making a good defile there."[132] Washington again harangued the men, calling them to duty. Spirits in the American forces were high as the troops braced for a British attack.

Grant reported to General Harvey in London:

> The Rebells Army was posted at New Port with Christine Creek up their Left, the Heights of Wilmington & Brandy Wine River upon their Right, the Delaware in their Rear, Redoubts & Abbaties in their Front. Washington expecting that the attack would be made as He wished upon the New Port side, was determined to Risk an Action to save Philadelphia which was avowedly & in all their publick orders the object of all their Efforts. The Rebell Genl. & his Council agreed in opinion that a more advantegious Position could not be found, to prevent our penetrating into their darling Province.[133]

But no attack came. In the predawn hours of September 8, the Crown Forces struck camp and marched northward to Newark as a strange glow filled the northern sky. "The whole moved 2 hours before daylight—a remarkable borealis," Captain Montrésor noted. Leaving the flat, sandy coastal plains of the Delmarva Peninsula, Howe's army crossed the fall line marked by Iron Hill and entered the hilly region beyond. "An amazing strong ground—marched this day about 12 miles to Head Quarters—a very strong country," the chief engineer commented. "At 1/4 past 7 this morning marching through Newark the weather was very cold indeed. Encamped this day at 1 o'clock . . . [on] the road from Newport to Lancaster in the way to New Garden."[134] Ens. Carl Rüffer of the Regiment von Mirbach described Newark as "a very pleasantly built city of about sixty houses, but completely uninhabited. Also, now and again, very pleasing country homes which previous to this time we had seldom encountered in this area because it is rather thinly settled."[135] James Parker observed, "The country is entirely deserted. We pass the Village of Newark, remarkable for Sedition & Presbeterian sermons, the inhabitants had all left their houses."[136]

In the American encampment, drums sounded "The General," the signal to strike camp. Lt. James McMichael of the Pennsylvania State Regiment wrote in his journal:

> September 8: At 3 A.M. the General was beat and all tents struck. All the regiments were paraded, the men properly formed with an officer at the head of every platoon, and after wheeling to the right, we remained under arms until 9 o'clock. Then the alarm guns were fired and the whole army drawn up in line of battle, on the east side of Red Clay Creek, with Gen. Greene's division to the right. Here we remained for some time, when Gen. Weedon's brigade (of which my regiment was a part), was detached to the front to bring on the attack. We crossed the creek and marched about a league [3 miles] to an eminence near Mr. McCannon's meeting house, and there awaited the approach of the enemy, who were within half a mile of us. They however encamped, which occasioned us to remain under arms all night, the sentries keeping up a constant fire.[137]

Beyond Newark, the British Army "crossed the White Clay Creek, which was surrounded on both sides by steep, rocky heights that formed a most frightful defile half an hour in length," Ewald wrote with apprehension. "I still cannot understand why Sullivan abandoned this position, where a hundred riflemen could have held up the army a whole day and killed many men." The Jägers had to go forward, fully expecting to be ambushed. "My hair stood on end as we crammed into the defile," the Jäger captain admitted, "for the precipitous rocks on both sides of the creek and along the defile were so steep that no one could scale them."[138] But not a shot was fired at them, and hardly a soul was to be seen in the immediate area.

"Everyone is pleased with the good march and the fact that it was kept a secret, thus cutting off Washington from Lancaster," a relieved Captain von Münchhausen noted in his diary. From the Nicholas House in Hockessin, Delaware, where Howe established headquarters, the captain reported, "When our vanguard arrived here, it seemed that the rebels were also on the move. We were only five miles away from them and only five miles from Newport. There was much activity in front of us. We saw two regiments coming from Newport on two different roads, with their flags flying, and in very good order, as if they were heading for the road to Lancaster." This was probably Weedon's Brigade. "I was ordered by the General to ride quickly so as to lead the Hessian jägers diagonally through the woods to cut off these troops, if possible. At the same time General

Howe, with the light infantry, marched directly toward them for the same purpose. But the rebels, who had become aware of all this, retreated quickly. Notwithstanding this, the jägers got close enough to send a few amusette balls at them."[139]

While on this march, the British light troops passed the home of Col. Samuel Patterson, commander of the 2nd Regiment of New Castle County Militia. "This day we got two Stand of Colours, a number of Regimental Swords, and five or six Stand of Arms &c. at Colonel Pattersons House; he made his escape as the Light Infantry appea'd," Lt. Henry Stirke of the 10th Light Infantry Company wrote in his diary.[140] One of the captured flags, of dark blue or green fringed silk with a canton of thirteen red and white stripes, is a rare survivor of the Revolution, thanks to a British officer who sent it home as a trophy. "I must tell you a Piece of good Luck I had a few Days before the Battle of the Brandywine," Capt. William Dansey of the 33rd wrote to his mother. "On a Flanking Party, I took the Horse, Arms, Colours and Drums belonging to a Rebel Colonel of the Delaware Militia, made his Brother prisoner, & caused all his Baggage to be taken, which the General very politely sent back again, but the Horse, Arms & Colours came to my share, the latter I hope to bring a Trophy to Brinsop," the Dansey estate near Hereford, England.[141]

The Patterson family's odyssey was by no means over. "Toward evening one of our patrols brought in a coach harnessed to six very fine horses," Ewald wrote slyly. "Found in the coach was Lady Patterson, the wife of an American colonel—a lady who before autumn had overtaken her beauty must have been attractive—together with her maid, a dainty blonde, and three Negro servants. The entire baggage was thoroughly searched, and everything belonging to the colonel was distributed among the jägers." His gallantry with an elderly lady of quality not failing, Ewald continued his tale, with tongue firmly in cheek:

> Since darkness now fell over this *partage d'Arlequin*, and these ladies did not dare continue their journey at night, they were put up for the night in our gypsy dwellings, which were mostly nothing but huts of brushwood. At daybreak, after we had treated the ladies to breakfast and had exchanged their six good horses for six very patient ones, they resumed their journey. They bid us farewell and we wished them a pleasant journey. I do not believe they had ever dreamed in all their lives of making a toilette under such circumstances.[142]

In response to the British march, the Continentals stood to arms for the better part of the day, waiting for Howe's army to appear in front. American scouts reported that the British had moved onto the main road between Wilmington and Lancaster, effectively turning Washington's right flank and rendering his entrenchments useless. Further, the head of the British column was now turning away from Wilmington and moving west toward Lancaster, Pennsylvania.

After Howe had set up headquarters at the Nicholas House, on the road between Wilmington and Lancaster, he prepared to cross the border into Pennsylvania. Capt. Lt. Francis Downman of the Royal Artillery complained:

> The rear guard to which I belonged, with the 2nd brigade of artillery, did not reach our ground till 11 o'clock at night, after a very disagreeable march of 16 hours without anything to eat, and almost suffocated with dust, owing to the vast train of baggage waggons and cattle that were in front. We did not meet with the smallest interference in our march from the rebels, for we took a different road to that which they expected, and where they had raised works and collected a force. Mr. Washington is now encamped about three miles from us on a very strong ground with 20,000 men. . . . Our General and other officers are going to reconnoitre with a very strong detachment. In all probability a day or two will decide the fate of America.[143]

That night, to shield Philadelphia and avoid being trapped on the Delmarva Peninsula, Washington's troops withdrew from their carefully prepared defenses and marched northward from Newport, crossing the border from New Castle County, Delaware, into Chester County, Pennsylvania. Somehow word got around that the British were heading for Chads's Ford on the Brandywine. "Our Army at that time expecting they would take their rout thro' this place, over Brandywine Bridge, entrenched themselves very well on the Eastern bank of Red Clay Creek, about a mile westward from Newport, where they had moved the day before & waited their approach in the highest spirits imaginable," President John McKinly of Delaware wrote from Wilmington on September 9, "but the enemy has for the present given them the slip, having moved farther north to pass Brandywine, at a Place called Chad's Ford, about 9 or 10 miles above this place." How McKinly knew this is not clear; he told Caesar Rodney that the British "were pursued, or rather attempted to be out-

THE SEAT OF WAR
SEPTEMBER 1777

PENNSYLVANIA

N

Faulkners
Swamp
Reading
Schuylkill River
Pennibecker's Mills
Jones Tavern
Parkers Ford
Trappe
French Creek
Powder Mill
Whitemarsh
Reading Furnace
Valley Forge
Bristol
Yellow Springs
White
Swedes Ford
Germantown
Red Lion
Horse
Tredyffrin
Leverings
Ford
Lancaster
Merion
Meeting
Downingtown
Boot
Paoli
Buck
Falls of Schuylkill
McClellan's Tavern
Turks Head
Dilworth
Middle
Philadelphia
Martin's
Aston
Darby Ferry
Cochrane's Tavern
Center
House
Chads's Ford
Chester
Kennett
Square
Oxford
New
London
Wilmington
Newark
Newport
NEW JERSEY
Susquehanna River
Nottingham
Christiana
Iron
Hill
Head
of
Elk
*Chesapeake
Bay*
*Delaware River
and Bay*
Johnson's Ferry
Turkey Point
MARYLAND
DELAWARE
Spesutie Is.

Map by Thomas J. McGuire

marched, headed & interrupted, in their rout by the whole Continental Troops under Genl. Washington who set off for that purpose from their lines at four o'clock this morng."[144] Lt. William Beatty of the 7th Maryland wrote in his diary, "The Enemy not thinking it Proper to Continue their March on the Road by Wilmington and new Port, But Push'd to Cross the Brandewine at Shad's ford obliged our Army to move that way. The 9th we began this March about 2 o'Clock in the morning."[145]

The Continentals passed over the arc boundary, a twelve-mile circle drawn from New Castle that had been carefully surveyed and marked by Mason and Dixon ten years earlier, and moved up the roads to Chads's Ford. Spirits were still high but had deflated somewhat from their near fever pitch at Newport.

Once over the Mason-Dixon line, the unofficial dividing line between the North and South, the cultural contrast between slave country and farms built by free labor was immediately noticeable. Although Delaware had up until recently been part of Pennsylvania, its culture below the fall line was—and still is—distinctly southern.

Chester County was one of the three original counties established in Pennsylvania by William Penn, and its seat, the village of Chester on the Delaware River, was the site of the earliest European settlement in the state, having been founded as Upland by the Swedes in the late 1630s. Its rolling hills were covered with thick hardwood forests of chestnut, hickory, and oak, and the well-watered limestone topsoil was some of the best on the continent. The eastern townships, settled largely by British Quakers for nearly a century or more, presented a glorious image of William Penn's Peaceable Kingdom.

Elkannah Watson, a New England soldier passing from Virginia to the Valley Forge encampment in the spring of 1778, described the region:

> Most of the slopes of the hill-sides are laid out into regular farms, and are under high cultivation. The verdure of the fields, and the neatness and superior tillage of the farms in the rich vales, were so grateful to the eye, after being long accustomed to southern aspects. . . . The contrast, so obvious and so strong, in the appearance of these farms and of the southern plantations, will strike every observer, and can be imputed to but one cause. Here we witness the impulses and results of honest industry, where freemen labor for themselves. There we see the feeble efforts of coerced labor, performed by the enervated slave, uninspired by personal interest, and unimpelled by a worthy ambition. These distinctions are perceptible even between Maryland and Pennsylvania, separated only by an imaginary line.[146]

To be sure, there were slaves in Pennsylvania and other northern states in the 1770s, but their numbers were small. Chester County, with a population of 21,000, had approximately 500 slaves, less than 4 percent of the population. The largest slaveholder was Judge William Moore of Charlestown Township, the chief justice of Chester County for more than forty years under the crown and a staunch Loyalist. Few Quakers owned slaves by the 1770s; Moore, an Anglican, still owned 10 slaves in 1780.

Charles Biddle, who became vice president of Pennsylvania in the 1780s, commented on the sharp differences in temperament. "It is a saying of the people of Maryland that in traveling from Pennsylvania to the southward, the first countryman's house you stop at where the landlord behaves with politeness to you, you may be assured you are out of Pennsylvania." Traditional southern culture has been famous for its hospitality and openness for centuries. By contrast, the hospitality in Pennsylvania, especially in the rural areas, was less welcoming and often cold and distant. This was partly due to the "quietism" of the Quakers and many of the German sects, who generally frowned upon outward display and, beyond commerce and marketing, mostly kept to themselves.

"On the other hand, the Pennsylvanians say, that in going from Maryland to Pennsylvania, the first farm you come to where you see a good barn, the fences all up, and in good order, you may be certain that you are out of Maryland." Neatness and cleanliness, especially among the Quakers, were next to godliness. "The fact is, in Pennsylvania, the people are generally industrious and seldom take notice of strangers. In Maryland, they are very hospitable, but indolent."[147]

Biddle recorded an interesting remark made in this same era by Judge Richard Peters, a prominent Philadelphian and chairman of the Pennsylvania Board of War. "Judge Peters says all the great and strange people we have in Pennsylvania are from Chester County."[148] The county had many extraordinary individuals who, in addition to being farmers or millers, were self-taught mathematicians, scientists, doctors, or craftsmen who made extraordinary clocks and cabinetry. Some possessed their own small libraries, and a respectable number were members of the American Philosophical Society.

Humphry Marshall of West Bradford Township, in the center of the county, was such a person. A first-generation Anglo-American Quaker, Marshall was trained as a stone mason but became a self-taught botanist and scientist. It must have been in the family bloodline: His first cousin was John Bartram, who was born in Chester County in 1699 and was still working in 1777. Through his own study, Bartram became America's leading botanist and was called the greatest natural botanist in the world by the Swedish scientist Linnaeus. Bartram was appointed Botanist Royal for North America by King George III and opened a remarkable botanical garden along the Schuylkill River near Philadelphia. He also built his stone house with his own hands. Humphry Marshall did the same, building a handsome stone mansion in 1772, complete with astronomical observatory. He then opened a botanical garden and arboretum, and shortly after the Revolution, he published *Arbustrum Americanum*, the first American treatise on trees.

The county abounded with such farmers. Wrote Elkannah Watson:

> On our journey to Valley Forge, a heavy storm, and roads almost impassable, compelled us to seek shelter at the house of an opulent farmer. Here we were received with the kindest hospitality, and found our host an intelligent, sensible man. He had a fine library, and was well informed on most subjects. His house was spacious and neat, and well supplied with the comforts and substantials of life. Independence, wealth, and contentment were conspicuous in everything, within and without the house. This man was but a specimen of his class—virtuous, affluent, and intelligent republican freemen.[149]

August and September were crucial months for both harvesting and planting in the farming cycle of the region. Buckwheat fields, planted in late July, were in bloom and were not harvested until October. Winter wheat and rye fields were plowed in early September to prepare for planting at the end of the month; they would be harvested the following July. Apples and peaches were ripe for picking; cherry trees, numerous in the area, yielded their fruit in June and July. Many farms also grew small amounts of flax to make linen and hemp for rope.

But the greatest agricultural product was "corn," used in the broad English sense to mean grain, mainly wheat, but including barley and oats as well. Maize, or Indian corn, which was used on most farms for hog fodder, was tall and green in early September. "Our house stands upon a hill, it commands a beautiful prospect of the Country around, and which a few weeks past the fields were waving with yellow Corn," Christopher Marshall wrote from Lancaster in mid-September. "Now the Indian Corn & Buckwheat makes a pleasing object, add to which the trees bending beneath the ripening Fruits, Herds of Cows, Oxen, and sheep fattening on luxuriant Pastures, yet my heart is heavy in the Contemplation of the distress that our once happy Land is now plunged in."[150]

It was this peaceful, prosperous world that the two armies invaded in September 1777, leaving a lasting mark. "Not just chusing to take the Bull by the horns we disappointed Washington and turned his Right the 8th by a forced march from Pencader by Newark to New Garden," General Grant reported, "a handsome Move of 14 Miles which He did not think us equal to, knowing the state of our carriages & in fact was so much disconcerted upon finding that We might by a subsequent Move get possession of the Heights of Wilmington, that He quit his Camp in the night & fled with precipitation over the Brandy Wine."[151]

The Continentals crossed the Brandywine to the eastern bank and took up positions on the heights, with their center at Chads's Ford. On the following day, September 10, they deployed along the creek a few miles above and below the ford, with scouting parties covering several Brandywine fording places, and began constructing artillery batteries.

Howe's troops began crossing the Mason-Dixon line into New Garden Township during the midday hours of September 9. "This region of Pennsylvania is extremely mountainous and traversed by thick forests; nevertheless it is very well cultivated and very fertile," Ewald commented. Unlike the area they had just come through, he noted, "Because we descended upon the inhabitants so quickly, contrary to their expectations, they had not left their plantations." He further added, "The inhabitants of this region are generally Quakers, who, since they did not want to participate in the war, did not flee, but arrived in crowds and asked for protection." Military intelligence was also provided: "We received positive information here that the greater part of the American army had entrenched behind the left bank of the Brandywine."[152] Lt. Heinrich von Feilitzsch of the Anspach Jägers commented, "I must note here in Pennsylvania, that the inhabitants are encountered everywhere. This province is more loyal to the King than all the others." He fatuously added, "Therefore nothing is taken from the inhabitants," which was not quite the case.[153]

The British Army moved along two roads toward the village of Kennett Square through some very rugged terrain. "Some deserters come in, Some country people. Some with their Waggons also two people from Phila. who say Washington is determined to risk a battle rather than give up that City," James Parker wrote. "At 12 M. the tents are struck & we march at one about 2 Miles along the Great Road & halt till 5 when Genl. How & Ld. Cornwallis With the light troops take to the Right. Genl. Kniphausen with the Artillery Baggage &c goes on to Kenetts Square where after a Very fatiguing March we arive at 12 at Night." The road to the right went through a very difficult and steep gorge along White Clay Creek, prompting Parker to make a comparison with the ancient battle of Caudine Forks, which ended with Rome's most humiliating defeat.

"Our tract for 5 or 6 miles was through a Trough having high Surrounding hills on each side & Answer my idea of the Coudinforks where the Roman General Posthumeus was attacted by Pontius, & was obliged to surrender with his Whole Army. Our Army is now as light as possible."[154]

"Our march this day about 6 miles through an amazingly strong country, being a succession of large hills, rather sudden with narrow vales, in short an entire defile," Montrésor observed. "Encamped on very strong ground where we joined Lt.-General Kniphuysen's division." He too noted, "Almost all the Inhabitants found at their houses."[155]

The roads were narrow, and rain in the night made moving so much baggage and artillery extremely difficult. Once Howe arrived at Kennett Square, he gathered intelligence from local Loyalists concerning Washington's position at Chads's Ford and decided that this was where he would confront the Continental Army in the fight for Philadelphia.

CHAPTER 4

"As heavy a Fire from the Musketry as perhaps has been known this war."

The Battle of Brandywine, September 11, 1777

September 11 dawned gray and dank, with fog shrouding the Brandy-wine Valley. Thursday was baking day on many of the local farms, as several civilian accounts attest, and the bake ovens were fired up with brushwood first thing in the morning for the all-day process. Normally a slight haze from cooking fires would have been puffing out of the large hearth chimneys and hanging in layers over the glens, but on this Thursday, the air was murky with the heavy volume of smoke collecting from hundreds of campfires. The atmosphere was tepid; this was not a pleasant, early-morning vapor, but the herald of a thick, late-summer day.

The two armies were about five miles apart, each spread out over several miles, with hundreds of pickets and numerous scouting parties between them. The actual total of soldiers present and fit for duty can only be estimated in round numbers, for surviving statistics in the British Army are spotty at best, and they are even more so for the American forces. "It will be easily conceived by those acquainted with military affairs," *The Annual Register* pointed out, "that all calculations of this nature, though founded upon the best official information, will far exceed, even at a much nearer distance than America, the real effective number that can ever be brought to action."[1]

Washington's force, generally estimated at 12,000 regulars and 3,000 militia, was encamped behind the hills of Birmingham Township on the east side of Brandywine Creek. His center was at Chads's Ford on the Great Nottingham Road, where the creek could be crossed on foot, and at Chads's Ferry, a few hundred yards south of the ford, where the water was deeper and a ferryman on a flat boat would pull goods and passengers across the water by means of a rope stretched from one bank to the other. The depth of the water here provided a natural defense. John Chads, the ferryman, was dead, but his widow, Elizabeth, known in the neighborhood as old "Aunt Betty Chads," still lived in their modest stone house perched on a knoll overlooking the ford. When Continental troops arrived two nights earlier and began tearing up the fences for firewood and fortifications, Aunt Betty refused to leave her home.

The bulk of Washington's army was stacked up behind the crossings for a few miles east. Greene's Division, composed of Weedon's and Muhlenberg's Virginia Brigades (2,500 troops), was posted in depth on the heights behind the ferry about half a mile south of the Great Road, forming the left center of the line. Gen. Francis Nash's Carolina Brigade (1,500) was also in this area. Wayne's Division, made up of the 1st and 2nd Pennsylvania Brigades (2,000), occupied the center ground on Greene's right, about 200 yards east of the ford; its right flank rested on the road. On the hill to Wayne's right and near the artillery park were Conway's Pennsylvania and Maxwell's New Jersey Brigades, in Stirling's Division, and Stephen's Virginians, in Woodford's and Scott's Brigades (2,500 total).

A four-gun earth-and-log lunette, a curved artillery battery alternately referred to as a breastwork or redoubt, was constructed on a knoll near the Chads House to cover the ford. This lunette contained the brass guns of Col. Thomas Proctor's Pennsylvania Artillery: two French 4-pounders, a Hessian 6-pounder (a rebored 3-pounder taken at Trenton), and a Philadelphia-made 8-inch howitzer capable of firing exploding shells. "The army encamped on the Brandewine on the right of Shads ford on the hier ground," wrote Jacob Nagle, a sixteen-year-old artilleryman in Proctor's unit. "Our artilery was ranged in front of an orcherd. The night before the Brittish arived the infantry hove up a brest work, so that the muzels of the guns would run over it." Nagle also described the terrain at the ford: "A cross the road on the left was a buckwheat field opposit to a wood and the Brandewine between them."[2]

Another four-gun battery was erected on a hill several hundred yards below the ford near Greene's left, covering the ferry. Across the creek, on the west side, a third log-and-earth battery and a long breastwork of fence rails were constructed facing the road toward Kennett Square, covering the main approach to the ford. A mile or so south of Greene's position behind the ferry was Maj. Gen. John Armstrong, with about 2,000 Pennsylvania Militia belonging to Potter's and Lacey's Brigades. These units were covering Pyle's and Gibson's Fords, protecting Washington's far-left flank.

Upstream a mile from Chads's Ford was Brinton's Ford, where Sullivan's Maryland Division (1,100), composed of Smallwood's and De Borre's Brigades, held ground. A temporary bridge made of wagons and fence rails probably stood in the water between the two fords, and a two-gun artillery battery was begun on a nearby hill to cover the crossings.[3]

Sullivan detached two units from his division to guard the next three fords above the right. Col. David Hall's Delaware Regiment (250) was detached from Smallwood's Brigade and sent to Jones's Ford, a mile above Brinton's. The two battalions of 2nd Canadian, or Congress's Own Regiment (400), commanded by Col. Moses Hazen, went to cover two crossings farther north. One battalion was posted at Wister's Ford, a mile and a half beyond Jones's; the other was sent yet another mile up to Buffington's Ford, just below where the western and eastern branches of the creek come together from their headwaters in upper Chester County. The area between the two branches is called the Forks of the Brandywine.

Proper reconnaissance in the American forces was strangely uncoordinated or flat-out lacking. "The proceedings of the battle of Brandywine suggested to me two or three important lessons," Col. Timothy Pickering wrote a few days afterward. "1. To reconnoitre thoroughly the post you take. . . . Before the battle of Brandywine, we had time to have viewed all the ground several miles on our right, but did not do it. . . . [2.] to have correct maps of the country. . . . [3.] You should have guides perfectly acquainted with every road. These men should be timely procured beforehand, and not be sought for just at the critical moment when you want them."[4]

All told, Washington's main force stretched along the left bank (east side) of the Brandywine for five miles, covering eight possible crossing places. His advance forces, made up primarily of Maxwell's Corps of Light Infantry (1,000), were posted west of the creek toward Kennett Square.

Several hundred Chester County militia with little or no training were also attached to Maxwell. The local militia's value here was to bolster the appearance of numbers and aid with scouting, but parties and whole companies of these troops seem to have been wandering through the area that morning, to little or no purpose. "On the morning of the Battle of Brandywine, we were marched down the west side of the creek near the Chad's Fording," Pvt. William Hutchinson of the 2nd Battalion of the Chester County Militia recalled. There the unit was "ordered to cross to the east side of the creek, which we did by wading, and marched up the stream about half a mile, where we lay upon a bottom, then clothed with woods, between the hill and the creek." The 2nd's commander, Capt. Allen Cunningham of London Grove Township, "was a gallant man, and we had full confidence both in his skill and courage."[5] Overall, though, "the militia of this country are not like the Jersey militia," Nathanael Greene told Kitty on September 10. "Fighting is a new thing with these, and many seems to have but a poor stomach for the business."[6]

Five miles west of Chads's Ford, in the fields and woods around the village of Kennett Square, the Crown Forces, generally estimated at 18,000, were up in the predawn hours, preparing to move at first light. The troops packed their blanket rolls and knapsacks; filled their canteens; checked their cartridge boxes, haversacks, and pockets for the full complement of sixty rounds of ammunition; and prepared for a long march. "The fatigues of this Day were excessive," Lt. Loftus Cliffe of the 46th remarked afterward. "If you knew the weight a poor soldier carries, the length of time he is obliged to be on foot for a train of Artillery to move 17 Miles, the Duties he goes thro when near an Enemy & that the whole night of the 9th we were marching, you would say we had done our duty on the 11th."[7] Lt. Martin Hunter of the 52nd noted, "The night before the battle twenty empty wagons were ordered to attend each battalion of Grenadiers and Light Infantry, to carry the wounded, which was always a preparation for battle."[8]

Civilians began to appear as events unfolded, watching both armies. Some were Loyalists and others were Patriots, but most were pacifist Quakers and country people who were simply spectators. Some of the Quakers willfully ignored the armies and went about their daily business, for Thursday was also the day for midweek Friends meetings. Others, like twenty-one-year-old Joseph Townsend from East Bradford Township, went out to see all of the activity before attending meeting. "Having curiosity, and fond of new things, William Townsend [Joseph's brother], myself, and some others rode alongside of the Brandywine for some distance to discover the approach of the British Army in case they should attempt to cross at any other of the fords on the creek between Jefferis' and Chadds," he recalled. "We fell in with many like ourselves but no intelligence could be obtained."[9]

Howe divided his army into two columns. The column heading straight for Chads's Ford was commanded by sixty-one-year-old Lt.-Gen. Baron Wilhelm Reichsfreiherr zu Inn-und Knyphausen, a dependable and able officer who had spent much of his career in the Prussian Army. "General Knyphausen was a noble specimen of a German baron, of the ordinary height & strong frame," a Philadelphian described him. In the best tradition of the Prussian officer corps, "there was a sabre mark on one of his cheeks extending from the eye to the chin."[10]

"At 5 o'clock in the Morning," von Knyphausen told Lord Germain, "I moved the Column from Kennets Square in the following Order: An officer & 15 Men of the Queen's Light Dragoons," followed by "Captain Ferguson's Riflemen, & the Queen's Rangers," numbering just over 400, and "the 1st & 2nd British Infantry under Major General Grant." The 1st British Infantry Brigade was composed of the battalion companies of the 4th, 23rd, 28th, and 49th Regiments, totaling 1,400 troops; the 2nd Brigade, made up of the 5th, 10th, 27th, and 40th Regiments, numbered about 1,300. Behind them was "the Remainder of the Queen's light Dragoons," about 200 troopers, and the 1st and 2nd Brigades of Royal Artillery, with six medium 12-pounders and four howitzers. They were followed by "the Baggage, Provision Train & Cattle of the whole Army covered by the 71st Regt.," Fraser's Highlanders, a Scottish regiment of 1,200 men divided into three battalions.

Blocking the road to Chads's Ford was Maxwell's Light Infantry. The main body was posted at Kennett Friends Meeting House, three miles east of Kennett Square. Out in front along the road between the meetinghouse and Welch's Tavern a mile west were four advance posts. "Three small detachments," commanded by lieutenant colonels of the Virginia Line—Richard Parker of the 10th Virginia Regiment, William Heth of the 3rd, and Charles Simms of the 12th—"were early in the morning separately and advantageously posted by the brigadier contiguous to the road, some distance in his front," Capt. Henry Lee wrote. Capt. Charles Porterfield of the 11th Virginia, "with a company of infantry, preceded

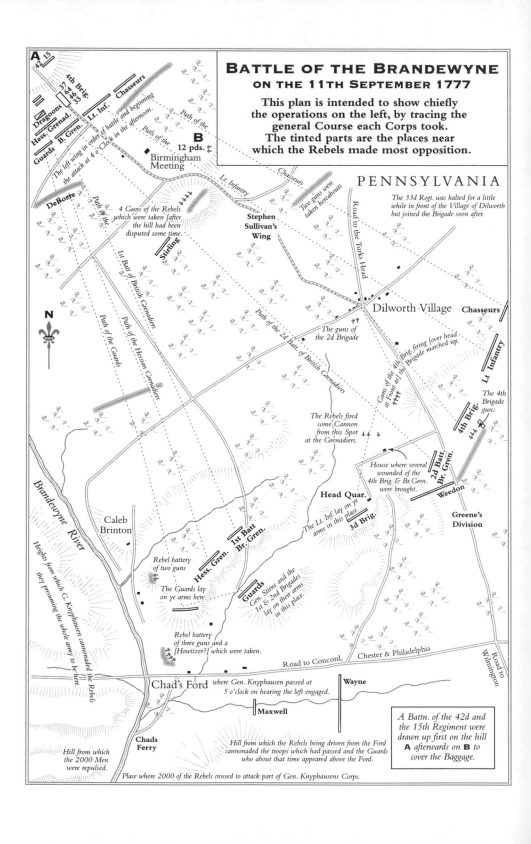

BATTLE OF THE BRANDEWYNE
ON THE 11TH SEPTEMBER 1777

This plan is intended to show chiefly the operations on the left, by tracing the general Course each Corps took. The tinted parts are the places near which the Rebels made most opposition.

A 15
42

4th Brig.
37
64
46
33

Dragoons
Hess. Grenad.
Guards B. Gren. Lt. Inf.
Chasseurs

The left wing in order of battle and beginning the attack at 4 o'Clock in the afternoon.

Path of the

DeBorre

B 12 pds.

Birmingham Meeting

Path of the

Lt. Infantry

Chasseurs

4 Guns of the Rebels which were taken [after the hill had been disputed some time.

Stephen Sullivan's Wing

Two guns were taken here abouts

PENNSYLVANIA

The 33d Regt. was halted for a little while in front of the Village of Dilworth but joined the Brigade soon after.

Road to the Turks Head

Stirling

N

1st Batt of British Grenadiers

Path of the Hessian Grenadiers

Path of the Guards

Path of the 2d Batt. of British Grenadiers

The guns of the 2d Brigade

Dilworth Village Chasseurs

Guns of the 4th Brig. firing [over head at Front as] the Brigade marched up.

Lt Infantry

4th Brig

The 4th Brigade guns

The Rebels fired some Cannon from this Spot at the Grenadiers.

House where several wounded of the 4th Brig. & Br. Gren. were brought.

2d Batt. Br. Gren.

Weedon

Greene's Division

Head Quar.

The Lt. Inf. lay on ye arms in this place.

3d Brig.

Brandewyne River

Heights from which G. Knyphausen cannonaded the whole army to be here.

Caleb Brinton

Rebel battery of two guns

The Guards lay on ye arms here.

1st Batt Br. Gren.

Hess. Gren.

Guards

Gen. Stirns and the 1st & 2nd Brigades lay on their arms in this place.

Rebel battery of three guns and a [Howitzer?] which were taken.

Road to Concord, Chester & Philadelphia

Road to Wilmington

Chad's Ford *where Gen. Knyphausen passed at 5 o'clock on hearing the left engaged.*

Wayne

Maxwell

A Battn. of the 42d and the 15th Regiment were drawn up first on the hill **A** afterwards on **B** to cover the Baggage.

Chads Ferry

Hill from which the 2000 Men were repulsed.

Hill from which the Rebels being driven from the Ford cannonaded the troops which had passed and the Guards who about that time appeared above the Ford.

Place where 2000 of the Rebels crossed to attack part of Gen. Knyphausens Corps.

these parties with orders to deliver his fire as soon as he should meet the van of the enemy, and then fall back."[11]

At the head of von Knyphausen's column was Capt. Patrick Ferguson with his small band of green-coated British riflemen. They were armed with Ferguson's breech-loading rifle, which was capable of firing up to six accurate shots per minute. "Gen. Knyphausen when I ask'd his orders was pleased to desire me to take my own way," Ferguson wrote, "as my whole detachment was under 90 men [and] was no great command."[12] Fanning out, the riflemen moved cautiously up the road from Kennett Square toward Welch's Tavern on the Great Nottingham Road. They were supported by 300 American Loyalists of the Queen's Rangers, also uniformed in green, under the command of a British officer, Capt. James Wemyss of the 40th Regiment. "Advancing on the Road to Chads's Ford" a mile or so from their camp, von Knyphausen reported, "I had hardly come up to Welch's Tavern when the advanced Corps viz. Captain Ferguson's Riflemen & the Queen's Rangers fell in with about 300 Riflemen of the Ennemy, who were posted in the Wood to the eastward of the Tavern."[13] Here the opening shots of the Battle of Brandywine were fired around 6 A.M.

"The first party we had to do with was an advanced Post of 150 men and some light horse, who threw away their fire and ran off, with the loss of three or four men and a horse whom we shot flying," Ferguson wrote.[14] Behind Ferguson were the Queen's Rangers. "We came in sight of the enemy at sunrise," Sgt. Stephen Jarvis of the Rangers recalled. "The first discharge of the enemy killed the horse of Major Grymes, who was leading the column, and wounded two men in the Division directly in my front, and in a few moments the Regiment became warmly engaged and several of our officers were badly wounded."[15]

Opposing them at the first fallback position was Lt. Col. Will Heth of the 3rd Virginia, leading 200 men. "I commanded as I mentioned before, a detachment of Light Infantry," he told Col. Daniel Morgan, "part of which under our valuable Friend Porterfield began the action with day light—he killd (him self) the first man who fell that day."[16] Using "shoot-and-scoot" tactics, Captain Porterfield and his detachment waited until the enemy was close, fired a volley, and then fell back to the next post. "This service was handsomely performed by Porterfield, and produced the desired effect," "Light-Horse Harry" Lee wrote. "The

British van pushed forward rapidly and incautiously, until it lined the front of the detachment commanded by Lieutenant-Colonel Simms, who poured in a close and destructive fire, and then retreated to the light corps. The leading officer of the enemy was killed [sic]; and the detachment suffered severely."[17] Heth commended Porterfield's skill: "His conduct through the whole day—was such, as has acquird him the greatest Honor—A great proportion of British Officers fell by a party under his command."[18]

"Such a set of base runaways never before presumed to disgrace a Gentlemans profession," Ferguson wrote of Maxwell's Corps. "In the course of two hours my lads underwent the fire of 2000 men who were kind enough to fire in general in the air and run away." Of the Loyalists, Ferguson said, "The Queen's Rangers Americans commanded by Rachel Wymess' husband seconded us with spirit and the line will do us the justice to allow that we kept them undisturbed and clear'd the way for them as fast as they could follow us."[19]

After firing a few volleys from their main position at Kennett Meeting, the Continental Light Infantry withdrew steadily down toward Chads's Ford, drawing the Rangers and Ferguson after them. "My Lads were so fatigued with dashing after the Rebels over all surfaces that I found it necessary to leave one half by turns in the rear with the column of march and work my way with the other—which as my whole detachment was under 90 men was no great command: however by avoiding the road, gaining their flanks, or keeping up a rattling fire from the ground or by bullying them we still got on."[20]

By the time the fighting reached the valley of the Brandywine, nearly two hours had elapsed, and the greencoats had taken numerous casualties. "Majr. Grymes's horse was shot under him, & our flanking parties were Attack'd on both sides," James Parker observed at a distance, "but drove the Rebels till within a half mile of the Creek, where they made a stand behind a breast work of some loggs they had made" near the artillery battery constructed on the west side of the Brandywine.[21]

As they descended toward the ford, some of Maxwell's Light Infantry performed a *ruse de guerre*, which infuriated the British riflemen and the Loyalists. The Queen's Rangers were lured close by a party of Continentals who pretended to surrender by turning their muskets upside down, but then fired at point-blank range. "The Queen's Rangers and Riffle

Corps at the head of Lieut. general Kniphausen's Column, advancing to the foot of a hill, saw the Enemy formed behind the fence, were deceived by the Rebels telling them, that they would deliver up their Arms; but upon their advancing they fired a volley upon our men, and took to their Heels, killed and wounded about thirty of them Corps," Sgt. Thomas Sullivan of the 49th wrote. "By that and the preceeding skirmishes they were much disabled, which occasioned our Brigade [i.e. the 1st Brigade: 4th, 23rd, 28th, 49th Regiments] to advance to the front, being separated (when we formed upon a little hill) by a small Creek, which ran between that & the opposite hill on which the Enemy took post."[22]

"Amongst other feats the troops behind us were witnesses," Ferguson noted with pride, "when my 30 Lads advanced to a breast work of 100 yards in extant well lined with men whose fire they received at twelve yards and when every body thought they were all destroy'd they Scrambled into the breast work and the Dogs ran away." The Continentals fell back by sections, providing covering fire as they withdrew: "We were Stop'd from following them by a heavy flanking fire from a very extensive breast work at 80 yards distance," Ferguson recalled. "I threw my party immediately on the ground, but Wemyss's, who had kept the road, being close to my rear, came under a part of it and had a fourth part of his men and officers killed and wounded"[23]

This tactic gave rise to the perception on the American side that British casualties were considerably higher than they actually were. "The fire from our People was not of long duration, as the Enemy pressed on in force, but was very severe," Washington wrote to Congress that afternoon. "What loss the Enemy sustained, cannot be ascertained with precision," he told John Hancock. "It is the general opinion, particularly of those who were engaged, that they had at least Three Hundred Men killed and wounded." As for Maxwell's loss, "it does not exceed fifty in the whole."[24]

Reinforcements for Maxwell arrived from across the creek. "Their numbers encreased," Ferguson noted. "This fire continued for some minutes very heavy until we Sicken'd [of] it, after which upon the Signal to rise my Lads like Bay's dead men Sprung up and not one hurt." Of his breech-loading rifle, Ferguson commented, "Such is the great advantage of an arm that will admit of being loaded and fired on the ground without exposing my men that I threw my people on the ground under pretty

Smart firing six times that morning without losing a man, although I had 1/4 part of those afterward kill'd or wounded."[25]

Maxwell's troops "formd on the declivity of a hill on clear ground & stood till Majr. Grymes Attackd them with ye Bayonets, when they broke fled to the Woods & heid [hid]," James Parker stated. The firing was intense at close range, and the Loyalists took more casualties, including Capt. Robert Murdon, who was killed. Parker continued:

> At this time Capt. Robt. Murdon fell, & many more Wounded, but they drove them over the Creek. While this passed on our Right Majr. Weems with part of the Regt. drove them through the woods on the left till they crossed the Creek also, when their Canon began from a battry in our front, & I [we?] took Stations on high Commanding ground on our left. Genl. Cleveland took post on a hill parallel to their front battery, & a Cannonade Continued for Some time, I believe without doing much damage on either side.[26]

The fighting had now gone on for the better part of the morning. "'Twas then about 10 o'clock," Sgt. Thomas Sullivan noted, "and the 2nd Brigade with all the Hessians and Artillery joined us, after we pursued the Rebels as close as we could without being in danger of their Cannon above the Ford, all the men lay upon their Arms in a close valley covered with wood."[27]

"About 8 or 9 o'clock this morning a very heavy fire began in front, which continued some time between our advanced corps and the rebels, who were posted very strongly in the woods and on the hills facing the ford of the creek," Captain Downman of the Royal Artillery wrote.

> The heavy artillery was ordered to make haste, and we galloped our horses some time, but were prevented from continuing the road by reason of trees being cut down and laid across. We turned into a wood and after a little difficulty got into a road that brought us to a very advantageous situation within shot of the rebel batteries on the other side of the creek. We immediately began to fire upon them from our 12 pounders and howitzers, and they returned it very smartly. This continued for some time, likewise a heavy fire of infantry and artillery in the woods to our right.[28]

There was a midmorning lull as both sides paused to regroup, and the fight downgraded to sniping and occasional cannon fire. From Proctor's battery at Chads's Ford, Jacob Nagle watched as "the adjudent rode down to the ford to water his horse." Mistaking the green uniforms of Ferguson's riflemen for Hessian Jägers, he observed that "a Hession laying in the brush fired at him and missed him but wounded the horse in the right shoulder. The horse stagered, the adjutent jumped off with his pistols in hand and run up to the spot, which was not more than 15 yards from him, and several of the artilery run down to him, but the Hission could not be found."

Nagle also observed a peculiar tactic of one of Maxwell's riflemen. "The Hessions and Morgans [*sic*] rifelmen being both in this wood and some of the American rifelmen in the buckwheat field, I took notice of one in a white frock laying on his back to lead his gun," using a crossed leg to steady the rifle barrel.

> On the edge of the wood next to the road was some trees cut down, and the Hessions got amongst them; this riffelman fired 7 or 8 shots at them as fast as they came there. The buckwheat being in bloom, they could not see him, but we ware on the highth over him. At length finding no more coming, he crawled on his hands and knees to the fence where he fell in with six more. They all rise and crossed the ford and went to the place he had been firing at them, as we supposed to overhall them.[29]

Patrick Ferguson also described the action that Nagle had witnessed:

> Whilst Knyphausen was forming the Line within a Mile of the Rebell Camp to wait for G. Howe's attack, their Rifle men were picking off our men very fast by random shots from a wood some hundred yards in front as it is easy to do execution upon such large objects. I had only 28 men with me (a few having been disabled by the Enemy the rest from Fatigue) who however proved Sufficient, for my Lads first dislodged them from the skirts of the Wood, then Drove them from a breast work within it, after which our purpose being answered we lay down at the furthest skirt of the wood—not unnecessarily to provock an attack, being so few without Support.

During this lull, one of the stranger and more controversial episodes of the battle took place. "We had not layn long when a Rebell Officer, remarkable by a Huzzar dress, passed towards our army within 100 yards of my right flank, not perceiving us." Hussars were light cavalry that originated in central Europe. Their peculiar clothing was Hungarian in style and garish, with a cylindrical cap topped by a hanging bag; a heavily laced jacket; a *pelisse*, a small, fur-trimmed jacket, slung over one shoulder; tight-fitting, laced breeches; and gaudy riding boots. It was a popular style among fashionable European cavalry officers. Ferguson, though, spotted someone else with the hussar:

> He was followed by another dressed in Dark Green or blue, mounted on a very good bay horse, with a remarkable large high cock'd hat. I ordered three good Shots to Steal near them and fire at them, but the idea disgusted me and I recalled them.
>
> The Huzzar in returning made a Circuit, but the other passed within 100 yards of us, upon which I advanced from the wood toward him. Upon my calling he stopd, but looking at me, proceeded. I again drew his Attention, and made Signs to him to Stop, levelling my piece at him, but he slowly continued his way. As I was within that distance at which in the quickest firing I have seldom missed a Sheet of paper and Could have lodged half a dozen balls in or about him before he was out of my reach, I had only to determine, but it was not pleasant to fire at the back of an unoffending individual who was acquitting himself very coolly of his duty, so I let him alone.

A few minutes after this, Ferguson was hit by a sharpshooter; the ball shattered his right elbow, a painful wound which did not heal for more than a year. He was taken to a hospital and related:

> The day after I had just been telling this Story to Some wounded officers who lay in the same room with me, when one of our Surgeons who had been dressing the wounded Rebell Officers come in and told us that they had been informing him that Genll Washington was all the morning with the Light Troops, generally in their front, and only attended by a French Officer in a huzzar Dress, he himself mounted and dressed as above described. The oddness of their dress had puzzled me and made me take notice of it.

He ended his story with a cryptic remark: "I am not Sorry that I did not know all the time who it was. Further this deponent saith not, as his bones were broke a few minutes after."[30]

Who the hussar was is not certain. Ferguson said he was told that the man was a French officer, possibly one of Lafayette's entourage. It is more likely that the officer was Count Casimir Pulaski, an impetuous Polish cavalryman who had left Philadelphia earlier, too impatient to wait for Congress to give him a commission. Pulaski, who wore a mustache and dressed in hussar clothing, could easily have been mistaken for a French officer. He was with Washington for much of the battle, and his bravery at the end of the day earned him command of the Continental Light Dragoons.[31]

The artillery of both sides now began to pound away at Chads's Ford. Sergeant Sullivan reported on the action:

> We played upon them with two 6 Pounders for half an hour, and drove them out of the breastworks which was made of loose wood, upon the declivity of the hill. The 2nd Brigade British [5th, 10th, 27th, 40th, 55th Regiments] formed on another hill upon our left and played their two six pounders also upon the Enemy's Battery at Chad'sford. As we crossed the brook they formed behind another fence at a field's distance, from whence we soon drove 'em, and a Battalion of Hessians which formed at the left of our Brigade, fell in with them as they retreated, taking them upon their Right flank, and after a smart pursuit from the Hessian Battallion, they crossed the Brandywine, and took post on that side; leaving a few men killed and more wounded behind.[32]

Capt. John Marshall of the 15th Virginia Regiment, part of Weedon's Brigade, viewed the fighting from the heights northeast of Chads's Ford. "By ten, Maxwell's corps, with little loss on either side, was driven over the Brandywine below the ford. Knyphausen, who commanded this column, paraded on the heights, reconnoitered the American army, and appeared to be making dispositions to force the passage of the river." The firing resumed on a smaller scale as numerous skirmishes with Knyphausen's force erupted. "A skirt of woods, with the river, divided him from Maxwell's corps, small parties of whom occasionally crossed over, and kept up a scattering fire, by which not much execution was done." Marshall witnessed one of the skirmishes: "At length one of these parties, led by Captains [Andrew] Waggoner [12th Virginia] and Porterfield, engaged the British flank guard very closely, killed a captain with ten or fifteen privates, drove them out of the wood, and were on the point of taking a field piece. The sharpness of the skirmish soon drew a large body of the British [the 10th and 40th Regiments] to that quarter, and the Americans were again driven over the Brandywine."[33]

Sgt. Thomas Sullivan's unit, the 49th, engaged in this skirmish, which he described as follows:

A Company of the 28th and a Company of our Regiment advanced upon the Hill to the right of the ford, and in front of the Enemy's left flank, in order to divert them, who were posted at 100 Yards distance in their front, behind trees, to the amount of 500, all chosen marksmen. A smart fire was maintained at both sides for two hours, without either party's quitting their Posts. Out of the two Companies there were about 20 men killed and wounded during that time; and two 6 Pounders [commanded by Lt. George Wilson of the Royal Artillery] were ordered up the hill to dislodge the Enemy if possible and assist the part engaged: Those guns played upon them for some time, but they were so concealed under the cover of the Trees, that it was to no purpose to endeavour to bring the Cannon to do any execution: In the mean time, by our Guns being in an open field, there was one man killed, and a man and a horse wounded.[34]

Artilleryman Jacob Nagle, across the ford with Proctor's battery, recalled, "The Brittish being in the open ploughed field, we could perceive when they saw the flash of our guns they would leave the gun 2 or 3 yards till the shot struck and then close. We then ceased about an hour, excepting a few shot at different times." Washington remained in the area, observing the fighting.

> About this time General Washington came riding up to Col Procter with his Life Guards with him and enquired how we came on. He informed the general that there was two field pieces on our left wing behind the wood which anoyed us very much and could not be seen except by the flash of the guns and he was then ordering four field pieces to play upon them. Accordingly they aimed for the flash of their guns, so direct, though they could not see the guns, that in 15 or 20 minutes we received no more shot from that quarter. Their guns were either dismounted, or otherwise it was two [sic] hot to remain there any longer.[35]

It was part of a ruse to draw Maxwell's men on, according to Sergeant Sullivan. "The Guns were ordered back and also the two Companies, in order to draw the Enemy after them from the trees, which scheme had the desired effect, for they quitted their post and advanced to the top of the hill, where they were attacked by four Companies of the 10th Battallion, in front, while the 40th made a charge upon their left flank, by going round the hill, and put them to an immediate rout. The 10th Battallion took up the ground the enemy left." Lt. Col. Thomas Musgrave, commanding the 40th, testified later that "at the Battle of Brandywine Lt. Wilson was attached to the 40th Regt. with two 3 pounders . . . upon the Brigade being ordered to form, there was a Wood thro' which he thought it might be difficult for the Guns to pass, he therefore ordered them to wait, but Lt. Wilson soon after brought them up, before he (Col. Musgrave) sent for them."[36]

The orderly book of Capt. James Wilson of the 49th Regiment was captured and sent to Washington, who reported to John Hancock that "Maxwell pushed over with his Corps, and drove them from their Ground with the loss of thirty Men left dead on the Spot, among them a Captn. Of the 49th."[37] Capt. James Wilson, though, was neither killed nor wounded; he either dropped his orderly book, or it was in someone else's possession. A few months later, "Capt. James Wilson of the 49th Regiment . . . deposed that at the Battle of Brandywine, Lt. Wilson was ordered with two Guns to support his Company which was then engaged, and was the principal means of first driving back the Enemy . . . that one of his Men were killed, and another wounded, & a horse in the Ammunition Waggon also wounded."[38]

As Knyphausen was pushing toward Chads's Ford, Sir William Howe and Lord Cornwallis were also well on the march, heading north with the main body of the army. Cornwallis's Division had encamped in a perpendicular fashion to Knyphausen; the head of this column was at Marlborough Friends Meeting, about three miles north of Kennett Square. The finest troops in Howe's army made up this force: the 1st and 2nd British Light Infantry Battalions (1,300), two squadrons of the 16th Queen's Light Dragoons (200), the 3rd Brigade of Artillery (six 6-pounders, four 12-pounders), the 1st and 2nd British Grenadier Battalions (1,400), the foot Jägers (500), three Hessian grenadier battalions (1,300), the Guards Brigade (1,000), the mounted Jägers (100), and the 3rd and 4th British Brigades (3,000).[39] Each brigade also had its own field artillery, typically consisting of two or four 3- or 4-pounder light guns. As cover, "a thick fog contributed greatly to our march," said Montrésor.[40]

The advance guard was made up of sixty Hessian foot Jägers led by Capt. Johann Ewald, fifteen mounted Jägers under Lt. Wilhelm von Hagen, Capt. James McPherson's Light Company of 42nd Royal Highlanders, and the Light Company of the 17th Regiment, commanded by Capt. William Scott. Guiding the column through the maze of narrow country roads were local Loyalists, including John Jackson, a clockmaker from East Marlborough, and Curtis Lewis, a blacksmith and large landowner in West Bradford Township, both of whom had scouted the fords of the Brandywine the night before. These men were under the direction of Joseph Galloway, Pennsylvania's leading Loyalist, who also accompanied General Howe. "Lord Cornwallis had sent me a guide who was a real geographical chart," Ewald commented, without naming the man. "I often spoke with him regarding the area which was beyond the horizon. His description was so good that I was often amazed at the knowledge this man possessed of the country."[41]

American patrols, both horse and foot, scoured the roads on the west side of the Brandywine above and below the Forks, looking for British activity. According to Ewald, "I had hardly marched half an hour when I ran into a warning post of the enemy," and skirmishing continued from place to place until noon.[42] Who made up this "warning post" and exactly where this skirmish occurred is not known, but reports began filtering back to Washington's headquarters that Cornwallis was marching up the Great Valley Road toward the Forks of the Brandywine.

Gen. John Sullivan, posted on the right of Washington's line, knew little if anything about what lay above his position at Brinton's Ford. "I enquired of His Excellency whether there were no Fords still higher up," he asserted, "to which, the persons who were then giving him information of the Country, replied there is none within twelve miles, the Roads leading to, & from which, are almost inaccesable." Washington issued instructions "that all the Light Horse of the Army were Ordered on the right Wing to give Information," but Sullivan claimed, almost unbelievably, "I had no Orders, or even Hints to look at any other places, but those mentiond, nor had I Light troops, or Light Horsemen furnished for the purpose." For communication, "I had but four Light Horsemen, two of which I kept at the upper Fords, to bring me Intelligence, the others I kept to send Intelligence to Head Quarters."[43]

"Washington in his Accounts to the Congress, owns He did not look for an Enemy in force" on his right, Gen. James Grant sneered, and "makes an excuse for not having prepared for & complains of his want of intelligence," adding with blistering sarcasm, "which in fact it was impossible for Him to procure unless Lord Cornwallis or I had sent it to Him."[44]

Sullivan received information about the flank march sometime during the morning from Col. Moses Hazen, who was covering fords three or more miles away. "It was ever my opinion that the enemy wou'd come round on our Right flank," Sullivan later insisted to John Hancock. "This opinion I often gave the general. I wrote him that morning that it was clearly my opinion: I sent him two messages to the same purpose in the forenoon & the very first intelligence I received, that they were actually coming that way, I instantly communicated to him."[45]

Sometime in the midmorning, one American infantry patrol from Sullivan's Division on the west side of the Brandywine came to the farm of Joel Baily, situated on a high hill overlooking Trimble's Ford on the western branch of the Brandywine, two miles above the Forks and about four miles northwest of Brinton's Ford. Baily was a well-to-do Quaker farmer, a member of Bradford Friends Meeting, who owned nearly 250 acres and a gristmill.[46] He was also one of "the great and strange people" of Chester County alluded to by Judge Peters. A self-taught mathematician and craftsman, Baily made clocks, built furniture, and occasionally did gunsmithing. He was also a surveyor and astronomer who had assisted Mason and Dixon in their famous survey ten years earlier, building levels for them and carefully recording important weather data.[47] Baily was part of a scientific team sent to observe the Transit of Venus at Cape Henlopen in 1769, for which he was elected to the American Philosophical Society.[48] Baily's first wife was a niece of the noted scientist Humphry Marshall, whose home, botanical garden, and observatory were located a mile north of Trimble's Ford on the Strasburg Road by Martin's Tavern.

The patrol was commanded by twenty-two-year-old Capt. Mountjoy Bayly of the 7th Maryland Regiment.[49] According to Captain Bayly, Joel Baily was "a namesake of his own and a zealous loyalist." He described the farmhouse as comfortable, pleasantly situated on a high hill overlooking the western branch of the Brandywine.[50] The road to Trimble's Ford passed near the dwelling, and the Baily homestead was located on the right bank of the looping, twisting Brandywine, on the side of the creek that is alternately east and south, across from James Trimble's mill and farm.

The Marylanders in Captain Bayly's patrol apparently were dressed in red uniforms, possibly old Maryland Guard coats, for according to the captain, "The hospitable old farmer mistook the Maryland company for British, and greeted them with a hearty welcome." Baily was forty-five years old, but from the captain's description, he must have appeared considerably older. The patrol was provided with a meal, "of which they freely partook, and Mountjoy kept his aged host in pleasant conversation, without in any way correcting his misapprehension."

While they were enjoying the generosity of a well-stocked Chester County farm, the front of Cornwallis's Division came into view on the Great Valley Road, a mile or so away to the south. "The advance of the British column was seen approaching, when Capt. Bayley concluded it was about time for his Marylanders to be moving. He so stated to the hospitable old farmer, who thereupon urged him to remain, assuring him that the approaching troops were certainly good friends." With quick thinking, "Capt. Bayly, however, excused himself by alleging that the duty of his company was to keep some distance ahead of the column; and so he speedily made his escape from a rather critical position."[51]

Joel Baily's alleged loyalism did not prevent his farm from being plundered. As Cornwallis's troops headed down the hill to Trimble's Ford, some of them helped themselves to the bounty of the Baily farm. Though he did manage to receive £45 from two British officers for horses, Baily lost household items and clothing to the amount of nearly £140, including four horses with their harnesses, five "fat sheep," and 300 pounds of cheese.[52]

At this point, sometime between 9 and 11 A.M., the Crown Forces began crossing the western branch of the Brandywine into West Bradford Township, where their guide Curtis Lewis lived. The fog having burned off by this time, the king's troops would have seen a beautiful landscape under bright, sunny skies as they descended the hill from Baily's house, where the Brandywine meanders from the west and loops northward around the hill to the east and south. Rolling terrain, dotted with farm buildings and mills of stone and brick and log, some bright with whitewash, and rich with emerald meadows framed by rail fences, stretched into the distance. Buxom orchards and ripening cornfields carved out of the native woodlands lay spread before them.

About 200 yards west of the ford was the Great Valley Road, which headed north to Martin's Tavern, located at an important crossroads just over a mile away up a long, lazy ridge. The tavern keeper was Joseph Martin, a sixty-year-old former Quaker, whose eighteen-year-old son, Joseph Jr., was a casualty of war. Young Joseph had joined a Pennsylvania Associator Battalion of the Flying Camp the previous year, marched off to New York, and had not been seen since. Word reached the family that he had been taken prisoner at Fort Lee in November 1776 but died on his way home, as had many others from Chester County who were taken at Forts Washington and Lee.[53]

The tavern, also called the Center House because of its location in the then-geographic center of the county, was a substantial stone building, a gathering place in this crisis for militia and county officials. Col. John Hannum, commander of the 1st Battalion of Chester County Militia, took quarters there a day or two earlier as the invasion approached. Hannum's farm lay a few miles away, along the eastern branch of the Brandywine in East Bradford Township.

With Hannum was an important county official, his very close friend and relative by marriage, forty-six-year-old Thomas Cheyney, Esq. A large landowner in Thornbury Township, nearly ten miles away to the east, Squire Cheyney was a neighbor and close friend of Lt. Col. Persifor Frazer of the 5th Pennsylvania. He served for years in a variety of county government offices. In 1777, Cheyney was a Chester County sublieutenant, whose job it was to oversee the arrangement of the newly created militia. Together with Gen. Anthony Wayne, these individuals were among Chester County's leading patriots.

Also present at the Center House during the night was Maj. Joseph Spear of the 8th Battalion of Chester County Militia, who had been commissioned earlier that week, on September 6.[54] According to General Sullivan, "Genl. Washington had sent him out for the purpose of discovering whether the enemy were in that Quarter."[55] Spear evidently left Martin's Tavern in the predawn hours and rode south on the Great Valley Road, heading toward Welch's Tavern on the Great Nottingham Road, five or so miles away from Martin's.

Several hours after Spear left the Center House, Colonel Hannum and Squire Cheyney saddled up and headed south on the Great Valley Road. Passing down the long ridge through woods, the sight that met their eyes as they approached Trimble's Mill would have brought them up short. There across the Brandywine, on the hill above Trimble's Ford, was an amber cloud of dust, kicked up by thousands of moving feet. Under the cloud were Cornwallis's troops, a steady stream of British red and Hessian blue uniforms, touched with sparkles of silver and gold glinting from musket barrels and brass plates and buckles, pouring like a slow, smoking lava flow down the hill into the creek. Closer, in the flat fields of James Trimble on the west side of the ford, were the green and red coats of Ewald's Jägers and British light troops fanning out, followed by battalion after battalion of infantry, officers on horseback, squadrons of light dragoons, ammunition wagons, and gleaming brass fieldpieces pulled by scrawny horses dripping with sweat and creek water.

Cheyney and Hannum shifted direction and rode east around some of the nearby hills, where they spotted the front of the column temporarily halted but headed toward Jefferis's Ford, a little over two miles away. At this point, so local tradition maintains, Cheyney rode off in a hell-for-leather dash to warn Washington of the flank march.

In the same vicinity was another American patrol, which later that morning got into a firefight with some light troops at the rear of the column. This patrol of about seventy skirmishers was made up mostly of riflemen armed with Pennsylvania long rifles, possibly a detachment from Dunlap's Partizan Regiment. Their commander, Lt. Col. James Ross of Lancaster, dashed off a note to Washington:

Sept. 11 '77 Great Valley Road
Eleven oclock AM—

Dear General,

A large body of the enemy from every account 5000, with 16 or 18 field pieces, marched along this road just now. This road leads to Taylor's and Jeffries ferries on the Brandywine and to the Great Valley at the Sign of the Ship on the Lancaster Road to Philadelphia. There is also a road from Brandywine to Chester by Dilworth's Tavern. We are close on their rear with about 70 men. Captain Simpson lay in ambush with 20 men, and gave them three rounds within a small distance, in which two of his men were wounded, one mortally. I believe Gen. Howe is with this party as Joseph Galloway is here known by the inhabitants with many of whom he spoke, and told them that General Howe is with him.

Yours, James Ross Lieut. Col. D. P. Regt.[56]

This message made its way to Washington by noon. All morning, the commander in chief had been out along the front lines to reconnoiter and to see and be seen by the troops. "In the beginning of the action he rode from one end to the other of the line, cheering and encouraging the men," wrote Congressman Thomas Burke of North Carolina, who was present as an observer. "The men seemed animated by his presence; they could give no other vent to their feelings but by shouts of applause, which seemed to rend the air."[57] Lafayette, who was with Washington that morning, commented, "General Washington walked the length of his two lines, and was received with acclamations that should have promised victory."[58]

But the scattered reports of enemy activity near the Forks of the Brandywine had not been confirmed. At one point, sometime in the middle of the day, having received specific information of the flank movement from someone credible, possibly Squire Cheyney, Washington sent a terse and impatient note to Col. Theodorick Bland of the 1st Continental Light Dragoons, who was on patrol above the right wing:

Chads ford 11th Septr. 1777 20 Mints. after [   ] O'Clock

Sir,

I earnestly entreat a continuance of your vigilant attention to the movements of the Enemy and the earliest report not only of their movements, but of their numbers & the course they are pursuing. In a particular manner I wish you to gain satisfactory information of a body confidently reported to have gone up to a Ford Seven or Eight miles above this; It is said this Fact is certain. You will send up an intelligent, sensible Officer immediately with a Party to find out the truth—What number It consists of and the Road they are now on. be particular in these matters.[59]

By noon, Washington was back in the center near the Chads House, where Lord Stirling had taken quarters. Aunt Betty Chads's nephew, Amos House, "who then lived with her, and superintended the business of her farm," remembered that on that morning:

Gen. Washington, with a few attendants, rode up into the field above Mrs. Chads's dwelling, and was engaged, with the aid of glasses, in reconnoitering and endeavouring to ascertain the character and position of the hostile forces on the hills west of the stream. While they were thus engaged,

Amos House and two or three others were led by curiosity to approach and observe what was going on. Pretty soon, said Mr. House, some cannon-balls from the enemy's artillery began to drop in the field quite near to the company thus collected, when Gen. Washington remarked to the visitors, "Gentlemen, you perceive that we are attracting the notice of the enemy. I think you had better retire." The hint was respectfully and promptly attended to.[60]

Washington, indeed, had been spotted by an enemy: James Parker. "The hill on which our artillery was commanded a Very fine prospect of the Rebels ground, to this place the Genls. Kniphausen & Grant came," Parker wrote. "About 12 I saw Washington Come out of A farm house. I pointed him out to the Generals; he had Some of his Officers about him with two White flags." Ross's message, written at 11 that morning, had just arrived; Parker commented, "I was afterwards told by a Rebel, it was just at that time he got intelligence that Genl. Howe was crossing the B. Wine above him."

The bitterness of the civil war aspect of the War of Independence raged in full fury on a personal level at that moment. As a Virginian who had lost everything—his beautiful and valuable home in Norfolk destroyed, his business ruined, his wife and children left destitute and forced into charity—and having suffered months of harsh imprisonment, James Parker had no qualms about trying to kill George Washington. "I had in short enough to get a Canon fired at the Group," Parker told his friend Steuart, venomously adding, "my prayers went with the ball that it might finish Washington & the Rebelion together."[61]

Having received Ross's message, Washington decided on a bold strategy. He would send Sullivan across at Brinton's Ford to hit von Knyphausen's left, while Greene took his division and Maxwell's Light Corps across at Chads's Ferry and Ford to hit the Hessian general's center and right. With luck, he would crush one major part of Howe's army while the forces were separated and, for once, turn the tables on Howe.

"The Genl. sent me word to cross the Brandewine with my Division & attack the enemy's left while the army crossed below me to attack their Right," Sullivan stated.[62] The opportunity was too much to pass up. "It was satisfactorily concluded that only a part of the enemy's army was on the other side at Chads' Ford; and in consequence, preparations were made for attacking it," Colonel Pickering recalled. "Sullivan as well as Greene, was to cross over & attack, with the whole Army in two columns."[63]

The critical moment had arrived: "I think it was about eleven or twelve o'clock when General Greene was prepared with a division to cross over and attack the enemy at the ford," Timothy Pickering noted.[64] Washington was about to launch the main Continental Army's first major offensive of the war against the main British Army in the field.

Sullivan's advance guard went across at Brinton's Ford. "Colonel Ramsay, of the Maryland line, crossed the river, and skirmished with and drove the Yagers," wrote Lt. Col. Samuel Smith of the 4th Maryland Regiment in DeBorre's Brigade, mistaking Ferguson's green-clad English riflemen for Germans. "General Washington had determined to cross the river, and destroy that Division of the enemy; and every Regiment had been prepared to pass over."[65] A Hessian report confirmed, "Meanwhile the enemy caused a number of their troops belonging to the right wing to cross the river at Edwardsmill [Edward Brinton's Mill, at the ford] and advance." Greene's Division formed up "and showed signs of occupying the hills on this side of the river behind the morass with more troops," while Maxwell's Light Infantry "reinforced their outposts, who were standing in the woods that extended to the foot of these heights, so as to dispute the passage of the morass." To stop the American advance, "General Knyphausen ordered the Queen's Rangers to cross same, and attack the enemy in the wood on the other side of it."

A sharp light infantry skirmish erupted as Greene prepared to cross the creek. According to the Hessian report, Maxwell's force, "who consisted of nothing but sharpshooters, killed and wounded many of our men, but withdrew to the woods in the direction of Chatsesfort on this side of the Brandewyn when these advanced with levelled gun [charged bayonets] and the English Jägers [Ferguson's Riflemen] approached their left flank. In the meantime all the regiments had to cross the morass, the 4th and 5th Regiments had to march towards the passage across the Brandewyn river, so as to dislodge the enemy who were posted on this side of same and chase them across the water." Artillery fire from both sides erupted in support, "so as to cannonade the batteries on the other side of the river and keep the enemy away from the banks."[66]

About this same time, as Sullivan's troops were beginning to cross Brinton's Ford and skirmishing had begun, Maj. Joseph Spear arrived and reported to Sullivan that he had gone from Martin's Tavern all the way to Welch's Tavern, and through the intervening countryside, but did not encounter any British forces on the roads in or near the Forks of the Brandywine. "The account was confirmed by a Serjeant Tucker of the L. Horse," Sullivan revealed, "sent by me on purpose to make discoveries & had passed on as he said to Lancaster road [probably the Strasburg Road]." Still convinced that Howe was going to swing around the right, Sullivan continued: "This intelligence did by no means alter my opinion which was founded not upon any knowledge I had of the facts but upon an apprehension that Genl. Howe would take that advantage which any good officer in his situation would have done."[67] The general felt it was his duty to report all information received, regardless of his personal interpretation. "I therefore set down & wrote Major Spear's account, from his own mouth & forwarded it to His Excellency by a Light Horseman & order'd the major to follow himself."[68] Sullivan sent this fateful message to the commander in chief:

> Brintons Ford Sepr 11th 1777
>
> Dr. General
>
> Since I sent you the message by Major Morris I Saw Major Joseph Spear of the Militia who Came last night from This morning from a Tavern Called Martins on the Forks of the Brandywine—he came from thence to Welches Tavern & heard nothing of the Enemy about the Forks of the Brandywine & is Confident they are not in that Quarter So that Colo Hazens Information must be wrong. I have sent to that Quarter to know whether there is any foundation for the Report & shall give yr. Excy. the Earliest Information.[69]

How Spear managed this can be partly explained by timing: He must have passed down these roads before Cornwallis and von Knyphausen began their marches at 5 A.M. The words "last night from," crossed out and changed "to this morning," imply that the major left Martin's Center House before dawn. Where he was and what he was doing between the time he arrived at Welch's Tavern, which had to have been before 6 A.M., when von Knyphausen began his advance, and the time he made his report to Sullivan at Brinton's Ford, which would have been between noon and 1 P.M., are unknown.

Suggestions of treachery on the major's part, made many years later, were speculative and unfounded. At the same time, with all of the troop movements, patrols, and firing that morning, it is difficult to reconcile Spear's whereabouts during the intervening six hours or more. He must have been very slow, dallying somewhere, or thorough to a fault, investigating byways and side paths. The area he passed through has numerous lanes, woods, parallel roads, and abrupt hills; this was the terrain that Cornwallis used to screen his march, and it was well chosen. Concerning Spear's reliability, Washington commented afterward that "the Major's rank, reputation and knowledge of the Country, gave him a full claim to credit and attention."[70]

On receiving Spear's information, Washington hesitated, fearing that the reported maneuver was a feint to draw him across the Brandywine. It was possible that Howe was setting up a trap similar to the one a few months earlier at Short Hills: lure him out of his position in the high ground, then turn and catch him in a pincer movement. The commander in chief sent orders to Sullivan to pull back, confirm the reports, and wait for intelligence from Col. Theodorick Bland.

Sullivan's advance guard broke off the engagement and fell back across the creek, as did Maxwell; Greene never did cross the Brandywine. All Continental forces were now on the eastern side. "The enemy were driven from a very difficult neighbourhood with much trouble and a loss of brave men, but only into the road leading to the fort [ford] beyond Edwardsmill," a Hessian report confirmed. "As they had thus been entirely dislodged from this side of the Brandewyn, General von Knyphausen ordered his column to halt according to previous arrangement, until he could get news of the attack made by General Howe."[71]

Howe and the main body of the Crown Forces continued to move slowly and steadily through the Forks of the Brandywine. About noon, Ewald and the advance guard approached Jefferis's Ford. Surprised to find it unguarded, he crossed and then paused at the bottom of a long notch or defile between two high hills. A narrow road twisted its way to the top through the woods between the hills. Lord Cornwallis came to the head of the column, and Ewald expressed concern that it would be the perfect spot for an ambush.

A dozen Jägers fanned out and moved slowly up the road in pairs, carefully spacing themselves, fully prepared to react in case of attack. Ewald himself passed through "this terrible defile, which was over a thousand paces long," and could not believe that it was left unguarded. Cornwallis himself followed and was astonished that the patrol they had skirmished with earlier was not posted here. Ewald felt that "a hundred men could have held up either army the whole day."[72]

At the top of this high hill, a little over half a mile by foot from the ford, was a small hamlet called Sconneltown, consisting of nothing more than a wheelwright shop and a few houses. The road from the ford headed south to Birmingham Meeting House, three miles away. Another road turned left toward the Turk's Head Tavern, a few miles east.

Here at the wheelwright shop, the Birmingham Friends were holding their midweek meeting, because American forces had taken over their meetinghouse for use as a hospital. Joseph Townsend, a member of Birmingham Meeting, confirmed that "a considerable number of the soldiers were sick, in consequence of their long marches through the excessive heat of that season of the year."[73]

Townsend recalled that the meeting in the wheelwright shop was interrupted by a disturbance outside. Several members went out to see what the commotion was about; when they did not return, "suspicion arose that something serious had taken place," and the meeting ended. Townsend went out and "found it to be an alarm amongst some of our neighboring women that the English Army was coming and they murdered all before them—young and old." As Townsend and others calmed the women down, their "eyes were caught on a sudden by the appearance of the army coming out of the woods into the fields belonging to Emmor Jefferis on the west side of the Creek above the fording place." From the height at Sconneltown, the Friends could see the front of Cornwallis's column. "In a few minutes the fields were literally covered over with them, and they were hastening towards us. Their arms and bayonets being raised, shone as bright as silver, being a clear sky and the day exceeding warm."[74]

The visual impact of this force would have been spellbinding for the local people. Rural Pennsylvanians at that time generally dressed in drab colors, especially the Quakers, who favored plain clothing in shades of gray or brown. Except for those who had been to Yearly Meetings or market in Philadelphia, most country folks had never seen more than a few hundred people gathered in any one place. Here, coming across Jefferis's

Ford, was an extraordinary spectacle of martial pomp and arrogance, the very antithesis of Quaker culture—thousands of proud, combat-ready soldiers dressed in colorful uniforms and carrying gleaming weapons. Even with colors faded by the sun or washed out by rain, and despite the sweat and dust from marching, the British and Hessian troops were dazzling: Ewald and his Jägers at the head of the column, in green coats faced red, with brass buttons; McPherson and his Royal Highlanders in short red jackets and canvas trews (trousers), each sporting a "Kilmarnock" Highland bonnet, a dark blue tam topped with a red "touri," or pompom, above a wide headband bearing three rows of red, white, and green checkers, with one or two black ostrich plumes bobbing over the top. Behind them, acres and acres of British light infantrymen in short red jackets and plumed round hats, followed by leather-helmeted dragoons and shining brass artillery in the distance. And this was merely the front of the column.

The Birmingham Friends dispersed. Townsend, who lived up the road toward Turk's Head, immediately went home. With his parents away and his sisters home alone, he feared that the house might be plundered, or worse. But when no troops showed up, his curiosity got the better of him and he went back to Sconneltown, where he found the British Army marching south toward Birmingham.

Ewald and the advance guard had moved ahead, and just under a mile down the road, they came to Strode's Mill in a small valley. Cornwallis once again ordered him to halt while the army came up the defile from the ford, regiment by regiment, an operation that would take nearly two hours. "After crossing the second Branch of the Brandywine the Van of the Army halted upon the Heights on this side until the Rear came up," Capt. Archibald Robertson of the Engineers noted. "It then moved on in three Columns—The centre Column composed of the Jägers, two Battalions of Light Infantry," followed by the grenadiers, "two Battalions British and three Battalions of Hessian Grenadiers in the Road." About 400 yards to the west of the road, "the Brigade of Guards and 16th Regiment of light Dragoons formed the right Column," and to the east, "the 4th Brigade British the left Column, about 400 Yards distant on each side of the Road," with flankers fanned out hundreds of yards beyond the right and left columns. Behind this, "the third Brigade British formed the Reserve and moved along the Road in the Rear."[75] Townsend noted that "the space occupied by the nearer body and the flanking parties was near a mile and a half wide."[76]

"The regular march of the British army consisted of horse and foot, artillery, baggage, provision wagons, arms and ammunition, together with a host of plunderers and rabble that accompanied the army. . . . Their passing took nearly four hours." As the troops descended into the valley at Strode's Mill, Townsend and his brother began to approach the flanking party. "A soldier under arms cried out, 'Where are you going?' We replied, 'We wished to see the army &c. if there was no objection.' He observed, 'There was their Captain, we might speak to him.'"

The captain gave permission, and Joseph with several others were permitted to wander among the troops, where they found "little to be discovered but staff officers and a continued march of soldiers and occasionally a troop of horse passing—Great numbers of baggage wagons began to make their appearance, well guarded by proper officers and soldiers." Here the army stopped to rest; half a mile ahead on the far side of the valley was Osborne's Hill, one of the highest points in the area.

The view from the top of Osborne's Hill is commanding and spectacular; Townsend recalled that a British officer told him "with some rapture that 'you have got a hell of a fine country here which we have found to be the case ever since we landed at the head of the Elk.'" To the west, Brandywine Creek meandered one or two miles away on the British right. Buffington's and Wistar's Fords, where Hazen's two battalions were posted, were now behind the British right flank and nearly cut off. A mile ahead to the south was the Street Road, running east-west through several townships and crossing the Brandywine at Jones's Ford, where Hall's Delaware Regiment held ground. Several hundred yards beyond the Street Road on an open rise was Birmingham Friends Meeting House, a small, one-story fieldstone building flanked by trees, its adjoining burying ground surrounded by a stone wall about chest-high. The meetinghouse was occupied as a hospital by the commissaries and "those who had the charge of the disordered persons," meaning Continental hospital personnel.[77]

Troopers from the 1st Continental Light Dragoons, commanded by thirty-five-year-old Col. Theodorick Bland of Virginia, were also in the area, looking for British activity. Just after 1 P.M., they spotted Ewald's patrol on Osborne's Hill. Bland immediately sent a message to Washington at "1/4 past one oClock. . . . I have discovered a party of the Enemy on the heights just on the Right of two Widow Davis's who live close together on the Road calld the forks road, about half a mile to the Right of the Meeting house (Birmingham). There is a higher Hill to their front."[78]

The message was carried as quickly as possible to headquarters, four miles away down steep, winding roads. Bland also sent a message to Sullivan, three country miles away from Birmingham in another direction. Sullivan, who had been waiting to hear from the Virginia cavalryman, received the note at 2 P.M. and immediately scribbled to Washington, "Colo. Bland has this moment Sent Me word that the Enemy are in the Rear of My Right about two miles Coming Down—there is he Says about two Brigades of them." An ominous postscript warned, "He also Says he Saw a Dust Rise back in the Country for above an hour."[79]

Washington had been up since before dawn and out along the front all morning, and he and his staff had returned to headquarters at the Ring House around 1 P.M. for dinner. Bland's note arrived "about two o'clock," Pickering recalled. "I remember we had just dined at Head Quarters, & briskly started from thence."[80] Washington immediately ordered Stirling and Stephen to take their divisions, which were in reserve near headquarters, and head toward Birmingham. He also sent a message to Sullivan, ordering him to move in the same direction, rendezvous with Stirling and Stephen, and take command of the entire right wing.

The terrain in the area immediately north and east of Chads's Ford is exceptionally craggy and convoluted, with steep, thickly wooded hills and deep ravines; the roads are few and tortuous. There was no direct route north, nor was there any direct route between Sullivan and the other two divisions. Coordination of the American right wing was going to be on the fly.

About 1,500 New Jersey and Pennsylvania Continentals in Stirling's Division, along with artillery and dozens of ammunition wagons, quickly moved up a narrow, winding road toward Birmingham via the crossroads village of Dilworth, located on a plateau three miles away. Behind them were another 1,500 or so Virginians in Scott's and Woodford's brigades of Stephen's Division, choking on the dust cloud raised on this very warm and muggy afternoon. In addition to their muskets and accoutrements, including forty rounds of ammunition, the troops were also carrying blankets and knapsacks on their backs, a total of about sixty pounds of equipment per man. The rapid march and steep climb would have left them gasping by the time they reached Dilworth, a crossroads hamlet of a dozen buildings mostly built of stone, clustered at an important five-points intersection near a substantial brick tavern, Charles Dilworth's Sign of the Pennsylvania Farmer.

At the crossroads, the troops moved left on the road to Birmingham Meeting and the Forks of the Brandywine, heading west for another mile over gently rolling terrain interspersed with tall stands of old-growth trees and farm fields, some freshly plowed. The road meanders down through an area called Sandy Hollow, abruptly swings southwest for 200 yards, and just as quickly turns right at a Y intersection, where it heads northwest and then north past Birmingham Friends toward Osborne's Hill, nearly two miles away.

From Osborne's Hill, "the Enemy were observed at Birmingham Meeting, but moving and unsettled," noted Captain Robertson of the British Engineers.[81] A British Light Infantry officer wrote, "The Light Infy. having gain'd the Heights were order'd to halt & the different Corps doubled up waiting for the Rear." He noticed that "during this sev'ral Rebel Officers came to Reconnoitre, & from the Columns of Dust their Army was perceiv'd to be at no great Distance but from the Woods & the uneaveness of Ground in the Front it was not easy to conjecture of their Intentions."[82] The dust proved to be an effective indicator of large-scale troop movements for both sides that day.

Stirling placed his division on open, commanding ground half a mile south of Birmingham Meeting, extending southwest from the Y about 800 yards along a partially wooded ridge. Adam Stephen formed his division on Stirling's right along the Birmingham Road, extending back through woods toward Sandy Hollow. Five light fieldpieces, 3- and 4-pounders, were positioned on an open knoll in the center of the two divisions about 200 yards south of the Y, aimed up the road toward the meetinghouse. "They formed two lines in good order along their heights," von Münchhausen observed from Osborne's Hill. "We could see this because there were some barren places here and there on the hills, which they occupied."[83]

Meanwhile, at Brinton's Ford, "at half past Two I Received orders to march with my Division," Sullivan recalled, "to Join & take Command of that & Two others to oppose the Enemy who were coming Down on the Right flank of our army." Moving north along the left bank of the Brandywine, the Marylanders had to clamber up and down craggy hills through woods and thickets, across marshy creek bottoms, over meadows and cornfields, and along dusty farm lanes, hoping to find not only Stirling and Stephen, but the other half of their division, Hazen's, and the Delaware Regiment, as well. "I neither knew where the Enemy were or what Rout[e] the other Two Divisions were to take," Sullivan complained, "& of course could not Determine where I Should form a Junction with them."[84]

The 4,000 or so American troops moving to stop Cornwallis's 8,000 were going to have to blunder into him—and each other.

Much of this activity was visible from the British positions across the Brandywine between Brinton's and Chads's Ford. "At 2 o'Clock great Movements were observed in the Ennemy's Position on the opposite Side of the Creek," von Knyphausen reported. From Sullivan's Division, he saw that "four Battalions with Artillery from their Right filed off, to where the Attack to the left of our Army was to be made." Behind Chads's Ford, the Hessian commander could also see Stirling and Stephen heading out, for "the Road to Chester was covered with Waggons going this Way & that Way."[85]

The weakening of Washington's front did not go unnoticed. "We saw several battalions, some artillery, and some troops of dragoons file to the right to reinforce their right wing," Major Baurmeister observed, "and other changes in the line being made to give the necessary defensive strength to their left wing, which had been weakened by the removal of some of these troops."[86]

Back on the north side of Osborne's Hill, out of sight from Birmingham Hill, Cornwallis's force had halted to rest and eat. It was absolutely necessary; the column had been on the march for nearly eight hours, covering about twelve miles, and had forded the Brandywine twice, where "the men had to cross these two branches in up to three feet of water." Each crossing took two or more hours to complete.[87] The troops were "both sultry and dusty and rather fatigued, many remaining along the road on that account," according to Montrésor.[88] "Some of our best men were obliged to yield," Lieutenant Cliffe told his brother, "one of the 33rd droped dead."[89]

Heat was not the only problem for some of the troops. "Our rum too failed some days before the action," Lieutenant Hale of the 2nd Grenadier Battalion groaned, "and the quality of the different waters we were obliged to drink gave me the bloody flux, by which I was so weakened as to faint twice in the morning of the affair." His thoughtful battalion commander came to the rescue: "However I recovered strength sufficient to go through the fatigue of the afternoon, Col. Monckton supplied me with claret, in which I mixed Ipecacuanha and Rhubarb, a never failing medicine."[90]

The British commander in chief was thoughtful, too. "Sir Wm. Howe with a most Cheerful Countenance convers'd with his Officers & envited sev'ral to a slight refreshment provided on the Grass," wrote one officer. "The pleasing Behavior of that great Man on this Occasion had a great Effect on the Minds of all who beheld him." Even the best troops, knowing that they were heading into battle, were nervous and looked to their leaders for example. "Evry One that remembers the anxious Moments before an Engagement may conceive how animating the sight of the Commander in Chief in whose Looks nothing but Serenity & Confidence in his Troops is painted; in short, the Army reasum'd their March in full assurance of Success & Victory."[91]

About 3 P.M., Cornwallis's aide-de-camp, Capt. Alexander Ross, came to Ewald carrying orders to proceed. The advance guard headed down the south slope of Osborne's Hill on the road toward Birmingham Meeting. A mile ahead was the Street Road, beyond which, Ewald recalled, "about half past three, I caught sight of some infantry and horsemen behind a village on a hill in the distance, which was formed like an amphitheatre."[92] A Hessian Corps report chronicled the arrival and deployment of Stirling and Stephen: "The enemy had a body of about 1000 men standing on the hill on the other side of the Meetinghouse. A numerous body of Light cavalry appeared on their left, and soon after that a body of infantry consisting of about 2000 men with 5 guns, who joined the men on the hill; several battalions were also observed, who marched to the woods on the right and left, and uniting themselves with the above 3000 men presented a formidable front."[93]

After consulting with the senior British captain, McPherson of the 42nd, as well as Captain Scott of the 17th, Ewald deployed his foot Jägers in skirmish order out in front and on the flanks, with the 17th

Light Company on the left and the Royal Highlanders on the right. Lieutenant Hagen's mounted Jägers remained on the road in the center.

Ahead to the left, southeast of the Street Road and Birmingham Road, was a red brick farmhouse and several orchards owned by Samuel Jones. Beyond it was Birmingham Meeting House, near a few houses and farm buildings which Ewald mistakenly referred to as "the village of East Bradford." Adjacent to the building in front was the burial yard, an acre or so of open ground surrounded by a good stone wall about three feet high, extending to the road. There were no gravestones; the Friends considered them monuments to vanity, so the yard was empty, save for rows of slight mounds and depressions in the ground where the remains of early English and Welsh Quakers lay.

American light troops and dragoons were deployed in this area. As an advance guard, Col. Thomas Marshall's 3rd Virginia Regiment in Stephen's Division was sent forward to the meetinghouse from the far-right flank of the line. The 3rd Virginia took up positions behind the graveyard wall, with skirmishers down the hill near Jones's orchard at the corner of the Street Road and Birmingham Road. "The third regiment stood pre-eminent, part of Woodford's Brigade," Capt. Henry "Light-Horse Harry" Lee of Bland's Dragoons later wrote. "It occupied the right of the American line, and being advanced to a small eminence some little distance in the front, for the purpose of holding safe that flank, it received the first shock of the foe." Barely numbering 200, "the regiment, having been much reduced by previous service, did not amount to more than a battalion; but one field officer, the colonel, and four captains were with it."[94]

As the British advance guard approached, "Capt. Ewalt proposed charging a party of dragoons on the road, provided we secured his left flank," an officer of the 17th Light Company recounted. "This was assented to, and the two companies quitted the road for this purpose to gain an orchard on the flank," when they "received a fire from about 200 men in the orchard, which did no execution," at least among the British.[95] Two Jägers were hit. Ewald stated, "I reached the first houses of the village with the flankers of the jägers, and Lieutenant Hagen followed me with the horsemen. But unfortunately for us, the time this took favored the enemy and I received extremely heavy small-arms fire from the gardens and houses, through which, however, only two jägers were wounded. Everyone ran back, and I formed them again behind the fences and walls" along the Street Road "at a distance of two hundred paces from the village."[96] From behind, the British light companies "run up to the fence and halted, as it was evident tho' the enemy fell back they were well supported."[97]

Having advanced too far too fast, Ewald found himself unsupported, as had happened at Boundbrook the previous April. The Jägers and light bobs took cover below the fence along the Street Road embankment. "They shouted to me that the army was far behind, and I became not a little embarrassed to find myself quite alone with the advanced guard," the intrepid captain confessed. "But now that the business had begun, I still wanted to obtain information about these people who had let me go so easily."

Ewald decided to swing wide to the right and, out of range, reconnoiter a large hill that lay several hundred yards to the southwest. Taking two Highlanders and a mounted Jäger named Hoffman, "a very courageous fellow," he crossed the rolling, open fields and ascended the height. Over the crest, Ewald made a remarkable discovery. "I gazed in astonishment when I got up the hill," the one-eyed marksman recalled, "for I found behind it—three or four hundred paces away—an entire line deployed in the best order." It was the New Jersey and Pennsylvania troops of Stirling's Division, "several of whom waved to me with their hats but did not shoot." The Hessian captain remarked, "I kept composed, examined them closely, rode back, and reported it at once to Lord Cornwallis by the jäger Hoffman."

Circling back toward the advance guard, Ewald "crossed a road that led to the right through a light wood." This was the Street Road west of Birmingham. "I told a Scot to follow this road for a few hundred paces," toward Jones's Ford, just under a mile away. "I rode after him," Ewald continued and, looking northwest, "caught sight of a whole enemy column with guns marching through the valley in which Lord Cornwallis's column had been marching for some time, a quarter or half an hour [about a mile] away to the right."[98] These troops were Hazen's two battalions, now outflanked and nearly cut off by Cornwallis, pulling back from Wistar's and Buffington's Fords to rejoin the Delaware Regiment straight ahead at Jones's Ford.

At that same moment, coming up from Brinton's Ford to the south, the rest of Sullivan's Division arrived at the Street Road. "I began my march in five minutes after I Received my orders," Sullivan told John Hancock, "& had not marched a mile when I met Colo. Hazen with his Regiment which had been Stationed at a Ford three miles above me who Informed that the Enemy were Close upon his Heels & that I might Depend that the principal part of the British army were there." Sullivan complimented Hazen, a tough old French and Indian War veteran, for his observations: "Altho I knew the Reports Sent to head Quarters made them but two Brigades as I knew Colo. Hazen to be an old officer & a good Judge of Numbers I gave Credence to his Report in preference to the Intelligence before Received."

Then Sullivan spotted Ewald and the Highlanders. "While I was Conversing with Colo. Hazen & our Troops Still upon their march, the Enemy headed us in the Road about forty Rods [220 yards] from our advance Guard." He ordered his division off the road. "I then found it necessary to turn off to the Right to form & to get nearer to the other two Divisions which I that moment Discovered Drawn up on an Eminence both in the Rear & to the Right of the place I was then at."[99] Sullivan directed his division to move toward the front of the hill Ewald had just descended.

"Had I the battalion with me, I would have cut off this column," Ewald commented wistfully. Instead, "I rode back to my detachment and reported this event."[100] Lt. Col. Ludwig von Wurmb, commander of the Jäger Corps, told his superiors in Kassel that "Captain Ewald of the advance guard reported the enemy was approaching and they were forming up on a hilltop and that another column was approaching on the right." Ewald's report was sent to Lord Cornwallis, who was back on Osborne's Hill with General Howe. As soon as His Lordship received it, "Then the order was received to form the line."[101]

"He was on horseback, appeared tall and sat very erect," is how Joseph Townsend remembered Cornwallis, seeing him pass by earlier that afternoon. "His rich scarlet clothing loaded with gold lace, epaulettes &c occasioned him to make a brilliant and martial appearance." Now, as Townsend and some of his friends were wandering among the troops behind Osborne's Hill, he noticed a sudden stir: "They were resuming their march and the halt that they had made was only to refresh the horses."

Together with James Johnson, another local Quaker, Townsend "proceeded through the crowd on the public road untill [they] reached the advanced guard, who were of the German troops." The Hessian and Anspach Jägers were moving up the north face of Osborne's Hill toward the top, and Townsend was struck by a peculiar feature that often startled and frightened people when first seeing German soldiers: Many of them "wore their beard on their upper lips."[102] Most men in the English world of the late eighteenth century were clean-shaven, as were British troops. European armies followed different rules; the Hessians and many other German forces modeled themselves—uniforms, drill, maneuvers—after the Prussian Army. Like the Prussians, the Hessian grenadiers all wore stiff, blackened mustaches waxed into sharp points with "blackball" paste, giving them a uniform and sinister look. Among other German soldiers, such as the Jägers, it seems to have been left to personal preference, as Townsend observed.

Cornwallis's force now began moving into position. "At four in the afternoon our two battalions of light infantry and the Hessian jägers marched down the hill" on the Birmingham Road. "They marched first in a column, but later, when they approached the enemy, in line formation, deploying to the left," von Münchhausen reported. Behind the light troops, "soon after this the English grenadiers did the same in the center, almost at the same time." About 400 yards to the right of the road, "just a little later, the English Guards formed the right wing." In support of the front line, "behind the English grenadiers were the Hessian grenadiers; behind the light infantry and the jägers was the 4th English brigade. The 3rd English brigade was in reserve on top of the hill." Near Howe, who was observing from the top of Osborne's Hill, were the 16th Queen's Light Dragoons. "The two squadrons of dragoons, who were close to us," von Münchhausen stated, "halted behind the left wing of the Hessian grenadiers."[103]

After descending the hill, the light troops continued up the road in a column. Halfway to the Street Road, the Jägers swung to the left and headed about 800 yards east into broken, wooded terrain. With them were "two English 3-pounders," light cannons known as "grasshoppers," "which were covered by the Hessian Jäger Lieutenant Balthasar Mertz with thirty grenadiers." There were also two amusettes, large, heavy muskets capable of lobbing 1-inch balls several hundred yards. "The Jäger Corps had the honor to man the extreme left wing and consisted, after the departure of the detachments under Captain Ewald and the cavalry, which because of the difficult terrain could not follow us, to something over 300 men."[104]

The 1,300 troops in the two British light infantry battalions followed the Jägers and moved quickly into the area just east of the Birmingham Road. The fourteen companies of Maj. John Maitland's 2nd Light Infantry Battalion deployed on the right of the Jägers in some woods and open fields a few hundred yards out, while Lt. Col. Robert Abercromby's 1st Light Infantry Battalion, also fourteen companies, formed in the fenced fields along the road, their right flank resting on the road itself. On the hill behind them in support were the four regular regiments of Gen. James Agnew's 4th British Brigade, another 1,500 troops.

The light bobs were arranged in files four men deep, with arm's-length intervals between them. From this formation, the troops could quickly move into "extended order," from five to fifty yards apart. This permitted the great flexibility that was the hallmark of light infantry tactics and enabled the men to spread out and take cover rapidly as the situation required, for, as one light infantry officer put it, "in danger men like all animals croud together."[105]

As the light troops were moving into position on the left, the two British grenadier battalions, about 1,400 men, came down the hill on the Birmingham Road and began deploying to the right of the road, forming the center of Cornwallis's line. Lt. Col. William Medows's 1st Battalion of sixteen companies swung to the right and headed across fields and fences a few hundred yards west of the road, while the fifteen companies in the 2nd Battalion under Col. Henry Monckton took up their initial position in a line less than 100 yards behind Medows, forming a "column of battalions," with the Birmingham Road on their left.

About 400 yards west of the road, Gen. Edward Mathew's brigade of Guards came over Osborne's Hill in a column 1,000 strong to take the position of honor, the right flank. The 1st Guards Battalion swung to the right and deployed, while the 2nd Battalion fell in on their left, next to Monckton and Medows. Like the light infantry on the left, the Guards were advanced about 200 yards ahead of the grenadier battalions. The Guards Light Company fanned along the front, while the Guards Grenadier Company held the most prestigious position in line, "the right of the right." Both flank companies were commanded by Sir George Osborn.[106]

The scene was spellbinding. "Being now in front of the army we walked inconsiderately," Joseph Townsend remarked, as he and Johnson went into a field to the left, southeast of the Birmingham Road, about halfway between Osborne's Hill and the Street Road. "On turning our faces back we had a grand view of the army as they advanced over and down the south side of Osborns Hill and the lands of James Carter, scarce a vacant place left."[107] From the Birmingham Road west, Cornwallis's front was half a mile wide—and that was only half of his first line. Brigade artillery, ammunition wagons, officers and their aides on horseback—"almost the whole face of the country around appeared to be covered and alive with these objects."

"While we were amusing ourselves with the wonderful curiosity before us," Townsend recalled, "to our great astonishment and surprise the firing of the musketry took place."[108] Ahead, Ewald and the advance guard were still deployed at Jones's orchard and could see the army forming up behind them. It was now approaching 4:30, nearly forty-five minutes since he had first skirmished with the 3rd Virginia. The waiting was unbearable, and with enemy skirmishers only a few yards away, Ewald took matters into his own hands. "As soon as the army had drawn near to me by three or four hundred paces, and I received no orders," he admitted, "I attacked the village and the church on the hill."[109]

"The advance-guard . . . having arrived at the Street Road . . . [was] fired upon by a Company of Americans who were stationed in the orchard north of Samuel Jones' dwelling house," Townsend observed from several hundred yards away, well out of musket range. Using classic light tactics, "the attack was immediately returned by the Hessians by their slipping up the bank of the road, along side of the orchard, and using the fences as a breastwork through which they fired upon the Company who commenced the attack."[110] This maneuver allowed the Jägers move up the embankment along the Birmingham Road and outflank the Virginians, hitting them on their left.

Overwhelmed by the sheer spectacle unfolding around him, Townsend confessed, "From the distance we were from them (though in full view untill the smoke of the firing covered them from our sight) I was under no apprehension of danger especially when there was such a tremendous force coming on and ready to engage in the action." But he and his friends were directly in the path of the main body of Jägers and light infantry, who were still forming. Common sense finally took hold of Townsend: "Finding that my curiosity had exceeded the bounds of prudence," he said, he made his way back toward the Birmingham Road. There, he "was met by several companies of soldiers" from the main force of light troops "who were ordered into the fields to form and prepare for the approaching engagement." As he came to the road, "a German officer ordered the fence to be taken down." Townsend wrote, "As I was nearest the spot I had to [be] subject to his orders, as he flourished a drawn sword over my head with others who stood nearby."[111]

As he was removing the rails, the young Quaker suddenly realized that his taking down the fence might be a violation of the Friends' testimony against active participation in war. Fortunately for Townsend, "as the hurry was great and the rushing forward of so many men under arms, [he] found no difficulty in retiring undiscovered and was soon out of reach of those called immediately into action."[112] The "rushing forward" described by Townsend was how light troops, in squads and companies, moved into action—at a trot.

Across the road and back toward Osborne's Hill, the regular British troops formed for battle in what was called "open order": two ranks deep, with the files spaced at arm's length from each other, rather than shoulder to shoulder. A year earlier, as the New York Campaign was about to begin, Howe announced in the General Orders that "the Infantry of the Army without exception are ordered upon all occasions to form two Deep, with the Files at 18 inches Interval till further Orders."[113] Colonel von Donop confirmed that this was still in effect when he wrote to the prince of Prussia on September 2, 1777, less than two weeks before Brandywine: "I hope . . . that we—(I mean the English)—may be a bit more closely drawn together for the attack. For unless we are, I cannot yet reassure myself that infantry with its files four feet apart can capture intrenchments by escalade, or hold its ground against cavalry."[114]

The three Hessian grenadier battalions—von Minnegerode, von Lengerke, and von Linsing—1,300 blue-clad troops wearing tall, gleaming brass or tin mitre caps, all under von Donop's command, were drawn up in support behind the Guards and British grenadiers. "We occupied a height in the Brandywine Mountains, and made a short halt towards three o'clock," stated a von Minnegerode Battalion report. "Then we moved on and after going about a mile we had to march forward with all possible dispatch, advance abreast in 2 divisions, and after we had passed through a wood and come out upon a height; the English Guards which formed the right wing . . . were supported by the Minnigerode Battalion in the 2nd line."[115] The von Lengerke battalion was positioned in the center of the Hessian line, with the left held by von Linsing.

The Hessian grenadiers continued using their traditional, Prussian-based tactics and troop formations—the same methodical slowness that Cresswell had observed a few months earlier in New York—and their maddeningly slow marching step.[116] "At Brandywine, when the first line formed, the Hessian Grenadiers were close in our rear, and began beating their march at the same time with us," Lieutenant Hale of the 2nd Grenadier Battalion wrote. "From that minute we saw them no more till the action was over, and only one man of them was wounded by a random shot which came over us." He smugly added, "They themselves make no scruple of owning our superiority over them, but palliate so mortifying a confession by saying 'Englishmen be the Divel for going on, but Hesse men be soldier.'"[117] A Hessian report confirmed Hale's observations about few Hessian casualties, but for different reasons: "The 3 battalions of Grenadiers have suffered little on this occasion, as they could not get a chance of firing on account of the enemy fleeing," conveniently neglecting to mention that rapidly advancing British bayonets had caused the Americans to flee.[118]

Regarding Hessian maneuvers, Hale told his parents, "I believe them steady, but their slowness is of the greatest disadvantage in a country almost covered with woods, and against an Enemy whose chief qualification is agility in running from fence to fence and thence keeping up an irregular but galling fire on troops who advance at the same pace as at their exercise." In the British forces, by contrast, "Light Infantry accustomed to fight from tree to tree, or charge even in the woods; and Grenadiers who after the first fire lose no time in loading again, but rush on, trusting entirely to that most decisive of weapons the bayonet; will ever be superior to any troops the Rebels can ever bring against them." Hale concluded by saying, "Such are the British, and such the method of fighting which has been attended with constant success."[119]

The British were about to once again demonstrate their successful method of adaptive tactics based on speed, use of the bayonet, and taking cover when necessary. Having learned much from Lexington and Concord and Breed's Hill in 1775, they modified their approach in the New York Campaign, with excellent results: tactical superiority and minimal casualties, as demonstrated at the Battle of Long Island on August 27, 1776. A few weeks later, as the British prepared to land on Manhattan, the General Orders stated, "The Soldiers are reminded of their evident Superiority on the 27th of August last, by charging the Rebels with Bayonets even in the Woods, where they thought themselves invincible." The American positions "are to be carried with little Loss by the same high spirited mode of Attack; the General therefore recommends to the Troops an intire Dependence on their Bayonets, with which they will always command that success their Bravery so well deserves."[120]

The serious discrepancies between American reports of tremendous British casualties at Brandywine and the small numbers officially reported may be partially explained by the actual tactics used by the British Army at this stage in the American war, which are largely misunderstood and repeatedly misrepresented in popular history. Lt. Loftus Cliffe of the 46th described some innovative tactics and maneuvers adopted by Capt. Matthew Johnson for his regiment's light company shortly after the Battle of Long Island:

> Johnson and his (46th) Company behaved amazingly, he goes thro his Manoevers by a Whistle, for which he has often been laughed at, they either form to right or left or squat or rise by a perticular whistle which his men are as well acquainted with as the Batallion with the word of Command, he being used to Woods fighting and having a quick Eye, had his Company down in the moment of the enemies present [i.e., the moment the enemy takes aim], & up again at the advantegious moment for their fire.[121]

In other words, these British troops repeatedly dropped to the ground by whistle signal as their opponents took aim and rose again once the volley was fired to push ahead with bayonets. No one laughed at Johnson and his whistle after that.

Of Brandywine, "my situation that Day was exactly simular to the command I had the 27th of August, upon Long Island," General Grant told General Harvey, "the plan for attack was much the same tho' upon a larger scale & of course more complicated."[122] It was helpful, too, having a commander in chief who was an expert in light infantry tactics.

Linear warfare was being adapted to conditions, not dispensed with, for it was still the most effective, large-scale method of combat with muzzle-loading, smoothbore muskets. Tradition, pomp, and pride still played a major role in battle, especially with the British grenadiers. They formed in front of Osborne's Hill. According to Lt. Martin Hunter, "It was here, before we attacked General Washington, that Colonel Meadows made the famous speech to the 1st Battalion of Grenadiers, which he commanded, 'Grenadiers, put on your caps; for damn'd fighting and drinking I'll match you against the world!'"[123]

The grenadiers took off the red cloth forage caps they had worn on the march, dropped their packs, and removed their impressive black bearskin caps (designed to pack flat) from their knapsacks, which were left on the ground in heaps.[124] Brushing up the fur, the grenadiers put on the caps, adding more than a foot of height to these elite troops, who were already the tallest men in the army. The grenadier's cap was held in place by tasseled white cords braided around an oval crimson patch on the upper part of the back and looping down behind his head under his queue, or ponytail, which was then tucked up beneath the cap rim. The red oval was often decorated with a regimental insignia or Roman numerals, and a polished, white metal grenade badge was fixed to the back below the patch. An embossed black-and-silver front plate bearing the king's crest and the royal cipher "GR" gleamed across the grenadier's forehead.

At approximately 4:30 P.M., "as soon as the third column had formed, the signal to march was drummed everywhere," von Münchhausen reported.[125] On the left, drums, trumpets, whistles, and small, brass hunting horns called "half-moons" sounded the advance for the light troops. The Jägers and light infantry, already positioned about 200 yards ahead of the rest of the line, advanced quickly in open order. On the far right, the Guards rapidly moved forward to the quickstep cadence of twenty-two fifers and drummers dressed in red coats faced with blue and festooned with special royal lace.

It was in the center, though, that the main spectacle of British pageantry was paraded in all of its spine-tingling glory. Sixty-two British fifers and drummers, resplendent in bearskin caps and uniform coats in reversed colors, decorated with a profusion of regimental lace, were massed between the grenadier battalions, the 1st Battalion in front and the 2nd Battalion behind. Fifers removed their instruments from fife cases, long cylinders of polished brass or painted tin worn on the right side below the waist, suspended by tasseled cords candy-striped in regimental colors, fixed on white leather slings over the left shoulder. Regimental badges and numbers—crowns, royal ciphers, Roman numerals—were engraved or brightly painted in regimental colors on the fife cases and on the fronts of the wooden-shelled drums. White ropes braced the sheepskin drumheads tightly on scarlet rims and dangled below in elegant braids.

The senior drum major inverted his mace and raised it vertically to his chest, upon which the drummers silently lifted both sticks horizontally to their nostrils, waiting for the word of command.

"*GRENADIERS!*" bellowed through the ranks, "*By Battalions!*" The drum major raised his mace high. "*To the FRONT! . . . QUI-I-I-CK . . . MARCH!*" Mace and drumsticks dropped in one crisp motion, and a visceral thunder of drums rumbled out as 1,200 grenadiers stepped off together in a mesmerizing, glittering mass. With muskets at the shoulder and flags streaming, the battalions swayed rhythmically forward toward the Street Road, the late-afternoon sun glinting from hundreds of bayonets and musket barrels in double ranks. The junior officers or subalterns, ensigns and lieutenants, carried light muskets called fusils or "fuzees" and marched alongside the men, while the captains marched out in front at the head of their companies. The field officers, majors and colonels, were mostly on horseback, with swords drawn and carried at the shoulder.

"We marched to the attack in two columns," Lt. Martin Hunter of the 2nd Light Infantry recalled, "the Grenadiers at the head of one, playing 'The Grenadiers March,' and the Light Infantry at the head of the other."[126]

After setting the cadence, the drum and fife majors called the tune and signaled their musicians. The drummers played a roll-off, the fifers raised their instruments to their lips, and the lilting strains of their belligerent quickstep, "The British Grenadiers," shrilled across the once peaceful Quaker landscape, above the relentless, reverberating throb of the drums:

> Some talk of Alexander, and some of Hercules,
> Of Conon, and Lysander, and some Miltiades;
> But of all the world's brave heroes,
> there's none that can compare,
> With a tow, row, row, row, to the British grenadiers.

> But of all the world's brave heroes,
> there's none that can compare,
> With a tow, row, row, row, row, to the British grenadiers.[127]

"Nothing could be more dreadfully pleasing than the line moving on to the attack," Lt. William Hale of the 2nd Grenadier Battalion told his parents. "The Grenadiers put on their Caps and struck up their march, believe me I would not exchange those three minutes of rapture to avoid ten thousand times the danger."[128] The Latin motto *Nec Aspera Terrent*— "Hardship does not deter us"—glittered from the front plates of the grenadier caps, the bold words embossed on a flowing scroll above the lion and crown of the royal crest. The sentiment was once more being put to the test as the advance brought the lines closer to the American artillery, which had a range of about 1,500 yards.

"The action began by a cannonade from the enemy, while our army was forming in line from column," Lieutenant Hunter noted.[129] Many of the guns in the American battery were French field pieces, with names like *La Inexorable* and *La Florisante* finely engraved on the barrels. Each had the Latin motto *Ultima Ratio Regum*—"The final argument of kings"— embossed on a scroll near the muzzle.[130] Three- and 4-pound solid shot began whizzing through the thick air toward the brilliant red lines, the apple-size iron balls bouncing along the ground or thudding into the soil with a shower of dirt and a cloud of dust. "Our army Still gained ground, although they had great Advantig of Ground and ther Canon keep a Constant fire on us," a British officer wrote. "Yet We Ne'er Wass daunted."[131]

> None of those ancient heroes e'er saw a cannon ball,
> Or knew the force of powder to slay their foes withal;
> But our Brave boys do know it,
> and banish all their fears,
> With a tow, row, row, row, row, the British grenadiers.
> But our Brave boys do know it,
> and banish all their fears,
> With a tow, row, row, row, row, the British grenadiers.

The Royal Artillery replied with 6- and 12-pound shot, firing in support, but failed to silence the Continental Artillery. Smoke began to layer the fields in a thick haze.

George Washington by Charles Willson Peale, painted after the Siege of Boston, 1776. Washington was forty-five years old in 1777 and had been appointed Commander in Chief on June 15, 1775. The Philadelphia Campaign began on June 13, 1777, as Washington entered his third year of command. The army he rebuilt in early 1777 was the third Continental Army authorized by Congress. *Brooklyn Museum of Art (Dick S. Ramsey Fund)*

Major General Marquis de Lafayette by Charles Willson Peale. Nineteen-year-old Lafayette arrived in America in 1777 and was commissioned a major general for political reasons, without pay or command. He joined Washington's staff on August 1, 1777, and was wounded through the leg at Brandywine, his first battle. His popularity with Washington and the army helped to cement relations with France.
Independence National Historical Park

Major General John Sullivan of New Hampshire. Sullivan commanded the Maryland Division in 1777 and was involved in one contentious episode after another. He was subject to court-martial inquiries for the 1777 Staten Island expedition and for Brandywine, where he was unfairly blamed for poor generalship. Both inquiries cleared him, but his luckless military career continued to be stormy.
Independence National Historical Park

Lieutenant General Sir William Howe was the second British commander in chief, replacing Gen. Thomas Gage in 1775 at Boston. He served in America until 1778 and was knighted after the 1776 campaign. He was successful in every major battle, but failed to follow up his victories, enabling Washington to regroup and continue the war. An enquiry into his conduct by the House of Commons in 1779 cleared his reputation. *Anne S. K. Brown Military Collection, Brown University Library*

Ensign William Augustus West, Viscount Cantelupe, miniature ca. 1778. Lord Cantelupe arrived in America in June 1777 and served nine months in the Brigade of Guards. His diary contains watercolors of the Battle of Brandywine and the Tredyffrin Camp, the only two known contemporary images of the campaign made in the field before the capture of Philadelphia. Cantelupe inherited the title Baron and Earl De la Warr upon his father's death in November 1777, symbolized by the coronet with the script D. *The Guards Museum, London*

General Sir George Osborn, Baronet, by George Romney, 1778. Osborn
was a captain and lieutenant colonel of the 3rd Regiment of Foot Guards,
and served in America during the New York and Philadelphia campaigns
as captain of the Grenadier Company of the Brigade of Guards. He was
also Muster Master General of the Foreign Troops, responsible for keeping
accounts of the Hessian and other German troops serving in the war. He
left Philadelphia with Lord Cornwallis in December 1777. This portrait
was painted shortly after he returned to England, when he was promoted
to general. *Private collection, United Kingdom*

"A Battery of Rebels opened on Brandywine Heights the 11th of September 1777 in the County of Birmingham," by Lord Cantalupe, 1777, depicting the Guards firing a volley up Battle Hill in Birmingham Township against Sullivan's Division.

Cliveden, a National Trust Historic Site

"Light Dragoon Encampment at Trydyffinn Pennsylvania 1777 Sept." by Lord Cantalupe, 1777, showing the 16th Light Dragoons camp behind the Guards camp on the afternoon of September 19. Note pup tents and wigwams, horses tethered to the fence and Trout Pen in the foreground. *Cliveden, a National Trust Historic Site*

"The Battle of Paoli, or Paoli Massacre" by Xavier della Gatta, 1782. Painted for a British officer, probably Lt. Martin Hunter, who is depicted in the left foreground, wrapping his wounded hand. His comrade Capt. William Wolfe lies dead nearby. Ferguson's Riflemen are the five green-uniformed soldiers in the center. American "booths" or wigwams are on the right amid the chaos and horror, and the 16th Dragoons saber Wayne's infantry on the left. *The American Revolution Center*

A Dansey Tent.

"A Dansey Tent." Capt. William Dansey of the 33rd Regiment wrote to his mother in 1778: "I am in good Health and Spirits for a Campaign and am look'd upon in the Army as the first equip'd Man in it, I have a Tent of a very singular construction intirely of my own Invention . . . It is what I can't well describe to you but if Peace comes you will see the Original as I had it pitch'd on the memorable Field of the Battle of Brandywine . . . I find I am writing on a Sheet I have been drawing on, but as it is a Draft of the Dansey Tent, pitch'd with a Firelock and four Bayonets." *Historical Society of Delaware*

Onward swept the grenadiers, unstoppable as they approached the Street Road. The front broadened as the Guards gradually shifted to the right and headed toward the hill that Sullivan's Division occupied. Step by step, the column of grenadier battalions steadily transformed into a single battle line as the 1st Battalion moved obliquely to the right while the 2nd Battalion continued straight ahead, its left flank hugging the Birmingham Road. "The Line moving on Exhibited the most Grand & Noble Sight imaginable," observed a British light infantry officer from across the road. "The Grenadiers beating their March as they advanc'd contributed greatly to the Dignity of the Approach."[132]

> The god of war was pleasèd, and great Bellona smiles,
>   To see these noble heroes, of our British isles,
>   And all the gods celestial,
>   descending from their spheres,
>   Beheld with admiration the British Grenadiers.
>   And all the gods celestial,
>   descending from their spheres,
>   Beheld with admiration the British Grenadiers.

Stirling's men could hear and see them coming from a mile away. "We Came in Sight of the Enemy who had Crossed the river & were coming down upon us," Lt. Ebenezer Elmer, a surgeon's mate of the 3rd New Jersey in Stirling's Division, wrote. "We formed about 4 oClock on an Eminence, the right being in ye woods. Presently a large Column Came on in front playing ye Granediers March & Now the Battle began which proved Excessive severe." Elmer noted, "The Enemy Came on with fury."[133]

On Cornwallis's left, the Hessian and Anspach Jägers advanced quickly and crossed the Street Road far ahead of the grenadiers, but they soon found themselves in difficult terrain, with opposition from American skirmishers. "I saw that the enemy wanted to form for us on a bare hill, so I had them greeted by our two amusettes and this was the beginning of General Howe's column's [participation]," Col. Ludwig von Wurmb reported. "We drove the enemy from this hill and they positioned themselves in a woods from which we dislodged them and then a second woods where we found ourselves 150 paces from their line which was on a height in a woods and we were at the bottom also in a woods, between us was an open field," in front of Stephen's position at Sandy Hollow. "Here they fired on us with two cannon with grape shot and, because of the terrible terrain and the woods, our cannon could not get close enough, and had to remain to the right."[134]

"The Jäger Corps found itself close to an enemy advance post with two 6-pounders and 600 men, which stood on a height, with woods in front of it," the Hessian Jäger Corps report stated. "Our two 3-pounders opened fire first, the Jägers attacked the enemy, drove them into a hedge, and dislodged them three different times before they retreated back to the main body of the army." The report went on to say that the main American force "was advantageously posted on a not especially steep height in front of the woods, with the right wing resting on a steep and deep ravine," the area just below Sandy Hollow. "That wing was directly opposite the Jägers, and in the same hedges from which the Jägers had driven the enemy corps; and the Jägers were engaged for over half an hour, with grapeshot and small arms, with a battalion of light infantry."[135]

When the British light infantry arrived at the Street Road, Ewald's party disbanded. "As soon as the line approached the advanced guard Lt. Col. Abercromby ordered the 17th light company to form on the right of the battalion, the 42nd on the left," while Ewald's Jägers "fought dispersed along the whole line."[136]

The Virginia skirmishers withdrew from Jones's orchard at the approach of the main British force and took cover with the rest of the 3rd Virginia behind the Friends graveyard wall. "When the Left of the Line came up to the Birmingham Meeting House about two hundred Rebels fired & fell Back," wrote a British light infantry officer. Then suddenly, from the hill beyond the Y in the road past the meetinghouse, "at that Instant five Pieces of Cannon open'd upon the Right of the 1st L. I. loaded with Grape Shot" at a range of 600 yards. Charges of thirty or so small iron balls packed in a linen bag (resembling a bunch of grapes) sprayed from each gun like a shower of iron hail. "As soon as the line came up to Dilworth Church the enemy opened a fire from five field pieces," an officer of the 17th Light Company wrote, noting, "The church yard wall being opposite the 17th light company, the captain determined to get over the fence into the road."

Once in the road, however, the light bobs were dangerously exposed to the American artillery. As the guns were reloaded, Captain Scott decided on a daring scheme: "Calling to the men to follow [he] run down the road and lodged the men without loss at the foot of the hill on which the guns were firing." Ducking and dodging, taking cover as needed, the 17th Light Infantry headed straight toward the battery, soon followed by the 4th and 38th Companies. Another light infantry officer confirmed that at the meetinghouse, "a High Stone Wall preventing their keeping up with the Battalion, those Companies leap'd over the Fence into the high Road which divided them from the British Grenadiers & in order the sooner to avoid the danger of the Shot ran down the Road & shelter'd themselves at the foot of the Hill." The volume of cannon fire was intense; one British officer noticed "the hedge on the left side of the road much cut with the grape shot."[137]

As for the 3rd Virginia, "one column moved upon it in front, while a second struck at its left," probably the light troops in the road. "Cut off from cooperation by the latter movement, it bravely sustained itself against superior numbers," Capt. Henry Lee wrote with much admiration and slight exaggeration, "never yielding one inch of ground, and expending thirty rounds a man, in forty-five minutes," from the time of the first skirmish with Ewald. "It was now ordered to fall back upon Woodford's right, which was handsomely accomplished by Colonel Marshall, although deprived of half his officers, where he renewed the sanguinary contest."[138] Lt. Col. T. Will Heth of the 3rd Virginia, who was with Maxwell's Corps at Chads's Ford at that moment, told Daniel Morgan, "I need not say more . . . than to assure you the 3rd. V. R. alone, prevented the British Grenadiers & Light Infantry advancing 3/4 of an Hour."[139]

Gentlemanly hyperbole notwithstanding, the 3rd Virginia performed with distinction, but it paid a terrible price. With only one field officer and four captains present, by the end of the day, Capt. John Chilton had been killed, and Capt. Philip Lee was mortally wounded; the other two captains, Thomas Blackwell and John Peyton, were both wounded but still fit for duty. "Marshall escaped unhurt, although his horse received two balls," Lee reported. "The subalterns suffered in proportion": Lt. Apollos Cooper and Ens. George Peyton were killed; Lt. William White was mortally wounded; and Lts. John Francis Mercer, John Blackwell, and Robert Peyton were all wounded. "Thirteen non-commissioned officers and sixty privates fell." But in consolation, "the opposing enemy was severely handled."[140]

Farther to the left, the 2nd Light Infantry Battalion found itself facing the same two guns that had the Jägers pinned down below Sandy Hollow. "Some skirmishing begun in the valley in which the enemy was drove," Captain Montrésor wrote, "upon gaining something further of the ascent the enemy began to amuse us with 2 guns." The chief engineer praised the stand made by Stephen's Division, as well as the mettle of the light bobs: "The ground on the left being the most difficult the rebels disputed it with the Light Infantry with great spirit, particularly their officers, this spot was a ploughed hill and they covered by its summit and flanked by a wood; however unfavourable the circumstances their ardour was such that they pushed in upon them under a very heavy fire."[141]

The light troops were all now under heavy fire and were stopped in their tracks. "Describe the Battle—'Twas not like those of Covent Garden or Drury Lane," Lt. Richard St. George of the 52nd quipped, referring to mock battles staged in London theaters. "There was a most infernal Fire of Cannon & musketry—smoak—incessant shouting—incline to the right! incline to the Left!—halt!—charge! &c.," as the light infantry maneuvered through the abrupt hills and hedges. The two American battalion guns on this hill covered Stephen's right flank, and the crews served them well.

With their own light 3-pounders stuck in a swamp behind them and out of action, the 2nd Light Infantry and the Jägers were pinned down in the woods at the bottom of a deep ravine, with "the balls ploughing up the ground. The Trees cracking over ones head, The branches riven by the artillery—The leaves falling as in autumn by the grape shot—The affair was general—The Misters on both sides shewd conduct. The action was brilliant."[142] St. George's friend, Lt. Martin Hunter, both of the 52nd Light Company in the 2nd Light Infantry, remembered, "The position the enemy had taken was very strong indeed—very commanding ground, a wood on their rear and flanks, a ravine and strong paling in front. The fields in America are all fenced in by paling."[143]

"We could not see the 2nd Battalion of Light Infantry because of the terrain," the Hessian Jäger Corps Journal stated, "and because we had received only a few orders, each commander had to act according to his best judgment." Flexible as they were, the light troops had difficulty negotiating their way through the tangled thickets and swampy lowlands. As for the British regular forces behind them, "the 3rd Brigade of Englanders likewise was to support the Jägers and Light Infantry in the second encounter. But, because of the uneven terrain and the movement toward the left by the column, we saw nothing of it during the battle."[144] The only way for the Jägers to break out would be to somehow get around the end of the American flank.

As all this was transpiring on the American right, Sullivan's Division was still not yet positioned properly on the left. On its first arrival, before the British advance, Sullivan had placed his troops on the front of a large, wooded hill about 400 yards west of Birmingham Meeting, only to find Stirling and Stephen on a ridge behind the hill nearly half a mile to his right. "I then rode up to Consult the other General officers," Sullivan explained, leaving his two brigades with only one general officer, Brig. Gen. Preudhomme de Borre, a sixty-year-old French general who barely spoke English and was greatly disliked by his troops, especially the officers.[145] De Borre wrote to Congress a few days after Brandywine, "I did not know your Language in my arrival in this country, I believed prudently I must Learn it. . . . I now know enough your Language to Weild my orders & to understand that I read."[146] The Marylanders wanted their native son Gen. William Smallwood to lead them, but he was down in Maryland that day attempting to organize the militia. The brave Col. Mordecai Gist was also away on the same duty, leaving the Maryland Line uninspired; now, at the critical moment, they were virtually leaderless.

As the British began to advance and their light troops moved quickly ahead toward the American right, Sullivan said that he and the other generals, Stirling and Stephen, "upon receiving Information that the Enemy were Endeavouring to out Flank us on the Right were unanimously of opinion that my Division Should be brought in to Join the others." Further, with the Jägers trying to extend their left to break the deadlock of being pinned down, Sullivan *correctly* observed "that the whole Should Incline further to the Right to prevent our being out flanked," meaning that Stephen and Stirling would have to shift to the right at Sandy Hollow.

The maneuvers at this stage of the battle became a major source of contention immediately afterward, resulting in a congressional recall of Sullivan (which was refused by Washington) pending an investigation. "There was some great *faux-pas* on the 11th," a disgusted Lt. Col. T. Will Heth of the 3rd Virginia wrote to Col. Daniel Morgan. "Our disaster was owing to the confusion Genl Sullivan threw our right wing into—He is calld the Evle-genius of America." Heth, who was with the Corps of Light Infantry that day, was not enamored with his own commander, Gen. William Maxwell of New Jersey, either, telling his fellow Virginian Morgan, "He is to be sure—a Damnd bitch of a General."[147]

Like Heth's comments, much of the criticism of Sullivan in this particular case was based on hearsay and on a letter published anonymously by Congressman Thomas Burke of North Carolina, who disliked Sullivan, as did many others in Congress. Tactless and ambitious, having been captured by the British at Long Island and used afterward—as a "decoy duck," in John Adams's words—to deliver a peace overture from Lord Howe, Sullivan was involved in one contentious episode after another, including squabbles about seniority and two threatened resignations. Viewed as a complainer, he was already facing an inquiry for the flash-in-the-pan Staten Island expedition a few weeks earlier. Beginning with the abandonment of Fort Ticonderoga, the military failures of 1777 unleashed storms of congressional criticism and recalls of commanders, and the hapless general became a lightning rod. Or as Sullivan himself put it, "I am the butt against which all the darts are leveled." He protested to John Adams, "How does this read? How will it sound when ringing in the public ear?"[148]

The maneuver here was inaccurately reported at the time and further distorted in the retelling, but the distortion was readily believed because of Sullivan's continuing propensity for disaster and the fact that Burke's letter was quickly published far and wide, within three weeks being printed in a Boston newspaper, copied by others, and even appearing in England in the *Gazette and New Daily Advertiser* on November 21, 1777—more than a week before Howe's official report of the battle even arrived in London. Through sheer repetition, it has become ingrained in many histories of the battle. "I never yet have pretended that my Disposition in the Late Battle was perfect," Sullivan lamely admitted to John Hancock. "I know it was very far from it but this I will venture to affirm . . . it was the best that time would allow me to make."[149]

The first inaccuracy was that Sullivan had "taken too large a circuit," meaning that in moving toward Birmingham to rendezvous with Stirling and Stephen, his division had somehow widely missed his assigned position. Given the distance, terrain, vague orders, and dismal lack of reconnaissance, the three divisions did remarkably well finding each other. Stirling and Stephen had roads to follow and were in tandem; Birmingham Meeting House, their point of rendezvous, was in plain view to them. By contrast, Sullivan had to move blindly cross-country, for the most part, while finding half of his division posted at the three upper fords three or more miles away, but he was able to find it and arrive within less than a mile of the other two forces.

"Sullivan to compleat his Blunder made a circuit of two Miles when one quarter in the direct road would have brought him to his ground," Burke wrote privately to Gov. Richard Caswell of North Carolina. The congressman was ill informed; the only direct road at Brinton's Ford led to Dilworth, two miles east of the ford and a mile away from Birmingham Meeting. Had Sullivan moved this way, he would have found the Birmingham Road congested with the Stirling-Stephen column, possibly causing more delay. He also would not have met up with the other half of his division posted at the three upper fords.

But Burke's criticisms did not stop with Sullivan. "I had an Opportunity of observing that our Troops and Inferior Officers are exceedingly good, but that our Major Generals (one only excepted) are totally inadequate," the congressman ranted on. "They were so disconcerted by the unexpected attack of the Enemy that they knew not what to do but to permit, (some say to order), a precipitate retreat."[150]

Ironically, a number of British and Hessian sources complimented the American position and the performance of most of the line. "Sullivan shewed a considerable share of judgment and ability in the execution of this commission," *The Annual Register for 1777* went so far as to say. "He took a very strong position on the commanding grounds above Birmingham church, with his left extending towards the Brandywine, his artillery advantageously disposed, and both flanks covered with very thick woods."[151]

Bad timing and poor training, compounded by low morale resulting from a lack of inspirational brigade-level leadership, were the main problems here, not "too large a circuit." In refuting this accusation made by the southern congressman based on hearsay, the New England general wrote:

> Sullivans division did not take too Large a Circuit as he Suggests but went on to meet the Enemy agreeable to their orders & were obliged to fall back, upon finding that the other Divisions which proceeded by Different Routs had taken ground & formed half a mile to the Rear of where

that Division had advanced. They were under a necessity of falling back & Filing off to the Right in order to form a Junction with the other Troops & before this could be completed They were attacked & Thrown into Confusion from which they never fully Recovered.[152]

Sullivan also had to gather as much of his division together as possible, since about half of his forces were posted at the upper fords. Hazen's Regiment, officially called the 2nd Canadian and also known as Congress's Own Regiment, was functioning as a light infantry unit for Sullivan, first by holding the upper fords, then by screening the division's movements. Hazen's experience as a Ranger officer in the French and Indian War followed by two years in the regular British Army, taken together with the composition of his unit, mostly Canadian frontiersmen, would qualify the 2nd Canadians as such. The day before Brandywine, Gen. de Borre protested that Sullivan "detached of my brigade the Congress regiment Who alone is the greatest half part of my brigade. I would go with them, general Sullivan Would that I remain With the 2. 4. & 6 mariland regiments Being other part of my brigade in all about 350 men." Then, as Sullivan moved toward Birmingham, de Borre again complained, "In our way I met the Congress regiment and Sent So Soon my brigade major to general Sullivan to have ordered for that regiment to join my brigade. The general has refused."[153]

After finding Hazen and the Delaware Regiment, and then spotting Ewald, Sullivan had immediately directed his division to the front of Birmingham Hill. "I ordered Colo. Hazens Regiment to pass a Hollow way, File off to the Right & face to Cover the Artillery while it was passing the Same Hollow way, the Rest of the Troops followed in the Rear to assist in Covering the Artillery." He added, "The Enemy Seeing this did not press on but gave me time to form my Division on an advantageous Height in a Line with the other Divisions but almost half a mile to the Left."[154] Then, after leaving his division to consult with the other generals, he sent orders to de Borre to shift the division to the right to come closer into line with the others.

The second and most often repeated inaccuracy is that Sullivan insisted his division be placed on the right of the battle line because he was the senior general, blindly preferring military protocol to the realities of a dangerous situation. Though it is true that his division was entitled to hold the position of honor on the right, he did *not* insist on this *precisely* because of the circumstances. "If part of the Division was not formed completely before the Engagement, The fault can not be imputed to Genl Sullivan," Brig. Gen. Thomas Conway testified, "who although he had a right to take the right of the Line, took the Left, in Order to save time, a proof that the Division of the Right, had full time to form."[155]

Sullivan, in fact, ordered his division to fall in on Stirling's left. In order to make room for the Marylanders, Stephen and Stirling had to shift their position to the right a few hundred yards. This they seem to have accomplished with little difficulty in the face of the British and Hessian light troops, who were still pinned down on the American right.

Watching Sullivan shift, apparently strengthening his right flank, "the sharp eye of General Howe noticed this as the firing started, and at once ordered the 4th Brigade to advance from the second line to the first line, on the left wing," von Münchhausen stated, where they would come up in support of the 2nd Light Infantry. "At the same time, the 3rd Brigade, which at first was in reserve, was ordered to take the place of the now advanced 4th Brigade." The shift caused a slight change in the British battle line; "the new front was somewhat more sloping."[156]

The British grenadiers were coming steadily across the Street Road at this point, half a mile away from Stirling, and the Guards were swiftly advancing on the American left. "While my Division was marching out & before it was possible for them to form to advantage," Sullivan stated, "The Enemy pressed on with Rapidity & attacked them, which threw them into Some kind of Confusion."[157]

An eyewitness to all of this was Gen. Thomas Conway, the contentious, Irish-born French general in command of the 3rd Pennsylvania Brigade in Stirling's Division. Conway, who was greatly disliked by many other American generals for a variety of reasons—one being the fact that he embarrassed them by regularly drilling his Pennsylvanians—was outspoken in his criticisms about the lack of coordination among Continental troops. "Genl Sullivan having come up with his division, when the Enemy was within half a mile of our front," Conway wrote, "the short time left to his troops in order to Form, was hardly sufficient, for well disciplined troops, and well exercised," meaning well-drilled troops, "and by no means sufficient for the troops of this Army, who appear to me to maneavre upon false Principles, and where I cannot discover as yet, The least notion of displaying Columns, and forming briskly upon all Emergencies."[158]

Another French general who was an eyewitness was Lafayette, here coming under severe fire for the first time. "M. de Lafayette, as a volunteer, had always accompanied the general [Washington] but since the left was quiet and the major thrust would come on the right, he obtained permission to join Sullivan," Lafayette wrote later. "At his arrival, which the troops appeared to appreciate, he found that the enemy had crossed the ford, and Sullivan's corps' had scarcely had time to form one line in front of a thinly wooded forest."[159]

With only one general actually present on the left of the wing, Chevalier Preudhomme de Borre, who commanded little, if any, respect from anyone, the Maryland Division executed a strange and confusing maneuver. This was probably the "too large a circuit" that was the basis for the rumors and accusations, but because it involved Sullivan's Division and he was overall commander of the right wing, the onus for the maneuver was placed on him, even though he was not personally leading it. Instead of a straightforward march to the right, the troops countermarched to the left and swung around the west side and back of the hill toward the ridge where Stirling's troops were positioned.

"Our division marched to join Lord Stirling who was on the ground where the enemy appeared, and where they seemed to intend their attack," Maj. John Hawkins Stone of the 1st Maryland Regiment in the 1st Brigade told William Paca. "By the time we reached the ground they had to cannonade the ground allotted to us, which was very bad, and the enemy within musket shot of it, before we were ordered to form the line of battle."[160]

Once in the valley between the hills, the 1st Brigade—Smallwood's, which had no general officer at that moment—was ordered to wheel to the left up the back of the hill and then countermarch into position. Essentially, most of the division seems to have moved in a complete circle, needlessly marching almost a mile and ending up with the 1st Brigade only a handful of yards from where it had started and the 2nd Brigade behind it in the valley, effectively cutting the division's front and firepower in half. All this occurred in the face of a large and well-organized attacking force.

The Guards appeared in front of the Maryland position, coming out of the light woods along the Street Road and supported by two medium 12-pounders. "Lord Cornwallis's men suddenly emerged from the woods in very good order," Lafayette observed. "Advancing across the plain, his first line opened a very brisk fire with cannon and muskets. The American fire was murderous, but both their right and left wings collapsed."[161]

Major Stone described his experience:

I marched in front of Gen'l Sullivan's Division, when I received orders from him to wheel to the left and take possession of a rising ground about 100 yards in our front, to which the enemy were marching rapidly. I wheeled off, but had not reached the ground, before we were attacked on all quarters, which prevented our forming regularly, and by wheeling to the left it doubled our division on the brigade immediately in the rear of the other. Thus we were in confusion, and no person to undue us to order, when the enemy pushed on and soon made us all run off.[162]

"Sullivan's Division, on the extreme left, were marched through a narrow lane," Lt. Col. Samuel Smith of the 4th Maryland in de Borre's Brigade related. "The First Brigade of it counter-marched through a gateway, to the top of a hill, under a galling fire from the enemy—thus bringing the rear to the front. Pressed by the enemy, they had no time to form, and gave way at all points." Smith's regiment was in the next line: "The Second Brigade was formed in a valley in its rear. It was said a retreat had been ordered; but Colonel Smith not knowing it, found himself, to his surprise—being on the left of the Regiment—with only Lieutenant Cromwell and about thirty men. Seeing no enemy, he retired deliberately."[163]

Gen. de Borre was unable to maintain any sort of control of his force. He told Congress:

I then am arrived upon the field of battle with about 350 men Who before to be placed, received a Discharge of the enemy. We have come back about 50 steps to be better to receive the ennemy who in that instant Schot a second Discharge. All my half brigade had Discharged also. & run away both oficers and soldiers & I find myself alone. I would rally them it was impossible to me & the same follow them.

I could not hold that brigade in my hand, I done my Duty to go and fetch them to bring again against the enemy. It is not my fault if the americanes troops run away to first fire of ennemy, it is enough unhappy for me to have had that disordered, the greatest proof of the precipitation with which all the division is run away, nobody of them is killed or wounded. I alone recieved a light wound in the cheek by a bal.[164]

De Borre was not entirely credible; Major Stone reported, "I lost 23 privates and 2 sergeants killed, wounded and taken, and one Captain (Ford) wounded; he will recover."[165] De Borre's case grew even more bizarre; later that evening, Col. Sam Smith said that the old French general "showed some scratches on his cheek, which he said had been done by the English firing fish-hooks, but more probably by the briars."[166]

"I gone & fetch them to bring again against the ennemy," de Borre continued, with an explanation as confused as the maneuvers themselves. "I find in my way some Soldiers, the rest was already upon a hill about a mile of the battle, where was also the Smallwood brigade who has been conducted by the general Sullivan in moving on to the ennemy, in my arrival upon that hill next that Division I moved on with had to go at Left of the ennemy to help our troops Who did made their retreat."[167]

Often more dangerous than well-directed enemy gunfire is friendly fire, especially from poorly led, panicking troops. "Of all the Maryland regiments only two ever had an opportunity to form, Gist's [3rd Maryland] and mine [1st Maryland]," Major Stone wrote, "and as soon as they began to fire, those who were in our rear could not be prevented from firing also." Some of de Borre's troops began firing into the back of the 1st Brigade. "In a few minutes we were attacked in front and flank, and by our people in the rear. Our men ran off in confusion, and were very hard to be rallied." Like many others, Stone was thoroughly disgusted with the whole performance caused by the lack of leadership in the Maryland Division: "Although my men did not behave so well as I expected, yet I can scarcely blame them when I consider their situation; nor are they censured by any part of the army. My horse threw [me] in the time of action, but I did not receive any great injury from it."[168]

Sullivan had used Hazen to screen the artillery as the division first moved into position. "Our regiment was posted on the right of the Army [at the fords], and was the first attacked and among the last to leave the field," Sgt. Maj. John Hawkins of Hazen's regiment wrote with spirit, if not complete accuracy. "A heavy fire of artillery and musketry was carried on by both sides the whole afternoon with scarcely any intermission. The enemy were much superior to us in numbers, as but a small part of our army were engaged, the greater part being away on the left. In justice to the brave officers and men of our regiment, Col. Hazen thought himself obliged to affirm, that no troops behaved better, nor any troops left the field in greater order."[169] Lt. Col. Samuel Smith confirmed, "Colonel Hazen's Regiment retreated in perfect order."[170]

Firing only a few volleys, relying on speed and the threat of the bayonet, the Guards advanced steadily under some musket and cannon fire. "The Guards receiv'd the fire of the Rebels from the Wood at the same time with the two Battalions of British Grenadiers," Captain Robertson of the Engineers noted, "and immediately charging them the Rebels gave way with the utmost precipitation."[171] On the far right, Sir George Osborn led the flank companies up the hill, but there wasn't much resistance as Sullivan's Division fell apart, with de Borre abandoned by his troops. "We attacked the left flank of the rebel army, and raining upon the brigades of Sullivan, a French General Deborre, and Maxwell with an impetuosity really that it would have been scarcely possible for them to resist," Sir George told his brother, "we saved much loss we might otherwise have sustained, and certainly made the enemy first give way," referring to the collapse of the Maryland Division. Not surprisingly, casualties in Osborn's command were very light: "I had but one Grenadier wounded, the Light Company who were with me had only three." At the end of the day, the Guards reported total casualties of one killed, five wounded, and two missing.[172]

Here in his first major battle, William Lord Cantelupe, with O'Hara's Company in the 2nd Battalion on the left wing of the Guards, advanced against the American position on Birmingham Hill. In his journal, shortly after the engagement, Cantelupe painted an image titled, *A Battery of the Rebels opened on Brandywine heights the 11th of September 1777 in the county of Birmingham.* The watercolor depicts the muzzle flashes of three cannons through a thick column of smoke on top of a wooded hill. A long battle line of redcoats behind a fence along a road fires a volley up the hill, and skirmishers from both sides have fanned out across the landscape. In the foreground, on the road behind the line of redcoats, are two sets of horses and wheeled vehicles, accompanied by figures in dark blue—the battalion artillery of the Guards. Farm buildings flank the battle line, and Cantelupe carefully delineated plowed fields, fences, even a haystack. It is the only known contemporary image of the Battle of Brandywine.[173]

While his division was collapsing on the left, Sullivan was on the hill where the five guns had pinned down the British light infantry. "I had taken post myself in the Centre with the artillery & ordered it to play briskly to Stop the progress of the Enemy & give the Broken Troops time to Rally & form in the Rear of where I was with the artillery," he told John Hancock. But repeated efforts on his part failed to bring the Marylanders back to order: "I sent off four Aid De Camps for this purpose & went myself But all in vain: no sooner did I form one party but that which I had before formed would Run off & Even at times when I though on Horseback and in front of them apprehended no Danger." Finally, with the British grenadiers approaching the center and the Marylanders in hopeless disorder, "I then left them to be Rallied if possible by their own officers & my aid De Camp & Repaired to the Hill where our artillery was which by this time began to feel the Effects of the Enemy's fire."[174]

Sullivan's proper place at that moment was in the center to direct the entire wing. The pounding drums and squealing fifes of the British grenadiers were relentlessly coming ever closer. The Royal Artillery thundered out in support; 6- and 12-pound shot hissed through the air and slammed into tree trunks with bone-shaking concussions, tearing down limbs and knocking men out, or landing among the Continentals with shocking, sickening results. Some were dismembered, others crushed to a pulp. Grapeshot flew in showers from the smaller battalion guns and wrought havoc in the woods, shredding branches and sending splinters ripping through the ranks. Battle smoke, dust, flesh and blood, falling leaves, and debris filled the air, along with the cries of the wounded and shouts of command from the Continental officers, their own fifes shrieking and drums beating out signals between volleys of musketry.

The Continental Artillery held firm, keeping the light bobs and Jägers at bay while blasting away at the oncoming grenadiers. Switching from round shot to grape, at a range of 600 yards they peppered the grenadier battalions, splintering the fences as they climbed over them and tearing into the hedges. A terrible harvest was gathered that September afternoon in the fertile green fields of Birmingham Township, as swaths of tall, proud men in bearskin caps and crimson uniforms spun and dropped or were violently thrown back, dismembered by showers of iron hail. Officers leading their companies also fell; of the ten British officers known to have been killed at Brandywine, seven were grenadiers, and seven other grenadier officers were wounded.[175]

Still the battalions pressed on at the quickstep, leaning forward into the smoke and musketry. The undulating hills occasionally shielded them from the effects of direct fire.

Just ahead and to the left of the grenadiers, the 17th Light Company was still pinned down in front of the main American battery, along with the 4th Light Company. One of the 17th officers carefully crept up the slope and "by a bend of the hill had a view of part of the enemys line opposite the grenadiers," though they were still more than a quarter mile away, "and opened a fire from about half the company on it, no more being able to form on the space." They were "presently joined by the 38th company," and a debate erupted over what to do next. "Some of their soldiers wanted to ascend the hill immediately," but the others "objected as too imprudent." Then "the 33rd company joined immediately afterwards, and the men of the three companies"—the 4th, 38th, and 33rd, perhaps 150 men total—"calling out up the hill, at their cannon, ascended the hill and had a glimpse of the enemys line as far as the eye could reach to the right and left."[176]

Another light infantry officer recalled, "The Inspiration & Courage of both Officers & Men inducing them to ascend the Height, the whole Rebel Line presented itself to View & so close that those who compos'd this spirited Attack had nothing to Expect but Slaughter."[177] The remaining ten companies of the 1st Light Infantry Battalion were 100 or so yards away to the left and rear, behind the fence on the northern side of the Birmingham Road just east of where it turned left at the Y. "Some firing might have taken place on the left, but as yet the heavy fire of musketry was not begun," one of them wrote. Here the light infantry tactics played a crucial role for the four companies on the front of the hill, as the "enemys guns were too far back on the height to annoy us, but their line advancing on us we were compelled to throw ourselves on our knees and bellies, and keep up a fire from the slope of the hill."[178]

"This Hill Commanded both the Right & Left of our Line & if carried by the Enemy I knew would Instantly bring on a Total Rout & make a Retreat very Difficult," said Sullivan. He told John Hancock, "I therefore Determined to hold it as Long as possible to give Lord Sterlings & General Stephens Divisions which yet stood firm as much assistance from the artillery as possible & to give Colo Hazens, Daytons [1st New Jersey] & Ogdens [3rd New Jersey] Regiments which Still Stood firm on our Left the Same advantage & to Cover the Broken Troops of my Division & give them an opportunity to Rally & come to our assistance which Some of them did & others could not by their officers be brought to do any thing but fly."[179]

On the hill that afternoon near the main battery was thirty-year-old Capt. Joseph McClellan, a native of nearby Middletown Township. The son of a Chester County farmer and tavern keeper, McClellan commanded a company in the 9th Pennsylvania Regiment in Conway's Brigade, Stirling's Division. "The position which his company occupied on the left wing of the line when formed, south of Birmingham Meeting-house. It was on the eminence immediately south of where the road turns at right angles to the east and west, about a quarter of a mile south of the meeting-house." McClellan recalled a particular episode involving a Highlander, probably from McPherson's 42nd Light Company in the 1st Light Infantry opposite them:

> He said when the British approached them, a stout man whom he took to be a Scotchman, and who was evidently under the influence of liquor, advanced recklessly and placed himself behind a little mound, made by the root of a tree which had been blown down. From this position, which was within pistol-shot of McClellan's company, the British soldier fired, and killed the sergeant, who was standing by Capt. McClellan's side. This, of course, attracted McClellan's notice.

As with British officers, many Continental officers carried and used firearms in battle, whether muskets, "fuzees," or in McClellan's case, a carbine.

> The American captains at that time were armed with carbines; subsequently they carried spontoons. Capt. McClellan, seeing his sergeant fall, and observing whence the fatal missile came, perceived that the man was reloading his piece as he lay crouched behind the mound, and partially protected by it, and determined to anticipate him. He discharged his carbine with deliberate aim, and said he saw the soldier roll over, evidently disabled, if not killed.[180]

The light bobs on the front of the hill could expect no immediate help from the other light troops on the left, for "the Yagers and 2nd L. I. having swampy and broken Ground to go over and besides oppos'd with great Number retarded their Advance." In the center, where Stirling's men held firm, "the British Grenadiers were likewise strongly oppos'd, & impeded by sev'ral Rail Fences."[181]

As they came closer, Stirling's infantry opened up on the grenadiers. "The fire of Musquetry all this time was as Incessant & Tremendous as ever had been remember'd," a British officer wrote.[182] Dr. Lewis Howell, a surgeon in the 2nd New Jersey Regiment, told his father that Stirling's Division had marched "to oppose Lord Cornwallis." He remarked, "We had been there but a short time when they appeared, and the heaviest firing I ever heard began, continuing a long time, every inch of ground being disputed."[183] On Stirling's left, the Jerseymen dug in their heels and held firm.

In addition to whole volleys, the troops on both sides engaged in what was known as "platoon-firing," where each regiment or battalion was divided into sections called, confusingly enough, grand divisions, subdivisions, and platoons. Rather than having the whole line empty its weapons at once, each section was to fire in sequence so that "a constant and perpetual fire" would be kept up. According to the rules of the day, "The first fire is from the . . . platoon on the right; the second fire, from the left; the third fire, from the right again; and so on alternately until the firing comes to the centre platoon." In this type of firing, both front and rear ranks of each section fired together, providing a solid burst of musketry from each. "The platoon-firing is such as must necessarily produce a general confusion, as well by the noise of those who command," meaning that shouted commands could get confused in the din of firing. The difficulty was in timing and coordination; some Continental units were able to execute "platoons" well, but many were not. "Even the king of Prussia himself," referring to Frederick the Great, an eighteenth-century military genius, "is of the same opinion; for he says, 'the platoon fire would, no doubt, be the best, if it could be executed.'"[184]

The peculiar sounds of this firing sequence were also called "platoons," and on a large scale, from a distance, they provided a seemingly endless ripping or crackling roar of musketry that carried for miles. The effect was not unlike the sound of sudden heavy, wind-driven rain on a window or hail on a metal roof.

At Chads's Ford, James Parker wrote, "I visited my friends of the Queens Rangers who had Suffered wounds, when I was delighted with the platoons of Genl. Howe on the rebels' right."[185] Across the creek,

Col. James Chambers of the 1st Pennsylvania commented that on the right wing, "The cannonade commenced about three o'clock, but soon gave way to small arms, which continued like an incessant clap of thunder, till within an hour of sunset."[186] Ten miles away, at the Seven Stars Tavern near Chester, Cornet Baylor Hill of Bland's Dragoons noted, "This day was the greatest Cannonade I ever heard, & greatest rore of Small Arms."[187]

In Philadelphia, the people and Congress could hear the battle. "It began a little before Nine in the Morning with a heavy Cannonade, which was very distinctly heard in Our State House yard about 30 miles from the Place of Action," Henry Marchant told the governor and Assembly of Rhode Island, "it lasted till dusk." Elbridge Gerry wrote of "a Cannonade, which We distinctly heard at this place & which was returned by our Army," and said that "a very warm engagement ensued, in which was as heavy a Fire from the Musketry as perhaps has been known this war in America." William Williams told his father-in-law, "A very heavy & tremendous Fire took place for considerable time; old officers & all I have seen say beyond what they conceived possible from Musquetry."[188]

The British grenadiers were now less than 100 yards away from Stirling's line. The drummers and fifers dispersed behind their companies to provide signals as well as a cadence and to assist the wounded when the time came. The two battalions, displayed in a long battle line, continued forward, clambering over fences and re-forming under fire. "When we got close to the rebels, they fired their cannon; they did not fire their small arms till we were within 40 paces of them, at which time they fired whole volleys and sustained a very heavy fire," von Münchhausen wrote. "The English, and especially the English grenadiers, advanced fearlessly and very quickly; fired a volley, and then ran furiously at the rebels with fixed bayonets."[189]

"The two Battalions of British Grenadiers got up to the Rails," Captain Robertson of the Engineers noted on his map, "when they received a heavy Fire from the Rebels in their Front; after crossing the Rails they immediately charged and drove the Rebels before them."[190] Captain Montrésor observed from an artillery position, "The British Grenadiers and Guards at the same time labouring under a smart and incessant fire from the Rebels out of a wood and above them, most nobly charged them without firing a shot and drove them before them," noting that as Stirling's Continentals withdrew, "they [were] covering their retreat with their Light Troops from one patch of woodland to another firing upon us, as we advanced into the cleared intervals until our Cannon surmounted the summits from one to another which effectually drove them beyond its Posts."[191]

On the right, at the head of the 1st Grenadier Battalion, "Lieutenant Colonel Medows distinguished himself most particularly on that day in leading on his grenadiers on horseback, with the intention of charging the enemy's line without firing," Capt. George Harris of the 5th Grenadier Company recalled. "In this situation he received a shot, in the act of waving his sword-arm just above the elbow, that went out at the back, knocking him off his horse, and the fall breaking his opposite collar-bone."[192] Medows toppled out of his saddle and fell hard to the ground, crumpled in a bleeding heap. Capt. Henry Lee of Virginia wrote, "The opposing enemy was severely handled; and the leading officer of one of the columns, with several others, was killed."[193]

Medows was not dead; the impact of the ball threw him backward and sideways to the ground with force, knocking him out cold. His friend Captain Harris, who himself had been wounded in the leg at Iron Hill, was following the army in a small carriage. "Taking a horse without a saddle, he had the honour to share in the glory of that day, but attended with the drawback of finding his gallant commander and friend most literally in the hands of the surgeon, having lost the use of both his own." Temporarily blinded by the shock of the fall, "the Colonel had not recovered his senses when Captain Harris came to him, but looking at him some time, and knowing his voice, he attempted to put out his hand, and not being able to use either, exclaimed, 'It's hard;' then, quite recovering his senses," and thinking of his sweetheart back in England, he said, "'It's lucky, Harris, poor Fanny does not know this;' evincing then, as in every other instance, that perfect coolness and indifference to accidents as they affected himself, and only feeling anxiety for his friends."[194] Seeing their brave commander shot off his horse no doubt added to the ardor of the grenadiers to push on with bayonets.

With the Marylanders on the American left gone, the center of the American line now began crumbling. "The Enemy Soon began to bend their principal force against the Hill & the fire was Close & heavy for a Long time & Soon became General," Sullivan stated. "Lord Sterling &

General Conway with their Aid de Camps were with me on the Hill & Exerted themselves beyond Description to keep up the Troops."[195] Lafayette, who was also there, remembered, "The general and many officers joined the central division, where M. de Lafayette was with Stirling, and where 800 men [of the 3rd, 6th, 9th, and 12th Pennsylvania Regiments] were brilliantly commanded by M. de Conway, an Irishman who had served in the French army. By separating that division from its two wings, and advancing across an open plain, where they lost many men, the enemy was able to concentrate its fire on the center."[196]

"Five times did the Enemy drive our Troops from the Hill & as often was it Regained & the Summit often disputed almost muzzle to muzzle," Sullivan reported. "How far I had a hand in this & whether I Endured the Hottest of the Enemys Fire I Chearfully Submit to the Gentlemen who were with me."[197] A British light infantry officer pinned down on the front of the hill confirmed Sullivan's valor: "[The] enemy repeatedly attempted to come on, but were always drove back by our fire altho' their general (Lincoln) [sic; Sullivan] very much exerted him[self]. At this time a most tremendous fire of musketry opened from both lines."[198]

The four light companies were becoming desperate, having fended off five American advances at close range and suffering heavy casualties. The 4th Light Company was commanded by twenty-eight-year-old Capt. Charles Cochrane, a career soldier who had entered the army as an ensign at age thirteen. Cochrane came to America in 1774 and was active in the campaigns since Lexington and Concord, where he went out on reconnaissance the night before the war started. It was his father-in-law, Maj. John Pitcairn of the Marines, who ordered the minutemen at Lexington to lay down their arms. Cochrane fought at Bunker Hill, where Pitcairn was killed, and he served through much of the New York Campaign of 1776 as captain of the 4th Grenadier Company. He took command of the light company after his predecessor, Captain Evelyn, was killed just before the Battle of White Plains. Now, "his company in the action at Brandywine lost an officer and 11 men in forcing that part of the rebel line where their five field pieces were."[199] In the face of determined American resistance, Cochrane and his comrades were trapped.

Then, out of the smoke and confusion, a bizarre character unexpectedly appeared, coming up the hill toward the light bobs. "Looking back to see how far the grenadier line was off from which alone we could receive immediate support, to my surprize I saw close to me Major Stuart of the 43rd, whose regt. being at Rhode island attended the army as a spectator."[200] Howe evidently did not know what to do with the hated Lord Bute's audacious and troublesome son, so Stuart seems to have gone wherever he pleased, looking for adventure. "He is very clever, exceedingly intelligent, takes great pains, and is as bold as a lion," is how Lt. Col. Allen Maclean, an old Scottish veteran, described Stuart in early 1777. "He is a fine young fellow, and I have lost my skill if he will not be one of the best officers in the King's service."[201] Stuart himself blithely told his father, "A ball gave me a pretty severe scratch in the cheek, and another went through the crown of my hat at the Brandy-Wine, or else I have escaped full well from all the dangers we have been in."[202]

"Recollecting the 43rd grenadier company was the left of their line," the 17th officer revealed, "we persuaded Major Stuart to run down the hill and prevail on that company to hasten to our support; he did so, but before he could return, to my inexpressible joy, saw Captain Cochrane of the 4th company on my left throw up his cap and cry 'Victory!'— and looking round saw the 43rd company hastening to our relief." As the American line began to break under the bayonet charge of Monckton's grenadiers, the four light infantry companies rose up and charged, followed by the rest of the 1st Light Infantry. "We dashed forward and passed the five pieces of cannon which the enemy had abandoned," the 17th officer boasted, "and made some few prisoners, the enemy running away from us, with too much speed to be overtaken."[203] Of the grenadiers, Robertson confirmed that "after crossing the Rails they immediately charged and drove the Rebels before them. At the same time the first Battn. of Light Infantry charged and took five Pieces of Cannon in their Front."[204]

Opposing the attack, "our men stood firing upon them most amazingly, killing almost all before them for near an hour till they got within 6 rod [30 to 35 yards] of each other," Lt. Ebenezer Elmer of the 3rd New Jersey wrote, referring to the British Light Infantry. Then, the British Grenadiers arrived: "A Column of the Enemy came upon our flank which Caused 'em to give way which soon extended all along ye line; we retreated & formed on ye first ground and gave 'em another fire & so continued on all ye way, but unfortunately for want of a proper Retreat 3 or 4 of our [artillery] pieces were left on ye first ground."[205]

One of the first accounts of the battle read by the British public appeared in the newspapers in December, including *Felix Farley's Bristol Journal.* "At the battle of Brandywine we had the most dreadful fire for one hour I ever saw," a grenadier officer wrote to a friend in Edinburgh. "I heard nothing equal to it all last war in Germany. At last we gave the rebels the bayonet, which soon dispersed them."[206]

Joseph Clark of New Jersey, on General Stephen's staff, noticed, "As their number was larger than was expected they streched their Line beyond ours, & flanked our right wing shortly after the action began. This occasioned the Line to break to prevent being surrounded, tho' the fireing while the action lasted was the warmest I believe that has been in America since the War begun." Clark, like many others, tried to collect accounts from different officers, as he seems to have been in the headquarters area near Chads's Ford, probably as a liaison officer. Reports of heavy British casualties were told, retold, and recirculated: "As our men on the left of the Line were pretty well stationed, they swept of[f] great numbers of the Enemy before they retreated and from the best accounts I could collect from the Officers in the Action the Enemy must have suffered very much from our people before they broke." He mentioned, significantly, "Tho' indeed Our people suffered pretty much in this action."[207]

The Chevalier Dubuysson, Lafayette's companion, was with the young Marquis and General Conway in the center. "Only the divisions of Lord Stirling and M. de Conway held out for any length of time," the twenty-five-year-old French volunteer wrote. "The Marquis de Lafayette joined the latter, where there were some Frenchmen. He dismounted and did his utmost to make the men charge with fixed bayonets." According to Dubuysson, "The Frenchmen personally attached their bayonets for them, and Lafayette pushed them in the back to make them charge. But the Americans are not suited for this type of combat, and never wanted to take it up. . . . Soon that brigade fled like the rest of the army." Dubuysson also noted, "It was there that Lafayette was wounded."[208]

Lafayette, writing in the third person, stated, "The confusion became extreme, and it was while M. de Lafayette was rallying the troops that a ball passed through his leg. At that moment the remaining forces gave way, and M. de Lafayette was fortunate to be able to mount a horse, thanks to Gimat, his aide-de-camp." After three painful weeks of convalescing, Lafayette told his wife, Adrienne, in a light-hearted way, "About that particular eleventh [of September], I have a tale to tell you." Revealing only that he was very slightly wounded, "I do not know how I received it," he wrote, not wanting her to worry. "In truth," he lied to her, "I did not expose myself to enemy fire. It was my first battle, so you see how rare battles are."[209] Barely out of his teens, one of the most popular and romantic American heroes thus was created in the midst of a collapsing battle line.

Across the field, Capt. William Dansey, commanding the 33rd Light Company in the 1st Light Infantry, was lightly wounded but in great pain. Terrified, he and his light bobs took cover under the showers of musket balls and grapeshot ripping up the ground and fences and comrades nearby. "I don't know how I shall end this Letter or when," he told his mother and girlfriend a month later. "I write to you and Miss Malit as soon as I was able to handle a Pen which I do now in Pain and can not bear to write long at a time, owing to a slight Wound I received. . . . I was shot thro' the joint of my right Thumb, which did not make me quit the Field or my Duty afterwards," he quickly reassured them. Reflecting on the danger of battle, he added, "You will be thankful with me that's no worse for where I expected to have lost my head I had liked to have lost my Thumb." The trauma of the experience was evident, both in this letter and the next, where he gave yet another indication of the sheer volume of gunfire. "Thank God it is no worse," he wrote a few days later. "I wou'd have given half a Dozen Thumbs to have been assured Life and Limb at the Time."[210]

It could have been much worse. Across the field in Stirling's New Jersey Line, Lt. John Shreve watched as "a cannon-ball went through Captain Stout and through a sergeant that stood behind him, and killed them both."[211] Coming up the slope, the 1st Light Infantry, now supported by the 2nd Grenadier Battalion, hit Conway's 3rd Pennsylvania Brigade on Stirling's right flank hard, and the momentum caused Stirling's line to unravel. "At the same time we were attacked on the right, another attack was made on the left, where our people fought them, retreating in good order," Dr. Howell of the 2nd New Jersey Regiment wrote. With Sullivan's Division gone in chaos, the 1st Grenadier Battalion was able to advance quickly toward Stirling's exposed left flank, forcing the New Jersey Brigade to pull back or face annihilation. "Our people at last gave way, not being supported, with the loss of very few wounded and killed, not exceeding twelve," the surgeon continued. "Colonel Shreve in that action was wounded in the thigh, but not mortally. Captain Stout was killed, and one sergeant. These are the only killed in our regiment." As for himself, Dr. Howell reported, "I shall inform you of my escape from the enemy, after having been among them, with the loss of my mare, saddle and bridle, and great coat and hat. With all my misfortunes I think myself happy, not to be taken prisoner."[212]

"I beleive before G. S. D. [General Sullivan's Division] was formed as they changed their ground on which they first draw up, a number of them was marching past my Regiment when the first fire began," recalled Col. Elias Dayton of the 3rd New Jersey Regiment, holding the center of Stirling's line. "Consequently I belive [they] never fired a gun, in half an hour at furtherst the whole of our men gave wey. The Enemy pursued briskly by which means A number of our wounded as allso some well men fell into their hands."[213]

With Stirling dislodged, the 2nd Light Infantry began to advance. Five companies managed to move up the hill across open ground toward Scott's Brigade on Stephen's left flank, which was uncovered by Stirling's withdrawal. Then Gen. James Agnew's 4th Brigade, four regiments of British regulars following the light infantry battalions, came up in support behind the 1st Light Infantry. The 4th Brigade had advanced in a column of battalions, with the 800 men of the 37th and 64th Regiments in front, followed by the 33rd and 46th, another 700. In mapping this intricate maneuver, Captain Robertson of the Engineers noted, "When the 4th Brigade which followed the Rear of the first Battalion Light Infantry gained the Hill" from which the five American guns had been firing, "the two Rear Battalions—the 33rd and 46th—filed off to their left in the Rear of the 5 Companies of the 2nd Battalion of Light Infantry, who by that time had got upon the Flank of the Rebels." The five companies got up to the Birmingham Road and moved in a column under trees through Sandy Hollow itself, where there was a gap of nearly 300 yards between Stirling's right and Stephen's left, probably caused by the earlier "Sullivan shift" and the terrain. Now, with support from the 33rd and 46th Regiments, they "facilitated the Charge made by the remainder of the 2nd Battalion of Light Infantry and Chasseurs [Jägers] across the Field" at Sandy Hollow.[214]

A quarter mile away on the far left of the British line, von Wurmb's Jägers were still bogged down in the ravine below Sandy Hollow by the fire from Woodford's Brigade. "By six o'clock our left wing still had not been able to advance," von Münchhausen stated. "Here the rebels fought very bravely and did not retreat until they heard in their rear General Knyphausen's fire coming nearer."[215] Lieutenant von Feilitzsch of the Anspach Jägers wrote, "The small arms fire was terrible, the counter-fire from the enemy, especially against us, was the most concentrated."[216]

Capt. Carl von Wreden, commanding the Hessian Jäger company on the left flank, decided on a daring solution that required bravery and skill. A squad of six marksmen led by a sergeant was sent to swing out wide around Woodford's right. "Sergeant Bickell of Captain Wreden's Company, who had the flanking battalion, moved left to a hill," Colonel von Wurmb reported to his superiors in Hesse-Cassel, "where he disrupted the enemy for a half hour."[217]

Sgt. Alexander Wilhelm Bickell was a twenty-five-year-old forester from the village of Bischhausen, near Eschwege in Hesse. He had volunteered for service in the Hessian Leib-Jäger Corps in 1772 and rose to the rank of sergeant by 1777. His portrait shows a handsome soldier with "an oval face, a strong-minted nose, light blue eyes," and though he had been clean-shaven, "a fast-growing beard, shown as a shadow."[218]

Taking six Jägers around Stephen's right flank, Bickell helped break the stubborn American defense with rifle fire from behind. The sharpshooters wrought havoc by steady, accurate harassing fire at long range. "During the action Colonel Wurmb fell on the flank of the enemy, and Sergeant Bickell with six jägers moved to his rear," Capt. Johann Ewald said, detailing the straw that broke the camel's back of Sullivan's last defense, "whereupon the entire right wing of the enemy fled to Dilworthtown."[219] For his valor, Bickell was rewarded with the rank of second lieutenant, a rare promotion of a soldier from the ranks to the officer corps.

"Then we heard the firing to our right become lively and detected movements among the enemy," von Wurmb reported, describing the momentum caused by the British bayonet charge at the other end of the line, "whereupon we attacked them in God's Name and drove them from their post."[220] Over the deafening roar of gunfire, the charge was sounded by the shrill piping of whistles, the long roll of beating drums, and the brassy wail of half-moon horns. "Lieutenant Colonel von Wurmb heard that the right wing was advancing," the Hessian Jäger Corps journal recorded. "Therefore, he had the call to attack sounded on the half moon, and the Jägers and the battalion of Light Infantry stormed up the height." The throaty battle cries of the men roared out also. British and American troops traditionally shouted, *"Huzza!"* ("huh-ZAH!"); the Germans, especially the Jägers, often used "the favorite cry of Frederick the Great—*'ALLONS! ALLONS!'* [*"Let's go! Let's go!"*]." The journal continued, "The enemy retreated in confusion, abandoning two cannons and an ammunition wagon, which the Light Infantry, because they had attacked on the less steep slope of the height, took possession of."[221]

As the whole British left swept forward, Lt. Martin Hunter of the 2nd Light Infantry also recognized the bravery of his opponents, Scott's and Woodford's Virginians. "They stood the charge till we came to the last paling. Their line then began to break, and a general retreat took place soon after, except from their guns, many of which were defended to the last; indeed, several officers were cut down at the guns." With the perspective of having been in the campaigns since Bunker Hill in 1775, Hunter added, "The Americans never fought so well before, and they fought to great advantage."[222] General Woodford himself was wounded, shot through the hand.

"As we were going up the hill, the English light infantry moved in 10 paces ahead of us and used the cannon, since we were very fatigued from the long march," Colonel von Wurmb observed somewhat ruefully. Arriving at the summit, the Jäger commander noted, "Many dead lay to our front," mostly from Woodford's Brigade.[223]

"The enemy had made a good disposition with one height after the other to his rear," Lieutenant von Feilitzsch confirmed, writing with slight hyperbole, "He stood fast and was certainly four times as strong as we were. However, all the English and Hessians conducted themselves as they are well-known to do. They attacked with great strength and with the bayonet." Jäger casualties were relatively light: Among the Anspachers, the lieutenant reported, "Our company suffered four wounded and five dead, including one officer," Lt. Carl von Forstner, "who will surely die later." Total Jäger casualties amounted to two officers and six men dead, and three sergeants and thirty-five men severely wounded. Von Feilitzsch piously added, "Once again, God has helped us."[224]

"The General fire of the Line Lasted an hour & forty minutes," Sullivan recounted, "fifty one minutes of which the Hill was Disputed almost Muzzle to Muzzle in Such a manner that General Conway who has Seen much Service Says he never Saw So Close & Severe a fire." At Sandy Hollow, "on the Right where General Stephen was," facing the Jägers and British light infantry, Sullivan said, "it was Long & Severe & on the Left Considerable—when we found the Right & Left oppressed by Numbers & giving way in all Quarters we were oblidged to Abandon the Hill we had So Long contended for," significantly adding, "but not till we had almost Covered the Ground between that & Bremingham meeting House with The Dead Bodies of the Enemy."[225]

Here again, a combination of actual British casualties, together with the British light infantry repeatedly dropping to the ground and holding firm, plus poor visibility as a result of the terrain, heavy smoke, clouds of dust, and sun glare—as by now the sun was making its protracted descent in the western sky, shining through the battle haze into the faces of the American forces—all contributed to the perception that British casualties were covering the ground. In the woods, late-afternoon sunlight streaming through full-leaf foliage and white smoke casts ever-changing beams and shafts of light as well as lengthening shadows. Because of this, together with the stress and mayhem of combat, visual distortion is a common feature of warfare and was one of the main reasons for the colorful uniforms and large battle flags of the period.

As the American line broke, General Howe, who had been observing the initial advance from Osborne's Hill, moved forward with his staff. Emmor Jefferis, a local farmer who owned the farm west of the Brandywine at Jefferis's Ford, "was compelled to guide the British Army towards Birmingham Meeting" earlier in the afternoon. "After the retreat commenced, Howe moved on after the army, taking Mr. Jefferis some distance with him." As they came near the fighting, "the bullets from the Americans whistled so sharply by him, that he could not refrain from dodging his head, as they passed." The terror exhibited by this middle-age Quaker countryman was so amusing that, "Sir William observing, called out very encouragingly—*'Don't be afraid Mr. Jefferis, they wont hurt you.'* Mr. J. however, took the earliest opportunity to quit the scene, and return home."[226]

"As usual, the General exposed himself fearlessly on this occasion," von Münchhausen noted with admiration. "He quickly rushed to each spot where he heard the strongest fire. Cannon balls and bullets passed close to him in numbers today." An old light infantryman himself, Howe's personal bravery under fire was, like Washington's, extraordinary, sometimes even foolhardy. "We all fear that, since he is so daring on any and all occasions," the Hessian aide commented apprehensively, "we are going to lose our best friend, and that England will lose America."[227]

But the battle was far from over. "At half after four O'Clock, the Enemy attacked Genl Sullivan, and the Action has been very violent ever since," Washington told Congress at 5 P.M. "It still continues." He informed John Hancock that at Chads's Ford, "there has been a Scattering loose fire between our parties on each side of the Creek, since the Action in the Morning, which just now became warm," and "a very severe Cannonade has begun here too." The intensity of the gunfire was such that he was moved to say, "I suppose we shall have a very hot Evening."[228] It proved to be one of the hottest evenings of the war.

"We remained in presence of the whole Rebell Army from Nine in the morning till after four in the afternoon," Grant wrote about the day at Chads's Ford, with "constant skirmishing or rather poping & frequently a Cannonade from both sides." He lauded his commander by saying, "Genl. Howe surely deserves great Credit for the Move, his Disposition was masterly, & He executed his Plan with ability." Not one to miss an opportunity for self-congratulation, Grant asserted that the plan had worked brilliantly, in his humble opinion, thanks to him, even though von Knyphausen was in command of the column. "Washington having no intelligence of the Disposition of the Army, was convinced that our whole force was opposite to Him," the Scottish general boasted, "& was confirmed in that opinion, by Detachments which I made in the course of the Day of the 4th, 5th, & 27th Regts. with Artillery to keep possession of the Heights upon our Left & to prevent the Rebells from passing the River upon that Flank," referring to Sullivan's aborted crossing at Brinton's Ford. "Those Regts. He consider'd as so many Brigades detached in order to pass the River in different Columns & was so much convinced of it, that He took no Care of his Right & only sent detached Corps to defend the Fords in my Front."

But the waiting took its toll on nerves, even those of the high and pompous. "I expected the Action to begin about two o'clock," Grant informed his friend. "I had made my mind up to that, but from two to four I became anxious," he admitted. "The minutes were Hours, I was uneasy & impatient."[229]

"Presently a total silence ensued," Captain Downman of the Royal Artillery wrote of the midafternoon at Chads's Ford, "General Knyphausen ordered us to leave off." The tension grew as the minutes ticked by. "We began to be uneasy about General Howe" after Sullivan's Division pulled away from Brinton's Ford, "for a great force of the rebels marched from the hills and woods before us towards him." Two hours later, "our doubts were eased, for we heard a firing on our left, at first gentle, but in a little [while] very heavy indeed both of cannon and musketry." About an hour after the firing started, "we saw the rebels," remnants of Sullivan's shattered division, "running in multitudes out of the woods. We now began again with all our artillery to play on the flying scoundrels; the fire was returned by them from all their batteries."[230]

In pursuit of Sullivan's retreating troops were the rapidly advancing Guards and Col. William Medows's 1st Grenadier Battalion, supported by the 16th Light Dragoons and followed at a distance by the slow but steady Hessian grenadiers. The Guards and British grenadiers had been gradually separating ever since they crossed the Street Road. The Hessian grenadiers were supposed to fill the gap, which was several hundred yards wide and growing at every step.

Then, as Sullivan's Division scattered, the two Guards battalions separated. The 1st Battalion swung wide to the right and swept along the heights of the Brandywine, with the 16th Dragoons in support, while the 2nd Battalion continued straight ahead. The three Hessian grenadier battalions lumbered on, attempting to fill the widening space between the Guards and the British grenadiers. "The Guards who formed the right wing and were supported by the Minnigerode Battalion in the 2nd line engaged the enemy," reported a Hessian officer of the Lengerke Grenadier Battalion, "and sent them flying through wood and field, over mountains and valleys until we joined the Knyphausen Corps at nightfall."[231]

The terrain was difficult, with one high, rocky climb and descent after another, though woods and soggy bottoms of creeks that emptied into the Brandywine floodplain. "In passing through a cornfield" somewhere in the midst of the retreat, Col. Samuel Smith of the 4th Maryland "discovered a flanking party of the enemy, which he checked by two fires from his small number and received one from them, by which he lost one man who was shot in the heel." In the ensuing confusion, "some of the men left him; and he retired, almost alone, to the top of a high hill, on which he halted, and collected nearly one thousand men; formed them into Companies; and remained until near sunset."[232]

Just beyond the road connecting Brinton's Ford and the village of Dilworth, "one Battalion of the Guards [the 2nd Battalion], the three Battalions of Hessian Grenadiers, and the first Battalion British Grenadiers halted, having in their Front a Ravine, and a woody rocky Hill almost impassable." These troops had reached the 270-foot precipice above Brinton's Run, about half a mile east of the ford. "The 16th of Light Dragoons who were on the right with the Guards, and who could never have an opportunity to charge from the closeness of the Country, were halted," swung to the left, "then marched up the Road to Dillworth to the left of the Army," two miles away.[233]

On the right, the 1st Guards Battalion, with Osborn's grenadiers and light bobs leading the way, filed to the right down a road that crossed Brinton's Run at the Brandywine floodplain halfway between Brinton's Ford and Chads's Ford. "We now saw our brave fellows under Howe push out of the woods after the rebels," Downman reported when the Guards appeared near Brinton's Ford. "We renew our fire from the artillery to scour the woods," pelting the retreating Marylanders with 12-pound shot ricocheting through the trees and 8-inch explosive shells from the royal howitzers. "They fly from all quarters," Downman wrote with enthusiasm, though, according to Jacob Nagle of the Continental Artillery, "While at a distance, the Brittish shells that they hove from their howetors never busted, which saved a good many men."[234] Down near Proctor's battery, Nagle witnessed "one shell, while the fuse was burning, a soldier run and nocked out the tube which provented it from bursting."[235]

"Our battery Soon opened about 600 or 700 Yards from theirs, when a very Warm thundering began," James Parker wrote. "The Rebels fired grape & exploding shells. Capt. Steuart who Commanded at our battery kept a warm fire for near a half hour."[236] Joseph Clark, the deputy muster master of Stephen's Division, confirmed that "the Batteries at the middle Ford opened upon each other with such fury as if the Elements had been in convulsion, the valley was filled with smoke, and now I grew seriously anxious for the Event: for an hour and a half, this horrid sport continued."[237]

Shortly after the report to Congress was written, Washington ordered Greene to pull his division, which consisted of Weedon's and Muhlenberg's Brigades, nearly all Virginians, away from Chads's Ferry and move toward the rear and right to reinforce Sullivan. Initially leaving Wayne, Maxwell, and Nash to hold Chads's Ford, the commander in chief himself headed up toward the trouble spot. "On the commencement of the action on the right," wrote Capt. John Marshall of the 15th Virginia, "General Washington pressed forward with Greene, to the support of that wing."[238]

Washington ordered the 2nd Brigade, Muhlenberg's, to take another route, as it could not "be up in time for service."[239] Weedon's Brigade headed east, then north toward Dilworth. Consisting of the 2nd, 3rd, 4th, 10th, and 14th Virginia Regiments and Col. Walter Stewart's Pennsylvania State Regiment, Weedon's troops made one of the all-time record-setting quick marches in military history. "I marched one brigade of my division, being upon the left wing, between three and four miles in forty-five minutes," Greene recounted, the troops double-timing up the same steep, winding roads that Stirling and Stephen had taken earlier. "When I came to the ground," the plateau southwest of Dilworth, "I found the whole of the troops routed and retreating precipitately, and in the most broken and confused manner."[240] Brig. Gen. George Weedon of Virginia wrote, "About 6, General Green's Division arrived to cover the Retreat." He added laconically, "One of his Brigades (Weedon's) gave the Enemy such a check as to produce the desired Effect."[241]

Before Washington headed to the right, Pickering recalled, "he charged me with an order, to deliver it to Genl. Nash of the No. Carolina brigade, at Chads' ford." The adjutant general did not say what was in the message, but it was probably orders for Nash to send his brigade to the right. "I delivered the order," Pickering remembered, "and just then fell in with Col. Fitzgerald, one of the Generals' aids, and we galloped to the right where the action had commenced, and as we proceeded, we heard heavy and uninterrupted discharges of musketry (and doubtless of artillery) but the peals of musketry were most striking."[242]

Sullivan's whole wing was now in full retreat from Sandy Hollow back toward Dilworth. "The weather was very warm, and tho' my knapsack was very light, was very cumbersome, as it swung about when walking or running, and in crossing fences was in the way so I cast it away from me," wrote Sgt. John Hawkins of Hazen's regiment, one of the last units to fall back, "and had I not done so would have been grabbed by one of the ill-looking Highlanders, a number of whom were fireing and advancing very brisk towards our rear." The faint skirl of bagpipes may have pierced the din as McPherson's Company of Royal Highlanders in the 1st Light Infantry Battalion pursued the Americans, as did the two companies of Fraser's 71st Highlanders in the 2nd Light Infantry. "The smoke was so very thick that about the close of the day I lost sight of our regiment," Hawkins lamented.[243]

No sooner did Greene pull away from the Chads's Ford area than the lower jaw of Howe's pincers began to close. "At 4 o'Clock by an uninter-rupted firing of Musketry, first we discovered the Commander in Chief's Approach & Attack upon the right of the Ennemy," von Knyphausen reported to Lord Germain. The Hessian general ordered two 12-pounders and two 6-pounders to be placed "near the Creek to cover the going over of the Troops."[244] At the same time, the attack column of nearly 5,000 troops was formed: the 4th and 5th Regiments in front, about 700 men; followed by the 2nd Battalion of the 71st Regiment, consisting of nearly 350 of Frazer's Highlanders detached from the other two battalions, who remained guarding the baggage; Ferguson's Riflemen and the Queen's Rangers, badly shot up and now numbering less than 300; and the 23rd Royal Welsh Fusiliers, numbering about 350. Behind them was "the Remainder of the 1st & 2nd Brigade," about 2,000 men, as well as a handful of "Light Dragoons, & Major General Stirn's Brigade" of four Hessian regiments, nearly 2,000 strong.[245] "Lieut. Genl. Knyphausen push'd his Troops (which had been assembled under cover of the Woods) across Chad's Ford, the 4th Regt. leading," Captain Robertson noted on his map.[246]

"About half after five in the Evening, a heavy Column of the Brittish Troops crossd Chads ford, at the Place on which our Division Genl. Waines solely was stationd," Lt. Col. Adam Hubley of the 10th Pennsyl-vania told his brother.[247] The British crossed the Brandywine both at the ford and the ferry, and then had to pass through more than 200 yards of swampy area east of the crossings, all the while under fire from Proctor's guns and Maxwell's light troops. "The Fourth Regiment led the Column and the Queen's Rangers followed," Sgt. Stephen Jarvis of the Rangers wrote, "the battery playing upon us with grape shot, which did much execution. The water took us up to our breasts, and was much stained with blood."[248]

"The 4th & 5th Regt., the 2nd Battaillon of the 71st, the British Riflemen & Queens Rangers having pass'd the Ford, which was about thirty Paces broad, continued their March on the Road," von Knyphausen explained.[249] Robertson wrote that "as they were obliged to advance in Column along the Road on Account of the Morass on their Flanks, they were galled by Musketry from the Woods on their right and by round and grape Shot from two Pieces of Cannon and an 8 inch Howitzer from the Battery in their Front."[250]

The troops, "when they came near the Battery, drew up to the left, & attack'd the ennemy in such a Manner as forced them to quit it," von Knyphausen reported.[251] The battalion companies of the 4th Regiment led the assault on the guns. "As the 4th Battalion (being the first) forded the River, under a heavy fire of Musquetry," Sgt. Thomas Sullivan of the 49th revealed that "the Enemy's Cannon missing fire in the Battery as they crossed, and before the Gunners could fire them off, the men of that Battallion put them to the Bayonets, and forced the Enemy from the Entrenchment."[252] James Parker told his friend in Edinburgh, "The 4th the 5 & the Queens Rangers Crossed the Creek & in 11 Minutes after they had parted with us they was in the Rebel fort. The 10th Regt. Cross'd next. I went with them."[253] Sergeant Jarvis of the Queen's Rangers recalled, "Immediately after our Regiment had crossed, two Companies (the Grenadiers and Capt. McKay's) was ordered to move to the left and take possession of a hill which the enemy was retiring from, and wait there until further orders."[254]

From another hill somewhere behind the American lines, "about sunset I saw a Collumn of the Enemy advance to one of our Batteries & take it," Joseph Clark observed. "Under cover of their Cannon they had crosed at the Ford & were advancing in a large body."[255] Using the base of the hill as cover (as the light infantry had done on Birmingham Hill), redcoats and greencoats moved below the muzzles of the guns around the front to the left of the battery and stormed it on its right flank. "The British advenced to the very works, though our artilery made a clear lane through them as they mounted the works, but they filled up the ranks again," Continental artilleryman Jacob Nagle wrote. "One noble officer," possibly Capt. John Rawdon of the 4th, "mounting the works, cried out, 'Come on my Brittons, the day is our own.' At that moment, one of Capt.

Joneses brass 9 lbr. [sic; 4-pounder] went off, and he was no more, with a number more."[256] None of the British officers killed in the battle were in that area at that time; Rawdon, the only 4th Regiment officer listed as a casualty, was wounded, but he survived.

Capt. James Moncrieff of the British Engineers "was in the front of a column which advanced to a redoubt," according to John Graves Simcoe, who was wounded at Brandywine. "There was a howitzer in it, loaded with grapeshot, pointed directly toward the column and a man standing by it, with a lighted match in his hand." Simcoe related that "Moncrief, with his usual presence of mind, called out 'I'll put you to death if you fire.' The Man threw down the match and ran off." Ironically, "had he fired he could equally have escaped."[257]

"When we began to retreat," Nagle recalled, "while the infantry covered us, we had a mash [marsh] or swampy ground to cross with the artillery to get into the road, and the horses being shot, the men could not drag the peaces out. Therefore we had to spike two pieces and a howetor [howitzer]." In the chaos of the fight, a fallen officer's horse caught Nagle's attention. "In the retreat I saw a beutiful charger, all white, in a field next the road with an elegant saddle and holsters, and gold lace housing, and his bridle broke off, and his rider gone. I made an attempt to ketch him, but he was skared, and the enemy keeping up a constant fire, I thought it best to leave him."[258]

The guns in Proctor's battery were abandoned. General Wayne "sent orders for our artillery to retreat—it was on my right," Col. James Chambers of the 1st Pennsylvania Regiment explained, "and ordered me to cover it with part of my regiment. It was done, but to my surprise the artillerymen had run and left the howitzer behind." Some guns made it away: "The two field pieces went up the road, protected by about sixty of my men, who had very warm work, but brought them safe. I then ordered another party to fly to the howitzer and bring it off." Capt. Thomas Buchanan and Lt. Michael Simpson of the 1st Pennsylvania and Lt. Thomas Douglass of the 4th Continental Artillery "went immediately to the gun, and the men followed their example, and I covered them with the few I had remaining," Chambers told Gen. Edward Hand. "But before this could be done, the main body of the foe came within thirty yards, and kept up the most terrible fire I suppose ever heard in America, though with very little loss on our side."[259]

"A colored man," referring to thirty-year-old Pvt. Edward "Ned" Hector of Capt. Hercules Courtenay's 3rd Company of Pennsylvania Artillery, "had charge of an ammunition wagon attached to Col. Proctor's regiment."[260] Most teamsters were hired civilians, and many were free men of color, but Ned Hector, or "Negro Hector" as one muster sheet reads, was an enlisted man in 1777. He was a bombardier, defined as "an artillery soldier, so called because they are always employed in mortar and howitzer duty."[261] As the British overran the battery, "an order was given by the proper officers to those having charge of the wagons, to abandon them to the enemy, and save themselves by flight." Ned was reported to have replied, "The enemy shall not have my team; I will save my horses and myself." As he withdrew with his wagon, "amid the confusion of the surrounding scene, he calmly gathered up a few stands of arms which had been left on the field by the retreating soldiers, and safely retired with his wagon, team and all, in face of the victorious foe." An act of valor by an American soldier of African descent "will soon be forgotten," his obituary stated years later, "and yet, many a monument has been 'reared to some proud son of earth' who less deserved it than 'poor old Ned.'"[262]

As Maxwell's Light Corps fell back, "many of them Ran to an Orchard to the right of the fort, from which they were Drove to a Meadow, where they made a Stand for some time in a ditch & a battry which till then was still not begun from a hill on our right," James Parker reported. "But nothing could stand before our lads, they routed them from the Meadow, & all afterwards was a mere Chace, so far I saw."[263]

At one point during the fighting in this area, Jacob Nagle had the fright of his life. "In the heat of the action close to the orchard that I already made mention of I see some men burien an officer who wore the same dress that my father wore, which was green turned up with read fasings [red facings] and gold lace. I was ready to faint. I run up to the officer and enquired what rigment he belonged to. He informed me he was a colo[nel] belonging to the Virginia Line, which gave me comfort but sorrowful."[264] Who the officer might have been is unknown.

Downstream at Chads's Ferry, "we were up to our middle in the River," Sgt. Thomas Sullivan of the 49th recounted, "and the rear line of the Enemy being posted upon a Hill on the other side of the Road, plaid upon us with four Pieces of Cannon during that attack."[265] This battery was about 800 yards south of Proctor's position, firing on the British right flank.

After crossing, Sgt. Sullivan noticed that the Americans, "who drawing up in the field and orchard just by, rallied afresh and fought Bayonet
to Bayonet." They were some of Maxwell's Light Corps, "but the rest of
the two Brigades, 71st and Rangers coming up," the rebels "were obliged
to retreat in the greatest confusion, leaving their Artillery & Ammunition
in the Field." The American advance troops on the left, facing the force
crossing Chads's Ferry, were probably some of the militia attached to
Maxwell and "made but a little stand on that side," according to Sergeant
Sullivan. "After they began to give way," the Irish sergeant witnessed a
grisly scene: "Part of them being attacked by the Rangers and 71st in a
Buck Wheat field was totally scivered [skewered] with the Bayonets before
they could clear the fence round it."[266] On a hill near Proctor's battery,
Sergeant Jarvis of the Queen's Rangers observed with grim satisfaction,
"From the eminence we had a most extensive view of the American Army,
and we saw our brave comrades cutting them up in great style."[267] Of his
rifle corps, Pat Ferguson painfully scribbled to his brother George with
his left hand that "they finished the day by killing or taking in conjunction with part of Wemyss' Rangers their own number of Rebels."[268]

Von Knyphausen noted that Proctor's position "was supported by the
Musketry of the Battaillons, that were formed behind the Battery."[269] Five
hundred yards east of the ford, the two Pennsylvania brigades of Wayne's
Division, nine regiments totaling about 2,000 men, were spread thin in
one battle line, with high hills on both flanks. Like several other Continental divisions, their command structure was "deranged." There should
have been three generals here—two brigadiers and one major general.
Instead, there was only one, Anthony Wayne, a brigadier who was acting
as a major general in place of Gen. Benjamin Lincoln.

The four regiments of the 2nd Brigade, commanded by a former
British officer, forty-four-year-old Col. Richard Humpton of York-
shire, England, was formed on the left, with Wayne's old regiment, the
5th Pennsylvania, holding the left flank. Made up largely of Chester
County men, the 5th Pennsylvania was led by Col. Francis Johnston of
Nottingham and Lt. Col. Persifor Frazer of nearby Thornbury. The
11th Pennsylvania was right next to the 5th, followed by the 8th and
4th Pennsylvania Regiments.

The 1st Brigade, commanded by twenty-eight-year-old Col. Thomas
Hartley of York, Pennsylvania, formed the division's right wing and was

composed of five regiments. The severely understrengthed 2nd Pennsylvania Regiment, barely 100 men, was commanded by Maj. William Williams and posted on the left. Next came the 10th Pennsylvania, then Hartley's Additional Continental Regiment in the center, adjoining the 7th Pennsylvania, the largest regiment in Wayne's command, with about 350 men.

Wayne's right flank rested on the Great Road; holding the "post of honor" on the right was the 1st Pennsylvania Regiment, composed mainly of Pennsylvania riflemen and commanded by Col. James Chambers. The 1st Pennsylvania was not only the senior regiment in the Pennsylvania Line, but also the first regular regiment in the U.S. Army. It was originally Thompson's Pennsylvania Rifle Battalion, the first regiment formed in response to Congress's authorization for a national, or Continental, army in June 1775. Many of its original personnel were still in the ranks. In January 1776, Thompson's was renamed the 1st Continental Regiment, out of twenty-six regiments, and in July of that year it became the 1st Pennsylvania. Here at Brandywine, its unusual regimental flag, one of the few still in existence, flew proudly in the center of the line. The flag was a large square of green silk with a small, red square in the center, on which was depicted a hunter holding a spear against a netted, rampant tiger. Below this was a scroll with the motto *Domari Nolo*, "I refuse to be subjugated."

The artillery park was on the hill above to the right, and Proctor's earthwork lunette battery was 200 yards in front of the park. "The troops that were on the right of our brigade, on the hill," Stirling's and Stephen's Divisions, "were drawn off, and left our right flank quite uncovered," Chambers told Edward Hand, the 1st Pennsylvania's previous commander, now a brigadier general in charge of Fort Pitt. "The enemy kept an unremitting fire from their artillery (and ours too played with great fury), until advancing under the thick smoke they took possession of the redoubt in front of our park," which was Proctor's battery. "As there were no troops to cover the artillery in the redoubt, the enemy was within thirty yards before being discovered; our men were forced to fly, and to leave three pieces behind."[270]

"The Brittish Troops came on with the Greatest boldness & bravery, and began a most heavy fire on us," Lt. Col. Adam Hubley of the 10th Pennsylvania wrote, assuring his brother John, "We returnd it a heavy."

The 10th Pennsylvania Regiment was posted to the left center of the 1st Brigade, next to Hartley's regiment, which was in the center. In the heavy exchange of fire, Maj. Lewis Bush of Hartley's regiment had his horse shot out from under him. No sooner did he remount than he toppled over, mortally wounded. "When he received his wound fell in my Arms," Hubley informed his brother.[271] Maj. Lewis Bush was the highest-ranking American soldier killed in the battle.

On Wayne's left, the 2nd Brigade was also slugging it out, enduring heavy musket and cannon fire. Lt. Gabriel Peterson of the 8th Pennsylvania, in the right center of the brigade, said that he was near twenty-nine-year-old Maj. Stephen Bayard "when he was struck down by a cannon ball, that broke a rifle gun of Sergt. [Thomas] Wyatt and his shoulder and then struck Bayard on the head and shoulder, and tumbled him over the ground for near two rods," about thirty feet. Peterson helped Bayard up. "He was frantic, and seemed much hurt, but being much engaged at the time," the lieutenant "could not render him any assistance."[272]

On Wayne's far-right flank, "Our brigade was drawn into line, with the park of artillery two hundred yards, in the rear of the redoubt," Chambers wrote. "Our park was ordered off then, and my right was exposed." Suddenly, filtering through the woods over the hill on the right of the Pennsylvania Line came red-clad troops, "the lads," as the Americans sometimes called their British opponents. "The enemy advanced on the hill, where our park was, and came within fifty yards of the hill above me," Chambers reported. It was the Guards, with Osborn's flank companies in the lead and the rest of the 1st Battalion on the way. "I then ordered my men to fire," said Chambers. The majority of the 1st Pennsylvania were veteran riflemen, so the gunfire would have been sharp and accurate. Prudently, the advance parties of the Guards pulled back until the rest of the battalion came up; or, as Chambers put it, "Two or three rounds made the lads clear the ground."[273]

"The Guards met with very little resistence and penetrated to the height overlooking the 4-gun battery of the rebels at Chad's Ford just as General Knyphausen had crossed," Capt. John André noted in his diary, indicating on his map the Guards' advance to both the battery and the hills overlooking Wayne's position.[274] Robertson carefully delineated that "one Battalion of the Guards filed off to their right," crossed Brinton's Run, "and forming at W," the hill where Sullivan's two-gun battery had been placed to cover Brinton's Ford and the bridge of wagons and rails that was probably thrown across the Brandywine, "advanced to X," the hill above Proctor's battery, "by which means they came upon the right Flank of the Rebels who had opposed Lieut. Genl. Knyphausen's Column, who now gave way on all sides, but Night coming on hindered a Pursuit."[275]

Coming up behind the Guards from Chads's Ford were hundreds of British troops, led by the Royal Welsh Fusiliers, their regimental flags embroidered with the three feathers and crown of the prince of Wales and the motto *Ich Dien,* "I serve." "The 23rd Regt. with the Remainder of the 1st & 2nd Brigade . . . got upon the Height a short Time after them where they every where met with dispersed parties of the Ennemy, that had fled from the Guards & Grenadiers, who occupied about the same Time a Height something more to the left," hovering above Wayne's right.[276]

Wayne was now seriously outnumbered and outflanked on both wings, with Guards and Welsh Fusiliers gathering on the right and several hundred vengeful Queen's Rangers and ferocious Highlanders of the 71st pressing on the center and left, all supported by two British brigades and Hessian musket battalions crossing the creek in strength. As darkness descended, the Pennsylvanians grudgingly withdrew about 600 yards to a height. Pvt. James Patten of the Pennsylvania Militia was in Dunlap's Partizan Regiment, attached to Maxwell's Corps. Patten "assisted at this battle in covering the retreat of Genl. Wayne and aided in drawing his cannon up a hill or steep to the heighths of that place."[277]

"I brought all the brigade artillery safely off, and I hope to see them again fired at the scoundrels," Chambers vowed. "Yet we retreated to the next height in good order, in the midst of a very heavy fire of cannon and small arms. Not thirty yards distant, we formed to receive them, but they did not choose to follow."[278] General von Knyphausen told Lord Germain that Wayne's men, "upon the troops coming up, retired from one Inclosure to the other, & were driven by the gallant Behaviour of the Troops back to the Heights to the left of the Road to Chester."[279] Colonel Hubley informed his brother, "The Action Lasted Nearly to Night when the Genl. thought proper to retire about 600 yds. on an Eminence opposite the Enemy, leaving the Enemy to bemoan the Loss of Considerable Numbers of their Vatren Soldiers, slain on the feild of Battle."[280]

"As all our Militia were at the lower Ford where was no action, & Genl. Green sent to reinforced at the upper Ford, we had not a very large party to oppose the Enemy at the middle Ford," Joseph Clark observed. Describing the Pennsylvania Line's withdrawal, he wrote, "The Body stationed across the Valley drew off to the right & formed farther back on an Eminence when an Engagement began with musketry & the Enemy gave way," probably referring to the advance companies of the Guards pulling back. "But as night was spreading its dusky shade thro' the gloomy valley, & our army was something broke it was necessary to leave the field of Action & take care of the Troops. Accordingly after sunset the party at the middle Ford drew off & marched down to Chester, where the whole army by appointment met. The sun was set when I left the Hill from whence I saw the fate of ye day."[281]

"Nothing but misconduct lost us the feild," referring to Sullivan's rumored blunder, "the men behav'd like Vetrans, and Fought with the Greatest bravery," Hubley wrote a few days after the battle. "Aboutt half an hour after knight we Moov'd of[f] the Eminence to which he had returnd & Marchd that Knight to Chester."[282]

As Knyphausen began to push across Chads's Ford, George Washington was galloping up toward Dilworth, along with Gen. Henry Knox, the chief of artillery; Count Casimir Pulaski; and others of the headquarters staff. Local tradition maintains that an elderly man named Joseph Brown was pressed into service to guide the commander in chief up the quickest route. Brown hesitated and tried to be excused. "One of Washington's suite dismounted from a fine charger, and told Brown if he did not instantly get on his horse and conduct the general by the nearest and best route to the place of action he would run him through on the spot."[283] Brown did as he was ordered, and they "leapt all the fences without difficulty, and was followed in like manner by the others." Washington was reported to have kept close beside Brown, repeating, *"Push along, old man— push along, old man."* Arriving near Dilworth, "Brown said the bullets were flying so thick that he felt very uncomfortable," and like Emmor Jefferis, he was able to scurry off.[284]

Moving ahead of Greene's Virginians, who were double-timing up from Chads's Ford, the commander in chief arrived in time to see Stirling's and Stephen's troops falling back, some pell-mell while others retained their formations. "I saw nothing of the disposition you had made," Washington later wrote to Sullivan, "not getting up till the action was, in a manner over; & then, employed in hurrying on a reinforcement, and looking out a fresh ground to form the Troops on, which, by this time, were beginning to give way."[285] In the distance, lines of British troops could be seen advancing through the smoke amidst sunbeams streaming horizontally through the trees behind them.

Col. Timothy Pickering arrived shortly afterward. Several hundred yards southwest of Dilworth, he wrote, "I found the General near the southeastern quarter of a very large clear field, at the further side of which, I saw the enemy advancing in line," probably Monckton's 2nd Grenadier Battalion.[286] Washington was across the Wilmington Road from a large, medieval-looking stone dwelling, William Brinton's "Great House," built in 1704, the ancestral home of the extensive Brinton family. Daylight was starting to fade; sunset on September 11, 1777, was precisely at 6:15 P.M. "The sun shone, and was perhaps 15 or 20 minutes above the horizon," the adjutant general recalled. "A few rods in our front, was a small rising in the ground; and General Knox asked—'Will your Excellency have the artillery drawn up here?' I heard no answer; nor did I see any body of infantry to support it."[287]

Two guns were positioned and began bombarding the British lines at long range. "Orders were given to the 2nd Battalion of Grenadiers and 4th Brigade to incline to their left, and a Halt was made" at the Birmingham Road just west of Dilworth "to give time to the Artillery to come up," Capt. Archibald Robertson noted.[288] Across the field, as the British moved forward, Pickering remembered, "We retired. Some of our troops were formed behind a rail fence. The enemy continued to advance." Three Royal Artillery 12-pounders opened fire; the rounds hissed through the air and tore into the Continentals with terrible results. "A shot from their artillery I saw cut down a file of those troops," Pickering recalled.[289]

"The Rebels were discover'd behind the Fence in Front, with two Pieces of Cannon, with which they cannonaded the Troops" at the Birmingham Road, Robertson wrote, "but our 12 pounders which had got up to [the road], firing a few rounds," forced the Americans back about 200 yards to another fence, "where they again cannonaded the 4th Brigade."[290] Pickering revealed, "We retreated further. Col. Richard Kidder Meade, one of the General's aids, rode up to him about this time, and asked 'if Weedon's (or Muhlenberg's) brigade, which had not yet been engaged, should be ordered up?'" Though Pickering did not hear Washington's reply, the answer was affirmative.[291]

The situation was absolute chaos. "We had the whole British force to contend with, that had just before routed our right wing," Greene wrote.[292] Fortunately for him, the British paused momentarily. After storming the hill and capturing the five American guns, His Majesty's troops were disorganized and needed to regroup; they were also exhausted. A British light infantry officer confirmed that the rebels "were pursued closely, but the fatigue of the day having been very great & the Men encumber'd with their Blankets &c, it soon became necessary to halt."[293]

"The men being blown, we halted and formed to a fence," a 17th light infantry officer revealed, "and were immediately joined by the 2nd grenadiers to our right." The four light companies who had stormed the hill under the guns were still separated from the 1st Battalion, and Lord Bute's intrepid son was with them. "[Our] own battalion kept away more to the left; as soon as the men were fit to go on, out of gratitude to Major Stuart we desired to elect him our chief, and meant to have gone on under his command," but spontaneous promotions by acclamation were not allowed, even in as innovative a group as the light infantry. Stuart's ascent to chief had been buoyed up by the euphoria of shared dangers and glory, and just as quickly it was scotched: "Before we could move, Col. Abercromby galloped to us, and we joined the battalion."[294]

On the far left, the Jägers, too, were exhausted. "We had no cavalry, our people were very fatigued, and in only a moment, the enemy were out of sight," a Hessian report stated. "Therefore, we made no prisoners . . . and of the enemy we saw many dead and wounded." As the British reorganized and prepared to move on, the Jägers stayed on the extreme left. "The 2nd Battalion of Light Infantry had attacked so far to the right, we stood at a great distance from the army and not until about seven o'clock in the evening, on order, were we rejoined to the army at Dilworth."[295]

The American forces took advantage of the reprieve. Count Casimir Pulaski, the impetuous Polish cavalryman, bought some time with a small handful of dragoons. "At the time when our right wing was turned by the victorious enemy pressing upon us, and the rapid retreat of the right and the centre of our army became the consequence, Count Pulaski proposed to General Washington to give him the command of his body guard, consisting of about thirty horsemen. This was readily granted, and Pulaski

with his usual intrepidity and judgment, led them to the charge and succeeded in retarding the advance of the enemy."[296] In recognition of his ini-
tiative and bravery, Pulaski was afterward commissioned brigadier general
of all the Continental Light Horse by Congress.

"The enemy, however, moved with caution which gave those men who
were obliged to give way, an opportunity to make their retreat with
safety," Col. John Stone of the 1st Maryland wrote afterward. "Never
was a more constant and heavy fire while it lasted, and I was much amazed
when I knew the numbers that were killed and wounded," he added,
amazed that they weren't higher. "We retreated about a quarter of a mile
and rallied all the men we could, when we were reinforced by Greene's and
Nash's corps, who had not till that time got up. Greene had his men
posted on a good piece of ground, which they maintained for some time,
and I dare say did great execution."[297] Lt. Ebenezer Elmer, a surgeon's
mate with the 3rd New Jersey, recalled, "Genl. Greens Division being a
reserve were sent & part of Nash's Brigade were sent to their assistance
on ye right but it was almost night before they came up, they gave the
Enemy some smart fire & it Coming on night they retired also."[298]

Weedon arrived around 6 P.M. and his troops took up positions about
a mile southeast of Dilworth. American forces retreating through the
crossroads hamlet fired at the 4th Brigade, "two Regiments of which, the
33rd and 46th, were ordered to scour the Village of Dillworth, and then
formed in the Field" just outside, west of the Wilmington Road.[299] Lt.
Loftus Cliffe of the 46th told his brother, "Half of our Brigade 33 &
46 ordered to the left to take possession of the village of Dilworth were
ready to obey when informed that our 2d Grenadier Battalion were out
flanked and must give way if not immediately supported," adding with
pride, "we had the Honour" to come to their assistance.[300]

The 2nd Grenadier Battalion had walked into a deadly surprise. As
the British confidently advanced, having scattered one rebel line after
another, Weedon quickly set up a trap to enfilade them. Retreating Continentals formed on a cleared rise about 100 yards east of and parallel to
the Wilmington Road, near the intersection with Harvey Road, the road
used by the troops to come up from Chads's Ford. Weedon formed his
line behind them another 300 yards along a fence line on the reverse slope
of the rise, still parallel to the road, but swung his right flank inward at
a 90-degree angle along a second fence and some woods running toward

the road. Other American forces, probably part of Weedon's and possibly some of Nash's Brigade, who were following Weedon, formed a concave line south of the intersection, with their left extending 500 yards into some woods and their right flank resting near the road to Wilmington, protecting the army's line of retreat. Both American wings were on the reverse slope and out of sight of the advancing redcoats. Any British forces moving near the road could now be surprised and enfiladed, or fired upon from three sides.

Col. Charles Cotesworth Pinckney of South Carolina, on leave from his unit in Charleston, appears to have attached himself to the headquarters staff at Brandywine. Pinckney was with Washington when Sullivan rode up to the commander in chief to report on the situation. It was "in the Evening, about the time that General Weedon's Brigade, was brought up to the Right," Pinckney testified. Sullivan "appeared to me to behave with the greatest Calmness, and Bravery." Refuting later charges that the hapless New Hampshire general "behaved like a madman," the South Carolinian stated, "At that time I had Occasion to Observe his Behaviour, as I was then with General Washington, and heard General Sullivan, tell him that all the Superior Officers of his Division had behaved exceedingly well," evidently not knowing what had become of de Borre. As commander of the entire wing, Sullivan asked Pinckney to ride over to Weedon and ask him to place Col. Alexander Spottswood's 2nd Virginia Regiment and the 10th Virginia under Col. Edward Stevens "in the Plough'd Field, on our right, & form them there." After delivering the message to Weedon, Pinckney returned to the commander in chief, where, he said, "I was informed that General Sullivan while I was delivering his Orders, had his Horse shot under him."[301]

The task was now to cover the Continental Army's line of retreat. Capt. Joseph McClellan of the 9th Pennsylvania Regiment, in Conway's Brigade, Stirling's Division, stated that "the last he saw of Gen. Washington that day was in the Wilmington road, about a mile below Dilworthtown. The general finding some officers there during the retreat, rode up and inquired if any of them were acquainted with the country between that place and Chester. Capt. McClellan, being a native of the county . . . replied in the affirmative, whereupon Gen. Washington desired him to collect as many of the dispersed soldiery as possible and rendezvous at Chester the next morning."[302]

It was now dusk, but the action was about to get extremely hot. "On the approach of the Second Battalion of Grenadiers, the Rebels left the Hedge," the line near where Pickering earlier had seen Washington and Knox, "and were observed drawn up in the Field" on the rise about 800 yards away, east of the Wilmington Road.[303] This line was probably composed of remnants of Stirling's and Stephen's Divisions, who then withdrew further through Greene's Division. They were luring the British grenadiers into Weedon's trap.

As the sun sank below the horizon and the Americans seemed to melt into the twilight, Captain Ewald decided to gather his Jäger vanguard together. "Now, since I believed that the action had ended, I told Colonel Monckton, whom I knew quite well, that I wanted to ride with him and ordered the jäger officers to assemble the advanced guard." Apparently believing that the houses and farm buildings scattered along the Wilmington Road south of Dilworth were part of the village, Ewald wrote, "We had hardly reached the village when we received intense grapeshot and musketry fire which threw the grenadiers into disorder, but they recovered themselves quickly, deployed, and attacked the village."[304] Capt.-Lt. John Peebles of the 2nd Grenadier Battalion stated that "they came upon a second and more extensive line of the Enemys best Troops drawn up and posted to great advantage, here they sustain'd a warm attack for some time & pour'd a heavy fire on the British Troops as they came up."[305] Howe's chief engineer, Captain Montrésor, recalled that the British "pursued them through Dilworth Town and drove them for one mile & a 1/2 beyond it, to the skirt of a wood, where they had collected and from whence they poured out on us particularly on the Guards [*sic*; Grenadiers] and 4th Brigade, the heaviest fire (for a time) during the action."[306] Sullivan confirmed, "Weedens Brigade was the only part of Greens Division which was Ingaged. They Sustained a heavy fire for near 20 minutes when they were posted (about Sunset) to Cover the Retreat of our Army & had it not been for this the Retreat must have been attended with great Loss."[307]

Monckton's grenadiers had entered the left concave pincer of Weedon's trap; the British commander asked Ewald "to ride back and get assistance."[308]

"We took the front and attacked the enemy," wrote Lt. James McMichael of the Pennsylvania State Regiment, part of Weedon's Brigade, "and being engaged with their grand army, we at first were obliged to retreat a few yards and formed in an open field, when we fought without giving way on either side until dark. Our ammunition almost expended, firing ceased on both sides, when we received orders to proceed to Chester." McMichael went on to say, "This day for a severe and successive engagement exceeded all I ever saw. Our regiment fought at one stand about an hour under incessant fire, and yet the loss was less than at Long Island; neither were we so near each other as at Princeton, our common distance being about 50 yards."[309]

Timothy Pickering witnessed this regiment in action. "I saw Col. Walter Stewart's Pennsylvania regiment engaged with the enemy," he wrote. "This regiment was close up to the edge of a thick wood in its front, and firing briskly." The twenty-one-year-old "Irish Beauty" was no mere pretty boy; Pickering saw "Stewart on foot, in its rear, animating his men." He continued, "But although I was within 30 or 40 yards of this regiment, I could not see any troops of the enemy at whom they were firing."[310] The rapidly descending darkness and remarkable, strobe-like effect of the gunflashes and smoke in the dark would have made it difficult to see.

In the final glimmers of twilight, Ewald found assistance for the grenadiers. "In the distance I saw red coats and discovered that it was General Agnew with his brigade. I requested him to support the grenadiers, and pointed out a hill which, if he gained it, the enemy could not take the grenadiers in the flank." This was the clear rise that Stirling's and Stephen's men had fired from and then vanished over. It was about 300 yards to the left of the 2nd Grenadiers, just east of the Wilmington Road. Agnew advanced up the slope, unaware that Weedon's men were below the summit on the other side, positioned like an inverted wedge along a fence in his front and around his left flank. "He followed, and he no sooner reached the hill than we ran into several American regiments, which were just about to take the grenadiers in the flank and rear," Ewald recalled. "At this point there was terrible firing, and half of the Englishmen and nearly all of the officers of these two regiments (they were the 46th and 64th) were slain."[311]

Ewald's description vividly captures the intensity of the final phase of the Battle of Brandywine, though as in many of the accounts, his perception of losses was distorted. It is possible that some of these British troops threw themselves to the ground, as the light infantry had done, but many of them were, in fact, shot down. The 46th's losses were negligible, but the 64th Regiment of Foot, 420 strong, took the brunt of the firing and was decimated, losing just over 10 percent of its strength. Seven officers, including one ensign, four lieutenants, and thirty-nine-year-old Maj. Robert McLeroth, were hit, of which six fell wounded; Capt. Henry Nairn, a forty-two-year-old veteran with more than twenty years of service, was killed, as were four privates; and five sergeants and thirty-one privates were listed as wounded, for a total of forty-seven casualties, the largest reported loss for a single British regiment at Brandywine.[312] An officer of the 17th Light Company confirmed, "A considerable Body which form'd part of the Rebels second Line & which remain'd in order to cover their Retreat being perceiv'd by the 4th Brigade, they advanc'd with great Spirit in the Attack assisted by the 2nd LI, part of the 1st LI & 2nd Grenadiers. The heat of the Action fell chiefly on the 64th Regt. who suffer'd considerably, enduring with the utmost steadiness a very heavy fire, which lasted till Dark, when the Rebels retreated in great Panick taking the Road to Chester."[313] Archibald Robertson noted, "The second Battalion of Grenadiers advanced, and the 4th Brigade wheel'd up to their left in the position" where Weedon's right flank turned at 90 degrees to enfilade, "when a very heavy Fire commenced from Hedges and Woods where the Rebels had retired, from which they were very soon driven on all sides, but it being by this time almost Dark, unacquainted with the Ground, and the Troops very much fatigued, it was impossible to pursue further the Advantage they had gained."[314]

"I certainly believe that the affair would have turned out to be an even more dirty one if an English artillery officer had not hurried up with two light 6-pounders," the battalion guns of the 4th Brigade, "and fired on the enemy's flank with grapeshot," Ewald commented, "whereupon the enemy retreated to Chester. Night fell over this story and the hot day came to an end."[315] Montrésor clarified the details: As chief engineer, "I directed the position and attack of most of the field train," the heavy 6- and 12-pounders, "and late in the evening, when the action was near concluded, a very heavy fire was received by our Grenadiers from 6,000 Rebels, Washington's Rearguard, when Col. Monckton requested me to ride through it to Brigadier-General Agnew's Brigade, and his 4 Twelve

Pounders; which I did time enough to support them; and by my fixing the four 12 pounders, Routed the Enemy."[316]

Peebles, across the Wilmington Road with the 2nd Grenadiers, wrote, "We briskly attack'd ye enemy & after a close fire for some minutes charged them again and drove them into the woods in the greatest confusion."[317] After coming to the rescue of the grenadiers, said Lt. Loftus Cliffe of the 46th, "we had the Honour & with our fire closed the Day. The fatigues of this Day were excessive."[318] Lt. Martin Hunter in the 2nd Light Infantry observed, "A very considerable body of the enemy formed in a wood to cover their retreat, but were immediately attacked by the 33rd Regiment and Light Infantry, and totally defeated." This was Weedon's angled right flank. "It was now near dark, and our army so very much fatigued that we could not follow up our victory; indeed, it could not have been attended with much success, in a country so much intersected with rivers and woods, and it is always very difficult to come up with a retreating army with infantry."[319]

"The sun set when I left the Hill from whence I saw the fate of the day," Joseph Clark of Stephen's Division wrote. "His Excellency I saw within 200 yards of the Enemy, with but a small party about with him & they drawing off from their station; our Army broke at the right & night coming on adding a gloom to our misfortunes. Amidst the noise of Cannon, the hurry of people, & waggons driving in confusion from the field, I came off with a heart full of Distress."[320] Timothy Pickering recounted, "Very soon after this, the General retired still farther. The sun had for some time disappeared: it began to grow dusky: and as we proceeded, in retiring, the General said to me—'Why 'tis a perfect rout.'"[321]

The British did not pursue any further; the field was dark by 6:45, illuminated by starlight and a bright yellow moon high in the southwestern sky. Ens. George Inman of the 17th Light Company wrote of him and his men, "[We] began the attack after 4 in the afternoon and before nine were able to sitt down and refresh ourselves with some cold Pork and Grogg, on the Ground the Enemy had first posted themselves, which we enjoyed much, as our march before the attack was better than 18 miles."[322] An officer of the 2nd Light Infantry Battalion wrote, "They all gave way, leaving 15 [sic; 11] pieces of brass cannon, 2 Iron ditto, 70 Wagons of ammunition, baggage and provisions 150, with horses completed at 4 for each gun and wagon, but night came on, and brave Howe not knowing the country was obliged to halt that night." The Jägers and part of the 2nd Light Infantry Battalion came to a halt on the far left, at the 1704 Brinton Great House on the Wilmington Road. The same officer wrote that "Genl. Sir William Erskine [was with] the Flying Army [the light troops] on the left of the Grand Army, the Brigadier Generals commanding their different brigades in station."[323]

A story came down through the Brintons, who have been a prominent and numerous family in the area since the 1680s, that "about the time the Americans had retired and left the invaders masters of the Brandywine battle-ground, Sir William Erskine, quarter-master-general of the British army, came, with some of his companions, to the house of Edward Brinton, Esq., near Dilworthtown." Edward was a first-generation American, the son of William Brinton Jr., who came from Staffordshire, England, with his parents in 1684. William built the impressive stone house with steep, high gables in 1704, the same year Edward was born.

> [General Erskine] took possession of the parlor, and caused his servant to produce some bottles of wine from his baggage, when the company sat down, and had a jolly time over their liquor. Edward Brinton was then an aged man [he was seventy-three years old], had long held the commission of judge and justice of the peace from George II, and was the respected ancestor of many families. . . . When the visitors had thus regaled themselves after the fatigues of the day, Sir William addressed the venerable squire, saying, "Well, old gentleman, what do you think of these times?" The worthy patriarch of Birmingham replied, very frankly, "Our people may have been a little rash sometimes, but I do think the mother-country has treated us very badly." "Indeed, sir," said Sir William, "I think so, too; and had it not been for your Declaration of Independence, I never would have drawn my sword in America."[324]

Grant had the final word. "General Sunset saved the Rebell Artillery & prevented a pursuit, but they retreated in the utmost confusion to Chester & many of them never stopt till they got to Philedelphia," he told General Harvey. "Thus ended the 11th of September."[325]

CHAPTER 5

"Now prepare thyself, Pennsylvania, to meet the Lord thy God!"

THE FALL OF PHILADELPHIA, SEPTEMBER 12–25, 1777

"At Midnight, Chester, September 11, 1777 . . . I am sorry to inform you, that in this day's engagement, we have been obliged to leave the enemy masters of the field," Washington notified John Hancock. "I have directed the Troops to assemble behind Chester, where they are now arranging for the Night."[1] The Concord Road between Dilworth and Chester was a scene of horror and confusion, but not panic, as Washington's troops withdrew from the field. Stragglers by the hundreds swarmed through the moonlit countryside, exhausted, hungry, many of them wounded and bleeding.

"My first recollections of the War were of the Battle of Brandywine," Phebe Mendenhall Thomas remembered nearly a century later. "We heard the guns all day and Mother would say whenever we heard a great volley of noise, 'Dear me, what are they doing?' But they let us know what they had been doing in the evening. Father said it was a great battle near, he could only judge where, by the directions of the sound."

Phebe was seven years old when the battle took place. Despite the passing of the decades, she retained vivid memories of that day, especially of the evening as the Continental Army retreated past her family's home about four miles east of Dilworth on the road to Chester in Concord Township. "In the evening a great company of American soldiers came. Father told us to shut up the front of the house and come back to the kitchen. They came flocking into the yard, and sat down on the cider press, trough and benches, and every place they could find. They seemed so tired," Phebe distinctly remembered. "Father said, 'bring bread and cheese and cut for them.' They were so hungry."

The neighbors, who were Mendenhall cousins, came to help. "Margaret, Stephen's wife, came running in with her 2 children," she recalled. "Stephen was away off at the other end of the place and knew nothing of it. As it happened both houses, ours and Stephen's, had baked that day, and we cut up all the bread and cheese we had. I know, I got no supper and they had to bake bread on the iron," meaning that quick breads such as cornbread or rye and Indian meal ("rye 'n' Injun") were baked on the hearth in deep-lidded iron pans called Dutch ovens.[2]

The distraction and fear caused by the sounds of battle produced some interesting consequences to the baking in the Osborne household over in Westtown Township, near where Cornwallis's attack had begun. "An aged colored woman, named Grace, lived with Peter Osborne in the house," and she revealed that several friends and neighbors had gone there to avoid the armies. To feed everyone, "several women were engaged in making pies," and Grace recalled that "at each report of cannon and volley of musquetry, they would all leave their employment and fly to the door, perhaps just as they had fixed their under-crust on the plate; returning, would place the lid or cover on without putting any fruit in their pie, not being conscious of any mistake until they came to eat them."[3]

A few miles north of the Osborne home, young Thomas Cope recalled that "in the night after the battle, the family where we were— our uncle Nathan Cope's," in East Bradford Township—"were aroused out of their sleep by a small party of Americans who demanded shelter & something to eat." More than sixty years later, he clearly remembered that "having eaten some pye & milk, they hastily withdrew." Nine years old at the time, Cope recognized the company commander from his hometown of Lancaster. "When gone, I told Uncle I knew one of them, Col. Ross, of the Lancaster Militia." This was Lt. Col. James Ross, whose rifle detachment had skirmished with the rear of Cornwallis's column earlier in the day. "He was a handsome man, but in a sad plight, being destitute of hat & coat & his hands and face besmeared with gunpowder."[4]

The acrid, sulfurous smoke produced by black gunpowder quickly dries the mouth, throat, and nasal passages, and everyone inhales it continuously during battle. Infantrymen not only inhale the smoke, but also swallow quantities of the powder itself as a result of the musket-loading procedure. The ammunition was made up in paper cartridges, which had to be bitten open, resulting in the blackening of the soldier's mouth, especially at the right corner as the teeth held and tore the cartridge while the right hand pulled it away, smearing the gritty powder across the face and hands. In the haste and chaos of fighting, powder also spilled into the soldier's mouth, sometimes in large amounts if the biting was not done carefully—hardly possible in the heat of battle. A compound of potassium nitrate, sulfur, and charcoal, black powder is very salty and astringent. Together with the marching, shouting, and stress produced by battle, a maddening thirst was a constant companion of the combat soldier.

Down at the Painter farm, near the intersection of the Great Nottingham Road and the Wilmington Road (later called Painter's Crossing), Jane Carter Painter had been baking too. Her grandson William recalled that "the American army passed by the Painter house, and his grandmother, a staunch patriot, making bread, the soldiers, hungry and tired, ate all the dough and drank the well dry."[5] It was no exaggeration. Artilleryman Jacob Nagle wrote, "It coming on night, I was famishing with drouth [drought, i.e., thirst]. Coming to a well, but could not get near it for the mob of soldiers, but falling in with one of the artillerymen, he worked his way through them and brought me water in his canteen. Otherwise I should of fell on the road."[6]

Many of the American wounded were brought along with the army, though scores had to be left behind on the field. "Then after a bit a Captain came on his horse," Phebe Mendenhall recounted. "He was wounded and had his servant and a Doctor. He wanted to stay all night. Father didn't want him to stay, for he told him he expected the English would be along in the morning, and would tear us all to pieces, but they didn't mind that. They took him off his horse, brought him in and they staid. The girls brought him a bed, and he laid there in the common house and the Doctor staid with him. The servant slept in the barn. They all got their suppers too."

The captain had been shot in the thigh. In an era before antibiotics, sterilization, or anesthesia, wounds typically festered and became inflamed. The shock of the injury, especially from a lead musket ball, blunt and heavy, also aggravated thirst. "Next morning the wounded man was too bad to get on his horse. They got the horse there, and the girls helped to lift him, but he couldn't get on. Father didn't want him there when the English came. As the wounded man was laying there, Adam came running in and said 'The Red-Coats are coming! The Red-Coats are coming!' The poor sick man raised up and called for mercy. The Doctor hid under the porch, but it was only one of the neighbors that had a reddish-brown coat."

The horror stories of British and Hessian behavior that had circulated for the past year, first from North Jersey, then from Head of Elk and the Newark area, were enough to convince sixty-four-year-old Robert Mendenhall that his family was in mortal danger should any American military personnel be found on his premises. He and his third wife, Ester Temple, little Phebe's stepmother, had married only six months earlier. "Mother and Father sat up all the night," Phebe remembered; the next morning, "finding that the Captain couldn't ride (he had a bullet in his thigh), Father geared up a great black horse we had, a noble fellow, to the carriage, and they took him to the Black Horse," a tavern outside of Chester.

"Oh! How glad I was to see father come home," Phebe exclaimed. "He had just put the horse away, when the English came, sure enough, but they didn't come to the house. We were so afraid while Father was away, but he wasn't gone long. I remember when I saw him coming I couldn't think what made the gears all white, but it was the foam" from the horse sweating and overheating. "It was 10 miles to the Black Horse and back, and he had driven very fast."[7]

The trauma of the day was vivid, especially for the Quaker adults, who had their worst fears about war and military behavior confirmed, and then some. Their quiet, peaceable kingdom had been invaded; many of their fields were ruined, trampled, soaked in blood, and strewn with the hideous human wreckage of battle. The dead and wounded now lay starkly illuminated in a ghastly moonlight where they fell. Broken fences and shattered trees, dead horses, abandoned wagons, bits of clothing, blankets, shoes, and hundreds of muskets told of the course of battle for miles. Stories abounded of forced participation in military activity, such as that of Emmor Jefferis and Joseph Brown, pressed to serve as guides by the commanders of both armies.

Col. Samuel Smith of the 4th Maryland Regiment admitted in his memoirs that he "applied to a Quaker Farmer, to guide him to the road leading to Chester, which he refused; but a pistol having been pointed at his breast, he complied. On being thanked he replied, 'I want no thanks, thee forced me.'"[8] Smith later revealed the details that he "assured him he was a dead man if he did not get his horse instantly and show the way to Chester. The Friend was alarmed, and, exclaiming, '*What a dreadful man thou art!*' went and saddled his horse and prepared to set out."

But the Maryland colonel was not finished. "'Now,' said Col. Smith, 'I have not entire confidence in your fidelity, but I tell you explicitly, that if you do not conduct me clear of the enemy, the moment I discover your treachery, I will blow your brains out.' The terrified farmer exclaimed, 'Why, thou art the most desperate man I ever did see!'" The Quaker showed him to the road "and was dismissed with proper acknowledgements for the favor."[9]

A few miles away to the northeast, eight-year-old Sally Frazer was worried about her father and especially her mother, thirty-two-year-old Polly. "She was riding about all day," first to find her aged mother at the house of her cranky Quaker stepfather, John Pierce, halfway between Thornbury and Chads's Ford; then she "came home once, but was off again and did not return till dark." Sally was home all day with her two younger brothers and sister, together with Polly Fellows, a woman who had lived with the Frazers for years, and three slaves, "black Rachel and two black men who worked on the farm [and] made up my family." The last time Sally had seen her father was in early August, when he managed to take a few days' leave while the army was waiting for news of the British fleet. Unknown to the little girl, her mother was now one month pregnant.

"We heard musketry with an occasional discharge of heavy artillery through the day," Sally recalled vividly, "but particularly towards evening." Even more striking was the sound of platoon-firing. "There was a continual discharge of small arms heard at our house," she said, the memory still sharp more than half a century later. "My Father was in the engagement sure enough."

Lt. Col. Persifor Frazer had been holding the line at Chads's Ford with the 5th Pennsylvania. As the troops retreated in the dark, "he then mounted a wounded soldier on his horse and walked by his side to the Seven Stars tavern in Ashtown [Aston] township, where he put the soldier into a wagon going to Chester. He then rode home 5 or 6 miles and went to bed."

Before the colonel turned in, an ominous episode occurred. Earlier that day, "two very genteel looking men" had come to the house and asked to stay overnight. With all of the disruption and displaced persons in the area, they were permitted to stay. When Percy arrived, "it was late and the strangers had gone to bed." Polly went outside to embrace her husband and help remove his battle-stained uniform, drenched with sweat and grime, as well as blood from the wounded soldier. Frazer's personal servant, an Irishman named Harvey, carried the colonel's saddle into the house. He made noise going up the stairs and woke the strangers, "who called out, asking 'who had come?'" Harvey answered that his master had come home. "They arose immediately, went out," probably through a back door while the Frazers were out front, "saddled their horses, and before anyone knew of it were off." Polly remembered, "We never learned who they were"; Percy thought they were probably "some dreadful good-for-nothing Tories."

Much too early the next morning, the exhausted colonel was awakened by a little girl's shrill, hysterical screams, "Oh, my Daddy's killed, my dear Daddy's killed!" It was Sally; she had come downstairs and looked out the front door, where she saw a battle-stained blue-and-white uniform coat with silver epaulettes hanging on the fence outside. "At early morning I got up and seeing my fathers Regimental coat all stained and daubed with blood I set up the murder shout as I thought he must have been killed," she recalled vividly. To her relief, "turning round [she] saw her father behind her brought from his room by her cries." The reunion was very brief, for "as soon as his horse was prepared," Lieutenant Colonel Frazer "mounted and rode off to the army."[10]

That morning, the full impact of the battle became evident. "Friday 12th Sept. Head Qrs. at Dilworth.—party's sent out to look for wounded & bury the dead," Captain-Lieutenant Peebles of the Grenadiers wrote. "The loss on our side between 5 & 600 killed & wounded, that of the Rebels I suppose twice as much besides 4 or 500 prisoners & Deserters." The dead were buried in pits near where they fell, sometimes individually, more often in groups. Buildings of all types were converted into makeshift hospitals, even before the shooting had stopped. "An Hospital at Dilworth & houses adjacent," Peebles noted.[11] Birmingham Meeting House had its doors torn off to serve as operating tables, according to Joseph Townsend, and he was pressed into service to assist with the wounded while the battle was still in progress. After witnessing an amputation, he was able to slip away in the darkness and confusion of the night. The dead of both sides found in the vicinity, together with the amputated limbs, were buried in a large trench dug in the walled burial yard.[12] The names and number of the dead are unknown.

Howe established general headquarters in a house just over a mile south of Dilworth. Search parties combed the woods and the fields for the next few days, picking up the dead and wounded from both sides. The official British and Hessian casualty list claimed 3 captains, 5 lieutenants, 7 sergeants, and 78 rank and file killed, for a total of 93 dead. In addition, 49 officers, 40 sergeants, 4 drummers, and 395 rank and file were wounded, and 6 missing, for a grand total of 587 casualties. American estimates of British losses run as high as 2,000, based on distant observation and sketchy, unreliable reports.[13]

"This victory cost us about 400 men killed & wounded, the latter of which prevented our moving forwards to profit of our advantage for several days," Capt. Richard Fitzpatrick wrote to his brother, John Lord Ossory. "Some foolish people were much elated with this event and an insufferable torrent of nonsense was talked for some time afterwards, such as that the whole army must disperse, that it was impossible they should ever recover so severe a blow, &c &c but these silly fellows were soon convinced they had no foundation for their opinions, Washington still continued to talk high language."[14] Of the Americans, Howe reported to Lord Germain that "their loss was considerable in officers killed and wounded, and they had about 300 men killed, 600 wounded, and near 400 made prisoners."[15] Other British estimates of American losses run as high as 2,000. "The Nomber Killed & wonded And taken ware About 1000 or 1100 Hundred And they ware Comming in Dayly & taking them prisner," Lt. Gilbert Purdy reported. His unit was charged with the task of burial, and he wrote, "In the time we Laid their the Dead that was Buryed By Us on the Day After the Batle ware 55 By our Betalion Besides What was Buryed By the rest of the Army."[16] An officer of the 2nd Light Infantry Battalion wrote in his memorandum book on the twelfth, "Orders Wass Given for to Revew the ground to Beruie the dead and the Surgens to attend the Wounded. The Enemy had 502 dead in the field. We had 30 beried the Next Morning. The Wounded In not as yet Asserted. We took 400 Prisners that Night and the Next day."[17]

In Philadelphia that morning, Mrs. Margaret Stedman wrote to her friend Mrs. Elizabeth Fergusson at Graeme Park, "Friday 11 O'Clock—Jemmy is this moment came from the Coffee House, where he saw on the book that eight hundred of our People fell yesterday, and as our army continues to retreat this way . . . Some of the wounded are coming and the Town is all in confusion." The real numbers may never be known.

"Gracious God, look down upon us and send help from above," Margaret prayed, "every face you see, looks wild and pale with fear and amazement, and quite overwhelmed with distress. Some flying and some moving one way some another and the slaughter some think much greater than what is yet made public." Yet in the midst of it all, she did notice something odd: "Strange it is tho' at no greater distance than Chester, the accounts should be so very various, that one can't be certain of anything."[18] The rumor mill was working overtime.

The sheer number of American wounded left on the field or found in buildings nearby prompted General Howe to request Washington to send American surgeons to care for the wounded prisoners. Under a flag of truce, Dr. Benjamin Rush, the surgeon general of the Army's Middle Department and a signer of the Declaration of Independence, together with several other doctors, made his way to Dilworth. "I attended in the rear at the battle of Brandywine, and had nearly fallen into the hands of the enemy by my delay in helping off the wounded," Rush wrote in his autobiography. "A few days after the battle I went with several surgeons into the British camp with a flag from Genl. Washington to dress the wounded belonging to the American Army who were left on the field of battle. Here I saw and was introduced to a number of British officers. Several of them treated me with great politeness."

Some old familiar Philadelphia faces were also present. "I saw likewise within the British lines and conversed for some time with Jos. Galloway and several other American citizens who had joined the British army." He noted the professionalism of the British regulars, especially regarding camp security—"I was much struck in observing the difference between the discipline and order of the British and Americans"—and wrote about it to John Adams, criticizing the lack of discipline in the Continental forces: "I lamented this upon my return. It gave offense and was ascribed to fear and to lack of attachment to the cause of my country."[19]

Captain Fitzpatrick was evidently one of the officers with whom Rush spoke. "Their Principal Surgeon, a very clever fellow who was a Member of Congress, & who came in with a flag of truce to visit the wounded prisoners, a few days after the engagement spoke with the greatest confidence, acknowledged the defeat to have been complete," Fitzpatrick told his brother. The Guards camp was only a few hundred yards east of Dilworth, where the main hospital was located.

Most revealing to Fitzpatrick, though, was Rush's attitude about the effect of the defeat on the American cause. Rush "declared that all possibility of accommodation much less of satisfaction was as remote the day after the battle as it ever had been since the declaration of independency; before which they all (both whigs & tories,) agree that a few concessions on our side would have put an end to the whole business."[20]

Spirits were, indeed, still high among the die-hard rebels. "Those who expect to reap the blessings of freedom, must, like men, undergo the fatigues of supporting it," began an essay written the day after Brandywine. "The event of yesterday was one of those kind of alarms which is just sufficient to rouse us to duty, without being of consequence enough to depress our fortitude."

The essay appeared in the Philadelphia papers shortly afterward. "It is not a field of a few acres of ground, but a cause, that we are defending," the writer reminded his readers, "and whether we defeat the enemy in one battle, or by degrees, the consequences will be the same." Reflecting on the desperate days of Trenton and Princeton, he told them, "Look back at the events of last winter and the present year, there you will find that the enemy's successes always contributed to reduce them," and recalled, "Howe has been once on the banks of the Delaware, and from thence driven back with loss and disgrace: and why not be again driven from the Schuylkill?"

"Shall a band of ten or twelve thousand robbers, who are this day fifteen hundred or two thousand men less in strength than they were yesterday, conquer America, or subdue even a single state?" he asked rhetorically. "Men who are sincere in defending their freedom, will always feel concern at every circumstance which seems to make against them. . . . But the dejection lasts only for a moment; they soon rise out of it with additional vigor; the glow of hope, courage and fortitude, will, in a little time, supply the place of every inferior passion, and kindle the whole heart into heroism."

"I close this paper with a short address to General Howe," this former English tax collector, a recent immigrant, poignantly stated. "You, sir, are only lingering out the period that shall bring with it your defeat," he warned the general. "We know the cause which we are engaged in, and though a passionate fondness for it may make us grieve at every injury which threatens it, yet, when the moment of concern is over, the determination to duty returns."

"We are not moved by the gloomy smile of a worthless king, but by the ardent glow of generous patriotism. We fight not to enslave, but to set a country free, and to make room upon the earth for honest men to live in. In such a case we are sure that we are right; and we leave to you the despairing reflection of being the tool of a miserable tyrant." The essay was signed, "COMMON SENSE, PHILADELPHIA, September 12, 1777." Thomas Paine, writing what has become known as "The Crisis #4," had once more wielded his pen in support of American liberty.[21]

The battle was heard for miles around. "This morning we heard heavy and long continuing cannonading some thirty miles away on Brandwine Crick, where the two armies were engaged in a hard struggle," Rev. Henry Muhlenberg had written at Trappe, above the Schuylkill River, on the eleventh. His son, Brig. Gen. Peter Muhlenberg, whose Virginia brigade had been in reserve, saw little or no action. The following day, the pastor said, "We received one report after another to the effect that the losses in the American army were considerable. Now prepare thyself, Pennsylvania, to meet the Lord thy God!"

Muhlenberg witnessed something else on September 12: "This afternoon six wagons with guards passed by; they are to take the most prominent Quakers of Philadelphia, who have been arrested, to Augusta County, in Virginia."[22]

The wagons were on their way to Reading and eventually to Winchester, Virginia. September 11 had been a very distressing day on a personal level for some of the leading Quaker families in Philadelphia. As the sounds of battle echoed in the distance, twenty-two men were sent out of the city, including Elizabeth Drinker's husband, Henry; Sarah Logan Fisher's husband, Thomas; James Pemberton; and Israel Pemberton. They had been arrested in early September under suspicion of being enemies to the United States and confined to the Masonic Lodge. Now, on Congress's recommendation, they were being sent far away.

The move was based on false papers allegedly "found" by Gen. John Sullivan in North Jersey that hinted at a Quaker plot to aid the British Army. No formal charges were ever leveled against them, but in the crisis, Congress and the Supreme Executive Council agreed to remove them, fearing treachery. "We have been obliged to attempt to humble the Pride of some Jesuits who call themselves Quakers, but who love Money and Land better than Liberty or Religion," John Adams told Abigail bluntly on September 8. "The Hypocrites are endeavouring to raise the Cry of Persecution, and to give this Matter a religious Turn, but they cant succeed. The World knows them and their Communications," he coldly observed. "American Independence has disappointed them, which makes them hate it," Adams added venomously, "yet the Dastards dare not avow their Hatred to it, it seems," referring to their refusal to "take the Test" and swear allegiance.[23]

South of the city that same day, after a few hours' rest, Washington's forces headed up from Chester toward Philadelphia. There was only minor panic as news of the defeat spread. "Numbers of the Inhabitants are removing from the City, but the Confusion and Tumult, is much less than I could have supposed, considering the very Critical Situation of Affairs," Dr. James Hutchinson, a Philadelphia surgeon, wrote to his uncle James Pemberton, one of the exiled Quakers. "I must however refer thee to the Bearer for News, as accounts and reports are so various, and different, that nothing can be said with certainty."[24]

Howe again failed to follow up a major victory with vigorous pursuit. Instead, the Continental Army, though battered, withdrew unhindered and marched north through Darby to the Schuylkill River at the Middle Ferry, where a floating bridge built on pontoon boats was located. There they crossed, leaving part of the army on the west side as a screen. Instead of heading into the city, which was a mile and a half ahead to the east, the troops turned left and marched north five miles up the left bank of the river to the Falls of Schuylkill near Germantown, thus avoiding the chaos and distractions of Philadelphia.

The Schuylkill was the last natural obstacle between Philadelphia and the British Army. It was fairly shallow but swift flowing, even in dry weather, for the water level dropped more than one hundred feet in twenty miles. The Falls of Schuylkill were rapids that passed through large boulders where the river dropped some thirty feet, and before dams

raised the water level and obliterated the rapids, they were quite picturesque. The river had no permanent bridges, and until the floating bridge
was installed, Philadelphia was directly accessible from the west only by
three ferries—the Upper, Middle, and Lower—and by a number of
fords farther up.

"The Enemy by the best accounts have lain still this day to bury their
Dead, to take care of their wounded &c.," Congressman Eliphalet Dyer
wrote on the twelfth, "but are expected very soon to Move & supposed to
pass Schuylkill about 15 miles above this City at a smooth shallow ford
way there called Sweeds ford."[25] Most of the Schuylkill fords were narrow
and tortuous, winding around on a gravelly river bottom and using islands
or mudflats in the river. Swedes Ford was wide and shallow, with a hard,
stony bottom, so the crossing was direct, and it lay in a valley that was also
wide and shallow. The Schuylkill is surrounded by high hills through most
of its path, and many of the ford roads wandered down steep inclines,
where a large army crossing the river would find itself vulnerable to a well-
positioned opponent. The hills around Swedes Ford were more gradual
and provided much more space for a large force to maneuver quickly.

At the Falls Camp, the Continentals rested on the thirteenth, cleaned
their weapons, and received new ammunition. The inhabitants of Germantown once again braced for the usual damage resulting from large
numbers of soldiers in the neighborhood. "The Army being encamped
at, and near Germantown, made it necessary for one to go up there,"
Hutchinson told Pemberton. "Thy House was General Sullivan's Head
Quarters; I remained there with him till Yesterday, when the Army
recrossed the Schuylkill, and I returned to Philadelphia." Overall, the
Pemberton property was spared. "Thy House, Garden, and Orchard,
have not sustained any damage, but above 150 Pannels of thy Fence is
destroyed, and burnt," the doctor informed his uncle. "Most of the
Neighbours shared the same, (and many of them a much worse) fate,
particularly Dr. Bensel, several Cornfields are entirely destroyed."[26]

Rumors abounded in the American camp that the British Army could
not move because of severe casualties. There was some truth to this, for
there were not enough horses and wagons to move the wounded and the
army's baggage at the same time.

Howe's forces repositioned themselves around Dilworth, and Gen.
James Grant was sent to Concord with two British brigades and the

remains of the Queen's Rangers, a unit that had lost nearly 20 percent of its strength in the battle. "The 12th in the morning I was detached with two Brigades, a Squadron of Dragoons and a Provincial Corps, by way of making a forward Move against the Enemy, tho' in fact not expecting to find them," he told General Harvey.[27]

Grant's force arrived at the Mendenhall farm just as Phebe's father had returned from delivering the wounded officer to the Black Horse Tavern. "Well, as I said, he just got the horse put away, when we saw the Red-Coats coming," Phebe recalled. "One big officer came to ask if there was any way of avoiding the big hill." She clearly remembered the scrawny British artillery horses, many still suffering from the effects of the voyage: "They had the poorest little horses to pull their big guns, they couldn't pull them up the big hill by the barn." But Phebe's father dreaded the worst, and "he told the officer he wanted to go to the house to get his hat, and besides he'd left no one at the house, but women and children, and that he'd heard their men sometimes behaved very badly." Much to his surprise and joy, "the officer turned to a man behind him and said 'Go guard the gentleman's house'."

The soldier, a dragoon, galloped to the house and posted himself at the entrance. It was fortunate, for a belligerent British camp follower soon arrived. "While he was there, a woman came with a can, and tried to get in at the gate. He refused to let her come in, but she was a right soldier, and would push in, so he struck her a right blow with his sword. Mother ran out and said, 'don't hurt her, maybe she wants something.' Sure enough she wanted milk, so Lizzie took some out and filled her can. We couldn't tell what the man could mean sitting there on his horse, saying nothing. However, after a bit Father came, and then he rode away."[28]

The Guards, who had encamped near the Ring House east of Chads's Ford on the night of the battle, "marched 2 miles farther to Dilworth, & there encamped," Lord Cantelupe noted in his diary. Like many of the officers, the young ensign wandered over the battlefield during the next few days, retracing the course of the action. One morning, going to a spot where the Guards had struck Sullivan's Division "on Brandywine Heights," he took out his diary and created a souvenir by painting a watercolor of the battle.[29] It is presently the only known contemporary image made of this large and important battle.

Later that day, a detachment of the Guards descended on the Frazer farm, about four miles east of their camp at Dilworth. Before the battle, Frazer had sent the baggage of several regiments in Wayne's Division to the farm for safekeeping. By doing this, the colonel had placed his own family and property in jeopardy. The two men who had left the house so abruptly the night before no doubt informed the British of the farm's location. Now, as the Guards detachment approached the house, a mad scramble ensued to hide valuables and evacuate several rebel officers.

As Polly Frazer remembered it, "A British officer, tho' not the commander of the party, entered and accosted me in broad Scotch with 'where are the damned rebels?' In those days when I was frightened I always became angry. . . . I said to him that I knew of no Rebels.—there was not I believed a *Scotchman* about the place. At this he flew into a great rage and used abusive language."

Following the advance party was a large foraging detail. "The Commander of the party (which consisted of 200 foot and 50 horse) now came up. He divided the horse into two Companies.—Stationing them at a considerable distance from the house but so as to completely surround it. They were in great fear that the Riflemen who they had heard were in the neighbourhood should surprise them. They had seen Major Christy," Capt. John Christie of her husband's unit, the 5th Pennsylvania, "as they came up the hill, go into the woods and knew the American uniform and they thought that he might be one of a party not far off, did not tend to lessen their fears."

The commander, whom Mrs. Frazer remembered as "Captain De West," was "a Captain of the Guard and ranked equal with a Colonel," which accurately describes the ranking system in the Guards. As there was no Captain De West in the Guards, it is probable that the officer was Capt. and Lt. Col. West Hyde of Sir George Osborn's Grenadier Company.

The captain "came into the house just as one of the men was going to strike me," Polly said. "They had got at the liquor and were drunk—the officers were obliged to drive them off with their swords." The captain told Polly that "he had understood the house was full of arms and ammunition." She replied, "I know of no ammunition in the house." The officer "then opened the case of the clock hoping to find money; he found an old musket with the lock broken off, this he jammed up into the works and broke them to pieces."

Considering the fact that the British had come across a number of Continental baggage wagons at the Frazer farm, it is remarkable that the entire premises was not completely destroyed, as happened to the homes of several other rebel officers in the Philadelphia region. But the Guards captain did show consideration to Mrs. Frazer, though this was of little comfort to the family, as their home was ransacked. "He then told me to show him every thing that belonged to me and that it should not be touched, which I did."

Then the army baggage was found. "When he saw the baggage which was packed in chests and ammunition boxes, turning to me, he said, 'you told me there was no ammunition,' and breaking them open found only the soldiers clothes. Now it became a scene of pillage and confusion,— they plundered the house—what they could not carry away they destroyed: took the beautiful swords worn by the officers on parade, carried off the clothes, one man put on five shirts."[30]

The Frazers owned several slaves, one of whom was Rachel, "a Mulatto Wench, about 32 years old, middle sized, one arm shorter than the other."[31] "While tearing about up stairs," the British troops "took a suit of plaid worsted curtains I had that belonged to a field bedstead—this they threw at poor Rachel saying, 'here nigger is a petticoat for you;' she, poor creature, being frightened partly to death thinking she was obliged to put it on, in her efforts to get her head thro' a slit became completely entangled to their great amusement."

All the horses and grain in the barn were taken away. "I had orders to take *Mr* Frazer prisoner and burn the house and barn to the ground, but these I give you," the captain told Polly. Furious, she further tempted fate by retorting, "I can't Sir, thank you for what is my own, and if such were your orders you would not dare to disobey them." The house was left in disarray, and a few smaller items were pilfered, including some glass "cream buckets" brought from England by Polly's grandfather when he emigrated. But all in all, it could have been much worse.[32] The Frazer home was spared, as was the family, though badly rattled. But news of the raid did make it into the camp scuttlebutt. "A Number of Swords are taken at the house of a Rebel Colo. Fraser, & Several Quires of paper Money," James Parker noted in his journal.[33]

Later that afternoon, Howe dispatched the 71st Regiment, Frazer's Highlanders, to Wilmington, Delaware, about ten miles southeast of

Dilworth. Except for one of the three regular battalions and the flank companies, this large unit of about 1,000 men had been kept in reserve during the battle, assigned to guard the army's baggage. The older and more famous Scottish unit, the 42nd Royal Highlanders (the "Black Watch"), had also been kept out of the battle, its battalion companies serving as the headquarters guard. "The 71st Regiment . . . having been heretofore composed of three battalions, was now formed into two, marched to Wilmington, dispersed some enemy militia, and found seven iron guns in a trench." The purpose of seizing Wilmington was to create a point of rendezvous with the fleet, which had sailed back down the Chesapeake. Sir William "had been assured by Admiral Howe that he would have several ships at Wilmington on September 15th at the latest."[34] The British would establish a general hospital at Wilmington and transport their wounded there, where they would then be transferred to hospital ships.

The Highlanders found an unexpected prize at Wilmington in the form of the rebel president of the state, John McKinly, who was home. "Several Circumstance concurred to render my staying at Wilmington, necessary to the publick whilst the Enemy were moving toward Philada.," McKinly told the President of Congress later, "& being more solicitous to perform my Duty, than for my own personal Safety, I was unexpectedly made a Prisoner in my own House there on the Night succeeding the 12th Day of September last, by the 71st British Regiment, said to consist at that time of 900 Men, who were detached to take possession of that place for the accommodation of such of their Army as were wounded the day preceeding, at the Battle of Brandywine." McKinly reminded Congress, "I sustained at this time some heavy losses of private property."[35]

Hessian troops under the command of Col. Johann von Loos, including the Combined Battalion, which was composed of the remains of the regiments defeated at Trenton, were sent to Wilmington two days later to escort the wounded and many prisoners. "We started at 6 o'clock on the morning of the 14th and escorted the wounded belonging to our army and 350 prisoners to Wilmington, a beautiful little town surrounded by two rivers, the Brandywine and Christine, both of which flow into the Delaware close to this place," a Hessian report eloquently stated.

On the march thither we destroyed a magazine belonging to the rebels containing arms, cartridge pouches, and clothing. Colonel MacDonald with 3 Battalions Scotch Highlanders had already taken possession of Wilmington; the small rebel garrison had been surprised by him in the night. In a fort in the direction of the Delaware, we found 7 guns. All the troops which were now under command of Colonel von Loos encamped on a height before the town, and fortified themselves as well as circumstances permitted, as we had not much Artillery with us.[36]

In one of his letters to his friend Charles Steuart in Edinburgh, James Parker compiled a remarkable list of the breakdown of American prisoners by nationality:

To give an idea of what the Rebels are Composed of please know that the 315 Rebel prisoners we sent from Dillworth to Wilmington were as follows:

English	65
Scots	9
Irish	134
German	16
Italian	3
Swiss	1
Russ	1
Gernsey	1
French	3
American	82
	315[37]

Lord Cornwallis was sent toward Chester via Concord with the British grenadier and light infantry battalions. "The 13th Marched to Chester and on the Roade fell in With Several Out houses and Barns full of Wounded men Who tould us that If We keep on that Night We Should have put a total End to the Rebelion," an officer of the 2nd Light Infantry Battalion wrote.[38] Cornwallis rendezvoused with Grant's force at Concord and advanced to the heights of Aston, just outside Chester. Some British patrols went into Chester without opposition; this was the extent of Howe's pursuit of Washington.

Plundering once again became a serious problem, and Lord Cornwallis resorted to hanging two soldiers in the Aston camp. "A Light Infantry man of the 5th. & a Grenadier of the 28th were executed today at 11 o'clock in front of 1st Grenadiers for mauroding," Captain-Lieutenant Peebles wrote in his diary. Significantly, he added, "The 1st. Examples made, tho often threaten'd, & many deserved it."[39] Despite the severity of the punishment, the practice persisted, though not nearly as widespread, as authorized and unauthorized foraging parties continued to scour the region.

The Gibbons farm in Westtown Township, not far from the Frazer plantation, was cleaned out of livestock by several foraging parties. Forty-one-year-old James Gibbons was a Quaker and a self-educated Renaissance man, another of the "great and strange" people of Chester County. In addition to being a farmer, he was a classical scholar who was fluent in Latin and Greek as well as French and Spanish, and a mathematician and surveyor who served as the county treasurer and as a representative in the Pennsylvania Assembly. His forty-year-old brother, Col. William Gibbons, was commander of the 7th Battalion of the Chester County Militia and was good friends with John Hannum and Thomas Cheyney.

Jane Sheward Gibbons, their seventy-five-year-old mother, was a tall and dignified Quaker widow, "the queen of the county," as one contemporary put it. She went to Howe's headquarters to try to recover a favorite cow that had been taken and was allowed to apply to Howe in person. Howe courteously listened to her request, and then asked her to state her name.

"My name is Jane Gibbons," she said.

"Have you not a son in the rebel army?" Howe questioned.

"I have a son in George Washington's army," Jane replied. William's decision to take up arms had no doubt been the source of much grief to this Quaker family.

"I am afraid, madam," Howe told "the queen of the county," "that you love your *cow* better than your *king!*" Biting her tongue, Mrs. Gibbons quietly said, "I bid thee farewell," and left. Shortly after, "the cow escaped from the enemy, and found her way back to her kind mistress."

The Gibbons farm had other visits. A well-educated British officer leading one foraging party came into the Gibbons house and, seeing shelves filled with books, said to James, "You are a clergyman, I fancy?"

"No, I am not," Gibbons replied.

"A doctor, perhaps?"

"I am not a doctor," Gibbons answered.

"Pray, then," the officer said, "what is your profession?"

"I am a Chester County farmer."

"But these are not farmer's books!" protested the officer, who was examining some of them.

"What dost thou know about them?" Mr. Gibbons asked.

"Oh," the officer said, "they are old and familiar friends."

The British officer and the Quaker farmer then had "a long and very pleasant conversation" on the subject of education in England and America. At the end, the British officer reached out his hand and said, "This has been the most agreeable hour I have spent in your country. I did not expect to find classical scholars in the woods of America."[40]

While Howe's forces continued to sit at Dilworth and Aston, and with them no closer to Philadelphia than the outskirts of Chester, Washington decided to leave the Falls Camp on September 14 and go on the offensive. He ordered the floating bridge to be detached and pulled to the eastern side of Middle Ferry, "as the Enemy (being now advanced near Chester) will probably detach a party of light Troops to take possession of it." Initially planning to move the army up to Swedes Ford, he instead decided to cross at Levering's Ford, about halfway between Swedes Ford and the city, and move onto the Lancaster Road, the main direct route between Philadelphia and Lancaster. This would enable the army to obstruct Howe's advance to the Schuylkill by marching up to the Great Valley toward Downingtown and taking up positions blocking the road to Swedes Ford.

French engineers headed by Col. Louis Le Bègue de Presle du Portail were sent by Washington to Gen. John Armstrong of the Pennsylvania Militia, with orders to fortify Swedes Ford with a redoubt and heavy cannon. "Colo. Du Portail and his Officers will attend you for this purpose," Washington told the Pennsylvania general. Knowing some of the difficulties of dealing with professional military engineers, especially with the ongoing squabbles between Frenchmen, he told Armstrong, "As it is not expected that these Works will have occasion to stand a long defence, they should be as such as can with the least labour and in the shortest time be completed, only that part of them which is opposed to cannon, need be of any considerable thickness and the whole of them should be rather calculated for dispatch than any unnecessary Decorations or Regularity which Engineers are frequently too fond of."[41]

Contentions between the English speakers and the French officers were one ongoing source of tension in the army; jealousies and rivalries among the French engineers concerning the Delaware River defenses at Forts Mifflin and Mercer had been growing ever more divisive. Duportail and others had been in conflict with the Chevalier de Coudray, appointed as a major general and inspector general of ordnance and military manufactories by Congress to oversee the river defenses. Phillipe Charles Jean Baptiste, Tronson de Coudray, often called du Coudray or simply Coudray, was able and well connected but also imperious. He had arrived from France with an entourage of eighteen officers and ten sergeants and was a continual source of political turmoil. "I believe M. Du Coudray has done us the most damage, because he has disgusted the whole Congress," Dubuysson wrote. "He arrived here with the airs of a lord." When Duportail and other engineers arrived, de Coudray "was unmasked . . . he reviles all the Frenchmen, even the Marquis de Lafayette, to whom he wrote a very rude letter."[42]

Faced with more of the same infighting, which promised only to worsen, few were heartbroken when fate intervened. On the morning of September 16, "Cloudy and some Rain, about 11 oClock General Coutree [de Coudray] set off with Nine French officers towards the Camp, over Schuylkill," Jacob Hiltzheimer wrote in his diary, "but he the Said French Genl. Kep on his Horse, in the Boat Crossing. His Horse Leped over board, and thereby Drowned the General. In the Evening went to Schuylkill and Seen Said Genl. Taken up out of the water."[43] The controversial Frenchman had foolishly decided to ride his horse onto the ferryboat at the Lower Ferry. The high-spirited animal kept going, taking the high-spirited general with him. Though he managed to get free from his stirrups, his aides were unable to rescue him. "This Morning, Genl. De Coudray, in attempting to cross the Schuylkill, was unfortunately drowned," Hancock wrote to Washington, "and was this Afternoon interred at the public Expence."[44] Lafayette remarked, "The loss of this muddle-headed man was perhaps a happy accident."[45]

Washington's army recrossed the Schuylkill at Levering's Ford to head back into Chester County, "the water being nearly up to the waist," Timothy Pickering wrote. "We lost here much time, by reason of mens stripping off their stocking & shoes & some of them their breeches," he grumbled. "It was a pleasant day, & had the men marched directly over by platoons without stripping, no harm could have ensued, their cloaths would have dried by night on their march, & the bottom would not have hurt their feet." The adjutant general was extremely annoyed by a poor display of leadership, for "the officers too discovered a delicacy quite unbecoming soldiers; quitting their platoons, & some getting horses of their acquaintences to ride over, and others getting over in a canoe. They would have better done their duty had they kept to their platoons & led in their men."[46]

The Continentals "proceeded on—passed till we came to Merion Meeting House," Sgt. John Hawkins of Congress's Own Regiment wrote, "where we turned into the Lancaster Road" near the eighth milestone "and kept on till we came near the Eleventh Mile Stone where we halted in the Woods and rested this night."[47] The Sign of the Buck, or Widow Miller's Tavern, eleven miles from Philadelphia, became general headquarters. The front of the army continued as far as Radnor Meeting at the fourteenth milestone, where Anthony Wayne wrote to Gen. Thomas Mifflin, "The Enemy, sore from the Others days Action lay in a Supine State—part at Dilworths, part at Chads's ford, & the Remainder Advance at Concord. We Intend to push for the White Horse," a tavern in the Great Valley a dozen or so miles ahead, near where the Swedes Ford Road connects with the Lancaster Road.

Wayne had a rhetorical question for Mifflin about Howe's forces: "May they not steal a March and pass the fords in the Vicinity of the Falls unless we immediately March down and Give them Battle?" he asked in his usual bellicose style. "Come then and push the Matter and take your fate with your most humble and very obedient servant, Anty. Wayne."[48]

From the Buck that evening, Washington wrote to Gen. William Smallwood, who was supposed to have brought the Maryland Militia up to the main army several days before. Smallwood faced more problems than anyone could imagine: no food, few weapons, badly made ammunition, no tents or blankets—not even officers' commissions or regulations for the Marylanders. Hundreds of those who initially turned out went home, and dozens were leaving hourly. He wrote repeatedly to those in authority—Gov. Thomas Johnson, Congressman Samuel Chase, William Paca, and Washington—describing the chaos. Yet from the Buck, he received a letter that said, "His Excellency begs you will push on as expeditiously as possible with what troops you now have, leaving those in your rear to follow, and that you will either annoy or harass the Enemy on their Flank or Rear."[49]

Smallwood received this letter at Oxford Meeting House in southern Chester County, more than fifty miles away, the following day. His militia force of 1,400 was only half armed, with no artillery, little ammunition, and no training. Worse yet, they had to forage every day for provisions, as the Commissary Department had failed them every step of the way. "I will do all in my Power to comply with our Instructions," he replied, "but the Condition of my Troops, their Number, the state of their arms, Discipline and Military Stores, I am Apprehensive will not enable me to render that essential Service." The Maryland general feared that Howe's army, less than thirty miles away, "may detach a Body of Infantry with their light Horse to Attack and disperse the Militia." He reminded Washington, "Your Excelly. Is too well acquainted with Militia to place much Dependence in them when opposed to regular and veteran Troops, without Regular Forces to support them." Besides, under the circumstances, "it will not be in my Power to bring these Troops for these three Days to come on the Enemy's Rear." Smallwood added, "Your Excy. will excuse the freedom I have taken in offering my sentiments."[50]

Washington had a number of other immediate problems to deal with as far as generals were concerned. Congress voted to recall Sullivan from active field command on September 14, pending an inquiry into his performance at Brandywine; this was on top of the Staten Island fiasco, which inquiry was also pending. Gen. Preudhomme de Borre, insulted that he too was going to be the subject of an investigation, submitted his resignation. No tears were shed at de Borre's departure; however, the Maryland Line was now in a serious managerial crisis. "Tho' I would willingly pay every attention to the Resolutions of Congress, yet in the late instance respecting the recall of Genl. Sullivan, I must defer giving any order about it," Washington told John Hancock. "Our Situation at this time is critical and delicate . . . to derange the Army by withdrawing so many General Officers from it, may and must be attended with many disagreeable, if not ruinous, Consequences." Recalling Sullivan would leave the entire Maryland Division without a single general officer. Washington went on to say, "I cannot be answerable for the consequences which may arise from a want of Officers to assist me."[51] Congress reluctantly agreed, and Sullivan's inquiries were put off until the campaign slowed down.

The Continental Army continued its march up the Lancaster Road on September 15. The day dawned with gray skies, and the atmosphere became more unsettled as a major Nor'easter made its way slowly up the coast. The troops marched about twelve miles, and Washington took up quarters in the Malin House in East Whiteland Township, where the Swedes Ford Road and Lancaster Road intersect. Three miles farther west, advance parties of the army moved to the vicinity of the White Horse Tavern, while the rear of the army stretched three miles back from Malin's to the General Paoli Tavern in Tredyffrin Township.

"At 6 AM we marched to the Sorrel Horse, the Spread Eagle, and to Paoli, where we encamped," Lt. James McMichael of the Pennsylvania State Regiment wrote in his diary on September 15, naming some of the taverns they passed on the way.[52] The Paoli Tavern was named in honor of Gen. Pasquale Paoli, a Corsican patriot who had fought for Corsica's independence and was the hero of the Whigs, both in England and America. In between general headquarters at Malin's and the Paoli Tavern was the Adm. Warren Tavern, named for the British naval hero Sir Peter Warren. "Marchd to the Warren on Lancaster road," Ens. George Ewing of the 3rd New Jersey Regiment wrote in his journal, noting where Stirling's Division encamped.

The army was about to enter a phase of campaigning that would try the men to their limits of physical endurance in the defense of Philadelphia. "Were I to describe the hardships and difficulties we underwent from this time untill the 4 of October no person but those who were with us would credit my relation," Ewing observed. "Therefore I chuse to pass it over in silence rather than those who should se this work should think me guilty of an Hyperbole."[53]

The Crown Forces remained encamped in the vicinity of Dilworth and Aston until the night of September 15. "At 4 o'clock P. M. learnt that the rebel army which had crossed the Schuylkill at Philadelphia had repassed it to this side of Levering's Ford and were pursuing the road to Lancaster," Montrésor wrote. Howe decided that this would be the time to move, and he ordered Lord Cornwallis to march from the "Ashtown Camp" toward the Great Valley by way of Goshen Friends Meeting, where the two columns would rendezvous. Montrésor noted, "This night at 8, the body with Lord Cornwallis moved from near Chester towards the Lancaster Road."[54]

Cornwallis had both grenadier and both light infantry battalions with him at Aston, near Chester, along with Grant's two brigades, and he began advancing up the Edgemont Road toward the rendezvous at Goshen Meeting. "We turn'd off at the sign of the 7 stars into the Lancaster road"—actually the Edgemont Road, which led to the Lancaster Road—"& march'd about 2 miles over very rough road & halted till day light, ye 16th" wrote Captain-Lieutenant Peebles, "when we moved on for 9 or 10 miles & made a halt."[55] The weather was turning stormy and the roads were rutted, churned into a dense paste by the movement of thousands of feet.

American scouts were on the lookout for British activity in this area. Lt. Col. Persifor Frazer and Maj. John Harper of the 2nd Pennsylvania Brigade, who was a neighbor, along with Frazer's brother-in-law Jacob Vernon, were on the Edgemont Road not far from the Frazer farm. Stopping at the Blue Ball Tavern for refreshments, "Major Harper looking from the window saw a number of horsemen coming up the road who from their uniform he supposed were part of a company of Virginia Light horse." Some troopers of Moylan's 4th Continental Light Dragoons wore captured uniforms of the 8th and 24th Regiments, both royal regiments, with blue facings. They were constantly causing confusion and alarm; Washington at one point had ordered the men to wear linen hunting shirts over the coats.[56] But evidently Harper now presumed that dragoons in red coats faced with blue were Virginians and not the 16th Queen's Own Light Dragoons—who also wore red coats faced with blue. "When the mistake was discovered Uncle Jacob Vernon jumped out of a window. . . . The others attempting to do so, were fired upon, the house surrounded and they captured, their swords and horses taken from them and themselves compelled to proceed with their captors."[57]

Lt. Henry Stirke of the 1st Light Infantry Battalion confirmed, "This morning a party of Light Dragoons, with us, surpris'd at a house a Rebel Colonel and a Major of Brigade; 3 Light Dragoons was with them but made their escape out of a backdoor, leaving their Horses behind them."[58]

James Parker noted in his journal that day, "Colo. Frazer & his Brigade Majr. (formerly a Taylor) with three light [horse were take]n."[59]

Shortly after his capture, Persifor Frazer had an interesting meeting with General Grant. According to Elizabeth Smith, Frazer's granddaughter:

> Gen. Grant entered into a conversation with my Grandfather who was walking near him, and at length asked his name—Persifor Frazer. "That is a Scotch name," said the General (himself a Scotchman), "and should not be the name of a rebel." [Colonel Frazer replied,] "England has called other men rebels besides those who resist her government in America." "For that answer," said Grant, "you shall have your horse," and when it was brought he restored his sword also, and they rode along very pleasantly together for the remainder of the journey which was short. This occurred as they were passing the Goshen Quaker meeting house.

By a remarkable coincidence, "in the conversation Grandpa had with Gen. Grant they made themselves out to be cousins. Grant said his mother was a Frazer and cousin to our Great Grandfather."[60]

"The 15th Lord Cornwallis moved at eight at Night from Ash Town, the Genl. [Howe] marched the 16th in the morning from Dilworth & We met pretty early that Day at Goshen Meeting House," Grant told General Harvey, "but were obliged to wait till three o'clock for the Artillery & Baggage, both Columns then moved forward by different Routes towards the White Horse, upon the great Lancaster Road, where Washingtons Army was said to be encamped, having repassed the Shuylkill, upon our making Demonstration to Chester."[61]

Howe left Dilworth early that morning despite threatening gray skies and intermittent rain. The general was with von Knyphausen's column, which was marching towards Goshen Friends Meeting House and the Boot Tavern by way of the Turk's Head Tavern (now West Chester). The keeper of the Turk's Head, Jacob James, joined the British Army after Brandywine to serve as a guide. James proved to be extremely useful to Galloway and Howe over the next few months, serving as a guide, spying, recruiting, and even kidnapping. He was eventually commissioned captain of the Goshen Troop of Light Horse, a Loyalist unit.

"The Army marched from Brandywine to Goshen," Capt. John André wrote. "Some shots were fired on the Column at the Turk's Head five miles from Brandywine, where a soldier of the 33rd Regiment was killed and another wounded, an Officer was likewise slightly wounded."[62] Joseph Townsend recalled more details about the event:

> On the 16th of the 9th month 1777, as the British army was on their march from their ground of encampment at Birmingham . . . as they passed by the Turk's Head tavern, on their way to the Swedes Ford on the Schuylkill, they were fired upon by a scouting-party of the Americans, and two of their number were shot dead. Graves were immediately opened inside of the garden-fence near the intersection of the Philadelphia Road and their bodies deposited therein during the time of their march, which was performed in about four hours in the course of the forenoon, a tremendous rain taking place during the time.[63]

That morning, on the Lancaster Road, Washington's troops formed up and began ascending the South Valley Hill in two columns into Goshen Township. The left column, with Pennsylvania Militia and Continentals commanded by Anthony Wayne in the lead, moved on the Chester Road headed toward Goshen Meeting House and Cornwallis, while the right column, led by Maxwell's light corps augmented by militia, including Dunlap's "partizans," moved up the road toward the Boot Tavern. Washington planned to place his army on the top of the South Valley Hill to block the British advance toward the Schuylkill.

At the foot of the South Valley Hill near the White Horse Tavern, "Tuesday 16th Sepr. Struck Tents Cross'd the main Road [the Lancaster Road] and paraded in line of Battle in A Buckwheat Field expecting the enemy in order to give them battle," Capt. Robert Kirkwood of the Delaware Regiment wrote.[64] On the Boot Road near Goshen Meeting, "Every one Rejoiced, hoping to see Jonathan in a few hours," James Parker scribbled, delighted at another opportunity for battle with "Jonathan," one of the more pleasant nicknames the British had for Americans. "We were going Northerly, & the Rebels Westerly," Parker observed. "We would have met them at the Corner of an angle just in the teeth at the White horse Tavern, & Lord C. Wallace would have fall'n in with the Center of their line of March. But our hopes were blasted, tho', at that very time W———ton was on that Ground."[65]

Just north of the meetinghouse, skirmishing erupted between Cornwallis's vanguard and the Pennsylvania Militia on Washington's left flank. "About 3 O'Clock, the first Battn of Light Infantry, attack'd a body of

500 rebels, under the command of Genl Waine, posted behind a fence, on a hill, about half a mile from Goshen meeting House," Lt. Henry Stirke of the 1st Light Infantry Battalion wrote. "On our advancing very briskly," the Pennsylvania Militia "gave us one fire and run away, leaving 10 men kill'd and Wounded on the field." The light bobs suffered one man wounded.[66]

Advancing up the Boot Road with von Knyphausen's column while Cornwallis's force skirmished on the Chester Road, Parker noticed, "About two we heard a firing on our Right between L.C.W. & Some of their advanced party which did not continue long." Meanwhile, the Hessian Jägers at the head of von Knyphausen's force engaged Maxwell's light infantry and Dunlap's Pennsylvania riflemen just beyond the Boot Tavern on Washington's right. "About 3 the Yeakers on our front were Attackd, & a [heavy?] fire Supported a Cross a ploughd field, till some of our troops coming up drove off the Rebels, taking 8 prisoners." Parker wrote, noting, "This was at the entry Of the Great Vally by Thomas's Mill, difficult ground."[67]

Ewald and the Jägers were in the thick of the fight at the head of von Knyphausen's column. "The advance guard had hardly arrived at the Boot Tavern," about four miles northwest of Goshen Meeting House, "when they learned that an enemy corps of two to three thousand men had appeared on the left flank of the army." Col. Count Karl von Donop decided to personally lead the Jägers into action. Taking a party of Capt. Carl Wreden's foot and Capt. Richard Lorey's mounted Jägers, he advanced toward some of Maxwell's riflemen. "The colonel pursued them too far, through which mistake an enemy party passed between him and the army and cut off his retreat. Captain Lorey decided to break through with the horsemen to relieve the foot jägers, notwithstanding that the enemy had posted himself very favorably behind walls and fences and kept up a sustained rifle fire." After the colonel was safe, the Jägers had a chuckle at the colonel's expense. "The colonel got off with his skin.—That is not a trade for one to follow who has no knowledge of it," Ewald commented wryly. "We all laughed secretly over this partisan trick."[68]

Pvt. James Patten of Dunlap's "partizans" recalled that "a few days after the battle of Brandywine he was in an engagement with the British at a place near the White-horse tavern between Phila. and Lancaster; but owing to the tremendous rain that fell that day, the small armes were out of order and but little execution was done on either side."[69]

"The Light Troops of both Columns got into Skirmish with advanced Rebell Corps which were beat with ease, & without Loss," Grant wrote, "but the Blow could not be followed on account of the badness of the weather." Having spent years in Scotland, as well as in Cuba and in Florida as governor, he told General Harvey, "It was the heaviest Gale of Rain I ever saw in any Country, during which Washington, astonished at our unexpected move from Chester, fled in the utmost confusion & by that means according to intercepted Letters, He lost all his ammunition."[70]

Washington had placed himself badly. His back was to the Great Valley, and only two or three roads provided an escape route for 12,000 men down the South Valley Hill. Further, it had taken the men so long to get up the hill that morning that they were not properly placed. Pickering, who had been ordered to assist in arranging the right flank, rode back to the center as the skirmishing began and saw that the troops there were still not arranged.

"Sir, the advancing of the British is manifest by the reports of the musketry," the adjutant general told Washington. "The order of battle is not complete. If we are to fight the enemy on this ground, the troops ought to be immediately arranged." Pickering further reasoned, "If we are to take the high grounds on the other side of the valley, we ought to march immediately, or the enemy may fall upon us in the midst of our movement."[71] Washington agreed and ordered the army to withdraw into the Great Valley.

The Continentals slipped and slid quickly back down the South Valley Hill and took up positions north of the White Horse Tavern, "where they had a most favourable position being a prevailing gradual height in the valley."[72] As the Americans withdrew, the Jägers under Ewald became involved in some hand-to-hand fighting. "I believe it was about five o'clock in the afternoon, an extraordinary thunderstorm occurred, combined with the heaviest downpour in this world," he wrote. "General Knyphausen, who arrived at my company on horseback, ordered me to attack the people in the wood." The rifles on both sides began to misfire in the rain, so Ewald ordered the Jägers to charge with their hunting swords. "I reached the wood at top speed and came to close quarters with the enemy, who during the furious attack forgot that he had bayonets and quit the field, whereby the jägers captured four officers and some thirty men. The entire loss of the Jäger Corps in this fight consisted of five killed, seven wounded, and three missing."[73]

"All this time Morgans [*sic*; Dunlap's] riffelmen ware on the wings, next to the enemy, against the Hissions, as they could use their rifels, having bearskins over their locks, and every now and then you would give a crack at each other," Artilleryman Jacob Nagle, who had just turned sixteen, recollected. He observed the difference in sound between the weapons. The Jäger rifles, which had short barrels but were large in caliber, gave off a loud *BLAM!* when fired, whereas the Pennsylvania rifles, with longer barrels and of smaller caliber, made a higher-pitched snap. "We could always tell when a Hession fired, from our rifels, cracking so much lowder than our rifels."[74]

As the advance forces skirmished and the Continentals tried to get positioned, the deluge of rain brought the firing to an end. Both armies were saturated by the extraordinary volume of precipitation from this slow-moving tropical storm, and the firing petered out. The encounter became known as the "Battle of the Clouds."

The storm increased in fury. "It had threatned rain all day, & now it fell, a Mud deluge, the Roads so deep there was no bringing on the Artillery," Parker observed. "The Wind was at south East & every thing look'd like the Equinoctial storm, which it realy was. Here we were oblijed to halt." Talking with some of those captured by the Jägers, Parker was able to gather some intelligence. "The prisoners say they were part of 1000 Commanded by Genl. Potter," referring to James Potter's Pennsylvania Militia Brigade, attached to Maxwell's Corps, "& that Washington was expected to be At Donington that night."[75] Downingtown, five miles west of the Boot, was a militia rendezvous point and Chester County's largest inland town. Also called Milltown, it was a major commissary depot for flour and other food supplies. It was also halfway between Philadelphia and Lancaster, about thirty miles from each.

As darkness descended, Washington ordered the army to withdraw not to Downingtown, but toward Yellow Springs, six miles away up and over the North Valley Hill. "We began to March towards the Yellow springs where we Arrived About 2 o'Clock the next Morning," Lt. William Beatty of the 7th Maryland wrote. The roads were flooded and the creeks became torrents. "All the small Branches that we were Obliged to cross on this march were so rais'd by the Hard rain that they took us to the waists and under the Arms when we Waded them, None of our men preserv'd a single round of Ammunition that did not get thoroughly wet."[76]

The march took nearly fourteen hours. "We came to a regular decented hill, the ground being so soft that they had to onhich the horses from one piece of artillery and hitch them to another till they got them all up," Jacob Nagle recalled of the North Valley Hill. "The nights was so dark you could not tell the man next to you. I being a horseback, I kept close behind one of the ammunition waggons but dripping wet and shivering with cold."[77]

Howe took up quarters in the Boot Tavern, described by Captain von Münchhausen as "a miserable small house, called The-Boot-Sign."[78] As night fell, the royal forces hastily encamped along the roads and tried to find shelter and dry firewood as best as they could. The officers took refuge in local houses, while the troops crowded into barns, built wigwams out of fence rails and tree limbs, or took shelter in the woods. "The Troops ordered to pile their arms & make fires," John Peebles wrote, "but no shelter for a wieried soldier wet to the skin & under a heavy rain all night."[79] The Guards formed the left front flank of the encampment on the crest of the South Valley Hill about half a mile in front of Howe's headquarters, guarding a road that led across the Great Valley. The right front was held by the 1st Light Infantry Battalion on the hill overlooking the White Horse Tavern.

"As wet as water could make me, & cold without any chance of a dry place to sleep I went from the front to the Rear of the Army," James Parker wrote, slogging back up Boot Road toward Goshen Meeting House. "It was quite dark when I was by a glimmering led to a little hut where lived a Quaker Woman, who lent me a dry pitticoat; the Capts. McCloud & Calden of the Jersey Volunteers," a Loyalist unit, "found the Way here & here we staid all night in Goshen Township."[80]

Twenty miles or so away to the northeast, Col. Joseph Reed was at Swedes Ford, watching the Schuylkill rise by the minute. "We apprised you a few hours ago that the river was rising fast and was scarcely fordable," he told Washington at 6 P.M. "The heavy rains have since swelled it so much that it is now impassable . . . it will be twenty-four hours before it will be fordable for the footmen." No digging of fortifications was possible until the deluge stopped. "M. Portel has been up," he said, meaning the French engineer Col. Louis Duportail, "and will lay out the necessary works as soon as the weather will permit." Regarding the other crossings, he wrote, "The militia are collecting at this place and the fords lower down." As for the floating bridge at Middle Ferry, "the bridge is fully removed."[81]

Washington's forces began arriving at Yellow Springs before dawn, thoroughly soaked and utterly spent. "We had yesterday one of the Hardest Marches known by any Soldiers in our army," Col. Thomas Hartley, commander of the 1st Pennsylvania Brigade in Wayne's Division, told some friends in Lancaster. "Neither Floods, Storms, Myres, Nor any Thing else, prevented us from effecting the Point."[82] With their ammunition completely ruined, the army's firepower was gone, largely because of faulty cartridge boxes that were not waterproof. "Nearly all the musket cartridges of the army that had been delivered to the men were damaged, consisting of about 400,000," Henry Knox told his wife, Lucy. "This was a most terrible stroke to us, and owing entirely to the badness of the cartouch-boxes which had been provided for the army."[83] Washington had repeatedly complained of this, advocating tin boxes if proper leather could not be had. But shortages of materials of all types, rampant inflation, and the sort of shoddy materials and incompetence too often associated with hasty government contracts and unscrupulous contractors plagued the army. The British forces, by contrast, were equipped with heavy leather cartridge boxes featuring a double flap and lined with felt, which were much more water resistant.

To put some distance between his sodden forces and the British, as well as to secure new ammunition, Washington decided to move the army farther north, to Warwick Furnace in the French Creek Valley. With French Creek over its banks, the only safe way to cross was to march five miles east to the Reading Road, where there was a bridge, and then nine miles west to Warwick. Once the rain stopped, the Continentals began a grueling march on roads that were nearly impassable.

To screen the rear of his march and keep an eye on Howe, Washington left Wayne's Pennsylvania Division near Yellow Springs at "Camp three miles from the Red Lion," a tavern in Uwchlan (pronounced "YOO-klin") Township. "The two Armies have been maneuvering these two Days," Colonel Hartley wrote to friends in Lancaster on September 17. "You will soon hear something of Consequence." But he did warn his friends: "The Enemy are plundering all before them—I hope the Military Virtue of this Country will soon make them repent their Rashness."[84]

As for the British, they had waited out the storm in Goshen. But under the cover of darkness and teeming rain, and encouraged by the confusion of the hasty encampment, plundering resumed, and this time some of the Guards were caught right in the middle of it.

On the morning of the seventeenth, Sir George Osborn discovered a major problem in his company. Several grenadiers were missing; two of them, Robert Eliot and Luke Redman, were "taken prisoner Sept. 17, 1777, at Goshen, Pa.," probably while out plundering.[85] Two others, Robert Hicks and Thomas Burrows, were caught with plunder by Osborn and Capt. Richard Fitzpatrick.

"Having found several of the Grenadiers of the Guards absent at the Morning Roll calling," Sir George testified at their court-martial two days later, "and having reason to imagine that they had gone to a house at some considerable distance from the front of the encampment," Osborn and Fitzpatrick "walked on to the corner of the wood, to endeavour to find if any of the Grenadiers were coming that way with plunder, and in a very short time, Captain Fitzpatrick, who had stopp'd the two prisoners, call'd to him." Sir George "found upon them the plunder mentioned in the annexed List, and the Prisoners very much intoxicated with liquor; that some inhabitants came soon after to claim some of the goods."

The quartermaster of the 1st Guards Battalion, George Beecher, identified one of the inhabitants as Evan Evans, an old man who, like many of the local people, was of Welsh descent. This area of Chester County was part of William Penn's original "Welch Tract," 40,000 acres stretching from the Schuylkill through the Great Valley to "Uwchlan," Welsh for "the upper land" at the end of the tract. Evans was a member of the Evans family of Uwchlan Township who lived near the Red Lion Tavern about five miles north of the British camp on the other side of the Great Valley. Sir George noted that the grenadiers "had gone to a house at some considerable distance from the front of the encampment." The court found both Burrows and Hicks guilty; they were sentenced "to receive five hundred lashes each on their bare backs with cats of nine tails."[86]

The fear of being plundered caused some local families to flee the area or hide their valuables, especially silver, which, other than livestock, was often the most valuable disposable item possessed by Chester County families. But most inhabitants stayed at their homes, as Captain Montrésor noted when the army finally moved from Goshen on September 18: "Between 3 and 4 this morning (the Equinoxial Gale still continuing at N. East, with small rain) the Army marched from the boot 3 miles to the White Horse, where we joined Lord Cornwallis's column," which came down the South Valley Hill after several hours of delay caused by the artillery taking the wrong road and having to turn around. At the White Horse, the columns "halted an hour, and the whole army moved on towards Philadelphia, until we arrived at Randel Malins, being 2 1/2 miles further. There we struck off (the roads forking) the road to the Swedes Ford to Treduffrin."

The army once again divided, and "Lord Cornwallis's column continuing the Philadelphia Main Road from the Forks at Randel Malins (which was Washington's Headquarters the night before last) which road runs nearly parallel with the Swedes Ford Road," but eventually ascends to the top of the South Valley Hill. Cornwallis's men marched on the Lancaster Road past the Admiral Warren and General Paoli Taverns. "We found the Inhabitants in general at their Homes."[87]

Howe was with von Knyphausen's column on the Swedes Ford Road, which continued east in the Great Valley to Tredyffrin Township. "The roads were extremely bad," von Münchhausen noted, "partly because of the heavy rains and partly because Washington, with the large part of his army, artillery, and all his baggage, had passed this way last night, thus reaching his destination before Lord Cornwallis arrived at White Horse, all owing to the fatal mistake of our artillery."[88]

The Great Valley, or "Duffryn Mawr," as many of the Welsh locals called it, was the main part of the Welsh Tract. Most of the inhabitants were first- or second-generation Americans, but many of the older people still spoke Welsh. There were also a few English, a congregation of Scots-Irish Presbyterians, some German and Swiss "Mennonists and Omish," and a sprinkling of Africans in the region.

While many of the Welsh were Quaker, many others were Anglican or Baptist. The army passed a road to St. Peter-in-the-Great Valley, an Anglican church with a Welsh congregation but a Scottish minister. Rev. William Currie was a Loyalist, but his three sons joined the Continental Army. Currie was also pastor of St. David's Church in nearby Radnor, where Anthony Wayne was a parishioner. A few miles east of St. Peter's was the Great Valley Baptist Church, whose firebrand pastor was Rev. David Jones, the chaplain of Wayne's 1st Pennsylvania Brigade.

The British and Hessian forces marched past David Howell's Tavern, formerly the Sign of George III, where Maj. Gen. Charles Grey took up his quarters. Howe established general headquarters in Tredyffrin, Welsh for "the Valley Town," at the home of Samuel Jones, a little over a mile away and a few hundred yards west of the Great Valley Baptist Church.

"They call this region Great Valley because there are chains of high hills covered with woods on both sides of the valley," von Münchhausen noted. "The Valley Creek, part of which flows through our camp, has the best water I have tasted here in America."[89] Mills and small manufactories of various types used the numerous streams that were found throughout the valley.

Three miles downstream from the British camp, the rapidly flowing, sweet water of Valley Creek was utilized by an ironworks called the Valley Forge, where an American military magazine, or supply depot, was located. The forge was owned by a partnership of David Potts of the Potts family, noted Pennsylvania ironmasters, and Col. William Dewees of the Pennsylvania Militia. Whether military items were actually fabricated there is uncertain, but the state government began storing large quantities of iron goods there—axes, shovels, tomahawks, camp kettles—in the spring of 1777.

West of Valley Forge, a number of ironworks, such as Warwick Furnace and Hopewell Furnace, were casting cannons and ammunition for Congress in 1777, and the Continental Powder Mill was established on French Creek six miles from Valley Forge, together with the "Public Gun Manufactory" and "Public Gunlock Factory" under the supervision of scientist and clockmaker David Rittenhouse. The Valley Forge storehouses were convenient locations for finished goods, along with flour ground at the local mills, one of which was situated near where Valley Creek empties into the Schuylkill River a few hundred yards below the forge. The gristmill and a sawmill were owned by David Potts's brother Isaac, who also owned a small, elegant country house nearby.

With the British Army so close, Colonel Dewees wanted the supplies moved away quickly from his home and business. He compiled an inventory of hundreds of kettles, axes, shovels, and several thousand barrels of flour, all of which had to be moved across the Schuylkill River. None of his workers were available; they had been called up for militia duty. So Capt. "Light-Horse Harry" Lee and a handful of dragoons went to Valley Forge on the afternoon of September 18, along with Washington's aide, Lt. Col. Alexander Hamilton, to move or destroy the supplies. Two rafts and eight men were now available to move 4,000 barrels of flour, each barrel containing about 200 pounds, not to mention the tons of iron goods, which all needed to be hauled 400 yards to the river landing.

That evening, a British force of several hundred men, composed of two mounted squadrons of the 16th Light Dragoons and 200 dismounted dragoons led by Lt. Col. Harcourt, along with three companies of light infantry, marched four miles north to seize the magazine at Valley Forge. At the crest of the hill called Mount Joy, overlooking the forge area, Lee had posted two vedettes, or mounted sentries. "The fire of the vedettes announced the enemy's appearance," Lee wrote. Hamilton was near one of the flatboats, and "of the small party four with the lieutenant colonel jumped into the boat, the van of the enemy's horse in full view, pressing down the hill in pursuit of the two vedettes. Captain Lee, with the remaining two, took the decision to regain the bridge" over Valley Creek and rely on "the speed and soundness of his horse." Lee escaped, as did Hamilton. Gunfire erupted; one man in the boat was killed, another wounded. Hamilton's horse was shot and killed in the boat, and the commander of the British light infantry, Maj. Peter Craig, also had his horse shot.[90] The forge and storehouses were captured intact, along with one flatboat, and "the Battle of Valley Forge" was a British victory.

When Hamilton reached the other side of the river, he scribbled a message to John Hancock in Philadelphia: "If Congress have not yet left Philadelphia, they ought to do it immediately without fail, for the enemy have the means of throwing a party this night into the city." A few hours later, at 9 P.M., Hamilton again wrote to Hancock: "The enemy are on the road to Swedes ford, the main body about four miles from it." He told the president about the skirmish and the fact that the British had exactly two rafts at their disposal. "These two boats will convey 50 men across at a time so that in a few hours they may throw over a large party, perhaps sufficient to overmatch the militia who may be between them and the city."[91]

Hancock had received earlier intelligence from Joseph Burns, who had been sent by Anthony Wayne to reconnoiter the British positions. Burns was unable to get back to Wayne, so he went down to the city to report that Howe was within seven or eight miles of Swedes Ford. More alarming, though, was the fact that "some of the Pennsylvania light Horse on their return to Town had made Prisoners of two British Soldiers within eighteen miles of this City on the Lancaster Road."[92] These soldiers were from Cornwallis's column, camped on top of the South Valley Hill, and the head of the column was near the eighteenth milestone, less than two miles from the Spread Eagle Tavern. Two troopers of the 1st Troop of Philadelphia Light Horse, one of whom was John Donnaldson, "were sent out by General Armstrong to obtain intelligence of the Enemy— about 8 [sic; 2] miles from the Spread Eagle on the Lancaster road they observed a piquet of the British, & with the assistance of two young men of the neighbourhood brought off two soldiers in the face of the piquet— reported to General Armstrong that night at Vanduren's [Vanderin's] mill," located at the mouth of Wissahickon Creek just above the Falls of Schuylkill.[93] The information was quickly sent to town.

Philadelphia was a city already on edge, especially as news trickled in that Washington's army was now mired somewhere in the hills of northern Chester County with no ammunition. "I cannot help acquainting you, my dear General, that the distance of the army from the city" to a place "so remote has given great alarm, and very much discourages the militia," a frustrated Joseph Reed wrote to Washington at 9 P.M. from the Falls of Schuylkill. "I do not doubt you have sufficient reasons for a measure which seems so mysterious, but if you could consistently with your plans disclose them, it would have a happy effect on the minds of the people." He also told Washington that he would return the next morning to Swedes Ford, where they had "the works in great forwardness."[94] These were the only land works built to defend the city east of the Schuylkill.

But events and communications were moving at different paces, locked in a fateful waltz. Hamilton's news of the British advance to Valley Forge reached Philadelphia, twenty-two miles away, in three or four hours. "The morning of the 19th September . . . when about one oClock (& I was not in bed, nor had my Cloaths off for three Nights before) I Rec'd an Express from the General's aid De Camp recommending the immediate Removal of Congress, as the Enemy had it in their power to throw a party that Night into the City," Hancock told his wife, Dorothy. "I instantly gave the alarm, Rous'd the Members, collected my Waggons, Horses, Carriage &c and after having fix'd my Packages, Papers &c in the Waggons and Sent them off, about 3 oClock in the morning I Set off myself for Bristol."[95]

Now a panic began in the city, starting with the government leaders. "The Scene was equally droll & melancholy," Congressman Henry Laurens wrote. "Thousands of all Sorts in all appearances past by in such haste that very few could be prevailed on to answer to the Simple question what News?" According to Laurens, he was one of only a few patriots who kept a level head, given the information received. "I however would not fly, I stayed Breakfast & did not proceed till 8 oClock or past nor would I have gone then but returned once more into the City if I had not been under an engagement to take charge of the Marquis delafayette who lay wounded by a ball through his Leg at Bristol." But he admitted, "My bravery however was the effect of assurance for could I have believed the current report, I should have fled as fast as any Man, no Man can possibly have a greater reluctance to an intimacy with Sir William Howe than my Self."[96]

Two days later, having fled to Bristol and Trenton with most of the rest of Congress, John Adams wrote in disgust, "It was a false alarm which occasioned our Flight from Philadelphia. Not a Soldier of Howes has crossed the Schuylkill. Washington has again crossed it, which I think is a very injudicious Maneuvre." Figuring out what Washington was attempting to do, he commented, "If he had sent one Brigade of his regular troops to have heald the Militia it would have been enough. With such a Disposition, he might have cutt to Pieces, Hows Army, in attempting to cross at any of the Fords." Adams was also worried about Gates, "who seems to be acting the same timorous, defensive Part, which has involved us in so many disasters."

Adams had reached the end of his rope with the generals, Washington included. "Oh, Heaven!" he cried in frustration, "grant Us one great Soul! One leading Mind would extricate the best Cause, from that Ruin which seems to await it, for the Want of it." Calming down somewhat, he continued: "We have as good a Cause, as ever was fought for. We have great Resources. The People are well tempered." He confided in his diary, "One active masterly Capacity would bring order out of this Confusion and save this Country."[97]

As Congress fled the city, some Continental forces were on the move in Chester County. Washington's main force arrived at Warwick late on the seventeenth and early on the eighteenth, utterly exhausted; general headquarters was established at Reading Furnace, two miles farther on. From here, Washington began to formulate yet another plan to stop the British advance on Philadelphia.

With the Schuylkill still running high, Howe would be staying west of the river for a few more days. Washington decided to send Anthony Wayne's two Pennsylvania brigades, along with four light cannon from Randall's Independent Artillery and some dragoons from the 1st and 3rd Continental Light Dragoons, a total force of about 2,200 personnel, on a mission to get behind Howe's army. "Genl. Maxwell and Potter are order'd to do the same," Washington told Wayne, "being at Potts' Forge," the Valley Forge. "I could wish you and those Genl. Would act in conjunction, to make your advances more formidable." He added, "I shall follow as speedily as possible with jaded men," instructing Wayne, "Give me the earliest Information of every thing Interesting & of your moves that I may know how to govern mine by them." Wayne was told to harass the rear of the British line of march, and if possible, "the cutting of the Enemy's Baggage would be a great matter." He ended the orders with a warning: "Take care of Ambuscades."[98]

Washington had also ordered General Smallwood, who was still struggling to move his Maryland Militia up from the southern part of the county, to rejoin the main army rather than harass the rear of the Crown Forces. Smallwood was joined on the eighteenth by Col. Mordecai Gist, with 700 men from the Eastern Shore, along with three iron cannons. By September 19, this force of 2,100 Maryland troops was at James McClellan's Tavern in Sadsbury Township, about fifteen miles west of Downingtown.

Wayne's troops left Yellow Springs during the night of the eighteenth, and by dawn, the Pennsylvania Division was at the Paoli Tavern, ten miles east of Downingtown and only four miles behind the British camp at Tredyffrin. Wayne was a cattleman and tanner, as well as a farmer and surveyor. His home and 500-acre plantation, Waynesborough, which also contained a tannery, was less than a mile from the tavern, and he knew the area intimately—the roads, hills, and bypaths, some of which he had surveyed.

Following his instructions to keep the commander in chief informed, Wayne wrote two letters to Washington from the Paoli Tavern that morning, informing him that the British Army was lying still; "indeed their Supineness Answers every purpose of giving you time to get up." He told Washington that if they attempted to move, he would attack them. "There never was, nor never will be a finer Opportunity of giving the Enemy a fatal Blow than the Present," he instructed the commander in chief, "for Gods sake push on as fast as Possible."[99]

"I expect Genl. Maxwell on their left flank every Moment," the second letter stated, "and as I lay on their Right, we only want you in their Rear—to Complete Mr Hows buisness." Wayne reassured his commander, "I believe he knows nothing of my Situation—as I have taken every precaution to Prevent any intelligence getting to him." But in closing, he remarked, "I have not heard from you since last Night," an ominous indication that somewhere there was a breakdown in communication.[100]

Being an active leader in the community for much of his life, Wayne also knew that Chester County had many neutrals and Loyalists, some of whom, like Jacob James, were serving as guides for the British Army. James would have been well known to Wayne, for Wayne's old regiment, the 4th Pennsylvania Battalion, had been mustered at the Turk's Head Tavern in 1776 before it marched to New York. There were others, too, whom Wayne also knew personally: Nathaniel Vernon, the sheriff of Chester County, was serving Howe as a guide, together with his son Nathaniel Jr.; and another son, Job, was a captain in the 5th Pennsylvania Regiment. Additionally, Joseph Galloway was known all over Pennsylvania, and William Allen Jr., who had served in Canada as lieutenant colonel of the 2nd Pennsylvania Battalion the previous year alongside Wayne, was also with Howe. "Consider that Galloway, the Allens, &c are conducting the enemy thro the most torified tracts," Congressman James Lovell wrote in late September, "assisted by Sheriffs of counties who know all the paths accurately."[101]

As it turns out, some Continental dragoons deserted, and others were captured on September 19. "Many deserters come in daily, 160 horses are brought in today by the Queens dragoons," Parker noted.[102] Howe was alerted that Wayne was moving behind him before he arrived at his actual camp location. And shortly after his second letter was sent, Wayne suddenly moved his force away from the Paoli Tavern and marched almost two miles to a wooded hillside above the Warren Tavern. Why did he make this sudden move?

About noon on September 19, word arrived at the Tredyffrin general headquarters that the dragoons and light infantry at Valley Forge were under attack. Immediately, Howe sent Lord Cornwallis with both grenadier battalions and the 1st Light Infantry Battalion on the double to reinforce Valley Forge, four miles away to the north. All three of these units were encamped on top of the South Valley Hill along the Lancaster Road.

The drums of the 1st and 2nd Grenadier Battalions and the 1st Light Infantry beat "To Arms," and any scouts that Wayne had out would have heard the signal or spotted all the activity. As those units were camped along the Lancaster Road only four miles from the Paoli Tavern rather than down in the valley, it might have appeared to Wayne that he had been spotted. Pulling back to the heights above the Warren Tavern was a prudent move, and when Cornwallis's force headed in the other direction, Wayne may still have believed that he was undetected.

The new position was located "on some high Ground above the Warren Tavern on the Lancaster Road," Colonel Hartley wrote. "In Part of the Front was a small wood and a Corn Field—on the Right a small wood and some open Fields—there were Roads passing the Flanks." Most important, "Genl. Wayne being acquainted with the Country chose the ground himself."[103] Wayne stated that "the Ground we lay on was the Strongest and best suited for our Purpose, that could be found for many Miles." As for security, "the Disposition was perfect for Defence"—or so he thought.[104]

A second hasty movement for the two Pennsylvania brigades occurred early that evening. Wayne and his officers never explained why they suddenly ordered the men out the left of camp and west on a road along the crest of the South Valley Hill toward the White Horse Tavern, or why they returned to the same ground a few hours later. But at the Tredyffrin headquarters, "In the evening it was reported that General Wayne had been detached by General Washington with 800 men to make the region behind us insecure," von Münchhausen wrote in his diary. "Consequently, the 2nd battalion of light infantry and the English riflemen," the handful of Ferguson's Corps not killed or wounded at Brandywine, "were dispatched to break camp quietly and attempt to surprise these gentlemen."[105] According to von Münchhausen, two drunken soldiers fired at a picket, giving the alarm. Wayne's force pulled out, and the British retired without any further pursuit—for the moment.

Meanwhile, as Cornwallis arrived at Valley Forge, he could see rebels on the low hills across the Schuylkill River. "The Light Infantry & Grenadiers march'd in the Afternoon about 3 OClock to the Hill above the Valley forge which is near the Sckuylkill at the Mouth of Valley Creek," Captain-Lieutenant Peebles wrote. "Some Scouting partys of the Rebels seen hovering about, they Lit fires t'other side of the River." He also noted "a fine Prospect from this Hill," a spectacular view of the Schuylkill Valley from the crest of Mount Joy.[106] Some Hessian Jägers that went along with Sir William Erskine scouted the area west of Valley Forge but found no rebel forces there.

Those Americans who were visible were Maxwell's Light Infantry, together with some of Gen. James Potter's Pennsylvania Militia. The militiamen were nothing to worry about, but the light infantry could be trouble. The lack of proper uniforms in the Continental Army made positive identification of units difficult, for the militia dressed mostly in civilian clothing with some military accoutrements. The Continentals wore a mixed bag of civilian clothing and military uniforms in various colors, including captured red coats, and assorted accoutrements and headgear.

Back in the Tredyffrin Camp, von Münchhausen noted that after Cornwallis's force went to Valley Forge in the early afternoon, "the detachment under Colonel Harcourt," the 16th Light Dragoons, "came back here."[107] The dragoons set up their camp in a meadow just south of the hill where the Guards were encamped, near Howe's headquarters. A small stream, Trout Run, meandered between the two camps, and the dragoons tethered their horses to a nearby fence. Having been up for hours on end since the previous day, the horsemen set up small pup tents and built wigwams to rest on this warm, sunny afternoon.

All of this would be inconsequential save for the fact that Ensign Lord Cantelupe of the Guards found the scene interesting enough to paint it into his diary. "Light Dragoon Incampment at Trydyffinn Pensylvania 1777 Sept" is an extraordinary image of a moment in time, a peaceful moment during a busy and violent month. The details of carefully drawn trees, fences, plowed fields, and the wooded South Valley Hill are extraordinary. But the mundane record of which regiment was where at what time—the Guards were camped on this hillside only one full day, and the dragoons were there south of them in the afternoon—together with the shadows cast by the trees are the clues that reveal the moment in time: the midafternoon of September 19, 1777, in the Great Valley. This is the only image known at present of a camp drawn by an eyewitness during this campaign.[108]

Across the valley and just beyond the left edge of the picture was the Samuel Jones house, Howe's headquarters. As the day wore on, information arrived here that the main Continental Army was on the move toward the Schuylkill. Later that evening, an intercepted message from Washington to Wayne not only confirmed Wayne's presence, but also revealed that the main American army was marching to cross the Schuylkill at Parker's Ford. Washington planned to cross the river and come down in front of Howe to reinforce the American position at Swedes Ford and other crossing places, including Fatland Ford, Pawling's Ferry, Richardson's Ford, Long Ford, and Gordon's Ford, all of which were near Valley Forge. Washington was trying to block Howe's movement across the Schuylkill and, with Wayne in position, possibly catch him in a pincer movement.

This captured intelligence was almost too good to be true. Wayne, who had sent the two letters to Washington that morning virtually ordering the commander in chief to bring the army down, was unaware that Washington was actually moving the army *away* from him and across the Schuylkill. Wayne was going to be reinforced only by Smallwood's untrained, badly armed, and disgruntled militia, which barely managed to make it to Downingtown that evening.

Clearly the British outpost at Valley Forge was exposed, and after sizing up the situation, Howe decided to send the Guards there as reinforcements in the predawn hours of September 20. Under a bright full moon, the Guards marched up the Valley Forge Road to the Gulph Road, and then deployed on the north slope of Mount Joy between Valley Forge and Fatland Ford. The ford was located just over a mile northeast of the forge. Captain Montrésor, who had been reconnoitering the river fords along with other British engineers, wrote, "At 2 this morning the guards moved and posted themselves with the Light Infantry at the Valley Forge."[109] Capt. Archibald Robertson, who was also on reconnaissance, observed, "at Day Break The 2 Battalions of Guards took Post at Fat-

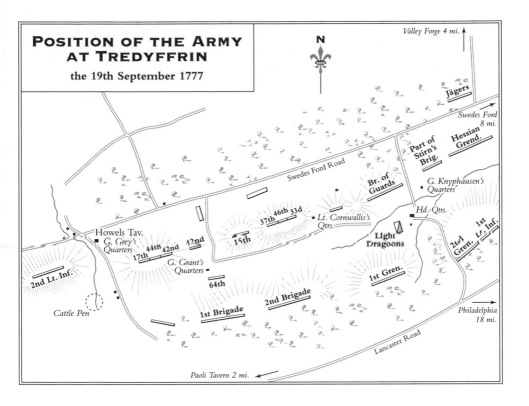

POSITION OF THE ARMY AT TREDYFFRIN
the 19th September 1777

land Ford and Found the Rebels had likeways taken Post on the Opposite side where they shewed a Brass 6 Pounder."[110] Cantelupe noted, "Marched from Trydyffin at 3 in the Morning about 3 miles And hutted on the banks of the Schuylkill River. Several shots fired by the Rebels across the river."[111] Montrésor confirmed, "This morning 5 rebel centries fired on the Guards who took the whole. They slightly wounded one of our officers," Capt. Charles Horneck of the 3rd Guards.[112]

The main Continental Army, now 7,000 men, marched sixteen miles from Reading Furnace that afternoon and crossed the Schuylkill at Parker's Ford that night. The river was still running high from the Battle of the Clouds storm, so the men linked arms and crossed the river in platoons. Once across, the Continentals headed to the Reading Road through Trappe, past Rev. Henry Muhlenberg's church and parsonage.

"The American troops marched through the Schulkiel, four miles from us, and came out on the road to Philadelphia at Augustus Church," Muhlenberg wrote as the army flooded into Trappe. "They had to wade through the river up to their chests. His Excellency General W was himself with the troops who marched passed here to the Perkiome. The passage of the troops lasted through the night and we had all kinds of visitors, officers, etc." His deepest sympathies were with the men and their condition, for "to get wet up to one's chest and then to march in the cold, foggy night while enduring hunger and thirst, etc. is hard for the poor men. It takes courage, health, etc." He was disgusted, though, for foul mouths were still in evidence. "Instead of prayers, what one hears from many of them is the horrible national vice: cursing." He noted, "At midnight a regiment camped on the street in front of my house. Some vegetables and chickens were taken, and a man with a flint came to my chamber, demanded bread, etc."[113]

The army mostly camped along the Perkiomen Creek that night. The following morning, September 20, they moved another ten to fifteen miles to take up positions along the left bank of the Schuylkill on a nine-mile-wide front from Gordon's Ford to Swedes Ford, hoping to shield both Reading and Philadelphia. Washington established general headquarters at Thompson's Tavern and proceeded to reconnoiter along the river. He also yet again chastised the men for plundering:

> General Orders: It is with the utmost concern, that the General observes, a continual straggling of soldiers on a march, who rob orchards and commit other disorders; and that many officers pay little or no attention to prevent a practice attended with such mischievous consequences, notwithstanding the orders relative thereto. The officers are reminded that it is their duty, and the General expects, that for the future, they know precisely, the number of men in their division or platoon; and where the time will admit of it, take a list of their names, previous to their marching; and that on a march they frequently look at their division to see if it be in order, and no man missing.[114]

All day, from the heights of Mount Joy, the British could see hundreds of Continental troops moving into position on the low hills across the river from Mount Joy. "There was now between us & Philadelphia a fordable river, the Schuylkill," Lt. Loftus Cliffe of the 46th told his brother Jack. "Mr. Washington detached a body of 1500 men under Gen: Wayne, to follow us & when to the hips in water in this ford to fall upon our rear; we were to cross over on the 21st and this body within 5 miles of us."[115] As the British consolidated their position at Valley Forge,

Howe prepared to move the main army toward the Schuylkill. He also decided to strike hard at Wayne's force hovering behind him.

Wayne and his two brigade commanders, Col. Thomas Hartley of the 1st Brigade and Col. Richard Humpton of the 2nd Brigade, reconnoitered the British camp at Tredyffrin during the day on September 20 and planned to advance toward them when Howe broke camp. "I had the fullest and Clearest Advice that the Enemy would March that Morning at 2 OClock for the River Schuylkill," Wayne wrote. "In Consequence of that Advice I had Reconnoitered a Road leading Immediately along the Right flank of the Enemy and that in Company with Coll. Humpton and Hartley and had the men laying on their arms to Move as soon as Gen. Smallwood should arrive."[116] That afternoon at four o'clock, Col. Daniel Brodhead of the 8th Pennsylvania noted, "The weather being Cloudy and threatening Rain we were Ordered to build Booths [wigwams] to Secure our Arms & go to Rest."[117]

The intrepid Pennsylvania general was waiting for the Maryland Militia, which was supposed to join him any minute. "We marched 20 odd miles yesterday, which marching in brigade, made it a little severe on the men, and fagged them," Capt. James Cox of the Baltimore Company wrote his wife from Downingtown on the twentieth. "We are now about marching, and expect to join General Wayne this day. Col. Gist has joined us, which makes us upwards of 2000 strong." He told her, "The enemy are pushing for Philadelphia as hard as they can, but I hope they will not get there. Howe stole a march on Gen. Washington the night before last, which I fear will prove to his disadvantage. A few days will determine the fate of Philadelphia."[118]

The British were aware that Wayne was somewhere between the Warren Tavern and the Paoli Tavern. Around the same time that Wayne was reconnoitering the British camp, "three Companies of our battalion were sent out under the command of Major Straubenzie to get all the information they could of the situation of General Wayne's encampment," Lt. Martin Hunter of the 2nd Light Infantry Battalion wrote. "They returned about four o'clock in the evening, and as soon as it was dark, the whole battalion got under arms."[119]

The British were preparing an unusual strategy: a silent surprise attack in the night, using bayonets and swords only. "This evening we visited some of our friends of the 2nd Batn. of L. Infantry who were encamped on a hill in the Rear," James Parker wrote. "Ye Major had seen Genl. Weans Camp, had got a guide," he revealed. "The lads were all in high spirits in hopes of a frolic that Night."[120]

A force of 1,200 British troops, composed of the 2nd Light Infantry Battalion, the 42nd Royal Highlanders, the 44th Regiment, the remains of Ferguson's Rifle Corps, and a dozen troopers from the 16th Light Dragoons, all commanded by Maj. Gen. Charles Grey, assembled on the Swedes Ford Road by 10 P.M. and began to march silently toward the Admiral Warren Tavern, taking all civilians along the route with them to prevent an alarm. Another detachment, about 500 men of the 40th and 55th Regiments, commanded by Lt. Col. Thomas Musgrave of the 40th, a former light infantry officer, moved up another route toward the Paoli Tavern to block Wayne's escape in that direction.

Anthony Wayne received at least two warnings that he might be attacked. "In the Evening Mr. Bartholamew came up, and spoke of the vicinity of the Enemy and their Numbers," Col. Thomas Hartley later testified. "An Old Man by the Name of Jones also visited us. . . . He had been down at the Paoli where he had seen a servant or some other Person who had been with the enemy, where the Soldiers had told him, that they would attack Genl. Wayne's Party that Night, that they would have done it the Night before had he not changed his Ground." After an early supper, Wayne was again out of camp reconnoitering; when he returned around 9 P.M., "he received the foregoing Information from Messrs. Bartholamew and Jones—Mr. Bartholamew insinuated that our Situation was a little Dangerous."[121]

The general mostly discounted the warning from old Mr. Jones, who had overheard a conversation at the Paoli Tavern that the camp might be attacked, though he did double the number of pickets and send out additional horse patrols. The camp had a total of six picket posts; most were a mile or so out of camp, four of them on the roads heading to Tredyffrin. Vedettes were sent up several main roads, and it was they who first spotted the British column on the Swedes Ford Road nearly two miles from camp.

Wayne never mentioned the other warning he received from "Mr. Bartholamew." Thirty-year-old Lt. Col. John Bartholomew of the Pennsylvania Militia lived on Swedes Ford Road just down the hill from the camp. He was well known to Wayne and reliable, having been an active

Whig in local politics for years. He also served in the Flying Camp during the New York Campaign in 1776. His brother Ben, a captain in the 5th Pennsylvania, was wounded at Brandywine.

Bartholomew convinced Hartley that an attack was imminent. While Wayne was out reconnoitering, Hartley wrote a letter at 6 P.M. to William Atlee in Lancaster. "This Division is now in the Post of Danger," he said, "the Mayn [i.e. main part] of our army has crossed the Skookyl—*I understand General Howe means to have us attacked to Morrow Mornng—perhaps he may do it*—he will find Frost—thoo he may have Success." Hartley went on to say, "This Manuovere of ours to get in their Rear—has surprized our Enemy's not a little—& especially as we have had the Impurtence [impertinence] to lie within long Cannon Shot of them—for two Days—General Smallwood will join Us to Night."[122]

Since the assault on Wayne's camp was to be a midnight operation, the British troops were ordered to unload their muskets or remove the flints so the weapons would not fire, fix bayonets, and march in absolute silence. "It was represented to the men that firing discovered us to the Enemy, hid them from us, killed our friends and produced a confusion favorable to the escape of the Rebels and perhaps productive of disgrace to ourselves," General Grey's aide Capt. John André wrote in his journal. "On the other hand, by not firing we knew the foe to be wherever fire appeared and a charge [of bayonets] ensured his destruction." There would be a further bonus: "Amongst the Enemy those in the rear would direct their fire against whoever fired in front, and they would destroy each other."[123]

Shortly before midnight, down in the valley two miles from camp, two American vedettes spotted Grey's column on the Swedes Ford Road near the Long Ford Road, the turnoff for the Warren Tavern. The dragoons challenged three times. The British did not answer, so the horsemen fired and fell back; one rode off to alert the camp. Turning right at the Warren Tavern and heading southwest up the road that ran by the camp's left flank, the dragoon warned Picket Posts #5 and #6 of the British approach. Picket #4, posted around a bend in the Lancaster Road at a notch in the hills called the Warren Gap, a few hundred yards east of the tavern, received no warning. This post guarded the upper Longfford Road, which ran up the hill and along the right flank of Wayne's camp.

"We knew nearly the spot where the Rebel Corps lay, but nothing of the disposition of their Camp," André wrote.[124] On arriving at the War-

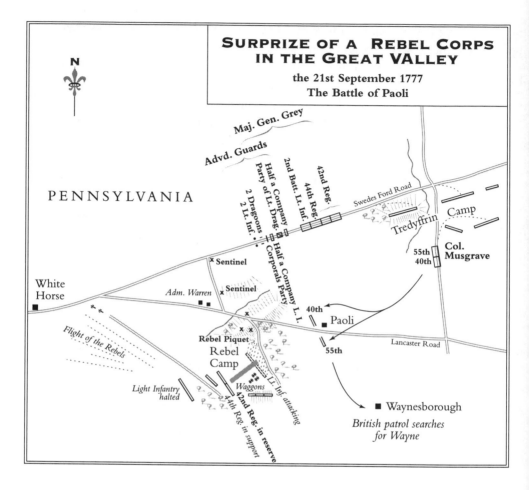

ren, the British were at a loss as to which way to turn on the Lancaster Road. "A little farther on the road there was a blacksmith's shop," Lt. Martin Hunter recalled. "A party was immediately sent to bring the blacksmith, who informed us that we were close to the camp, and that the picquet was only a few hundred yards up the road."[125]

Up in the camp, the vedette notified Wayne of the advance. After sending the dragoon back for confirmation, the general went out to alert the camp. "At about 12 o'clock Genl. Wayne came Riding along in the Rear of the 2d Brigade Calling out 'Turn out my Boys, the Lads are Comeing, we gave them a push with the Bayonet through the Smoak,'" Maj. Francis Mentges of the 11th Pennsylvania recalled, hearing Wayne shout a favorite battle cry of his. "The Troops turned out as quick as Could be Expected and Formed by Platoons, in less than five Minutes."[126]

Intermittent light rain began to fall as the British advance guard, made up of two dragoons, a company of light infantry and Ferguson's riflemen, approached Picket Post #4 on the Lancaster Road at the Warren Gap. This post was manned by Lt. Edward Fitz Randolph of the 4th Pennsylvania, with a sergeant, a corporal, and sixteen men who were spread out. "We had not marched a quarter of a mile when the enemy's picquet challenged, fired a volley, and retreated," Hunter recalled.[127] His friend Lt. Richard St. George wrote, "We then marched on briskly—still silent . . . a piquet fired upon us at a distance of fifteen yards miraculously without effect—This unfortunate Guard was instantly dispatched by the Riflemen's Swords."[128] André stated, "The sentries fired and ran off to the number of four at different intervals," meaning that they fired and fell back to the main post. The main picket fired a volley, exposing its position in the dark, "and most of them [were] killed in endeavouring to retreat."[129]

Hearing the firing from Picket #4, down the hill on his right more than half a mile away, Wayne realized that the British attack was coming from that direction. He ordered the 1st Pennsylvania Regiment, "which always takes the right," to wheel to the right and move into a narrow strip of woods between the camp and the upper Long Ford Road.[130] He detached the thirty-man light infantry company under Capt. James Wilson, who moved farther down the road to support Picket #4, whose men were falling back up the hill, firing as they retreated. Picket #3, commanded by Capt. John Doyle, was posted on the right of the camp, just over the crest of the South Valley Hill and across the Long Ford Road from the strip of woods where the 1st Pennsylvania was forming.

After annihilating Fitz Randolph's post, "General Grey then came to the head of the battalion and cried out, 'Dash, Light Infantry!' Without saying a word the whole battalion dashed into the wood," Hunter reported, "guided by the straggling fire of the picket that we followed close up."[131] St. George told his fiancée, "We rushd on thro a thick wood and receivd a smart fire from another unfortunate Piquet"—Picket #3, at the top of the hill—"as the first, instantly massacred."[132]

Wayne directed the artillery, which was posted on the right, to evacuate out the left, followed by the twenty or so baggage wagons parked in a line along the rear of the camp. He ordered the rest of the force to wheel by subplatoons to the right, and then march by files out the left side of the camp and take the road to the White Horse Tavern. Several lines of fences, which had been left up because of Washington's repeated orders, stood between Wayne's camp and the evacuation route to the White Horse. Openings had been made in a few fence sections the previous day, and the infantry proceeded out the left front as the artillery drove quickly down the back side of the camp, disappearing into the darkness. The head of the infantry column, with the 4th Pennsylvania Regiment of Col. Richard Humpton's 2nd Brigade in the lead, also vanished into the shadows. Wayne rode over to the right flank, where the 1st Pennsylvania, about 200 strong, was posted in the strip of woods to support the pickets and cover the withdrawal.

"By this Time the Enemy and we were not more than Ten Yards Distant," Wayne told Washington the next day. "A well directed fire mutually took Place, followed by a charge of Bayonet—Numbers fell on each side."[133] But the British weren't firing; the pickets and Wilson's light infantry were firing and falling back, and the 1st Pennsylvania evidently fired a volley at their own men, just as André had predicted would happen in the confusion. Worse yet, by firing, the 1st Pennsylvania had exposed its position in the woods, and the men were now desperately trying to reload in the dark.

Most of the 1st Pennsylvania were riflemen, and Wayne had tried repeatedly for months to exchange the rifles for muskets and bayonets. "In that Regiment there was Upwards of 200 Men, 60 of them had Bayonets," said Wayne.[134] Even in broad daylight, a rifle took considerably longer to load than a musket, because the tight-fitting ball had to be carefully forced down the barrel onto the rifling with a wooden ramrod and the help of a greased patch. Two types of powder—one for propellant and very fine powder for priming—from two different powder horns were required and had to be carefully measured, whereas only a single cartridge was needed for a musket. In the dark, with light rain falling and a silent enemy approaching steadily with fixed bayonets, the riflemen had no realistic chance at making a stand.

Back in camp, the 1st Brigade had wheeled into column behind the 2nd Brigade but for some reason had stopped moving. The campfires still flickered, silhouetting the line; the men were facing toward the left, their backs to the strip of woods on the right. The British light infantry silently trotted up the upper Long Ford Road, faced right, charged bayonets, and let out a terrifying "*HUZZA!*" It was "such a cheer as made the woods echo," according to Lieutenant Hunter.[135] They charged into the woods, and the 1st Pennsylvania fell back, scattering into the camp.

"Majr. Maitland being advanced Attack'd the picket guard with bayonets, who fired & fell back to their main body, part of whom were paraded, to have attack'd our rear at two oClock," James Parker wrote, "but this nocturnal Visit totally disconcerted their scheme."[136] The light infantry hit the rear of the column, which was revealed by the glow of the campfires. "They Came up upon our Right and left and by the light of our fires which was both in front and Rear of the line I Discovered the Enemy by their Clothes close after the infantry," Maj. Samuel Hay of the 7th Pennsylvania, the regiment at the rear of the column, wrote. "I then Ordered the Plattoons that was faced to fire which they did . . . but the Enemy got up Round us and wounded An officer and some of the Privates on the Parade before we Stired."[137]

"The enemy were completely surprised, some with arms, some without, running in all directions in the greatest confusion," Hunter wrote. The young lieutenant was among the few British casualties: "Captain Wolfe was killed, and I received a shot in my right hand soon after we entered the camp. I saw the fellow present at me, and was running up to him when he fired. He was immediately put to death."[138]

Hartley's Additional Regiment was in the column ahead of the 7th Pennsylvania. "The Seventh Regement having no Front towards the Enemy as well as my own Regiment—were attacked in their flank & Rear," Col. Thomas Hartley testified, "& tho' there were attempts made to form them with another Front, yet the Enemy were so amongst them that it was impracticable." The panic escalated as the men pushed and shoved those ahead of them in the stalled column through the opening in the fence. Many broke and ran into the woods in front of or behind the camp; others ended up pinned against the fence and bayoneted while madly scrambling to climb over it. "Confusion followed," Hartley wrote. "The Troops in the Rear pressed on those in the Front & the Passage on the Left being narrow sacrificed many of the Troops."[139]

The Battle of Paoli became known as the "Paoli Massacre" because of the atrocities committed by some of the British troops, such as frenzied, multiple bayoneting of Wayne's men and hacking some to pieces with swords after they had surrendered. "The greatest Cruelty was shewn on the side of the Enemy," Lt. Col. Adam Hubley of the 10th Pennsylvania, who was momentarily taken prisoner, noted with fury. "I with my own Eyes, see them, cut & hack some of our Poor men to pieces after they had fallen into their hands and scarcely shew the least Mercy to any."[140]

A Scottish light infantry officer, Capt. Sir James Baird of Frazer's Highlanders, was leading the 71st Light Infantry into the fray. The size of the regiment allowed for two light companies, dressed in full Highland kit, with Highland caps and kilts ("belted plaids"), and armed with broadswords in addition to muskets and bayonets.[141] "Here that Gallant Young Officer Sr. Jas. Beard, the scourge of Rebelion, had a very narrow escape," James Parker wrote, revealing one reason for the slaughter. "He push'd a rebel musket past his breast, which killed a Sergent behind him." Rage and fury took over Baird; armed with a Scottish broadsword, in addition to a fusil and bayonet, "he paid them, for he put 16 of them to death with his own hands."[142]

Behind the light infantry came a dozen troopers of the 16th Light Dragoons, charging across the camp, with the 44th Regiment fanning out to the left and into the rows of booths with another 350 bayonets. "Then followed a dreadful scene of Havock," Lieutenant St. George wrote. "The Light Dragoons came on sword in Hand. The Shreiks Groans Shouting imprecations deprecations, the Clashing of Swords & Bayonets &c &c &c . . . was more expressive of horror than all the Thunder of the artillery &c on the Day of Action."[143] Colonel Hartley recalled, "The Men were extremely intimidated with the Noise of the Enemys Horse." He also commented, "The Enemy [was] pressing so close on the left of the Retreat, which was chiefly my Brigade [the 1st], & so many Interuption of Fences that it was impossible to rally Any Men 'till we had got to some Distance from the Enemy." The four- or five-rail fences were stout, and the Continentals used them to form firing lines to cover the retreat; "at the Fences considerable opposition was made by some of the best Men," Hartley concluded, "but many of them suffered."[144]

Why was the front not moving? The artillery had galloped down the back of the camp and out onto the road along the left flank. The head of the infantry column reached the road at the same time and stopped to let them pass, when one of the guns broke down in the road, temporarily blocking the escape route. "One of the Pecies met with Misfortune near the field of Action" is how Wayne described the episode to Washington, "which Impeded us a Considerable time."[145] Lt. Col. Adam Hubley mentioned "[I] fell in with one of our field pieces (the carriage of which had lost the hind wheels)." After some delay, he was able to hitch a horse to the broken gun and drag it away, thereby freeing up the escape route. But by that time, the rear of the stalled column was disintegrating under a wave of cold steel. "The Enemy upon us, in our rear, and with their charg'd Bayonets, we push'd forward and got into a field adjoining the one in which we were Attacked," Hubley continued. "The Enemy being then almost mix'd with us, at the same time calling out 'No quarters!' &c, which in my humble Oppinion caused our Men to make a disparate and indeed obstinate stand. A most severe Bayoneting was the consequence."[146]

But the worst was yet to come. From the dark strip of woods on the right of the camp, a throaty, roaring shriek suddenly ripped through the night air in a terrifying counterpoint to the wail of bagpipes, as more than 600 Royal Highlanders of the 42nd advanced in two battalions without breaking ranks. In their first direct encounter with Wayne since June, when Wayne's Brigade and Morgan's Corps had peppered the British rear guard at Brunswick Bridge, the Royal Highlanders were about to take revenge. A veritable wall of bayonets swept across the field and camp, accompanied by a bloodcurdling chorus of Highland war yells.

The British "rushed in upon their Encampment, directed by the light of their fires, killed and wounded not less than 300 in their Huts and about their fires," Sgt. Thomas Sullivan of the 49th wrote. "The 42d. sat fire to them, as many of the Enemy would not come out, chusing rather to suffer in the Flames than to be killed by the Bayonet."[147] Lieutenant Hunter recalled that "the camp was immediately set on fire; the Light Infantry bayonetted every man they came up with." Hunter, who later served in India and the Napoleonic Wars, rising to the rank of lieutenant general, said, "This, with the cries of the wounded, formed altogether the most dreadful scene I ever beheld. Every man that fired was immediately put to death."[148]

"Fortune has not been sublime to our Division," Colonel Hartley wrote sorrowfully the next day. "The Enemy last Night at twelve oClock, attacked our little Force with about 4000 Men—Horse and Foot—

accompanied with all the Noise and Yells of Hell." Hartley was mistaken; only 1,200 British troops were in the attack. Darkness, surprise, and panic provided the rest. He described the chaos: "The Impetuosity of the Enemy was so great—our Men just raised from Sleep, moved disorderly—Confusion followed," then horror, as "Swords and Bayonets were the Weapons," and "many were killed on both sides—some times by Enemys and some Times by Friends," referring to the friendly fire on the right flank. "The Carnage was very great. This is a bloody Month."[149]

At the head of the column, Wayne rallied a few regiments around the 4th Pennsylvania, which was drawn up in some woods to provide cover fire. "Halt, boys, and give these assassins one fire!" shouted Maj. Marion Lamar of the 4th Pennsylvania.[150] Capt. Benjamin Burd saw Lamar "bayonetted on horseback a few yards from him."[151] The major fell from his horse, mortally wounded, the highest-ranking American killed at Paoli. The 4th then retired through some woods to a rise near the road to the White Horse Tavern and set up a line of defense, where Wayne hoped to rally the men.

Smallwood's 2,100 militiamen and three iron guns were coming up the road from the White Horse and were within less than a mile of the camp when the attack began. Prudently sizing up the situation, the general turned his badly armed, poorly trained, and skittish troops around and fell back to "about a Mile to an Advantageous Ground." As the force marched, they were fired upon by the enemy.[152] Some of the British light infantry had kept their weapons loaded upon the assurance of their commanding officer, Maj. John Maitland, that they would not fire. But now that the chase was on, they could not be restrained. "For two Miles We drove Them now and then firing scatteringly from behind fences & trees &c.," St. George wrote. "The flashes of the pieces had a fine effect in the Night."[153]

They had a fine effect on the militia, too. "One of our Men about the center of the Main Body was shot Dead by some of their Stragglers," Smallwood told Governor Johnson, "which threw great part of our Line in great Consternation, many flung down their Guns & Ran off, & have not been heard of since." In the confusion and panic, Smallwood was nearly killed by friendly fire as he tried to rally the militia. "The Rear taking us for British light Horse fired a Volley on us within 15 or 20 Foot, wounded several, and killed a light Horseman alongside of me in waiting for Orders," the general wrote. The horseman, Pvt. Jones Dean of Bland's Dragoons, was listed in the payrolls as "killed by the Militia 20th Septr." He was owed $8.33 for one month's pay.[154]

The Maryland Militia force all but disintegrated, despite Smallwood's and Gist's efforts. Hundreds of men threw away their muskets and equipment and disappeared into the countryside; more than 1,000 out of 2,100 deserted. "If our wrong headed Assembly cou'd only be here to see these Mens behavior," Smallwood complained to the governor in disgust, "and be a little pestered in restraining and regulating their conduct."[155]

Most of Wayne's force escaped, as did his four guns, and the men rendezvoused the next morning at the Red Lion Tavern in Uwchlan Township, nine miles from the scene of carnage. But nearly 300 Americans had been killed, wounded, or captured, about 15 percent of Wayne's force; British losses were 3 dead and 8 or so wounded. Lieutenant Colonel Hubley wrote the next day that he sent Maj. Caleb North of the 10th Pennsylvania, "with 4 of our Horsemen on the field who counted our Dead bodys; the enemy's were taken off, they were inform'd, in large numbers." The British took away their dead and wounded, as well as many of the wounded Americans, who were left at houses nearby. Two days later, Hubley told his friends in Lancaster, "We bury'd our Dead next day in the field of Battle, (52 brave fellows) All kill'd by the sword & Bayonet."[156]

British estimates of Wayne's losses tended to run higher. "500 were in a very little time put to rest without the least noise on our side, & 110 prisoners brought off," James Parker wrote. "It being night their Canon could not be found. The loss on our side was Capt. Wolf of the 40th, a sergeant & a private."[157] The British did take prisoners—between 70 and 80, most accounts state. Some of them were wounded, a few suffering a dozen or more stab wounds. Their experiences and condition provoked outrage and demands for revenge among the Pennsylvania troops.

The Battle of Paoli, or Paoli Massacre, had many other names immediately afterward, such as the "Attack near the White Horse" or "Action at the Warren," referring to two other taverns nearby. The British called it "Wayne's Affair," or the "affair of Peoli," in Sir George Osborn's words. The terms "massacre," "midnight slaughter," "bloody Highlanders," and "British barbarity" all became part of the Battle of Paoli lexicon. Capt. John McGowan of the 4th Pennsylvania, whose men were first hit at

Picket Post #4, referred to it as the "Payola Batle or Sticking Night."[158] Lt. Martin Hunter wrote, "The Americans ever after Wayne's Affair called us 'The Bloodhounds.'" He added with trepidation, "I don't think that our battalion slept very soundly after that night for a long time."[159]

Musgrave's force, the 40th and 55th battalion companies posted near the Paoli Tavern, did not engage in the battle. But at Wayne's home, Waynesborough, about a mile from the tavern, Wayne's brother-in-law Abraham Robinson told the general, "A number of the British troops surrounded your House in serch of you, but being disappointed in not finding you they took poor Robert & James." Remarkably, the British "behaved with the utmost politeness to the Women and said they only Wanted the General." Even more astonishing is the fact that "they did not disturb the least Article."[160]

The brutality of the night attack inspired much comment. "The affair of Peoli, which has struck more teror than any we have yet had, was conducted by Genl. Gray with the 42nd, 44th and one Battn. of Light Infantry, only in the same manner of the Hereditary Princes at Zerenburgh in 1760, without permitting a man to load," Sir George Osborn told his brother John. "It was a fair surprize in the night and the slaughter was exceeding great."[161] James Parker told Charles Steuart, "Genl. Wean, tho' an Old [fox?] but a Young General, taught now by experience, it is to be hop'd," he sneered, "will keep further from our rear."[162]

A few hours after Grey's force returned to Tredyffrin, the Royal Army broke camp and marched north to Valley Forge. "At 5 this morning the Army moved, marched 3 miles to the Valley Forge and 2 more to Moor[e] Hall making 5 miles and there encamped," Montrésor wrote. Moore Hall was the mansion and estate of seventy-eight-year-old Judge William Moore, the notoriously cantankerous chief justice of Chester County for more than forty under the crown and a die-hard Loyalist. But this was only the center of the British camp, where Howe established headquarters in a house just east of Moore Hall on Pickering Creek. The head of Howe's army continued another three or four miles west on the Nutt Road in Charlestown Township until it reached French Creek Bridge, which led to the Reading Road. "We found the houses full of military stores," the chief engineer observed, stores that had been hastily removed from Philadelphia and placed far and wide in the countryside. "This country abounds with Forage, but the cattle drove off."[163]

"We marched by the Valley Forge to Charles Town upon the Schuylkill, a very difficult Creek indeed much more formidable than the Brandy Wine if it had been defended," General Grant commented.[164] Just prior to this movement, Howe sent a trumpeter to Washington with a message requesting American surgeons to care for the captured wounded from Paoli, who were left at houses and taverns in the Tredyffrin area. The messenger took a long, roundabout route, going by way of Valley Forge and Moore Hall to Long Ford, then riding through most of the American camp to Washington's headquarters at Thompson's Tavern, across the Schuylkill in Norriton Township. "The main reason for sending this trumpeter off, probably was not only to acquaint Washington with the bad news," von Münchhausen speculated, "but also to have the trumpeter secure information on the depths of the water at Valley Forge." Moreover, "Giving Washington the news of Wayne's defeat before he might learn it himself, might induce him to leave his position and allow us to cross the Schuylkill unopposed."[165]

The trumpeter was also on a reconnaissance mission to gather information on the positioning of Washington's forces. "A flag of truce [was] sent out to desire Mr. Washington to bury those that were killed last night, and send Surgeons to the wounded," Captain-Lieutenant Peebles wrote from Valley Forge. "The flag came in upon a Camp of theirs about 3 miles up & on t'other side the river where he supposes there were about 3000." Peebles also commented about the American forces just across the river from the mouth of Valley Creek. "They have a guard just opposite to us here who ask'd for a truce for ye day, which was agreed to by our Guard, & they chatted to one another."[166]

The Guards remained in their position near Fatland Ford while the main army marched to French Creek Bridge, nearly seven miles to the west. The head of the column at French Creek became the army's left flank, and the Guards became the extreme right. There were four fords and two ferries across the Schuylkill in front of Howe: Gordon's, Long, Richardson's, and Fatland Fords; Pawling's Ferry; and Daviser's (Davis's or Dewees's) Ferry at Valley Creek. Washington's army was positioned to block all the crossings, in addition to Swedes Ford, five miles below Fatland.

The Crown Forces were now positioned halfway between Philadelphia and Reading, and the rebels could only guess which way Howe was going to move. Plenty of other fords were situated above and below

Washington's position. The British movements on September 21 seemed to point toward Reading, where the main Continental Army supply depot was located.

For the fifth time in less than three weeks, Washington's strategy had failed to stop the British advance toward Philadelphia. First his troops faced defeats in the battle at Cooch's Bridge and Iron Hill; then they were outflanked at Newport, Delaware; this was followed by the bloody defeats at Brandywine and then in the rain at Goshen; and finally there was the bloody night at Paoli. Howe was now pushing up a river with numerous twists, turns, and fording places, apparently to turn Washington's right flank yet again.

Late in the evening, British observers noticed major Continental troop movements away from the river fords. Washington was pulling back and shifting his army toward Reading, leaving only token forces to guard the fords. The next morning, September 22, British reconnaissance con-

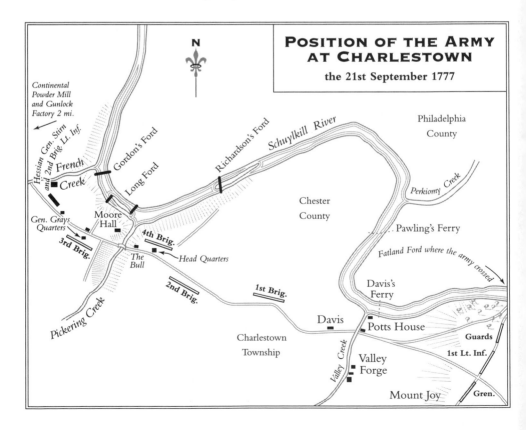

POSITION OF THE ARMY
AT CHARLESTOWN
the 21st September 1777

firmed that the Continental Army was moving toward Reading, and Howe decided to keep Washington headed in that direction with his own troop movements.

Ewald and a party of Jägers, Hessian grenadiers, and part of the British 2nd Light Infantry Battalion set out that morning on patrol and went up French Creek. A mile or so behind the army's left flank, they had a small skirmish with some local militiamen, who quickly ran off as the Jägers advanced. "I found a blown-up powder magazine and a rifle factory, in which several thousand pieces of fabricated and unfinished rifles and sabers of all kinds were stored," Ewald exclaimed.

He had stumbled upon the Continental Powder Mill that Congress had established earlier in the year on French Creek. After being created with great effort and expense, the mill had exploded in March 1777, shortly after beginning production. Peter DeHaven, a local man, had also established the Public Gun Manufactory and the Public Gun Lock Factory nearby to produce muskets for the Pennsylvania Board of War and the Committee of Safety. David Rittenhouse, the noted American mathematician and clockmaker, had been one of the chief supervisors of this project. Now, Ewald wrote that he "ordered everything smashed to pieces, set fire to the factory, and marched back."[167] An officer of the 2nd Light Infantry wrote, "the 2 Light Infentry on a Recnghting [reconnoitering] part[y] found a Pouder mill A Magzien and Some Armers Shops and Store houses Which they Burnt and Distroid all that Came to hand With Stores of Provishons and Furage."[168]

Shortly after Ewald's patrol went out, Gen. Sir William Erskine proceeded across French Creek Bridge and advanced up the Reading Road with a similar force of Jägers, light infantry, and light dragoons. After destroying the supplies, Ewald's force returned to French Creek Bridge "to cover General Erskin's withdrawal, who had gone 2 miles on the other side of same to reconnoitre the whole district."[169] This move helped confirm Washington's fear that Howe was once more attempting to get around his right flank, and perhaps seize Reading.

The final ruse came around 5 P.M., when a column of 200 Hessian grenadiers, led by Capt. Richard Lorey with 20 mounted Jägers and 60 foot Jägers under Capt. Carl von Wreden, and supported by British artillery fire, began to push across the Schuylkill at Gordon's Ford near the mouth of French Creek, six miles west of Valley Forge. This noisy movement was a feint, but it had the desired effect: American forces pulled away from the river fords and headed toward Reading. At dark, the Hessians pulled back, and orders went out from Howe's Charlestown headquarters that the whole army was to prepare to march "by the rising of the moon" at 10 P.M.—but not to Reading; they were to reverse their march and head to Fatland Ford, a mile or so east of Valley Forge.

The Guards were now the vanguard, and Sir George Osborn led the grenadier and light companies across the Schuylkill that night on the final leg of their march on Philadelphia. With the "affair of Peoli" still fresh in everyone's mind, Sir George told his brother, "I was ordered the night after to pass the Schuylkill with the Light Company and Grenadiers of the Guards only and was fortunate that our enemy had no inclination to retaliate for their late misfortune."[170]

The rest of the army followed, crossing the river by moonlight unhindered at both Fatland Ford and Richardson's Ford near Moore Hall. "We march'd between 1 & 2 oclock in the morning of the 23d. & cross'd the Sckuylkill at Fatland ford," Peebles stated, noting that the water was "up to a Grenadier's breetches pockets." As the men arrived on the other side, "the Troops took up ground as they arrived, made fires, & dryed themselves till about 7 or 8 oclock. They were put in motion again & march'd to the Eastward. HeadQrs at Norrington."

As the British Army left Chester County and entered Philadelphia County—Valley Creek formed the county line, and the Valley Forge was in Philadelphia County at that time—Peebles stated that "the Stores at Valley forge that could not be brought away were set on fire &ca."[171] The "&ca." was the forge itself and its related buildings—sheds, charcoal houses, storage facilities all were burned. "On leaving the ground of our last Encampment we set fire to the Valley Forge and destroyed it," Montrésor confirmed.[172]

Once the British crossed the river, the Pennsylvania militiamen who were posted at the small earthwork battery built by the French engineers at Swedes Ford abandoned the guns and fled. "We March to the ground joining the Sweeds ford where the Rebels expected we would have Crossed," James Parker noted on September 23. "Here they had thrown up Works, On Which they had three 12 pounders mounted on fieldpiece Carriages loaded & prim'd, but on hearing we had Crossd & pointed that way, they playd the Old game, Through the Woods Ladee, leaving their

Canon, some small Stores of liquor, ammunition, & their Potts with the potatoes half boil'd. Here we destroyed another pouder Mill."

Washington's army was gone—he had moved it to shield Reading, and it was encamped in New Hanover and Limerick Townships, several miles north of Trappe and nearly twenty miles away from Howe. Seeing Washington's former headquarters, Parker exulted, "On this days March we passed Thompsons Tavern adorned with the portrait of Washington with a blue Ribbon." The tavernkeeper, Col. Archibald Thompson, was a Philadelphia County sublieutenant and lieutenant colonel of the 5th Battalion of Philadelphia County Militia. "The soldiers very Soon finishd both his Excellency & ye house," Parker noted with glee as the portrait and premises were torched. The Crown Forces moved on to Stony Run, where Col. John Bull's plantation was situated. "Head quarters at the house of a Rebel Genl. Bull. We encamp a mile further on the Phila. Road now 18 Miles distant."[173]

Howe's army established camp along the southeast bank of Stony Run in Norriton Township, with the left resting on the Schuylkill near Swedes Ford and the right on the Germantown Road, five miles north of the ford. Plundering immediately resumed with a vengeance. "The army . . . has been well supplied with fresh meat and flour, and abundance of forage for the horses," Capt. Francis Downman of the Royal Artillery wrote. "Very few of the inhabitants have remained in their houses, those who have alone saving their effects. It is otherwise with the deserted houses."[174] This time several buildings were torched, including Colonel Bull's barn, whose house had become general headquarters.

"This Township of Norrington is very rebellious," Montrésor wrote the next day. "All the manufactures about this country seem to consist of Powder, Ball, Shot and Cannon, firearms, and swords."[175] The smoke from Bull's property and Thompson's Tavern further alarmed the inhabitants. "Toward evening we saw several high columns of smoke and we are told that the British had set fire to several houses belonging to some officers of the militia," Reverend Muhlenberg observed from Trappe, nearly ten miles away.[176]

Col. Joseph Reed also lived in the area. "I stayed at my house as long, or perhaps longer than was prudent," he wrote to Washington at 4 P.M. from Norriton Presbyterian Meeting House on the Germantown Road, across from David Rittenhouse's farm. "The enemy came there in about

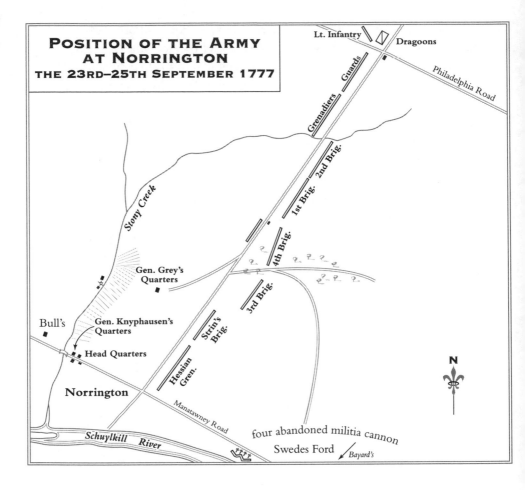

POSITION OF THE ARMY AT NORRINGTON
THE 23RD–25TH SEPTEMBER 1777

Lt. Infantry　Dragoons

Philadelphia Road

Grenadiers

Guards

1st Brig.　2nd Brig.

4th Brig.

Stony Creek

Gen. Grey's Quarters

3rd Brig.

Bull's

Gen. Knyphausen's Quarters

Strin's Brig.

Head Quarters

Hessian Gren.

Norrington

N

Manatawney Road

four abandoned militia cannon

Schuylkill River

Swedes Ford　Bayard's

fifteen minutes after. I have collected a small party here at the Meeting-House, about one mile above my own house." He told the commander in chief, "I shall remain here at present, and watch their motions, though I am puzzled to get persons to carry the intelligence I collect."[177]

Another important Pennsylvania official, Col. John Bayard, speaker of the new Pennsylvania Assembly and commander of the 1st Battalion of Philadelphia County Militia, had his property plundered in a very peculiar fashion. Earlier that year, he had moved his wife, Margaret, and fourteen children to a house in Plymouth Township, just below Swedes Ford, for safety. "A division of the British army was moving to Philadelphia by the way of the Swede's Ford; the road to be passed was the one on which our house stood," his eldest daughter recalled. "My mother engaged a few wagons to carry the furniture to places of safety, but could not, on such short notice, dispose of all the family stores. They had to be left for the plunder of the soldiery. She took her small children with her, and mournfully departed from her home."

Colonel Bayard was away at the time, on state business in Lancaster. That evening, "the enemy arrived and took possession of the house. . . . They found much that was gratifying, and some things which proved amusing in the way of destruction." Unlike the experience of the Gibbons family in Chester County, here "the library was a thing which could do them no good; they found many religious books, and concluded they belonged to some Presbyterian parson, and, of course, a rebel. They made a pile of them and amused themselves in shooting at them; in all directions, the fragments and some few volumes remaining scattered over the court yard."

There was also a large cache of wine in the house. "The wine was a great prize, and proved the means of saving the house which was doomed to destruction." In a comical twist of fate, "the officer, in gratitude for this unlooked for luxury, instead of ordering the house to be burnt, wrote a very polite note to my father, thanking him for his entertainment."[178]

Bayard's wine gladdened the hearts of Howe's officers. "September 24—This morning the light dragoons found another store of various provisions, including several barrels of wine," von Münchhausen said, "which upon orders of the General, was divided among the officers. Although it did not make even one full bottle for each officer, they were all happy for most of them had not had any wine for three weeks."[179]

Once again, plundering was by no means the sole propriety of the Crown Forces. "The militia troops who are encamped here must have wicked men among them," Rev. Henry Muhlenberg wrote on the twenty-third. "Some of them have broken into the house of the man who now owns my former farm, have broken chests and boxes to pieces, and have wrought havoc on the place. Others have smashed fences and rails and burned them, etc." He added, "It is a delicate matter in this kind of war in which father is arrayed against son, son against father, brother against brother, neighbor against neighbor, etc. No one can trust another."[180]

With Washington positioned on the hills of "Faulkner's Great Swamp" miles behind him, Howe headed toward Philadelphia in two columns with no opposition on September 25. "We March this morning at daylight. At 10 pass the strong ground of Chesnut hill, at 11 get to German-toun, a Village of one Street & two Miles in Length Inhabited Chiefly by German Stocking Weavers, Waggon Makers &c who are Chiefly of the Rebellious Cast, & look down on this Occasion," James Parker wrote, moving with the main column, which marched on the Germantown Road. "Most of the Rebels have left Philadelphia." He also noted, "Headquarters at the House of Mr. Logan at the south end of German Town."[181] Stenton, which had served as Washington's headquarters a lit-tle more than a month before as the Continental Army prepared to march through Philadelphia in order to defend it, once again assumed the role of general headquarters—this time for His Majesty's forces, which also prepared a march through the city with the intention to occupy it.

"This area is quite splendidly cultivated," Captain Ewald observed as the Jägers moved in the other column along the Ridge or Manatawney Road. As his men took up positions above Vanderin's Mill at the mouth of Wissahickon Creek, Ewald noted, "The inhabitants are mostly Ger-mans but were against us, the most ill-natured people in the world, who could hardly contain their anger and hostile sentiments." It was no won-der; many of the Germans belonged to pacifist religious sects such as the Mennonites, the German Baptists known as "Dunkers," or the Seventh-Day Adventists and went about their lives quietly. They had come largely from the Palatinate, a region along the Rhine River in western Germany that had been the scene of endless religious war and bloodshed over the past few centuries. Now, after three weeks with the noise of battle in the distance, columns of smoke on the horizon, and reports of mayhem in southeastern Pennsylvania, they were extremely apprehensive.

The news that Hessians accompanied Howe's army added a special element of cultural fear for the Pennsylvania Germans, who despised these militaristic, brutal slaves of the Landgraves of Hesse. "One old lady, who was sitting on a bench before her front door, answered me in pure Palantine German when I rode up to her and asked her for a glass of water," Ewald said. "Water I will give you," the old woman hissed, "but I must also ask you: What harm have we people done to you, that you Germans come over here to suck us dry and drive us out of house and home? We have heard enough here of your murderous burning," she tongue-lashed Ewald. "Will you do the same here as in New York and in the Jerseys?" she demanded to know, warning the Jäger captain, "You shall get your pay yet!"[182]

In Philadelphia, "this has been so far, a day of great Confusion in the City," Elizabeth Drinker wrote in her diary on the twenty-fifth. In the previous week, she had seen Congress and the state governments flee. The bells of the city—eight of the nine chimes in Christ Church steeple; the State House bell, later revered as the Liberty Bell; and several other church bells—had been taken down and sent away to prevent their seizure as scrap for cannon making. People by the hundreds were loading goods into wagons and fleeing, and the docks were busy with sloops and small gunboats from the Pennsylvania Navy, some carting off merchandise.

Parts of the scene were comical. Elizabeth watched as "ye Sign (Over ye Way) of G. Washingtn. [was] Taken down this Afternoon," the prudent move of a nervous neighbor. Considerably less amusing were the rumors of arson and plots to burn the city, as had happened to much of New York the previous September. "'Tis said that tar'd faggots &c are laid in several out Houses in different parts, with meschevious intent," she wrote apprehensively. Now, on September 25, "the English were within 4 or 5 miles of us . . . they are expected by some this Evening in the City. . . . Things seem very quiate and still." She also noted that "a great number of the lower sort of the People are gone out to them" and that Joseph Galloway had sent word "that the Inhabitants must take care of the Town this Night, and they would be in, in the Morning." The newest power shift had begun.

Later that night, as a steady rain fell and volunteers patrolled the streets, Elizabeth Drinker wrote, "all things appear peaceable at present, the Watch-Men crying the Hour without Molestation."[183]

The hour of Philadelphia's fall had come.

ENDNOTES

PROLOGUE

1. Persifor Frazer, *General Persifor Frazer: A Memoir Compiled Principally from His Own Papers by His Great-Grandson*, (Philadelphia: 1907), 155.

2. Thomas P. Cope, *Philadelphia Merchant: The Diary of Thomas P. Cope, 1800–1851*, edited by Eliza Cope Harrison (South Bend, IN: Gateway Editions, 1978), 401.

3. Ibid., watercolor illustration inset opposite 404. "This drawing is by Major John André of the British Army, when a prisoner, & living in my Fathers family in Lancaster. . . . I was at that time a small boy, but well remember André's bland manners, sporting with us children as if one of us. . . . I often played marbles & other boyish games with the Major. . . . Thos. P. Cope, Phila., 1851."

4. Ibid., 68, 142. Cope wrote: "My brother John, the eldest of five sons, was at that time a youth of very promising talents. His mind was uncultivated by education & experience, but his heart was affectionate & pure, his person attractive & his genius versatile, active & powerful. . . . A similarity of taste & character ripened into a mutual & ardent attachment between him & André. They formed a resolution to spend the residue of their days together. London, as affording the best hope to rising genius, was designed as the place of their permanent abode. André made known their intentions to my father & craved his approbation. . . . So firm & ardent was his attachment that he offered to abandon the army on condition of my father's consent to their plans. He went further; he offered wholly to defray John's expenses until they should both be settled in some honorable & lucrative employment. . . . John also pressed the suit, but he pressed in vain; neither argument, solicitation nor tears availed. Father was inflexible. . . . Whether by a private understanding between them, or whether it was the offspring of his own motion alone, I cannot remember, but John soon attempted to follow his friend to New York. His escape was private, but would

not long be concealed from his father, who went in search of him & . . . [overtook] him before he reached the British lines. . . . From that moment his character & pursuits assumed a new direction. The palette & pencil were thrown aside . . . No André to take him by the hand & lead him up the path of science. Home & study became equally irksome" (142, 144).

5. Ibid., 143.

CHAPTER 1

1. Letter, Germain to Knox, "1777, June 11. Stoneland Lodge"; Germain to Knox, June 24, 1777. Historical Manuscripts Commission, *Report on Manuscripts in Various Collections*, vol. VI (Dublin: His Majesty's Stationery Office, 1909: Reprint, Gregg Press, Boston, 1972), 130–31.

2. Letter, Thomas Forrest to Colonel Proctor, "McConkey's Ferry, 29th Dec'r, 1776," Samuel Hazard, *Pennsylvania Archives*, vol. 5 (Philadelphia: Joseph Severns & Co., 1853), 142. "Brass Caps" is a nickname for the Hessian grenadiers and fusiliers, who wore distinctive brass or tin "mitre" caps.

3. Letter, Gen. James Grant to the Honorable Richard Rigby, "Brunswick, 15th January 1777," James Grant of Ballindalloch Papers, National Archives of Scotland, Edinburgh. Microfilm in Library of Congress, reel 28.

4. Report, von Donop to Cornwallis, "*Cantonement Brunswig 6e. Janv. 1777*" ("Brunswick Cantonment, January 6, 1777), Grant Papers, reel 37. Translation from French by the author.

5. A summary of Sir George Osborn's examination can be found in "Parliament: Commons on Gen. Howe's Conduct," *Scots Magazine*, 41 (December 1779), 644.

6. Nicholas Cresswell, *The Journal of Nicholas Cresswell* (London: Jonathan Cape, 1925), 181.

7. *The Annual Register: or, a View of the History, Politics, and Literature, for the Year 1777*, 4th ed. (London: J. Dodsley in Pall Mall, 1794), 20. The *Register's* founder and chief editor was the Whig leader Edmund Burke, so its editorializing tended to be sympathetic to the American cause.

8. *The Annual Register: or, a View of the History, Politics, and Literature, for the Year 1776* (London: J. Dodsley in Pall Mall, 1777), 236.

9. Edward Gibbon, *Memoirs of My Life*, edited by B. Radice (1984), 160. Quoted in "Edward Gibbon, Historian of the Roman Empire," by Eugene Y. C. Ho, www.his.com/~z/gibho1.html.

10. Letter, Samuel Adams to Nathanael Greene, "Philad May 12 1777." Paul H. Smith, Gerald W. Gawalt, and Ronald M. Gephart, eds., *Letters of Delegates to Congress*, vol. 7 (Washington, DC: Library of Congress, 1981), 70.

11. Alexander Graydon, *Memoirs of a Life, Chiefly Passed in Pennsylvania, within the Last Sixty Years (1811)* (Edinburgh: William Blackwood, 1822), 298.

12. Johann Ewald, *Diary of the American War: A Hessian Journal, Captain Johann Ewald, Field Jager Corps,* translated and edited by Joseph Tustin (New Haven, CT: Yale University Press, 1979), 50–51.

13. Ibid., 51.

14. Letter, Howe to Grant, dated "N. York Jan 9th [1777] 11 o'clock A.M.," Grant Papers, reel 37.

15. G. Washington to Col. Jos. Reed, January 14, 1777. John C. Fitzpatrick, *The Writings of George Washington,* vol. 7 (Washington, DC: U.S. Government Printing Office, 1932), 15–16.

16. Ibid., 53.

17. Ibid., 66.

18. *Historical Anecdotes Civil and Military in a Series of Letters Written from America in the Years 1777 and 1778, &c.* (London: Printed for J. Bew, in Pater Noster Row, 1779), 5. Rare Book Collection, Library of Congress.

19. No. 2091, the King to Lord North, "Queens House Dec. 2, 1777," in Sir John Fortescue, *The Correspondence of King George the Third,* vol. 3, *July 1773–December 1777* (London: MacMillan and Co., 1928), 501.

20. Sir Danvers's wife, Lady Sarah Osborn (daughter of Lord Halifax), died from complications after the birth of her second son, John. Sir Danvers fell into deep depression over her death, and Lord Halifax tried to help his distraught son-in-law by securing him the governorship of New York, hoping that a change of scenery might give Danvers a new lease on life. Tragically, a few days after arriving in New York in 1753, Sir Danvers succumbed to despair and died of a self-inflicted wound. Danvers (formerly Salem Village), Massachusetts, is believed to be named after him.

21. Letter, Osborn to Germain, October 29, 1776. Public Record Office, London, CO 5/93-3, MS sheets 501–2.

22. With this language arrangement in mind, English-speaking officers often substituted the French preposition *de* for the German *von* in titles of officers and regiments. Thus General von Heister is often called de Heister in British writings.

On August 10, 1777, Osborn revealed his lack of fluency in German in a letter to his brother John, the British minister to Saxony stationed in Dresden: "How I envy your having been able to acquire the German language every day. I have an Harper on board, one of the Musick of the Regimen[t] de Ditforth, but I find no advantage but in the amusement of his musick. I shall wish much for my old servant from Dresden and shall be obliged for you to send out for him . . . I will always likewise have a German footman in my family, if it was only to prevent his [Sir George's son Johnny] being at the loss of the common expression I find myself in my present situation." Osborn Family Letters, vol. 3, 1771–1782, no. 98. Osborn's frequent use of French in his letters indicates a competency in that language.

23. Friedrich von Münchausen, *At General Howe's Side: The Diary of General William Howe's Aide-de-Camp, Captain Friedrich von Münchhausen*, translated and edited by Ernst Kipping and Samuel Stelle Smith (Monmouth Beach, NJ: Philip Freneau Press, 1974), 5.

24. Letter, Grant to Rigby, "New York Island 24th Septr. 1776," Grant Papers, reel 28.

25. "Letters Written during the American War of Independence" by Captain William Hale, Grenadier Company, 45th Regiment of Foot, *Regimental Annual* (the 1st Nottinghamshire Regiment/Sherwood Foresters) (United Kingdom, 1913), 37.

26. John Graves Simcoe, *A Journal of the Operations of the Queen's Rangers* ... (New York: Bartlett & Welford, 1844), 35.

27. Stephen Kemble, *Journals of Lieut.-Col. Stephen Kemble, 1773–1789, &c.*, new introduction and preface by George A. Billias (New York Historical Society, 1883; reprint, Boston: Gregg Press, 1972), 98. Kemble wrote on October 3, "The Ravages committed by the Hessians, and all Ranks of the Army, on the poor inhabitants of the Country, make their case deplorable; the Hessians destroy all the fruits of the Earth without regard to Loyalists or Rebels, the property of both being equally a prey to them, in which our Troops are too ready to follow their Example, and are but too much Licensed in it ... [the Hessians] Maraud throughout the Country, and take Hay and Oats wherever they find it, without the smallest means being used to restrain them, except a letter or two being wrote to their Officers, who pay no attention to them, and Publicly permit, or rather direct, these Depredations to be made" (91).

28. Martin Hunter, *The Journal of Gen. Sir Martin Hunter* ... , edited by James Hunter, Anne Hunter, and Elizabeth Bell (Edinburgh: Edinburgh Press, 1894), 26–27. Confirming these "pet" names, Capt. George Harris of the 5th Regiment's Grenadier Company wrote that when his unit arrived in Princeton shortly after the Trenton disaster, "You would have felt too much to be able to express your feelings, on seeing with what a warmth of friendship our children, as we call the light infantry, welcomed us, one and all crying, 'Let them come!' 'Lead us to them, we are sure of being supported.'" With unabashed emotion, he added, "It gave me a pleasure too fine to attempt expressing, and if you see a stain on the paper pray place the drops to the right motive, for the tears flowed even at the thought, so that I could not stop them." Stephen R. Lushington, *The Life and Services of General Lord Harris, G.C.B., During His Campaigns in America, the West*

Indies, and India, 2nd ed. (London: John W. Parker, 1845), letter/journal of Capt. George Harris, 5th Regiment Grenadier Company, 55.

29. "From Rariton, May 24, 1777," letter quoted in the *Pennsylvania Evening Post,* June 5, 1777, in William S. Stryker, ed., *New Jersey Archives,* 2nd ser., vol. I, *Extracts from American Newspapers, 1776–1777,* 391–92.

30. Philander Chase et. al., eds. *The Papers of George Washington: Revolutionary War Series,* vol. 9, (Charlottesville, VA: University Press of Virginia, 1998), 567–68.

31. Letter, John Adams to Nathanael Greene, "Philadelphia May 9 1777," in Nathanael Greene, *The Papers of General Nathanael Greene,* volume 2, *1 January 1777–16 October 1778,* edited by Richard K. Showman, Robert M. McCarthy, and Margaret Cobb (Chapel Hill, NC: University of North Carolina Press, 1980), 74.

32. Letter, Greene to Adams, "Camp Middlebrook May 28, 1777," Greene, *Papers,* 98.

33. Washington to Livingston, January 24, 1777, Fitzpatrick, *Washington,* 7, 56–57.

34. *Historical Anecdotes,* 4.

35. Fitzpatrick, *Washington* 7, 81.

36. George Washington Papers online at the Library of Congress, http://memory.loc.gov/ammem/gwhtml/. Ser. 3b, Varick Transcripts, image 323.

37. Eric Robson, ed., *Letters from America 1773 to 1780: Being the Letters of a Scots Officer, Sir James Murray, to His Home during the War of American Independence* (Manchester, UK: Manchester University Press, 1951), 38.

38. Ira D. Gruber, *John Peebles' American War: The Diary of a Scottish Grenadier, 1776–1782* (Mechanicsburg, PA: Stackpole Books, 1998), 98.

39. Letter, William Dansey to his mother, "On Board the *Chambre,* Amboy Mar. 15, 1777," Letters of Capt. William Dansey, Light Company, 33rd Regiment of Foot, Historical Society of Delaware, Wilmington. Punctuation added.

40. Fitzpatrick, *Washington* 7, 222–25.

41. Graydon, *Memoirs,* 279, 281.

42. Ewald, *Diary,* Introduction, xxiv–xxvi, 365–74. Ewald's original letters to Jeannette van Horne are in the Library of Congress. They are translated in Appendix 2 of Ewald, *Diary.*

43. The Bishop of Worcester to Lord North #135, "Lord North's Correspondence," *English Historical Review* 62 (1947): 235. The "Roll of the Age, Size, Service, &c." of the Brigade of Guards Grenadier Company, lists six men as "cordwainers," or shoemakers. Orders, Returns, Morning Reports and Accounts of British Troops, 1776–1781, film 9, reel I, M922 U.S. National Archives.

44. Hans Huth, "Letters from a Hessian Mercenary (Colonel von Donop to the Prince of Prussia)," *Pennsylvania Magazine of History and Biography* 62 (Octo-

ber, 1938): 497. Graydon says that Susan van Horne "had the opportunity of often seeing Colonel Donope, a Major Hendricks, and a Major Pauli, all of the German troops; the latter of whom was polite enough to take charge of her horse and chair . . ." Graydon, 279.

45. Graydon, 279.

46. Von Heister, fiche 45, FZ 57–58, in Count Carl von Donop, Journal of the Hessian Corps in America under General von Heister, 1776–June 1777, Hessian Documents of the American Revolution, Morristown National Historical Park, Morristown, New Jersey.

47. Ewald, *Diary*, 56–57.

48. Von Donop, Journal of the Hessian Corps, AA, 76–78. "En profound negligee" is a humorously exaggerated idiomatic expression based on the French term *en négligé*, which means "undressed." Adding the word *profond* makes the statement literally translate as "profoundly undressed." I have used the English idiom "in the buff" to convey the sense and flavor of von Donop's statement.

49. Ewald, *Diary*, 57.

50. Ibid., 57.

51. Chase, *Papers of Washington* 9, 188–89.

52. Greene, *Papers*, 57.

53. Chase, *Papers of Washington* 9, 171.

54. Greene, *Papers*, 2, 60.

55. Baurmeister Journal, Fiche 86, GZ 70.

56. Huth, "Letters," 498. *Grogge*, or grog, is watered rum, at that time a drink considered fit only for the lower classes and sailors, not for officers and gentlemen.

57. Henry J. Retzer, "Two Journeys to Pay and Clothe the Trenton Captives," *Schwalm* 8 (2005): 61.

58. Letter, Capt. James Moore to Col. Persifor Frazer, "Bonebrook Apl. 30th 1777," Frazer, *Frazer Memoir*, 224.

59. Letter, Osborn to Germain, "Rariton Near Brunswick May the 15th 1777," PRO, CO 5/93-3, MS sheet 426.

60. Letter, Lee to Jefferson, "Phila. May 20. 1777," Thomas Jefferson Papers, ser. I, General Correspondence, Images 846–47, loc.gov.

61. Cresswell, *Journal*, 220–21.

62. From Hessian GHQ New Brunswick: "last winter Colonel von Donop with the consent of General Howe, mounted 16 of his Jägers and put them under the orders of Captain Lorey." Von Donop, *Journal of the Hessian Corps*, von Heister, fiche 45, FZ 66,

63. Von Donop, *Journal of the Hessian Corps*, 86.

64. Ibid.

65. Thomas Glyn, *Ensign Glyns Journal on the American Service with the Detachment of 1000 Men of the Guards*, Manuscript Journal, 50a–51, Princeton University Library, Princeton, NJ.

66. Hale, 21. Grant lived very well, despite the conditions, which no doubt contributed to his unpopularity. John Peebles commented on April 1, "dined with Genl. Grant, the old fellow lives like a Prince." By contrast, Peebles noted two days earlier, "Din'd with Lord Cornwallis, a genteel Table & moderate." *Peebles Diary*, 107. An old Scottish veteran, Lt. Col. Allan Maclean, commander of the Royal Highland Emigrants, described the general in a letter that spring as "our countrywoman Mother James Grant." *New Records of the American Revolution: Letters of Charles Stuart* (privately printed, n.d.), 25. Library of Congress.

67. Letter, Grant to Harvey, June 7, 1777, Grant Papers, reel 28.

68. Charles J. Stillé, *Major-General Anthony Wayne and the Pennsylvania Line in the Continental Army* (Philadelphia: J. B. Lippincott, 1893), 71. Wayne was appointed brigadier general in February 1777, while stationed at Fort Ticonderoga with part of the Pennsylvania Line. The reorganization of the army and the Pennsylvania Line in this period is complex; see John B. B. Trussell, *The Pennsylvania Line: Regimental Organization and Operations, 1775–1783* (Harrisburg: Pennsylvania Historical and Museum Commission, 1977). Wayne arrived in Northern New Jersey sometime in early May and took command of the 1st Pennsylvania Brigade, which, along with the 2nd Pennsylvania Brigade, made up Maj. Gen. Benjamin Lincoln's Division.

69. Von Münchhausen, *Diary*, 13.

70. Graydon, *Memoirs*, 280.

71. Von Donop, *Journal of the Hessian Corps*, 90–91. Rev. Henry Muhlenberg of Trappe, Pennsylvania, wrote in his diary on June 11: "The dragoons surrounded him, and although he asked for pardon and offered to surrender, he was cruelly tortured, his eyes were knocked out, his nose was cut off, and finally he was killed by the stabs of seventeen men and his body left lying in the field. The American general washed the body of the said slain man, had him placed in a coffin, sent it to British headquarters, and in a letter inquired if this was an example of their method of waging war." Henry Melchior Muhlenberg, *The Journals of Henry Melchior Muhlenberg*, vol. 3, translated and edited by Theodore G. Tappert and John W. Doberstein (Philadelphia: The Muhlenberg Press, 1958), 51.

72. *Pennsylvania Evening Post*, June 12, in Stryker, *New Jersey Archives*, 397.

73. *The Papers of Alexander Hamilton*, vol. 1, Harold G. Syrett and Jacob E. Cooke, eds. (New York: Columbia University Press, 1961), 263.

74. Chase, *Papers of Washington* 9, 591.

75. Syrett and Cooke, *Papers of Hamilton*, 263.

76. Von Heister, Fiche 45, FZ 66.

77. Chase, *Papers of Washington* 9, 592.

78. Graydon, *Memoirs*, 280.

79. Letter, Grant to Harvey, June 7, 1777, Grant Papers, reel 28.

80. Letter, Wayne to Sharp Delaney, dated "Camp at Mount Prospect 7th June 1777," Stillé, *Wayne*, 65.

81. Cresswell, *Journal*, 229.

82. *Historical Anecdotes Civil and Military*, 40.

83. Germain to Knox, June 24, 1777, Historical Manuscripts Commission, *Report*, 131.

84. Mark M. Boatner, *Encyclopedia of the American Revolution* (New York: David McKay Company, 1966), s.v. "von Heister."

85. This was the name of the principality at the time of the Revolution. In recent times, it has been called Ansbach-Brandenburg-Bayreuth.

86. Cresswell, *Journal*, 231.

87. O'Hara was the officer who had the disagreeable duty of surrendering Cornwallis's army at Yorktown in 1781.

88. The original three regiments of Foot Guards were the 1st Guards, the Coldstream Guards, and the 3rd Guards (also known as the Scots Guards). Today there are five regiments, with the addition of the Welsh Guards and the Irish Guards, and they are collectively known as the Grenadier Guards, having received this name for their role in defeating the grenadiers of Napoleon's "Old Guard" at Waterloo in 1815.

89. Letter, Howe to Barrington, HQP, Carleton Papers, PRO 30/55, vol. 4.

90. Letter, Grant to Harvey, June 7, 1776, Grant Papers, reel 28.

91. Leslie Stephen and Sidney Lee, *The Dictionary of National Biography*, vol. 7 (Oxford, UK: Oxford University Press, 1922), 191–92; Henry B. Wheatley, *The Historical and the Posthumous Memoirs of Sir Nathaniel William Wraxall 1772–1784*, vol. 3, (London: Bickers and Son, Leicester Square, 1884), 56–58. Wraxall's memoirs were criticized at the time by his political enemies for being inaccurate. However, "one very strong testimony in favour of Wraxall was the letter which Sir George Osborn, for forty years equerry to George III, wrote to him: 'I have your first edition here, and have perused it again with much attention. I pledge my name that I personally know nine parts out of ten of your anecdotes to be perfectly correct. You are imprisoned for giving to future ages a perfect picture of our time, and as interesting as Clarendon.'" Vol. I.

92. Hessian Platte Grenadier Battalion Journal (Quartermaster Carl Bauer), in Bruce E. Burgoyne, *Enemy Views: The American Revolutionary War as Recorded by the Hessian Participants* (Bowie, MD.: Heritage Books, 1996), 141.

93. Diary entry June 12, Lt. Johann von Bardeleben, Hessian Regiment von Donop, Ibid., 141–42.

94. Gruber, *Peebles Diary*, 53.

95. Orderly Book and Journal of Capt. Robert Kirkwood, entries for June 10 and 11, 1777. Published as Robert Kirkwood, *The Journal and Order Book of Captain Robert Kirkwood of the Delaware Regiment of the Continental Line*, edited by Joseph Brown Turner (Wilmington, DE: Historical Society of Delaware, 1910), entries for June 10 and 11, 1777.

96. John Peebles, Journal of Capt.-Lt. John Peebles, Grenadier Company, 42nd Royal Highland Regiment, Public Records Office, Edinburgh, Scotland; Gruber, *Peebles Diary*.

97. Joesph Lee Boyle, *From Redcoat to Rebel: The Thomas Sullivan Journal* (Bowie, MD: Heritage Books, 1997), 116.

98. Diary of Ens. William Viscount Cantelupe, Grey Papers, University of Durham, United Kingdom, entry for June 13, 1777.

99. Peebles described the full composition of von Heister's column: "The 2nd Division under the Command of his Excellency Lt. Genl. DeHeister, Major Genls. Stirn, Vaughan & Gray, Brigr. Genls. Agnew & Leslie to March by the left—the 4 Companys of Light Infantry with Major Craig & Capt. Fergusons Rifle Company To join the Light Infantry of the Guards under the Command. of Lt. Col. Twistleton—four Grasshoppers [light cannon] to be Attached to this Corps—the Battalions. Of Guards with a Corps of Pioneers, 40th & 23rd Regts. Under the Command. of Lt. Colo: Trelawney to form the Advance Guard following Lt. Col: Twistletons Corps with 2 Medium 12 pounders. & two 6 pounders. Major Genl. Stirne with the 2nd & 4 Brigades with 2 Six pounders. to each, Majr. Genl. Vaughan with 3rd & 1st Brigade with 2 Six pounders. to each, 17th Dragoons with their dismounted—Brigadier Genl. Leslie with ye Brigade of 71st Regt. to assemble on the Prince Town road at 11 OClock in the rear of Ld. Cornwallis's Division & wait further Orders . . . The first Division March'd to Hillsborrow the 2nd to Middle Bush . . ." Gruber, *Peebles Diary*.

100. Archibald Robertson, *Archibald Robertson, Lieutenant General of the Royal Engineers: His Diaries and Sketches in America, 1762–1780*, edited by Harry Miller Lydenberg (New York: New York Public Library, 1930), 136–37.

101. Von Münchhausen, *Diary*, 16.

102. Letter, Col. James Chambers to Gen. Edward Hand, "Mount Prospect Camp, 18th June, 1777." John Blair Linn and William H. Egle, *Pennsylvania in the War of the Revolution, 1775–1783*, vol. 1 (Harrisburg, PA: Lane S. Hart, 1880), 313.

103. Fitzpatrick, *Washington* 7, 236–37.

104. Letter, Wayne to Peters, "Mount Prospect 17th June 1777," Wayne Papers, vol. 3, 101–10, HSP.

105. Letter, Wayne to the Pennsylvania Board of War, dated "Camp at Mount Prospect 3 June 1777," Stillé, *Wayne*, 65.

106. Henry Steele Commager and Richard B. Morris, eds., *The Spirit of Seventy Six: The Story of the American Revolution as Told by Participants* (New York: Bonanza Books, 1968), 536–37.

107. Letter, Charles Stuart to Lord Bute, "New York, July 10, 1777," *New Records*, 33.

108. Letter, John Adams to Abigail Adams, "Phyladelphia June 14, 1777," Smith, et. al., *Letters of Delegates*, vol. 7, 194–95.

109. John Andre, *Andre's Journal*, vol. I, edited by Henry Cabot Lodge (Boston: The Bibliophile Society, 1903), 39.

110. Von Münchhausen, *Diary*, 16.

111. Linn and Egle, *Pennsylvania*, 313.

112. *Historical Anecdotes Civil and Military*, 41–42.

113. Commager and Morris, *Spirit of Seventy Six*, 537.

114. Joseph Clark, Diary, entry for June 20, 1777, MS MG 256, New Jersey Historical Society.

115. Smith, et. al., *Letters of Delegates*, vol. 7, 195.

116. Letter, Percy to Polly Frazer, "Mount Pleasant near Bound Brook June 17, 1777," Frazer, *Frazer Memoir*, 139–40.

117. Letter, John Adams to Abigail Adams, "Philadelphia June 18, 1777," Smith, et. al., *Letters of Delegates*, vol. 7, 207.

118. Letter, Rush to Wayne, "Philadelphia June 18, 1777," Wayne Papers, vol. 3, 101–10.

119. Timothy Pickering, Pickering Papers, Microfilm reel 51 and 52, 142, Massachusetts Historical Society, Boston.

120. Kemble, *Journals*, 121.

121. Von Münchhausen, *Diary*, 18.

122. Johann Ewald, *Treatise on Partisan Warfare (Abhandlung Über den kleinen Krieg von Joh. Ewald), Cassel, 1785*, translated and edited by Robert A. Selig and David C. Skaggs (New York: Greenwood Press, 1991), 119.

123. Ewald, *Diary*, 65.

124. Pickering Papers, 142.

125. Commager and Morris, *Spirit of Seventy Six*, 537.

126. Letter, Percy to Polly Frazer, "June 20, 1777," Frazer, *Frazer Memoir*, 140.

127. Letter, Charles Stuart to Lord Bute, "New York, July 10, 1777," *New Records*, 32–33.

128. "Record of the Campaign of 1777," *New Records*, 49.

129. Letter, Grant to Harvey, "New York 10th July 1777," Grant Papers, reel 28/29.

130. Letter, John Adams to Abigail Adams, "Philadelphia June 21, 1777," Smith, et. al., *Letters of Delegates*, vol. 7, 240.

131. Cresswell, *Journal*, 283.

132. Entry for June 24, Kemble, *Journals*, 122.

133. *Historical Anecdotes Civil and Military*, 41–42.

134. Sarah Logan Fisher, edited by Nicholas Biddle Wainwright, "A Diary of Trifling Occurrences, Philadelphia, 1776–1778," *Pennsylvania Magazine of History and Biography* 82 (1958): 437.

135. Gruber, *Peebles Diary*, 117.

136. Letter, Charles Stuart to Lord Bute, "New York, July 10, 1777," *New Records*, 32.

137. Von Münchhausen, *Diary*, 18–19.

138. Boyle, *Thomas Sullivan Journal*, 119.

139. Letter, Percy to Polly Frazer, "Wednesday July 2, 1777," Frazer, *Frazer Memoir*, 142–43.

140. Cresswell, *Journal*, 240–41.

141. G. Washington to Congress, 11 PM June 22, Published by Order of Congress, *Pennsylvania Evening Post*, June 24, 1777, in Stryker, *New Jersey Archives*, 402–3.

142. Fitzpatrick, *Washington* 8, 295–96.

143. Letter, Harris to Gen. Edward Hand, "Cross Roads, (abt. 20 miles from Phila'da,) 13 August, 1777." Linn and Egle, *Pennsylvania*, 315. "Sawny" was a nickname for Scotsmen in the same way that "Paddy" was for Irishmen and "Taffy" was for Welshmen. Though Harris does not specify during which skirmish this comment was made, the fight at Brunswick Bridge involved Morgan's corps and some of Wayne's men, as well as Highlanders, as pointed out by both Cresswell and Peebles.

144. Cresswell, *Journal*, 241–42.

145. Burgoyne, *Enemy Views*, 151.

146. G. Washington to Congress, June 22, in Stryker, *New Jersey Archives*, 402–403.

147. Letter, Lewis Nicola to ———, "[Philadelphia] July 2, 1777," PaArch I, V, 410. Nicola was the town major of Philadelphia and commander of the Invalid Regiment. He obtained this information from Pvt. John Warrel, who was "a Deserter who came here yesterday morning having given some interesting intelligence. . . . he was pressed in London."

148. Cresswell, *Journal*, 240.

149. William Gordon, *The History of the Rise, Progress, and Establishment of the Independence of the United States of America . . .* , 2d Amer. ed., vol. 2 (New York: Samuel Campbell, 1794), 201.

150. Letter, Percy to Polly Frazer, "Camp at the Cloves July 18th 1777," Frazer, *Frazer Memoir*, 150. Sir George Osborn had informed Lord Germain on May 15, "The Hessian Grenadiers have lost within these two Months more

than 300 Men by a Putrid fever which got among them at Brunswick," PRO, CO 5/93-3, MS sheet 426.

151. Lillian B. Miller, Sidney Hart, and Toby A. Appel, eds., *The Selected Papers of Charles Willson Peale and His Family*, vol. I, *Charles Willson Peale: Artist in Revolutionary America, 1735–1791* (New Haven, CT: Yale University Press, 1983), 233–34.

152. Frazer, *Frazer Memoir*, 143.

153. Ibid.

154. *Annual Register for 1777*, 2d ed., 1781, 123.

155. Von Münchhausen, *Diary*, 19.

156. Edward William Harcourt, *The Harcourt Papers*, vol. 11 (Oxford: James Parker and Co., fifty copies printed for private circulation, 1880), 217.

157. Andre, *Journal*, 47.

158. Boyle, *Thomas Sullivan Journal*, 122.

159. Hunter, 27.

160. "Letter from Middle Brook, June 28," *Pennsylvania Journal*, July 2, 1777, in Stryker, *New Jersey Archives*, 415–16.

161. Richard Ketchum, "New War Letters of Banastre Tarleton," in *Narratives of the Revolution in New York* (New York: New York Historical Society, 1976), 134.

162. John Montrésor, *The Montrésor Journals, edited by G. D. Scull, Collections of the New York Historical Society*, vol. 14 (New York, 1882), 426. "Monthly Return of the 3 Regiments Guards . . . 1st July 1777" confirms that "Capt Finch Died of His Wounds 29th June 1777." Orders of British Troops.

163. Grant to Harvey, 10 July, Grant Papers.

164. Letter, Germain to Sir Wm. Howe, 3rd September 1777, HQP, Carleton Papers, PRO 30/55, vol. 6.

165. Grant to Harvey, 10 July, Grant Papers.

166. "Extract of a Letter from Philada. July 1st 11 Oclock AM," unknown to Samuel Chase; the extract is in Chase's handwriting and is in the papers of Richard Henry Lee. Smith, et. al., *Letters of Delegates*, vol. 7, 280–81.

167. Octavius Pickering and Charles Upham, *The Life of Timothy Pickering*, vol. I (Boston: Little, Brown, and Company, 1867), 144–45.

168. Grant to Harvey, 10 July, Grant Papers.

169. Dennis P. Ryan, ed., *A Salute to Courage: The American Revolution as Seen through Wartime Writings of Officers of the Continental Army and Navy* (New York: Columbia University Press, 1979), 82–83.

170. Letter, John Adams to Abigail Adams, "Philadelphia June 29 1777," Smith, et. al., *Letters of Delegates*, vol. 7, 262.

171. Boyle, *Thomas Sullivan Journal*, 122.

172. Montrésor, *Montrésor Journals*, 425.

173. Letter, Charles Stuart to Lord Bute, "New York, July 10, 1777," *New Records*, 33.

174. Fitzpatrick, *Washington* 8, 311.

175. Syrett and Cooke, *Papers of Hamilton*, 274–75.

176. Letter, Richard Fitzpatrick to his brother the Earl of Upper Ossory, dated "Camp Staten Island, July 5, 1777," Richard Fitzpatrick Papers, Miscellaneous Manuscripts 622, Library of Congress.

177. Pickering and Upham, *Life*, 145.

178. *Pennsylvania Gazette*, July 9, 1777, in Stryker, *New Jersey Archives*, 422.

179. André, *Journal*, 48.

180. Letter, Major Saml. Hay to Col. Irvine at Carlisle, dated "Morris Town, July 10, 1777," Irvine Papers 1777, Manuscript Division, Library of Congress.

181. Robertson, *Diaries*, 139.

182. Hessian Platte Grenadier Battalion Journal (Quartermaster Carl Bauer), *Enemy Views*, 152.

183. Ewald, *Diary*, 69.

184. Fitzpatrick, *Washington* 8, 315.

185. Grant to Harvey, 10 July, Grant Papers. Éclat is a French word meaning "burst" or "sudden uproar." In the sense of Grant's sentence and in the spirit of Grant's sardonic wit, it would best be translated idiomatically as "with a bang."

186. Ibid.

187. Letter, July 5, 1777, Fitzpatrick Papers

188. Montrésor, *Montrésor Journals*, 426.

189. Letter, July 5, 1777, Fitzpatrick Papers.

190. Letter "New York, July 10, 1777," *New Records*, 33.

191. Frazer, *Frazer Memoir*, 144.

192. Cresswell, *Journal*, 256–57; 252; 257; 259–60.

193. Entry for July 1, 1777, Kemble, *Journal*, 124.

CHAPTER 2

1. Fisher, 437.

2. Letter, Grier to Wayne, "Philada. July 5th 1777," Wayne Papers, vol. 3, 101–10.

3. Article quoted from *Virginia Gazette*, July 18, 1777. Fourth of July Celebrations Database by James R. Heintze, http://gurukul.american.edu/heintze/fourthhtm#Beginning. *Feux de joie*, "firings of joy," referred to a "running fire" of shots fired rapidly in sequence down a line of troops, starting at one end of the line. Each soldier fired his musket individually, the effect being similar to a string of firecrackers.

4. Letter, John Adams to Abigail Adams II, "Philadelphia, July 5th, 1777," Smith, et. al., *Letters of Delegates*, vol. 7, 293–94.

5. Ibid.

6. Letter, William Williams to Jonathan Trumbull Sr., "Philadelphia, July 5. 1777," Smith, et. al., *Letters of Delegates*, vol. 7, 303.

7. Letter, Adams to Abigail, July 5, 1777, Smith, et. al., *Letters of Delegates*, vol. 7, 294.

8. The Hessian band performed for hire for Congress and others while in captivity over the next few years. As odd as it may seem to modern minds, musicians were noncombatants by the rules of eighteenth-century warfare and were also "non-political" (i.e., "you pay, we play!"). Bandsmen were treated separately from regimental fifers and drummers, who were called "field music." The list of prisoners from Trenton included "5 Hautboys" from the Regiment von Loss-berg (Samuel and Wilhelm Hatteroth, Johannes Saechtling Sr. and Jr., and Johann Wickhard), "1 Hautboy" from the Regiment von Knyphausen (Philip Pfiel), and "4 Hautboys" from the Regiment von Rall (Emanuel Grau, Johannes Nickell, Johannes Sondermann, and one unidentified). [PaArch, 2nd ser., vol. I, 432–34; and Richard Barth, Dornemann, and Mark Schwalm, "The Trenton Prisoner List," *Schwalm* 3, I (1985), 1–21] . On many of the prisoner lists kept by American authorities, the first names of most of the German prisoners have been Anglicized—See Force Papers 9, 17,137, reel 104, LOC.

Hessian records indicate that Philip Pfiel "was released from prison by Hessian troops in Feb. 1777 and evidently returned to duty," but how, where, and when is a mystery. The same records show that he deserted in 1783. He stayed in Philadelphia, where his name changed to Philip Phile, and he composed the music for "The President's March," later called "Hail, Columbia," now used as the vice-president's march. See Robert M. Webler, "A Notable Hessian Deserter," *Schwalm* 8 (2005): 41.

9. Letter, Adams to Abigail, July 5, 1777, Smith, et. al., *Letters of Delegates*, vol. 7, 294.

10. Letter, Thomas Burke to Richard Caswell, "Philadelphia July 5th 1777," Smith, et. al., *Letters of Delegates* 7, 295. Sir George Osborn wrote to Lord Germain in May, "I found the Hessian Battalion, now under the Command of Colonel Loose [Loos], sick 183, deserted not one since their Misfortune at Trenton, they return Prisners of War 830 Private, 32 Officers, 84 N:Commissiond[.] they have reason to believe that not one of the Prisners have enlisted with the Rebels, excepting the Musick, and 30 Men who are reported by some German deserters to be engaged lately by a Lieutenant Farré (a near relation of Lt. Genl. Kniphausen) and is said to be with the Rebels at Newark." MS Let-

ter, Osborn to Germain, "Raritan near Brunswick, May the 15, 1777," PRO, CO 5/93-3, MS sheet 426.

11. Fisher, 437. Jacob Hiltzheimer wrote, "June 30 1777: Monday Rain all day, in afternoon went to Schuylkill Stables, which is full of Light horse, from thence went to Governor Penns woods to see the North Carolina Camp." Jacob Hiltzheimer Diary for 1777, B/H56d 1777–1778, American Philosophical Society, Philadelphia.

12. Phineas Pemberton, "Weather Observations," American Philosophical Society, Philadelphia.

13. Letter, John Adams to Abigail Adams, "Philadelphia July 1, 1777," Smith, et. al., *Letters of Delegates*, vol. 7, 278.

14. Christopher Marshall Remembrancer, vol. D, entry for June 9, 1777, Historical Society of Pennsylvania, Philadelphia. After the war, once the Protestant Episcopal Church was organized, the crown was replaced by a bishop's mitre decorated with thirteen star-shaped perforations.

15. Letter, Adams to Abigail, July 5, 1777, Smith, et. al., *Letters of Delegates*, vol. 7, 294. The New Moon began at 7:33 P.M. on July 4, 1777.

16. Letter, Williams to Trumbull, July 5, 1777, Smith, et. al., *Letters of Delegates*, vol. 7, 303.

17. Muhlenberg, *Journals* 3, 68.

18. Journal entry for September 3, 1776. Cresswell, *Journal*, 155.

19. Colonial Records, *Minutes of the Supreme Executive Council of Pennsylvania*, vol. 9 (Harrisburg, PA: Theo Fenn & Co., 1852), 37.

20. Letter, Grier to Wayne, July 5, 1777.

21. Letter, Williams to Trumbull, July 5, 1777, Smith, et. al., *Letters of Delegates*, vol. 7, 303.

22. Elizabeth Drinker, *The Diary of Elizabeth Drinker*, vol. I, edited by Elaine F. Crane (Boston: Northeastern University Press, 1991), 225.

23. Fisher, 438.

24. Muhlenberg, *Journals* 3, 56.

25. Osborn report to Lord George Germain, July 4. "I have the honor of acquainting your Lordship that part of the Reinforcement consisting of 1300 Troops from Anspach, 300 Hessian Chasseurs [Jägers], and 440 Hessian recruits are arrived. The Chasseurs are better Cloathed than they were last Year, their Arms and boots are in good order, the Chasseurs for the Reinforcement are chiefly Hessians, the Recruits are from Saxe, Hanover, & the County of Wirtembergh [Württemberg], hardly every other Man is a Hessian, they appear howe[ve]r neither too young nor too old to bear the fatigue of the Campaign." PRO, CO 5/93-3, MS sheet 428.

26. Letter, John Adams to Abigail Adams, "Philadelphia July 13, 1777," Smith et. al., *Letters of Delegates*, vol. 7, 340. Von Heister received his official letter of recall on June 28. Von Münchhausen wrote on July 1, "Late in the evening General Howe paid an unpleasant visit to General von Heister, to whom he had not talked since the latter's recall." Von Münchhausen, *Diary*, 20.

27. Letter, Fitzpatrick to his brother, "Camp upon Staten Island, July 5, 1777," Fitzpatrick Papers.

28. Osborn Letters 3, 98.

29. Letter, Fitzpatrick to his brother, July 5, 1777, Fitzpatrick Papers.

30. Entry for July 4, 1777, Kemble, *Journal*, 124.

31. Letter, Grant to Harvey, "New Brunswick 7th June 1777," Grant Papers, reel 28/29.

32. Sandy Hook Lighthouse is the oldest surviving lighthouse in continuous use in the United States. When constructed, it was 500 feet from the tip of the hook; because of tides and shifting sands, at present it is landlocked by more than a mile. "The lighthouse first cast forth its beam into the night June 11, 1764. A newspaper account of the time described the structure as being an '. . . octagonal Figure, having eight equal Sides; the Diameter at the Base 29 Feet; and at the top of the Wall, 15 Feet. The lanthorn is 7 feet high; the Circumference 33 feet. The whole Construction of the Lanthorn is Iron; the Top covered with Copper. There are 48 Oil Blazes. The Building from the surface is Nine Stories. The whole from Bottom to Top is 103 Feet.'" The attempts to douse the lantern occurred in the spring of 1776. "Sandy Hook Lighthouse," www.njlhs.burlco.org/sandyhk.htm.

33. Chase, *Papers of Washington*, 207–9.

34. Letter, Lt. Loftus Cliffe, 46th Regiment, to brother Jack Cliffe, "Camp near Philadelphia 24 October 1777," Cliffe Papers, Clements Library.

35. Cantelupe Diary, entry for July 8.

36. André, *Journal*, 55, 67.

37. Osborn Letters 3, 98.

38. Cantelupe Diary, entries for July 8 and July 23; "Embarkation Return of the Brigade of Foot Guards . . . 13th July 1777," Orders of British Troops.

39. Johann Conrad Döhla, *A Hessian Diary of the American Revolution by Johann Conrad Döhla*, translated by Bruce E. Burgoyne (Norman, OK: University of Oklahoma Press, 1990), 43–44n.

40. Ibid., 43–44.

41. Orderly Book, Captain Wilson's 49th Regiment, Washington Papers online.

42. Letter, William Dansey to his mother, "On Board the *Earl of Oxford*, 10 July 1777," Dansey Papers.

43. Von Münchhausen, *Diary*, 20.

44. "Mr. Joseph Galloway on the American War," *Scots Magazine* 41 (October 1779): 526–27.

45. *Annual Register for 1777*, 127.

46. Journal entry for June 19, 1777, Cresswell, *Journal*, 237.

47. Letter/Journal, James Parker to Charles Steuart, "New York July 16, 1777," Parker Family Papers 1760–95 (originals in Liverpool, England), film 45, reel 2, David Library. "Te Deum" was a long, elaborate medieval Christian hymn of Thanksgiving (*Te Deum laudimus*, "We praise thee, O God!), traditionally sung after a military victory.

48. *Encyclopaedia Britannica; or, A Dictionary of Arts and Sciences, Etc.*, vol. 2 (Edinburgh: A. Bell and Colin MacFarquhar, 1771), 21.

49. Huth, "Letters," 498.

50. Grant to Harvey, July 10, Grant Papers.

51. Letter, John Adams to James Warren, "Philadelphia June [*sic*; July] 11, 1777," Smith et. al., *Letters of Delegates*, vol. 7, 181–82. This letter is dated June 11 and is noted as a "recipient's copy." The contents of the letter, though, reveal that it is clearly July 11, as it mentions the British evacuation of New Jersey, which occurred on June 30. Adams's letter of July 11 to Abigail contains similar wording about Howe's intentions.

52. Letter, John Adams to Abigail, "Philadelphia July 11, 1777," Smith et. al., *Letters of Delegates*, vol. 7, 334.

53. *Magee's Weekly Packet*, Dublin, Saturday, August 9, 1777, no. 8, British Library Newspaper Archive.

54. Letter, Fitzpatrick to his brother, July 8, 1777, Fitzpatrick Letters.

55. Von Münchhausen, *Diary*, 21. Others had privately expressed their opinions of the British generals. Lt. Col. Allan Maclean had written in February, "General Howe is a very honest man, and I believe a very disinterested one. Brave he certainly is and would make a very good executive officer under another's command, but he is not by any means equal to a C. in C . . . He has, moreover, got none but very silly fellows about him—a great parcel of old women—most of them improper for the American service. I could be very ludicrous on this occasion, but it is truly too serious a matter that brave men's lives should be sacrificed to be commanded by such generals. For excepting Earl Percy, Lord Cornwallis, both Lt. Generals, and the Brigadier Generals Leslie and Sir William Erskine, the rest are useless." Quoted in Commager and Morris, *Spirit of Seventy Six*, 523.

56. Letter, Frazer to his wife Polly, "Camp at the Cloves, July 18th 1777," Frazer, *Frazer Memoir*, 148–49.

57. Pickering and Upham, *Life of Pickering*, vol. 1, 147. Versions of suppawn appeared all over rural America well into the twentieth century. "Indian pud-

ding" in New England and grits in the South are variations. For further discussion and an illustration of how suppawn was eaten in the Hudson Valley area, see Peter G. Rose, *The Sensible Cook: Dutch Foodways in the Old and New World* (Syracuse, NY: Syracuse University Press, 1989), 31–34.

58. Letter, Frazer to his wife Polly, "July 18, 1777."

59. Letter, Col. John H. Stone to Gov. Thos. Johnson, "Camp at Crumb Pond below Peeks Kills July 24th 1777," William H. Browne, *Archives of Maryland*, vol. 16, *Journal and Correspondence of the Council of Safety/State Council 1777–1778* (Baltimore: Maryland Historical Society, 1897), 319–20.

60. Letter, John Adams to Abigail, "May 22 [1777] 4 O Clock in the Morning," Smith et. al., *Letters of Delegates*, vol. 7, 103.

61. Letter, Nathanael Greene to Jacob Greene, "Camp at Middlebrook, June 4, 1777," Greene, *Papers* 2, 104.

62. Letter, John Adams to Nathanael Greene, "Philadelphia July 7, 1777," Smith et. al., *Letters of Delegates*, vol. 7, 305–7.

63. Alfred J. Morrison, *Travels in the Confederation 1783–1784*, from the German of Johann David Schoepf (Philadelphia: William J. Campbell, 1911), 107. Schoepf arrived in America in June 1777 as a surgeon with the Ansbach-Brandenburg-Bayreuth reinforcements. He stayed in the army until 1783, and then went on his own tour of America and published his observations in Germany in 1788. For some letters that he wrote while in the army, see *Schwalm* 7, no. 2 (2002), 14–20. Schoepf spends several pages decrying the "bastard tongue" of the Pennsylvania Germans, and cites a number of examples.

64. Cresswell, *Journal*, 271.

65. Letter, Jedediah Huntington to Jabez Huntington, "Peeks Kill 28 July 1777," *Huntington Papers: Correspondence of the Brothers Joshua and Jedediah Huntington during the Period of the American Revolution, Collections of the Connecticut Historical Society* vol. 20 (Hartford, CT: Connecticut Historial Society, 1923), 355–56.

66. Letter, John Adams to Abigail Adams, "Philadelphia Aug. 6, 1777," Smith et. al., *Letters of Delegates*, vol. 7, 433.

67. Muhlenberg, *Journals* 3, 68.

68. Letter, John Chester to Joshua Huntington, "Wethersfield [Conn.] July 23d. A.D. 1777," *Huntington Papers*, 66. Ironically, Admiral Byng was a near neighbor and close friend of Sir George Osborn's father, Sir Danvers Osborn.

69. Letter, John Adams to Abigail Adams, "Philadelphia August 19, 1777," Smith, et. al., *Letters of Delegates*, vol. 7, 506.

70. Letter, John Adams to Abigail Adams, "Fryday July 18, 1777," Smith et. al, *Letters of Delegates*, vol. 7, 350–51.

71. Frazer, *Frazer Memoir*, 148.

72. Letter, Jedediah Huntington to Jabez Huntington, "Peeks Kill 16 July 1777," *Huntington Papers*, 350.

73. Letter, John Adams to Abigail, "Philadelphia August 8. 1777," Smith et. al., *Letters of Delegates*, vol. 7, 439.

74. Letter, Jedediah Huntington to Andrew Huntington, "Peeks Kill 20th July 1777," *Huntington Papers*, 352.

75. Ambrose Serle, *The American Journal of Ambrose Serle, Secretary to Lord Howe, 1776–1778*, edited by Edward H. Tatum Jr. (San Marino, CA: Huntington Library, 1940; reprint, New York: Arno Press, 1969), 239–40.

76. Letter, Forman to Congress, "Middletown, county of Monmouth, June 20 1777 [*sic*]" Written on the bottom of the letter is "(Copy T. M. [probably Timothy Matlack]" and "(The date I presume should have been July instead of June. T. M.)." Hazard, *Pennsylvania Archives*, 435–36.

77. Letter, Forman to Congress, "Shrewsbury [NJ], 23 July 1777," Hazard, *Pennsylvania Archives*, 439–40.

78. Serle, *Journal*, 240. Sandy Hook Lighthouse is still in service after 240 years, the oldest surviving lighthouse in the United States.

79. Cresswell, *Journal*, 273.

80. Letter, Forman to Congress, July 23, 1777.

81. "Memorandum of Lt. Gilbt. Purdy for the Year 1777," Z 20/C21/ 1975/U2, National Archives of Canada, Ottawa.

82. Parker Family Papers, film 45, reel 2.

83. Letter, Hale to his parents, "Head of Elk River, Maryland, 30th August 1777," Hale, "Letters," 21.

84. Letter, Instructions to Capt. John Hunn, "In Council, July 24, 1777," Hazard, *Pennsylvania Archives*, 450; also see Colonial Records, *Minutes*, 250–51. "An order was drawn on David Rittenhouse Esq'r., in favour of Capt. Hunn, for the Sum of One Hundred Pounds, to hire expresses & Pay such Expenses as may accrue, and for which sum he is to account to the Board." For a brief biography of Hunn, see *Pennsylvania Magazine of History and Biography*, 11 (1887): 218–19.

85. *The Oxford English Dictionary* defines *cripple* as "U.S. (local) A dense thicket in swampy or low-lying ground" and cites 1675 and 1705 sources, both of which relate to land in New Jersey. A *spong* is "a long narrow piece or strip of land," source obscure. Both words have been used by locals ("Pineys") in the Pine Barrens since the seventeenth century. "In the vernacular, a low, wet area where the Atlantic white cedars grow is called a cripple. If no cedars grow there, the wet area is called a spong, which is pronounced to rhyme with 'sung.' Some people define spongs and cripples a little differently, saying that water always flows in a cripple but there is water in a spong only after a rain. Others say that

any lowland area where high-bush blueberries grow is a spong." John McPhee, *The Pine Barrens* (New York: Farrar, Straus, Giroux, 1981), 54–55.

86. Journal of Thomas Hopkins, manager of the Friendship Salt Works at Egg Harbor, August 11 and August 24, 1780, Historical Society of Pennsylvania, quoted in Arthur D. Pierce, *Smugglers' Woods*, (New Brunswick, NJ: Rutgers University Press, 1960), 240, 242.

87. Vickers Journal, quoted in ibid., 6.

88. Letter, Fithian to Rev. Enoch Green, quoted in ibid., 159.

89. Letter, Hunn to Wharton, "Cape May, July 30th, Eleven o'clock," Hazard, *Pennsylvania Archives*, 467.

90. Benjamin West, *The New-England Almanack, or Lady's and Gentleman's Diary for the Year of Our Lord Christ 1777* (Providence, RI: Printed and sold by John Carter), 8.

91. Montrésor, *Montrésor Journals*, 429–30. The land at N 39.48" is Island Beach, just over two miles above Barnegat Light and thirty-six miles north of Great Egg Harbor, which is at 39.18". Montrésor stated that the latitude at noon was N 39.48", and that later that afternoon they spotted Great Egg Harbor. The notations are remarkably good, given the ever-improving charts of the period, the distance and visibility, as well as the size and constant movement of the fleet at the mercy of the wind and tides.

92. Metchie J. E. Budka, *Under Their Vine and Fig Tree: Travels through America in 1797–1799, 1805, with Some Further Account of Life in New Jersey* by Julian Ursyn Niemcewicz (Elizabeth, NJ: Grassmann Publishing Co., 1965), 219–22. Niemcewicz was a companion of Tadeuz Kosciusko on his visit to America in the late 1790s. In June 1799, Niemcewicz visited Peck's Beach as part of a nature expedition and left a detailed description. At that time, there was one house on the island, occupied by a "poor family." His description is memorable, especially of the "million mosquitoes," of which he said, "They are at once uninvited physicians and musicians, passing through fire and smoke with their lancets and clarinets." The nearby salt marshes also breed greenheads [*Tabanus nigrovittatus*], voracious flies whose painful bites draw blood. Peck's Beach is the site of Ocean City, New Jersey.

93. Letter, Hunn to Wharton, "Cape May, July 26, 1777"; Letter, Stillwell to Wharton, "Cape May, July 26th, 1777"; "An Account of the Arms, &c. taken from the Enemy on Fryday July 25, 1777," Hazard, *Pennsylvania Archives*, 453–54. The purpose of the expedition is not given, but most likely it was to secure fresh beef. Yo ho ho!

94. Note, Dr. John McGinnis to Colonel Bradford, "Little Egg Harbor Saturday July 26th 1777," Washington Papers online, ser. 4, General Correspondence, images 157–58.

95. Letter, Thomas Mifflin to Washington, "Philadelphia Sunday Morning [July 27th] 9 oClock," Washington Papers online, ser. 4, General Correspondence, image 180.

96. Hiltzheimer Diary for 1777. Hiltzheimer was a well-known horse merchant, who handled procurement of horses for the army and militia. In the 1790s he sold horses to President Washington, who was one of the best horsemen and most astute horse dealers in the country. As a note of historical interest, Hiltzheimer wrote in his diary the next day, "this afternoon paid Jacob Graff, Junr. for the House & Lott at the corner of Seventh & High [Market] Streets & Recd. the Deed for the same, the sum pd. him is £1775." This was the boardinghouse where Thomas Jefferson wrote the Declaration of Independence.

97. Muhlenberg, *Journals* 3, 62–63.

98. Drinker, *Diary*, 226.

99. Letter, Washington to Thomas Mifflin, "Flemington [NJ] July 28th 1777," Washington Papers online, ser. 4, General Correspondence, image 200–201.

100. Montrésor, *Montrésor Journals*, 430.

101. Cantelupe Diary, entry for July 28.

102. Letter, Hunn to Wharton, "Cape May, July 29th 1777," Hazard, *Pennsylvania Archives*, 462–63.

103. Letter, John Adams to Abigail Adams, "Philadelphia July 30, 1777," Smith et. al., *Letters of Delegates*, vol. 7, 395.

104. Letter, Hunn to Wharton, "Cape May, July 30th, Eleven o'clock," Hazard, *Pennsylvania Archives*, 467. On Friday, August 1, the Supreme Executive Council ordered David Rittenhouse to draw an order "in favor of Abraham Bennett, for the Sum of Seven Pounds ten Shillings, for riding express from Cape May to this City, on public business." Colonial Records, *Minutes*, 257.

105. Letter, Hunn to Wharton, "Cape May, July 30, 1777, 5 P.M.," Hazard, *Pennsylvania Archives*, 468.

106. Cantelupe Diary, entry for July 30.

107. Montrésor, *Montrésor Journals*, 430–31. The remark about the "Pennsylvania shore" is not entirely erroneous. The state of Delaware was originally part of Pennsylvania, granted to William Penn by King James II as coastline for Pennsylvania, and was referred to in the eighteenth century as "the Three Lower Counties" or "the Three Delaware Counties."

108. The Cape Henlopen lighthouse stood until 1926, when it collapsed into the sea after 160 years of service. Its site was chosen by Henry Fisher, the river pilot. Originally it was said to have been a quarter mile from the water, but the shifting sands of the cape finally brought the house down. When it fell, it was the second-oldest lighthouse in the country. Numerous fireplaces in the

Lewes area are said to be built from its stones. See Hazel D. Brittingham, "The Fall of the Cape Henlopen Lighthouse," in *The Delaware Estuary: Rediscovering a Forgotten Resource*, edited by Tracey Bryant and Jonathan R. Pennock (Newark, DE: University of Delaware Sea Grant College Program, 1988), 40–41. This work is a fascinating study of the history and ecological development of the Delaware River and Bay.

109. Letter, Hall to Rodney, "* O'Clock A. M. Lewestown, August 2nd, 1777," *Delaware Archives, Revolutionary War*, vol. 3 (Wilmington, DE: Charles Story Co., 1919), 1380.

110. Letter, Henry Fisher to State Navy Board, "Wednesday Morning, 10 o'clock, July ye 30th, 1777," Hazard, *Pennsylvania Archives*, 465.

111. Letter, Colonel Richardson to Continental Board of War, "Sussex County [Del.] 9th August 1777," Caesar Rodney, *Letters to and from Caesar Rodney 1756–1784*, edited by George Herbert Ryden (Philadelphia: University of Pennsylvania Press, 1933), 211n.

112. Letter, Rodney to Hancock, "Dover July 30th 1777—5 Oclock," ibid., 201–2.

113. Letter, Hancock to Washington, "Philada. July 31t. 1777. 5 O'Clock A. M.," ibid., n. 1.

114. Fisher to State Navy Board, July 30, 1777; Hancock to Washington, "Philada. July 31t. 1777. 5 O'Clock A.M," n. 1. There is a discrepancy between the two versions of the letter from Rodney, which suggests that at least two letters were sent to make sure that one got through. In the Pennsylvania Archives I printed source, the notation at the bottom is written, "Fifteen minutes before six o'clock, and forwarded at 6 o'clock," and endorsed by General Mifflin. Although this letter is endorsed as being received at 5:45 and forwarded at 6, it is clear from Rodney's letter to Hancock that this same news arrived in Dover at 5 P.M. on July 30, and Sarah Logan Fisher's account that the alarm guns fired at 6 A.M. on the thiry-first suggest that Mifflin received it at 6 A.M. on the thiry-first, not 6 P.M. on the thirtieth as it might appear at first glance.

115. Chase, *Papers of Washington* 10, 466–68.

116. Fisher, 439.

117. Muhlenberg, *Journals* 3, 63.

118. Resolution of Congress, July 31, 1777, Hazard, *Pennsylvania Archives*, 469–70.

119. Supreme Executive Council to Congress, 31st July 1777, Hazard, *Pennsylvania Archives*, 471–72.

120. "July 31: Thursday Clear. at 10 oClock at Night His Excelly. Genl. Washington came to Town with abut 200 Light horse." Hiltzheimer diary. A

letter from Washington to Greene dated August 1, 1777, is headed "City Tavern Philadelpha.," Washington Papers online, ser. 4, General Correspondence, image 292.

121. Letter, Percy to Polly Frazer, "Camp near Howells Ferry July 29th 1777," Frazer, *Frazer Memoir*, 151. Coryell's Ferry is now Lambertville, New Jersey, and New Hope, Pennsylvania.

122. Denys Hay, "The Denouement of General Howe's Campaign of 1777," *English Historical Review*, vol. 74 (1964): 503. Hamond's papers are in the University of Virginia Library and contain his unpublished autobiography, which provides the only eyewitness account of the meeting on the *Eagle*. At the time and for many years afterward, Hamond was blamed for persuading the Howes to sail to the Chesapeake, thus prolonging the campaign by nearly a month. By using his autobiography and other primary documents, the author bears out the fact that Howe's decision was confirmed by Hamond's information, not made by it.

123. Ibid., 504–5.

124. Serle, *Journal*, 241.

125. Bruce E. Burgoyne, ed. and trans., *Diaries of Two Ansbach Jägers*, Diaries of Lt. Heinrich von Feilitzsch and Lt. Christian Bartholomai. (Bowie, MD: Heritage Press, 1997), 12.

126. Osborn Letters, 98.

127. Letter, Washington to Gen. George Clinton, "Chester Augt. 1, 1777," Washington Papers online, ser. 4, General Correspondence, image 298.

128. Letter, Postscript July 8, 1777, Fitzpatrick to his brother, "Camp upon Staten Island, July 5, 1777," Fitzpatrick Letters.

129. "Memoir by the Chevalier Dubuysson," September 12, 1777, Le Marquis de Lafayette, *Lafayette in the Age of the American Revolution, Selected Letters and Papers, 1776–1790*, vol. 1, edited by Stanley Idzerda, Robert R. Crout, Linda J. Pike, and Mary Ann Quinn (Ithaca, NY: Cornell University Press, 1977), 80. The purple sash was to be worn under the coat and over the shoulder. See Harold L. Peterson, *The Book of the Continental Soldier* (Harrisburg, PA: Stackpole Books, 1968), 242.

130. Note, John Heinn [Hunn] to John Hancock, "Cape May July 31 1777," Washington Papers online, ser. 4, General Correspondence, image 259; copy enclosed by Hancock in an MS Letter, Hancock to Washington, "Philada., 1 Augt. 1777. 7 o'clock PM," ibid., image 281. Hunn stated that this was the fifth express that he sent. In addition to Abraham Bennett and Benjamin Jones, the following individuals were paid seven pounds ten shillings for riding express between Philadelphia and Cape May: James Wilson, Matthew Weldon, and David Hand. Colonial Record, *Minutes*, 258–59.

131. Letter, Washington to Anthony Walton White, dated "Head Quarters Wilmington 1 August 1777." Chase, *Papers of Washington* 10, 485.

132. Letter, Washington to McDougall, "Chester on Delaware Augt. 1, 1777 10 Oclock P.M." Washington Papers online, ser. 4, General Correspondence, image 298.

133. Letter, Washington to Greene, "Head Q Chester August 1st 1777," written and signed by Alexander Hamilton, Washington Papers online, ser. 4, General Correspondence, image 294.

134. Von Münchhausen, *Diary*, 23.

135. Letter, Henry Fisher to ?, "Lewis Town, Aug. 2 1777. 8 o'clock, A.M.," quoted in *Pennsylvania Packet*, August 5. William James Morgan, ed., *Naval Documents of the American Revolution*, vol. 9 (Washington, DC: Naval History Division, Department of the Navy, 1980), 695–96.

136. Letter, Henry Laurens to John Lewis Gervais, "Philada., 5th August 1777," Smith, et. al., *Letters of Delegates*, vol. 7, 419.

137. Fisher, 440. Joseph Addison's *Cato* was one of the most popular British plays of the eighteenth century. It was a favorite of George Washington's and was performed by officers at the Valley Forge encampment in 1778. The line quoted is from act 1 scene 1, where two of Cato's sons speak. Joseph Addison, *Cato. A Tragedy* (London: Printed for the Booksellers, 1739), 204.

138. Letter, John Adams to Abigail Adams, "Philadelphia August 2, 1777 Saturday," Smith et. al., *Letters of Delegates*, vol. 7, 403.

139. Letter, James Lovell to William Whipple, "Friday August 1st 1777, 10 at night," Smith et. al., *Letters of Delegates*, vol. 7, 403.

140. Letter, Tench Tilghman to Col. Daniel Morgan, "Philada. 1st Augt. 1777," Washington Papers online, ser. 4, General Correspondence, image 315.

141. Letter, Wharton to Colonel Galbraith, "Philadelphia, 2nd August 1777," Hazard, *Pennsylvania Archives*, 480–81.

142. Pemberton Weather Data, 1777, American Philosophical Society, Philadelphia. Also U.S. Naval Observatory Astronomical Applications Department, aa.usno.navy.mil.

143. James McMichael, "Diary of Lt. James McMichael of the Pennsylvania Line, 1776–1778," *Pennsylvania Magazine of History and Biography* 16 (1892): 146. *The General* was a drum signal to strike camp and prepare for a march.

144. Fisher, 440.

145. Ibid., 440–41.

146. Pemberton Weather Data, 1777.

147. Fisher, 441.

148. Muhlenberg Orderly Book, entry "Germantown August 6 1777," *Pennsylvania Magazine of History and Biography* 34, 337.

149. McMichael, "Diary," 146.

150. Philip Katcher, *Uniforms of the Continental Army* (York, PA: George Shumway Publisher, 1981), 154–55; Martin, Joseph Plumb, *Private Yankee Doodle*, edited by George F. Scheer (Boston: Little, Brown and Co., 1962), 187. Lt. Col. St. George Tucker wrote on July 5, 1781, "At an entertainment given by the Marquis [de Lafayette] yesterday, I had the pleasure of seeing Col. [Walter] Stewart . . . He is the same pretty fellow that he ever was, and wears a plume almost as large as General Wayne himself. I wrote you before that the Pennsylvania line abounded in these decorations. I will venture to say that all the ostriches that ever appeared on the table of Heliogabalus would be insufficient to furnish the whole army in the same profuse style, for the feathers appear before you can well discover the shoulders to which the head that supports them is annexed." William Henry Egle, *Notes and Queries Historical and Genealogical, etc.*, vol. 2 (Harrisburg, PA: Harrisburg Publishing Company, 1895), 234–35. For visual confirmation of Stewart's personal appearance (including the above-described plume), see Charles Willson Peale's 1781 portrait of Stewart, reproduced in Charles F. Montgomery and Patricia Kane, *American Art: 1750–1800, Towards Independence* (New Haven, CT: Yale University Art Gallery, 1976), 95. Private Collection, Philadelphia Museum of Art.

151. McMichael, "Diary," 146.

152. Letter, Henry Laurens to John Loveday, "Philadelphia 9th August 1777," Smith et. al., *Letters of Delegates*, vol. 7, 449.

153. Letter, John Adams to Abigail Adams, "Philadelphia Aug. 6. 1777 Wednesday," Smith et. al., *Letters of Delegates*, vol. 7, 432.

154. Lafayette, *Letters and Papers*, vol. I, 91.

155. Pickering and Upham, *Life of Pickering*, vol. I, 150–51.

156. Fisher, 441.

157. Letter, James Lovell to William Whipple, "Philadelphia 11th Aug 1777," Smith et. al., *Letters of Delegates*, vol. 7, 459.

158. Letter, John Adams to Abigail, "Aug. 11.1777," Smith et. al., *Letters of Delegates*, vol. 7, 450.

159. Osborn Letters, 98.

160. "Narrative of Captain Andrew Snape Hamond," Morgan, *Naval Documents*, vol. 9, 363.

161. Von Münchhausen, *Diary*, 23.

162. Montrésor, *Montrésor Journals*, 434–35.

163. Letter, Cliffe to brother Jack, October 24, 1777. "Use brought us to relish our Salt Pork," i.e., "The circumstances made us learn to enjoy salt pork."

164. Letter, Grant to Harvey, "Head of Elk 31st August 1777," Grant Papers, reel 28/29.

165. Letter, Hale to his parents, "Head of Elk River, Maryland, 30th August 1777," Hale, "Letters," 21, 23.

166. Montrésor, *Montrésor Journals*, 435.

167. Von Feilitzsch, 12.

168. Osborn Letters, 98. In this same letter to his brother in Dresden, Osborn, the muster master general of the foreign troops, revealed that he did not speak or understand German: "How I envy your having been able to acquire the German language every day. I have an Harper on board, one of the Musick of the Regimen[t] de Ditforth, but I find no advantage but in the amusement of his musick."

169. Von Münchhausen, *Diary*, 23.

170. Letter, John Adams to Abigail Adams, "Philadelphia August 14, 1777," Smith et. al., *Letters of Delegates*, vol. 7, 479–80.

171. *Annual Register for 1777*, 126.

172. Muhlenberg, *Journals*, 66.

173. Montrésor, *Montrésor Journals*, 435.

174. Ronald Hoffman, Sally D. Mason, and Eleanor S. Carcy, eds., *Dear Papa, Dear Charley*, Letters of Charles Carroll of Annapolis and Charles Carroll of Carrollton, vol. 2 (Chapel Hill, NC: University of North Carolina Press, 2001), 1040.

175. Letter, John Adams to Abigail, "Phila. Aug. 13 1777," Smith et. al., *Letters of Delegates*, vol. 7, 474.

176. Letter, Adams to Abigail, August 14, 1777, Smith et. al., *Letters of Delegates*, vol. 7, 479–80.

177. Letter, Lee to Mann Page, "Philadelphia 17th Augt. 1777," Smith et. al., *Letters of Delegates*, vol. 7, 499.

178. Serle, *Journal*, 241–42.

179. Montrésor, *Montrésor Journals*, 436.

180. Robertson, *Diaries*, 141.

181. Parker Family Papers, August 16.

182. Letter, William Dansey to his mother, "In a Wood near Head of Elk, Maryland Aug 30th 1777," Dansey Papers.

183. Letter, Cliffe to brother Jack, October 24, 1777.

184. Osborn Letters, 98.

185. *London Chronicle* (November 18, 1777), 5, col. 1.

186. Serle, *Journal*, 245.

187. Montrésor, *Montrésor Journals*, 440–41, 438.

188. Von Feilitzsch, 15.

189. Boyle, *Thomas Sullivan Journal*, 125; von Münchhausen, *Diary* 23–24.

190. Montrésor, *Montrésor Journals*, 438. A butt is a 126-gallon cask.

191. Letter, John Adams to Abigail Adams, "Philadelphia August 29, 1777 Fryday," Smith et. al., *Letters of Delegates*, vol. 7, 567.

192. Letter, Charles Stuart to Lord Bute, "September 1777," *New Records*, 45.

193. Serle, *Journal*, 244.

194. "July 23rd, 1777: Annapolis has assumed a very different Appearance since Your Excellency left it." Extract of a letter from Mr. Eddis to Governor Eden, PRO Colonial Office 5/722, 9, quoted in Morgan, *Naval Documents*, 321–22.

195. Osborn Letters, 98.

196. Von Münchhausen, *Diary*, 26. Continental flags in this period did not follow any set pattern or fixed color scheme. It is possible that the red in the stripes was of a deep hue or the stripes were red, white, and blue. A contemporary British drawing of Fort Mifflin near Philadelphia shows a large flag with red, white, and blue stripes; were this the case with the Annapolis flags, the red and blue stripes together might appear as purple at a distance. None of the descriptions mention stars being on the Annapolis flags.

197. *London Chronicle* (November 18, 1777), 5, col. 1.

198. Minutes for Thursday, August 21, 1777, Brown, *Archives of Maryland*, vol. 16, 340.

199. Elmer T. Clark, J. Manning Potts, and Richard Morris, eds., *The Journal and Letters of Francis Asbury*, vol. 1, *The Journal, 1171–1793* (London: Epworth Press, 1958), 247. Asbury was sent to America by John Wesley in 1771 and is considered the leader in establishing the Methodist Church in America.

200. Letter, Col. Nathaniel Smith to Governor Johnson, "Baltimore the 22d. August 1777," Brown, *Archives of Maryland*, vol. 16, 340–41. In 1794, threatened by war with the British, "the fort at Whetstone Point was repaired by the inhabitants of the town, and the Star Fort of brickwork added. The ground was afterwards ceded to the United States, and the work called Fort McHenry, in honor of Colonel James McHenry of Maryland, then Secretary of War." J. Thomas Scharf, *The Chronicles of Baltimore, etc.* (Baltimore: Turnbull Brothers, 1874), 272.

201. Scharf, *Chronicles*, 166. "1769. Messrs. David Shields, James Cox, Gerard Hopkins, George Lindenberger, John Deaver and others, aided by a general subscription, procured an engine for the extinguishment of fires, which was called 'The Mechanical Company.'" Ibid., 64.

202. Letter, Mary Cox to Darby Lux, "Baltimore April 15, 1779," MS Collection 1909, James Cox Papers, Maryland Historical Society [MHS].

203. MS Notice, "Head Quarters the 24 August [1777], signed And. Buchanan," Cox Papers.

204. Letter, Benjamin Rumsey to Gov. Thos. Johnson, "24 Augt. 1777, Joppa," Brown, *Archives of Maryland*, vol. 16, 342–43.

205. Letter, Stuart to Lord Bute, "Chesapeake Bay, on Board a Transport, Aug. 21 1777," Morgan, *Naval Documents* 9, 780–81.

206. Parker Family Papers, entry for August 21.

207. Montrésor, *Montrésor Journals*, 442.

208. Letter, Grant to Harvey, "Head of Elk 31st August 1777," Grant Papers, reel 28/29.

209. Montrésor, *Montrésor Journals*, 441.

210. Letter, Aquila Hall to Governor Thomas Johnson, "Sunday 10 Oclock August the 24th 1777," Morgan, *Naval Documents* 9, 795.

211. Montrésor, *Montrésor Journals*, 441.

212. Letter, Grant to Harvey, "Head of Elk 31st August 1777", Grant Papers, reel 28/29.

213. Logbook, HMS *Isis*, entry for Sunday, August 24, 1777, ADM 52/1809, PRO, National Archives, Kew.

CHAPTER 3

1. Fisher, 443.

2. Letter, John Adams to Abigail, "Philadelphia August 20th 1777," Smith et. al., *Letters of Delegates*, vol. 7, 517.

3. Blockley Township is now the Overbrook and Wynnefield sections of West Philadelphia.

4. Hazard, *Pennsylvania Archives*, vol. 3, 118–19. "General Orders Reported by Town Major Lewis Nicola: August 12th, 1777. The Captain Commanding Colonel White's 4th Georgia Regiment must immediately send the Persons concerned in the murder of a Soldier, of said Regiment, to Philadelphia, under a Guard of a Serjeant, a Corporal and eight men. The Prisoners to be Hand-Cuffed and brought to the Town Major. The Surgeon and all other witnesses to attend at the same time." Hazard, *Pennsylvania Archives*, 548.

5. Marshall Remembrancer, entries for August 30 and September 6.

6. Letter, Percy to Polly Frazer, "Cross Roads Bucks County July [*sic*; August] 13/th, 1777," Frazer, *Frazer Memoir*, 151.

7. Letter, Walter Stewart to Horatio Gates, "Camp at Cross Roads, Augt. 13th, 1777," Gates Papers, film 23, reel 5, 62–63.

8. Letter, Richard Henry Lee to Landon Carter?, "Philadelphia 19th Aught 1777," Smith et. al., *Letters of Delegates*, vol. 7, 513–14.

9. Letter, Benjamin Harrison to Washington, "Philad. Augst. 20 1777," Smith et. al., *Letters of Delegates*, vol. 7, 519.

10. Muhlenberg, *Journals*, 69. According to the *Oxford English Dictionary*, a pelagian is "a believer in the doctrines of Pelagius or his followers, esp. in the denial

of the transmission of original sin, and in the principle that human will is capable of good without the assistance of divine grace."

11. Letter, Percy Frazer to Polly, "Graeme Park Augt. 21, 1777," Frazer, *Frazer Memoir*, 152.

12. Letter, John Adams to Abigail, "Philadelphia August 21, 1777," Smith et. al., *Letters of Delegates*, vol. 7, 521.

13. Letter, Chase to Johnson, "Philada. Augst. 23rd 1777," Smith et. al., *Letters of Delegates*, vol. 7, 534.

14. Letter, GW to Nash, "August 22, 1777 Sunset"; Letter, GW to Putnam "Head Qrs. Bucks County, August 22, 1777," Fitzpatrick, *Washington* 9, 115–16.

15. Resolution of Congress, "In Congress, Augt. 22nd, 1777," Hazard, *Pennsylvania Archives*, vol. 5, 539.

16. Letter, Percy Frazer to Polly, "Graeme Park Augt. 22nd, Night," Frazer, *Frazer Memoir*, 152.

17. Fisher, 443.

18. Letter, Dr. Rush to Wayne, "Philad. June 5th 1777," Stillé, *Wayne*, 69.

19. Letter, John Adams to Charles Adams, "Philadelphia 30 March 1777," Morgan, *Naval Documents* 8, 227–28.

20. Letter, Richard Henry Lee to Robert Morris, "Baltimore March 1, 1777," Morgan, *Naval Documents* 8, 10.

21. Colonial Records, *Minutes* 9, 278–79.

22. Letter, Percy Frazer to Polly, "Camp at the Cloves. July 18 1777," Frazer, *Frazer Memoir*, 149.

23. Graydon, *Memoirs*, 299–301.

24. Letter, GW to Hancock, "August 23, 1777," Fitzpatrick, *Washington* 9, 127–28.

25. Graydon, *Memoirs*, 307–8.

26. Letter, John Adams to Abigail, "Philadelphia August 23rd 1777," Smith et. al., *Letters of Delegates*, vol. 7, 533.

27. Letter, John Adams to Abigail, "Philadelphia August 1. 1777," Smith et. al., *Letters of Delegates*, vol. 7, 400.

28. Letter, John Adams to Abigail, "Philadelphia, August 24, 1777," Smith et. al., *Letters of Delegates*, vol. 7, 538.

29. General Orders August 23, 1777, Fitzpatrick, *Washington* 9, 127.

30. Letter, Henry Marchant to Nicholas Cooke, "Philadelphia August 24th 1777," Smith et. al., *Letters of Delegates*, vol. 7, 541.

31. Graydon, *Memoirs*, 308.

32. Letter, Christopher Marshall to his children, "Lancaster Augst. 25th, 1777," Marshall Letterbook, case 36, Historical Society of Pennsylvania, Philadelphia.

33. "Journal of H.M. Armed Ship *Vigilant*, Captain John Henry," Morgan, *Naval Documents*, vol. 9, 810.

34. Ibid., 811.

35. Von Münchhausen, *Diary*, 26.

36. Journal entry for August 29, Parker Family Papers, reel 2.

37. Von Münchhausen, *Diary*, 26.

38. Ewald, *Diary*, 75.

39. Grant to Harvey, August 31, 1777, reel 28, Grant Papers.

40. Letter, Murray to Mrs Smyth, "Head of Elke, Maryland, Sept. 1st 1777," Robson, *Letters*, 47.

41. Burgoyne, *Diaries*, 16.

42. Gruber, *Peebles Diary*, 127–28.

43. Letter, Fitzpatrick to the Countess of Ossory, "Head of Elk, September 1, 1777," *PMHB* 1 (1877): 289n.

44. Journal Entry for August 26, Parker Family Papers, reel 2. Words missing because of holes in manuscript are supplied in brackets.

45. Carl L. Baurmeister, *Letters from Major Baurmeister to Colonel von Jungkenn Written During the Philadelphia Campaign 1777–1778*, edited by Bernhard A. Uhlendorf and Edna Vosper (Philadelphia: Historical Society of Pennsylvania, 1937), 7.

46. Letter to his parents, "Head of Elk River, Maryland, 30th August 1777," Hale, "Letters," 21.

47. Burgoyne, *Enemy Views*, 171.

48. Montrésor, *Montrésor Journals*, 442.

49. Hale, "Letters," 21.

50. Montrésor, *Montrésor Journals*, 442.

51. Clark, Potts, and Morris, *Asbury Journal*, 247.

52. Serle, *Journal*, 246.

53. Montrésor, *Montrésor Journals*, 442, 443.

54. Carl L. Baurmeitser, *Revolution in America: Confidential Letters and Journals 1776–1784 of Adjutant General Major Baurmeister of the Hessian Forces*, translated and edited by Bernhard A. Uhlendorf (New Brunswick, NJ: Rutgers University Press, 1957), 98

55. Von Münchhausen, *Diary*, 28.

56. Serle, *Journal*, 245–46.

57. Baurmeister, *Letters*, 7.

58. André, *Journal*, 71.

59. Letter, Loftus Cliffe to his brother Jack, "Camp near Philadelphia 24 October 1777," Cliffe Papers. Nabobs were Englishmen who returned from India immensely rich, wallowing in luxury.

60. Kemble, *Journals*, 477–78.

61. Printed Proclamation "By His Excellency Sir William Howe, K. B., 27th Day of August 1777," André, *Journal*, 72, insert.

62. Ewald, *Diary*, 75.

63. Francis Downman, *The Services of Lieut.-Colonel Francis Downman, R.A . . . Between the Years 1758 and 1784*, edited by F.A. Whinyates (Woolwich: Royal Artillery Institution, 1898), 30.

64. Kemble, *Journals*, 479.

65. Baurmeister, *Letters*, 7.

66. Letter, Jesse Hollingsworth to Governor Johnson, "August 29th 4 P.M.," from "4 miles North of the Enemy's Camp on the high lands above the Head of Elk." Brown, *Archives of Maryland*, 349.

67. Ewald, *Diary*, 76.

68. Montrésor, *Montrésor Journals*, 443.

69. Grant, August 31, 1777.

70. Ewald, *Diary*, 76.

71. "Return of the Number of Men, Women & Children Victualled the 5th of September 1777 at the Head of Elk": Guides & Pioners 172 men, 3 wagons, 2 women, 2 children. Daniel Wier, *Copies of Letters from Danl. Wier, Esq., Commissary to the Army in America to J. Robinson, Esq., Secretary to the Lords Commissioners of the Treasury, and Copies of Letters from John Robinson, Esq., in Answer thereto in the Year 1777*, Letterbook 1777, Dreer Collection, case 36, Historical Society of Pennsylvania, Philadelphia.

72. Gilbert Purdy Diary, entry for August 28, "Memorandum of Lt. Gilbt. Purdy for the Year 1777," Z 20/C21/1975/U2, National Archives of Canada, Ottawa, Ontario.

73. Downman, *Services*, 30.

74. Montrésor, *Montrésor Journals*, 444.

75. Downman, *Services*, 30.

76. General Orders, "Head Quarters at Derby [Darby], August 24, 1777," Fitzpatrick, *Washington* 9, 129–30.

77. Boatner, *Encyclopedia*, 1054.

78. Letter, John Sullivan to Hancock, "Camp on Perkiomi September 27th 1777." Hammond, *Letters and Papers of Major-General John Sullivan*, vol. 1, 1771–1777 (Concord, NH: New Hampshire Historical Society, 1930), 549.

79. Letter, John Adams to Abigail, "Philadelphia August 26th, 1777," Smith et. al., *Letters of Delegates*, vol. 7, 554.

80. Pickering Journal, entry for August 26, 1777. Pickering Papers.

81. Lafayette, *Letters and Papers*, vol. 1, 92. The owner of the farmhouse was Robert Alexander, a Maryland Loyalist. Washington wrote to Landon Carter on October 27, "I assure you, that It is not my wish to avoid any danger which duty requires me to encounter[;] I can as confidently add, that it is not my intention

to run unnecessary risques. In the instance given by you, I was acting precisely in the line of my duty, but not in the dangerous situation you have been led to believe. I was reconnoitring, but I had a strong party of Horse with me. I was, (as I afterwards found) in a disaffected House at the head of Elk, but I was equally guarded agt friend and Foe." Chase, *Papers of Washington*, vol. 12, 26–27.

82. Von Münchhausen, *Diary*, 26.

83. McMichael, "Diary," 148.

84. Greene, *Papers* 2, 148.

85. Letter, Armstrong to Wharton, "Chester, 29th August 1777," Hazard, *Pennsylvania Archives*, vol. 5, 563–64.

86. Deposition of Pvt. James Patten, Pennsylvania Militia and Maxwell's Corps of Light Infantry, Revolutionary War Pension Files, film 27, National Archives, Washington, DC.

87. Von Münchhausen, *Diary*, 26.

88. Hale, "Letters," 22–23.

89. Letter, Dansey to his mother, "In a Wood near Head of Elk Maryland 30 August 1777," Dansey Papers.

90. Montrésor, *Montrésor Journals*, 443.

91. "Prisoners with the Rebels of the Detachmt. from the Brigade of Foot Guards, April 1778," Orders of British Troops.

92. Kemble, *Journals*, 480–81.

93. Charles Stuart, *A Prime Minister and His Son: From the Correspondence of the Third Earl of Bute and Lt. General The Honourable Sir Charles Stuart, KB*, edited by Mrs. E. Stuart Wortley (London: John Murray, 1925), 116.

94. Serle, *Journal*, 246.

95. Letter, Fitzpatrick, *PMHB* I, (1877): 289n. Sir John Fielding was one of the founders of London's first police patrols, the Bow Street Runners, founded about 1750. Jack Ketch was a seventeenth-century executioner famous for "bungled beheadings."

96. Gruber, *Peebles Diary*, 129.

97. Letter, Thompson to Paca and John Cadwallader, "Warwick, 30 Augt. 1777," MS Collection 1986, Maryland Historical Society.

98. Letter, Murray to Mrs. Betty Smyth, "Head of Elke, Maryland, 1st Sept. 1777," Robson, *Letters*, 48.

99. Fitzpatrick, *Washington* 9, 166–67; 162.

100. Montrésor, *Montrésor Journals*, 447.

101. General Orders, "Head Quarters, Wilmington, September 4, 1777," Fitzpatrick, *Washington* 9, 178–79.

102. Letter, Timothy Pickering to Mrs. [Rebecca] Pickering, "Wilmington, August 29th, 1777," Pickering and Upham, *Life of Pickering*, 152–53.

103. Letter, Stewart to Gates, "New Port [DE], September 2, 1777," Commager and Morris, *Spirit of Seventy Six*, 610.

104. John C. Dann, *The Revolution Remembered* (Chicago: The University of Chicago Press, 1980), 147.

105. Letter, Anthony Wayne to Polly, "Blue Bell [Tavern, near Darby], 26th Augt. 1777," Stillé, *Wayne*, 74.

106. Commager and Morris, *Spirit of Seventy Six*, 611. This is possibly the first documented use of the term "mad" in reference to Wayne, who acquired the nickname "Mad Anthony" by the end of the war.

107. Stillé, *Wayne*, 75–76.

108. Downman, *Services*, 32.

109. Montrésor, *Montrésor Journals*, 446.

110. Ewald, *Diary*, 77, 78.

111. Letter, Lt. Friedrich von Wangenheim to Baron von Wangenheim, "Camp at Amboy on Jersey, 24 June 1777," Bruce Burgoyne, "The Hesse Cassel Field Jager Corps," *Schwalm* 5, no. 3 (1995): 3.

112. "Journal kept by the Distinguished Hessian Field Jäger Corps, etc.," translated by Bruce Burgoyne, *Schwalm* 3, no. 3 (1987): 47.

113. Gruber, *Peebles Diary*, 129.

114. Baurmeister, *Revolution*, 102.

115. Purdy Diary, entry for September 3.

116. Montrésor, *Montrésor Journals*, 446–47.

117. "Revolutionary Pension Records of Morris Co. NJ," *Proceedings of the New Jersey Historical Society*, n. s., vol. 1 (1916). "About a year ago there was rescued from rubbish in Morristown a manuscript account book without covers which was found to contain court records of certificates presented by petitioners for pensions based upon Revolutionary War service . . . The dates run from 1779 to 1795" (89). "The deposition of Sarah Frost taken on oath . . . Saith that on the 22d day of Septr 1777 She the Said Deponant delivered Rachel Dallas the Wife of Archibald Dallas of her Son Archibald Dallas and further saith not.

"Whereupon the court adjudged that Rachel Cory late Widow of Archibald Dallas is entitled to the half pay of her late husband Capt. Archibald Dallas Deceased from the 5th. day of Sept. 1777, to the 28th day of January 1779 and that her Son Archibald Dallas or his Legal representative is entitled to draw the half pay of his Father Archibald Dallas from the said 28th day of January 1779, until he arrives at the age of eight years if he lives until that time which will terminate the 22d day of Sept. 1785" (95–96).

118. Capt. J. H. C. Smith, History of the 1st City Troop, based largely on the recollections of Trooper John Donnaldson, 1st City Troop Archives, Philadelphia.

119. Letter, Howe to Grant, "Aikins Tavern, Nine o'clock P. M., Wednesday, Sep. 3," Grant Papers, reel 37.

120. Letter, Washington to Hancock, "Wilmington, 8 o'clock P. M., September 3, 1777," Fitzpatrick, *Washington* 9, 173.

121. Lafayette, *Letters and Papers* 1, 94.

122. Letter, Henry Laurens to John Lewis Gervais, "5th September 1777," Smith et. al., *Letters of Delegates* 7, 612.

123. B. Floyd Flickinger, "The Diary of Lieutenant William Heth while a Prisoner in Quebec," *Annual Papers of Winchester Virginia Historical Society* 1 (1931): 33. Heth personally delivered a petition to Washington requesting that Maxwell be removed from command of the Light Infantry on September 30.

124. Cantelupe Diary, entry for September 3, 1777.

125. Osborn Letters, 100.

126. Gruber, *Peebles Diary*, 130.

127. Fitzpatrick, *Washington* 9, 181–82.

128. George Weedon, *Valley Forge Orderly Book of General George Weedon . . . 1777–78*, edited by Samuel Pennypacker (New York: Dodd, Mead and Company, 1902), 37–38.

129. Clark MS.

130. William Beatty Journal, 1776–1781. MS 1814, Maryland Historical Society.

131. Dann, *Revolution Remembered*, 147.

132. Ewald, *Diary*, 80.

133. Letter, Grant to Harvey, "Philadelphia 20th Octr. 1777," Grant Papers, reel 28.

134. Montrésor, *Montrésor Journals*, 448.

135. Rüffer, Regiment von Mirbach, *Enemy Views*, 172.

136. Parker Family Papers, journal entry for Sept. 8.

137. McMichael, "Diary," 149.

138. Ewald, *Diary*, 80.

139. Von Münchhausen, *Diary*, 30.

140. Henry Strike, "A British Officer's Revolutionary War Journal, 1776–1778," edited by S. Sydney Bradford, *Maryland Historical Magazine* 56, no. 2 (June 1961): 169.

141. Letter, William Dansey to his mother, "October 11, 1777" Manuscript Dept. HSD. The flag and Dansey's letters were acquired by the Historical Society of Delaware in the 1920s when the last of the Danseys died and the family possessions were sold at auction. Brinsop Court is still a farming estate in western England outside Hereford in Herefordshire, not far from the Welsh border. The house dates to the 1200s, and only five families have lived there in all that time, including the Danseys, who occupied it for 200-plus years.

According to the inscription on a memorial plaque found in Little Hereford Church, a few miles north of Leominster, Capt. Dansey Dansey died in 1774 at age sixty-six. He inherited the estate Brinsop Court from his uncle, Capt. William Dansey, "the last of that line," and he adopted the surname Dansey. The plaque was erected by his wife, Martha, and his only son, William. Capt. Dansey Dansey was a career soldier, as was son William, who died in Santo Domingo, as the following note in the Dansey papers indicates: "Sacred to the Memory of Catherine second Daughter of the Revd. Alexander Malet A. N. and Relict of William Dansey of Brinsop Court in the County of Hereford Esqr. Aid-de-Camp to His Majesty George the 3rd, Lieut. Colonel of the 49th Regiment, and Commandant of Cape Nicola Mole, in the Island of St. Domingo where he died Novr. 18th 1793, a victim to the Zeal with which he discharged his Duty regardless of the effects of an insalubrious and destructive climate. She died, Novr. 21st, 1825, Aged 81." Dansey Papers, HSD.

142. Ewald, *Diary*, 80.

143. Downman, *Services*, 32.

144. Letter, McKinly to Rodney, "Wilmington 9 Septr 1777," *Delaware Archives*, 1414–15.

145. Beatty Journal, 109.

146. Winslow C. Watson, *Men and Times of the Revolution; or, Memoirs of Elkannah Watson, etc.* (New York: Dana and Company, 1856), 61–62. [loc.gov Travels in America, 1750–1920]

147. Charles Biddle, *Autobiography of Charles Biddle, Vice-President of the Supreme Executive Council of Pennsylvania, 1745–1821* (Philadelphia: E. Claxton and Co., 1883), 148–49.

148. Ibid., 274.

149. Watson, *Men and Times*, 62.

150. Letter, Marshall to "Respected Ffriend, September 20, 1777," Marshall Letterbook, case 36.

151. Grant, October 20, 1777.

152. Ewald, *Diary*, 79–81.

153. Burgoyne, *Enemy Views*, 171.

154. Parker Family Papers, journal entry for September 9. The Caudine Forks was a deep gorge in Italy. During the Second Samnite War in 321 B.C., the Romans suffered a severe defeat after the Samnites, led by C. Pontius, blocked one end of the gorge, lured the Roman forces commanded by Posthumis into the trap, and then blocked the exit. The Roman Army was forced to accept a humiliating defeat without a battle. See Livy, *History of Rome*, book IX. The author is indebted to John Mackenzie of Britishbattles.com for his assistance in identifying this reference.

155. Montrésor, *Montrésor Journals*, 449.

CHAPTER 4

1. *Annual Register of 1776*, 166.

2. John C. Dann, *The Nagle Journal* (New York: Weidenfeld & Nicolson, 1988), 6.

3. Contemporary documentary evidence for this bridge is sketchy and uncertain. Von Knyphausen wrote Lord George Germain, "The Queen's Rangers were ordered to pass the Morass [at Chads's Ford] immediately . . . Whereupon the[y] ran off into the Wood near the creek on the Road to Chads's Ford. During this I had ordered the Brigades to follow over the Morass, The 4th and 5th Regt. to draw up to the left, across the Road to Brandywine Creek's Bridge & dislodge the Enemy in their Front. Brigadier General Cleveland posted two heavy & two light 12 pounders on the Height on this Road, & two Six pounders further downwards, where the 27th was placed. At 11 o'Clock the Ennemy were driven back over the Creek evacuating their very advantageous Posts of this Side—The most obstinate Resistance, they made was on the Road to Brandywine Creek's Bridge; but the gallant & spirited Behaviour of the 4th & 5th Regt. forced them soon to leave their Ground . . . I look upon it as my Duty, particularly to mention . . . the high Spirit & Ardour shewn by the 4th & 5th Regiment on *the Road to Brandywine Creek's Bridge* as well, as in the Attack upon the 1st Battery, which they forced." Letter, von Knyphausen to Germain, "Camp near Philadelphia Octbr. 21st 1777," CO 5/ 94, pt. 2, 442, PRO/British National Archives, Kew. This letter, written in English, while probably a translation from von Knyphausen's German or French, makes clear distinctions between Chads's Ford and Brandywine Creek Bridge. His description places it north of the ford, where the 4th and 5th Regiments were originally placed.

Tustin's translation of Capt. Johann Ewald's description refers to "the plank bridge." Ewald, however, was not with this column and based his description of this part of the battle on the accounts of others. While not a word-for-word copy, the similarity of Ewald's description to von Knyphausen's letter suggests that he wrote down the official headquarters version of this attack; this is a good source for someone attempting to keep a journal of events.

Later evidence is tantalizing, if elusive. When Lafayette returned to visit Brandywine on July 26, 1824, "The general received the greetings of the people, and viewed the interesting heights around Chads' Ford, and the field where the armies encamped the night before the battle, and pointed out the positions of Gens. Wayne and Maxwell's brigades. *He inquired if any one could point out where the bridge of rails was across the Brandywine, but no one was able to give him the information*" (Futhey and Cope, 130).

Finally, a topographical map prepared in December 1863 by Henry L. Whiting of the U.S. Coast Survey for the defense of Philadelphia (in case of another Confederate invasion), proposed fortifications near Chadds's Ford. The map marks the "Point where British crossed, in force, by Temporary bridge of trees and rails," located near the mouth of Brinton's Run, about half a mile below Brinton's Ford (http://memory.loc.gov/cgi-bin/map_item.pl, Library of Congress). The two-gun battery to the north of Chadds's Ford would have covered this position very well.

Unfortunately, no contemporary maps of the Battle of Brandywine show this bridge, and further primary documentation is elusive.

4. Pickering and Upham, *Life of Pickering,* 160.

5. Dann, *Revolution Remembered,* 149.

6. Greene, *Papers 2,* 154–56.

7. Letter, Cliffe to Brother Jack, October 24, 1777.

8. Hunter, *Journal,* 28.

9. Narrative, "Some account of the adventures of one day—the memorable September 11th, 1777, by Joseph Townsend of Baltimore. Some account of the British Army under the command of Genl. Howe and the battle of Brandywine which came to the knowledge and personal observation of the subscriber Joseph Townsend," in a cover labeled *A Manuscript Account of the Battle of Brandywine September 11th 1777 by Joseph Townsend,* with the inscription, "This was found among the effects of General Joshua Evans of Paoli[.] I think that it was published in 1846." MS 13292, Julius F. Sachse Collection, MS Collection, Chester County Historical Society.

Townsend's account was first published in 1846 by the Historical Society of Pennsylvania. That version is faithful to the original manuscript. The published version—in J. Smith Futhey and Gilbert Cope, *History of Chester County* (Philadelphia: Louis and Everts, 1881)—though essentially the same, has been edited and "corrected"; some wording and punctuation is different. For unknown reasons, words and phrases have been inserted, changing details here and there, resulting in distortion. Who inserted them or why is unknown; likewise, where the added information came from is not stated.

It is possible that Townsend wrote more than one manuscript. In January 2002, an anonymous eight-page manuscript narrative titled "A short sketch of the movement of General Howe's Army [insert: after he landed on Turkey Point at the head of the Chesapeak Bay] up to the 11th of September 1777" came up for bid at HCA Auction (item 0025) on the Internet. Excerpts of the narrative were published on the website, and it is clearly another version of Townsend's account. Attempts to acquire further information or a full transcript of the account went unanswered, and I don't know the present [2005] whereabouts of the manuscript.

Comparing the two published versions and the original manuscript, along with the primary accounts from other participants, it is clear that Futhey and Cope's editing has distorted much of the original. Hereafter, the text will rely on the original unedited manuscript, and the differences will appear in the notes.

10. Jacob Mordecai, "Addenda to Watson's Annals," *Pennsylvania Magazine of History and Biography* 98 (1974): 165.

11. Henry Lee, *Memoirs of the War in the Southern Department of the United States* (New York: University Publishing Company, 1869), 89.

12. Letter, Patrick Ferguson to George Ferguson, "Off Newcastle [DE] Octr. 18th 1777," quoted in DeWitt Bailey, *British Military Flintlock Rifles* (Lincoln, RI: Andrew Mowbray Publishers, 2002), 49.

13. Von Knyphausen to Germain.

14. Bailey, *British Flintlock Rifles*, 49.

15. Extract from the *Journal of Stephen Jarvis*, On-Line Institute for Advanced Loyalist Studies, www.royalprovincial.com, originally published in *Journal of American History* I (1907).

16. Flickinger, "Diary of Heth," 31.

17. Lee, *Memoirs*, 89.

18. Flickinger, "Diary of Heth," 31.

19. Bailey, *British Flintlock Rifles*, 49.

20. Ibid.

21. Parker Family Papers, journal entry for September 11.

22. Boyle, *Thomas Sullivan Journal*, 130.

23. Letter, Patrick Ferguson to George Ferguson, 8 Oct. 1777, Laing Manuscripts, 2, 456, University of Edinburgh, Scotland.

24. Letter, George Washington to the President of Congress, "Chads Ford, 5 O'Clock PM, September 11, 1777," Fitzpatrick, *Washington* 9, 206.

25. Bailey, *British Flintlock Rifles*, 49–50.

26. Parker Family Papers.

27. Boyle, *Thomas Sullivan Journal*, 131.

28. Downman, *Services*, 33.

29. Dann, *Nagle*, 8. The firing position described by Nagle was used by a British rifleman, Sgt. Thomas Plunkett of the 95th, in 1809. "On 3 January 1809, during the retreat to Corunna, Tom Plunkett of the 95th Rifles shot the French General Auguste Colbert. To do so, he lay on his back with the sling of his Baker rifle over his right foot, one of the positions taught for accurate shooting. When Colbert's orderly bravely charged to avenge his master, Plunkett reloaded in time to shoot him too." Caption of an illustration of the event, Richard Holmes, *Redcoat* (London: HarperCollins Publishers, 2001), 44.

30. Hugh F. Rankin, "An Officer out of His Time: Correspondence of Major Patrick Ferguson, 1779–1780, in *Sources of American Independence: Selected Manuscripts from the Collections of the William L. Clements Library*, edited by Howard Peckham, vol. 2 (Chicago: The University of Chicago Press, 1978), 299–301.

31. The Chevalier Dubuysson arrived near Charleston with "the Marquis de Lafayette, the Baron de Kalb, six officers, and two servants" on June 20, 1777. Dubuysson says that when they left for Philadelphia about June 25, "Our procession was led by one of the Marquis's servants, *dressed as a hussar*. The Marquis's carriage was a sort of uncovered settee, supported by four springs, with a forecarriage. Beside his carriage he had a servant on horseback, to perform the functions of a squire. The Baron de Kalb was in the same carriage. The two colonels, Lafayette's advisers, followed in a second two-wheeled carriage. The third carriage was for the aides-de-camp, and the fourth was for our baggage. The column ended with a Negro on horseback." Lafayette, *Letters and Papers*, vol. I, 73, 76.

32. Boyle, *Thomas Sullivan Journal*, 130–31.

33. John Marshall, *The Life of George Washington*, vol. 2 (New York: Wm. Wise, 1925), 299–300.

34. Boyle, *Thomas Sullivan Journal*, 131.

35. Dann, *Nagle*, 7.

36. Boyle, *Thomas Sullivan Journal*, 131. Court-Martial Testimony, March 31, 1778-PRO, W.O. 71: 85. Lieutenant Wilson was charged with cowardice on a later occasion, but several officers testified to his bravery. He was found innocent of the charge of cowardice but guilty of leaving his gun inappropriately.

37. Fitzpatrick, *Washington* 9, 206–7. Wilson's Orderly Book may be viewed online in the Washington Papers online, loc.gov.

38. Court-Martial Testimony, March 31, 1778-PRO, W.O. 71: 85.

39. The order of march is from "Correspondence of General von Knyphausen, Letter G, Microfiche 56, Hessian Papers," 72. The number and type of guns of the 3rd Brigade Artillery is from ibid., 65. The estimated troop strengths are from "Return of the Number of Men, Women & Children Victualled the 5th of September 1777 at the Head of Elk," Wier Letters. These numbers are rounded off, based on Commissary Wier's numbers given at Head of Elk a week earlier. The actual number of men fit for duty certainly would have been smaller, allowing for sickness, casualties, and not-uncommon inflation of commissary statistics. The total for these units based on Wier's figures is 9,200. Montrésor estimated 7,000, but he did not mention the 3rd and 4th British Brigades or the Hessian grenadiers. The actual numbers fit for duty were probably about 8,000.

40. Montrésor, *Montrésor Journals*, 449.

41. Ewald, *Diary*, 84.

42. Ibid., 83.

43. Hammond, *Sullivan*, vol. I, 549.

44. Letter, Grant to Harvey, "Philadelphia 20th Octr. 1777," Grant Papers, reel 28.

45. Letter, Sullivan to Hancock, "Camp at Perkiominy October 6, 1777," Hammond, *Sullivan*, 475–76.

46. This tract is now in Pocopson Township, which was formed in 1849 from parts of the surrounding townships. The Baily farm was later known as Bragg's Hill, and the road to the ford, now partially private, is called Bragg's Hill Road.

47. Joel Baily built large levels for the rods used in measuring distances. He also recorded daily temperatures for four months. See A. Hughlett Mason, *The Journal of Charles Mason and Jeremiah Dixon* (Philadelphia: American Philosophical Society, 1969), 58, 172, 173, 196. The temperature records were vital in measuring, for a brass standard rod had been sent from England, and several fir rods had also been sent. The survey required constant measurement of the rods against the standard, and the temperatures determined deviation in sizes as they expanded and contracted. Baily recorded the lowest temperature ever in Chester County, −22F in February, 1767. Charles Mason noted on June 21, 1767, "The height of the Fahrenheit Thermometer hung in the Shade on the North Side of a House standing on a Hill, about three Miles Eastward of Mr. Harland's. This is the same Thermometer as is taken account of for four months past by myself. The following [data] is by Mr. Joel Bayley [*sic*]." The "House standing on a Hill" was Baily's house, where Capt. Mountjoy Bayly, whose last name was alternately spelled Baily and Bayley, though he himself spelled it Bayly, encountered Joel on September 11, 1777.

48. Gilbert Cope, *Genealogy of the Baily Family . . . Descendants of Joel Baily* (Lancaster, PA: Wickersham Printing Co., 1912), 38–39. Mason and Dixon began their survey at John Harlan's house, located about two miles west of the Baily farm. There they placed the famous Star Gazer's Stone, marking the starting point to begin their measurements fifteen miles south to the east-west line. The survey lasted from 1764 to 1768, with Mason and Dixon returning to the Harlan House each winter to rest and go over their calculations. See also Arthur E. James, *Chester County Clocks and Their Makers* (Exton, PA: Schiffler Publishing Co., 1947).

49. Mountjoy Bayly served for years as doorkeeper of the Senate and sergeant-at-arms. "Mountjoy Bayley—Captain, 7th Maryland Regiment, Colonel John Gunby, Smallwood's Brigade, enlisted 3rd Dec. 1776, resigned 14 Sept. 1778," *Archives of Maryland, Muster Rolls etc. of the Maryland Troops in the American Rev-*

olution (Baltimore: Maryland Historical Society, 1900), 189. He died in 1836. Francis Heitman, *Historical Register of Officers of the Continental Army* (Baltimore: Genealogical Publishing Co., 1982), 81.

50. Futhey and Cope, *Chester County*, 80.

51. Ibid. This story of the encounter with Joel Baily came from Mountjoy Bayly by way of Dr. William Darlington, one of Chester County's earliest historians and a sometime member of Congress: "In the spring of 1822, during the session of the Seventeenth Congress, the compiler of these notes happened to be passing an evening with some friends at the residence of old Mountjoy Bayly, sergeant-at-arms of the United States Senate."

52. British Depredations Book, Chester County Historical Society.

53. The Revolutionary War's most famous private soldier, Joseph Plumb Martin of the 8th Connecticut Regiment, nicknamed "Private Yankee Doodle," visited this tavern in April 1778, while stationed at Downingtown on foraging duty during the Valley Forge encampment: "several of our party went to a tavern in the neighborhood. We here gambled a little for some liquor by throwing a small dart or stick, armed at one end with a pin, at a mark on the ceiling of the room. While I was at this amusement I found that the landlord and I bore the same name, and upon further discourse I found that he had a son about my age, whose given name was the same as mine. This son was taken prisoner at Fort Lee, on the Hudson River, in the year 1776, and died on his way home. These good people were almost willing to persuade themselves that I was their son. There were two very pretty girls, sisters to the deceased young man, who seemed wonderfully taken up with me, called me 'brother,' and I fared none the worse for my name. I used often, afterwards, in my cruises to that part of the state, to call in as I passed, and was always well treated by the whole family. The landlord used to fill my canteen with whiskey or peach or cider brandy to enable me, as he said, to climb the Welch mountains. I always went there with pleasure and left with regret. I often wished afterwards that I could find more namesakes." Martin, *Private Yankee Doodle*, 115. Joseph Martin Jr. in fact had not died; he was taken prisoner and finally came home in 1780 after being exchanged. One can only imagine the family's reaction to having a long-lost son, given up for dead, return to his family. He became a shoemaker and married Joel Baily's daughter Hannah in 1782.

54. Hazard, *Pennsylvania Archives* 5, 810.

55. Hammond, *Sullivan*, 476.

56. Washington Papers online, ser. 4, Correspondence, Sept–Oct. 1777, image 143. The notation after Ross's signature, "D. P. Regt." is a mystery; it may very well stand for "Dunlap's Pennsylvania Regiment" or possibly "Dunlap's Partizan Regiment." ("I have formed a Rifle Regt, and put a Coll. Dunlap at

the head of it, a prudent man, and not unacquainted with the business of a Partizan," Maj. Gen. John Armstrong told the Council on August 29. Hazard, *Pennsylvania Archives* 5, 563–64.)

On September 11, 1777, James Ross was the lieutenant colonel of the 8th Pennsylvania, promoted the previous June. Prior to that, he had served since the beginning of the war in the Pennsylvania Line with the same unit, the 1st Pennsylvania, which in 1777 was still largely a rifle regiment (captain, Thompson's Rifle Battalion, 1775; major, 1st Continental Regiment, 1776; lieutenant-colonel, 1st Pennsylvania, 1777). Capt. Michael Simpson had also served in the 1st Pennsylvania, and most of the 1st Pennsylvania continued to function as riflemen and were excellent scouts and skirmishers.

The conjecture is based on the following circumstantial evidence. The exact makeup of Dunlap's regiment is not known; it formed in late August 1777 and lasted barely a month. It was composed of 300 Pennsylvania militia riflemen, drawn from many sources. It would make sense to have them organized and led by experienced regular army officers, since Morgan's Rifle Corps had been sent to the Northern Army. Dunlap's was attached to Maxwell's LI Corps and may have been screening his right flank on the morning of September 11. This patrol would have been to the right of Maxwell's main body (posted near Kennett Meeting) when the Great Valley Road skirmish took place. Ross may have been put in command of this patrol because of his general knowledge of the area (he was from Lancaster, thirty miles west), dependability, and rifle expertise.

Further, Gen. Thomas Conway had proposed the following idea to the Council two weeks before Dunlap's regiment was formed: "15th August, 1777 . . . Having the honour to Command a Pennsylvania Brigade (3rd Brigade, 3rd, 6th, 9th, and 12 Pa. Regts.), I think it my Duty to inform you of the situation of the troops entrusted to me. The four Pennsylvania Regiments in Brigade are Very Weak—one is two hundred men strong, the three others are upon an average, one hundred and sixty . . . it is thought, with some foundation, *there a good many men have been Debauch'd by the Militia, where they have been persuaded to serve as substitutes*; this injures the army very much and makes it impossible for the Regiments to fill up; the militia, in general, hurt the army, and are absolutely good for nothing. I have seen it clearly in this campaign, it will arise chiefly from the foolish confidence putt in Militia . . . It is next to madness to imagine that undisciplined troops will make anything of a tolerable stand in the field against troops, any way officer'd and disciplined, therefore, my opinion is that you should attach to each Pennsylvania Regiment a Militia Company, During the remainder of the Campaign, under the Denomination of State Granedeers, or State Volunteers, or Light Infantry. I am sure they will render more service than six times the number of Militia together; proper regulations might be made to make this agreeable to the Militia, and it would do some service to the army, as I am pretty sure that the other States would soon follow the salutary example." Hazard, *Pennsylvania Archives* 5, 522–23. (Anthony Wayne told Washington on September 2, "Upon Mature Consideration I believe it will not answer to Annex the Militia to our Brigades—I wish it may not take place." Stillé, *Wayne*, 76.)

The italicized comment in Conway's letter indicates that some of the men serving in the militia did, in fact, have experience in the regular army; Graydon, Frazer, and others complained repeatedly of how difficult it was to raise Continental troops for full three-year enlistments when militiamen could serve shorter terms with better pay.

Regarding this issue in the summer of 1777, Graydon later wrote, "Uniforms and epaulets, with militia titles and paper money, making numbers of persons gentlemen who had never been so before, kept up every where throughout the country the spirit of opposition; and, if these were not real patriotism, they were very good substitutes for it. Could there, in fact, be any comparison between the condition of a daily drudge in agricultural and mechanical labour, and that of a spruce militia-man living without work, and, at the same time, having plenty of continental dollars in his pocket! How could he be otherwise than well affected to such a cause!" Graydon, *Memoirs*, 301–2.

57. Printed in England in the *Gazette and New Daily Advertiser* (November 21, 1777), 2, cols. 3, 4; headed "Boston, October 2," probably from the *Independent Chronicle*, Boston. This letter "By a Gentleman of Distinction" was widely published in America and made its way to England. It contained criticism of Sullivan that effectively smeared that general's reputation and led to a second court of inquiry into Sullivan's conduct. Burke revealed himself as the author after Sullivan fired off indignant letters to Congress.

58. Lafayette, *Letters and Papers* I, 94. James Parker told Charles Steuart, "Sept. 12: I was told by a [captured?] Rebel, that during the interval Yesterday, Washington rode twice along the line, he told those in the Center where this man was, that our troops were ——— to the right . . ." Parker Family Papers, reel 2.

59. Dispatch, Washington to Bland, "Chads ford 11th Septr. 1777 20 Mints. after [—] O'Clock," Autograph Collection, CCHS. The critical time on this note is missing, as the heading is crammed into the upper right corner of the document, some of which is missing, thus rendering parts of the inscription illegible. A notation on the bottom, written in another hand, labels this paper as "Orders written during the battle of Brandywine hour and minute 20 minutes to 4 oclock." The contents of this message and subsequent events of the battle makes 3:40 P.M. highly unlikely, since Washington had already ordered three divisions to move out nearly two hours earlier in response to Bland's note of 1:15 P.M. This

message may also have been written subsequent to Squire Cheyney's arrival and information. Firm documentation of Cheyney's story remains elusive.

60. Futhey and Cope, *Chester County*, 80. This anecdote was collected and recorded by Chester County's first historian, Dr. William Darlington, ca. 1800. Parker's primary account is a remarkable confirmation of what might otherwise be considered an apocryphal tale.

61. Parker Family Papers, reel 2.

62. Hammond, *Sullivan*, 475–76.

63. Pickering Papers, reel 52, 184–85.

64. Pickering and Upham, *Life of Pickering*, vol. 2, 81.

65. "The Papers of General Samuel Smith," *Historical Magazine* 7, 2nd ser., no. 2 (1870): 85.

66. Von Donop, *Journal of the Hessian Corps*, Letter Z, Hessian Corps Report, 83–87.

67. Letter, Sullivan to Hancock, "Camp at Perkiominy October 6th 1777," Hammond, *Sullivan*, 475–76.

68. Ibid.

69. Washington Papers online, ser. 4, Correspondence, Sept–Oct. 1777, image 145.

70. Letter, George Washington to J. Sullivan, "Head Quarters October 24th 1777," Washington Papers online, ser. 3b, Varick Transcripts, Letter Book 4, images 223–24. Congressman Thomas Burke, who was present at Brandywine and extremely critical of Sullivan, wrote on September 17, "General Sullivan was informed by a Country man, a Major of Militia, that he had come along the road which immediately led from that ford and had seen no Enemy, where-upon he dispatched Information to General Washington that he was Convinced from the Countryman's Intelligence that no Enemy was upon that Rout[e] . . . [Sullivan] relied on the Information of a Country man who passed along One road while the Enemy were marching on the other." Letter, Thomas Burke to Richard Caswell, "Philadelphia Sept 17, 1777," Smith et. al., *Letters of Delegates* 7, 680–81.

71. Von Donop, *Journal of the Hessian Corps*, Letter Z, Hessian Corps Report, 83–87.

72. Ewald, *Diary*, 84.

73. Townsend MS.

74. Ibid.

75. Map key, Archibald Robertson, Battle of Brandywine, manuscript map, RCIN 734026.A, King's Map Collection, Royal Library, Windsor Castle, UK.

76. Townsend MS. The Futhey and Cope published version gives a consid-erably different spacing of the British force: "The space occupied by the main

body and the flanking parties was near half a mile wide." Futhey and Cope, *Chester County*, 75.

77. Townsend MS.

78. Washington Papers online, ser. 4, General Correspondence, image 131.

79. Ibid., image 147.

80. Pickering Papers, reel 52, 184–85.

81. Robertson Map Key.

82. British Journal 1776–1778, Journal of Officer B, Sol Feinstone Collection, David Library of the American Revolution. The contents of the journal indicate that he was an officer of the 17th Light Company.

83. Von Münchhausen, *Diary*, 31.

84. Hammond, *Sullivan*, 463.

85. Letter, von Knyphausen to Germain, dated "Camp near Philadelphia Octbr 21st 1777," PRO, CO/94: 440.

86. Baurmeister, *Letters*, 11–15.

87. Von Münchhausen, *Diary*, 31. Some later American writers have derided this halt as "stopping for lunch," "halting because it was dinner time," or worse yet, the British "stopping for tea," pandering to ridiculous stereotypes. In fact, given the length of the march, the heat, and the hilly terrain, attempting any sort of attack without food and rest at this stage would have been unthinkable. Rested, fed, and well-motivated troops perform surprisingly better than exhausted, famished, and coerced soldiers, as the subsequent attack so clearly demonstrated.

88. Montrésor, *Montrésor Journals*, 449.

89. Letter, Cliffe to Jack, October 24, 1777.

90. Hale, Letter to his parents, "Philadelphia 23 March 1778," Hale, "Letters," 37.

91. Officer B.

92. Ewald, *Diary*, 84.

93. Von Donop, *Journal of the Hessian Corps*, Letter Z.

94. Lee, *Memoirs*, 89–90.

95. Officer B, attached memo.

96. Ewald, *Diary*, 85.

97. Officer B, attached memo.

98. Ewald, *Diary*, 85–86.

99. Hammond, *Sullivan*, 463.

100. Ewald, *Diary*, 86.

101. Letter, Lt. Col. Ludwig von Wurmb to Gen. Friedrich von Jungkenn, Court Chamberlain of Hessen Kassel, "In Camp at Schuylkill Falls, Five miles from Philadelphia, 14 October 1777"; Henry Retzer and Donald Londahl-

Smidt, "The Philadelphia Campaign, 1777–1778: Letters and Reports from the von Jungkenn Papers. Part I– 1777," *Schwalm* 6, no. 2 (1998): 10.

102. Townsend MS. "Which was a novelty in that part of the country" is added to the sentence in the Futhey and Cope version. Futhey & Cope, *Chester County*, 75–76. Mustaches were such an ingrained feature of German soldiers in the eighteenth century that to this day, men of the pacifist Amish faith grow beards after marriage in accordance with the Old Testament but do not wear mustaches as an avoidance of pride and militarism. For the same reason, the men of this community, who were severely persecuted in the seventeenth and eighteenth centuries in Germany and Switzerland for refusing military service, do not wear lapels or buttons on their coats.

103. Von Münchhausen, *Diary*, 31.

104. Hesse-Cassel Jäger Corps Report, Burgoyne, *Enemy Views*, 173–74.

105. Attached to the 17th Regiment officer's journal is a manuscript list of questions and comments headed "Examination of the Dundass System, answered according to the practice of the 1st Battalion Light Infantry," attached to a Memorandum on the Battle of Brandywine: "Number of ranks: [*Dundass: Company to form three deep*]. Answer: Usual order two men. Men instructed to form single rank or four deep. [*Dundass: Distance of files—Files lightly to touch*]. Answer: Files by day always loose; usual order 11 inches. Open order arms Length; extended order from five yards to fifty." British Journal 1776–1778, Notes of a Light Infantry Officer of the 17th Regiment of Foot, Sol Feinstone Collection, David Library of the American Revolution.

106. "The Brigade of Guards have always been with the advanced part of the army . . . at the battle of Brandywine we attacked the left flank of the rebel army . . . *I had but one Grenadier wounded, the Light Company who were with me had only three . . . I was ordered the night after [Paoli] to pass the —— [Schuylkill] with the Light Company and Grenadiers of the Guards only . . .*" George to John Osborn, "Camp near —— [Germantown?] September 30, 1777," Osborn Letters, no. 100.

107. Townsend MS. The version published in Futhey and Cope says that Townsend and his companions went into the field *southwest* of the road; the manuscript says "southeast," as does the 1846 published account. This is significant in the sense that Townsend later says that a German officer ordered him to take down bars of a fence along Birmingham Road to let troops through. If he was, in fact, west or southwest of the road, he would have been in the path of the British grenadiers. Here, on the east or southeast side of the road, he was faced with the Hessian and Anspach Jägers and British light infantry. The German officer was probably a Jäger officer.

108. Townsend MS.

109. Ewald, *Diary*, 86.

110. Townsend MS. The Futhey and Cope published account says, "Samuel Jones's *brick* dwelling-house" and "Hessians, who, *stepping up* the bank of the road . . ." Futhey & Cope, *Chester County*, 76. The Jones house, much modified in the mid-nineteenth century, still stands, its eighteenth-century brick shell encased in a white stucco Victorian Italianate country villa.

111. Townsend MS. The Futhey and Cope published version says, "a German officer, on horseback." Futhey & Cope, *Chester County*, 76. Again, the details included or left out by editing can change the whole picture. Perhaps the officer was mounted, which would make him a high-ranking officer, such as Lieutenant Colonel von Wurmb. Or he may have also been on foot, as many of the junior officers were. In Tustin's translation of Ewald's diary, he speculates, not unreasonably, in note 65 (p. 393) that the officer may have been Ewald. This is unlikely, however, as Ewald was up ahead at the orchard with a handful of Jägers, and this was the main body of light troops deploying for battle several hundred yards away, as Townsend's account demonstrates.

112. Townsend manuscript.

113. Thomas Glyn, "Ensign Glyn's Journal on the American Service with the Detachment of 1,000 Men of the Guards," entry for August 18, 1776, Princeton University Library, Princeton, New Jersey.

114. Huth, "Letters," 499.

115. Microfiche #232, letter K, Journal of the Hessian Grenadier Battalion von Minnegerode.

116. "CADENCE, in *tactics*, implies a very regular and uniform method of marching, by the drum and music, beating time: it may not be improperly called mathematical marching; for after the length of the step is determined, the time and distance may be found. *It is by a continual practice and attention to this, that the Prussians have arrived at that point of perfection, so much admired in their evolutions*" [emphasis added]. Smith, *Universal Military Dictionary*, 38.

117. An anonymous British officer echoed similar sentiments in a letter published in London in early 1777 (and reprinted in the *Pennsylvania Packet* in 1778): "From the LONDON MAGAZINE, for April 1777. The following letter, whilst it confesses the excesses and desolations committed last winter in New Jersey, by the army under General Howe, shews what opinion the British officers entertain of their German auxiliaries. It is plainly the effusion of an English officer.[:] 'You will easily imagine, that, differing as we do in language, manners and ideas, English and Hessians did not coalesce into one corps; not but that there was great communication and constant visiting, especially among the principal officers; but these were rather national civilities than personal kindnesses, and our younger people hardly kept up any communication with them at all. That rather affected to despise the thriftiness of the Hessian prudence,

as a something base and sordid. *The Hessian, naturally fierce, was not backward to return the disdain, and affected to consider the volatile spirit with which our youngsters went to war, as unsoldierly, and talked of themselves as the body on whom the success of the war was to depend'"* [emphasis added]. *Pennsylvania Packet,* January 7, 1778, Accessible Archives online, Item #61522.

118. "Of the von Linsing Battalion, Lieutenants Dupuy and von Baumbach were slightly wounded, and some noncommissioned officers besides; the von Lengerke Battalion lost a fine grenadier, who was suffocated during the attack on account of the rapid march and the great heat." Microfiche 334, Letter Z, Reports to General von Ditfurth, 198–99.

119. Letter, Hale to his parents, "Philadelphia, 23rd March 1778," Hale, "Letters," 36.

120. Glyn, 11–11a.

121. Letter, Loftus Cliffe to brother Jack, "Camp York Island [Manhattan] September 21st 1776," Cliffe Papers.

122. Letter, Grant to Harvey, "Philadelphia 20th Octr. 1777," Grant Papers, reel 37.

123. Hunter, *Journal,* 29–30.

124. Joseph Townsend returned to Osborne's Hill once the attack was under way. He recalled, "part of some of the fields in front of us contained great heaps of blankets and bagage thrown together to relieve the men for action." Townsend MS.

125. Von Münchhausen, *Diary,* 31–32.

126. Hunter, *Journal,* 29–30. Hunter inadvertently included the Guards and grenadiers together as one column.

127. "Song CXXI, The British Grenadiers," *The Musical Miscellany: A Selection of Scots, English, and Irish Songs, set to Music* (Perth, Scotland: Printed by J. Brown, 1786), 232–33. As with many songs of the period ("Yankee Doodle," for example), the words, tune, and tempo have changed over the years, and even contemporary versions have variations. Occasionally the question arises among students and scholars of this period as to whether "The Grenadiers March" and "The British Grenadiers" are the same tune, since there were and are, in fact, two distinctly different tunes with these titles still in use by the British Army. "The Grenadiers March," also called "The Grenadiers March Past," is a solemn, slow march in three-quarter time, used for Trooping of the Colours, whereas "The British Grenadiers" is a lively, two-two quickstep. See B. Bruce-Briggs, "'The Grenadiers March' in Colonial Massachusetts," *Notes and Documents of Journal of the Society for Army Historical Research* 81, no. 57 (Autumn, 2003): 282–83, n. 1678, where this question is satisfactorily answered with contemporary songs and titles, including patriotic songs with American words, such as "A Song on Lib-

erty" and "Gen. Washington" ("War and Washington"). The tune played at Brandywine was, no doubt, "The British Grenadiers." Two more verses of this song appear on the next page.

128. Hale, "Letters," 24.

129. Hunter, *Journal*, 29–30.

130. See Parker Journal entry for September 12 for the names of guns captured at Brandywine. "Ultima Ratio Regum" is found on most French cannon barrels of the period.

131. The original, arcane text reads, "Soon atter [after] the Line Wass formed the Army Moved on to Wards the Hights on Which Enemy Wass posted on. The first Line attacked Instantly which the Enemy advance Line gave Way our army Still gained ground all the [although] they had great Advantig of Ground and ther Canon keep a Constant fire on us. Yet We Near [ne'er] Wass danted." Memmorandum List for 1777, Washington Papers online. This anonymous officer was probably from the 2nd Battalion of Light Infantry.

132. Officer B.

133. "Extracts from the Journal of Surgeon Ebenezer Elmer of the New Jersey Continental Line, September 11–19, 1777," *Pennsylvania Magazine of History and Biography* 35 (1911): 104–5.

134. *Schwalm* 6, no. 2 (1998): 10.

135. Burgoyne, *Enemy Views*, 173–74.

136. Officer B, attached memo; Ewald, *Diary*, 86.

137. Officer B, attached memo.

138. Lee, *Memoirs*, 89–90.

139. Flickinger, "Diary of Heth," 31–32.

140. Lee, *Memoirs*, 89–90.

141. Montrésor, *Montrésor Journals*, 450.

142. Letter, "From the Camp on the Field of Battle near Delworth on the heights of Brandy Wine September 11th at Night," Wayne Papers, vol. 4. This unsigned and unfinished letter was captured by Wayne's forces after they overran the camp of the 2nd Light Infantry Battalion at Germantown on October 4. After careful, exhaustive research, Steve Gilbert of Wisconsin was able to conclude from clues found in the text that the author was Lt. Richard St. George Mansergh St. George of the 52nd Light Company, who was wounded in the head at Germantown. See Hunter's *Journal*.

143. Hunter, *Journal*, 29–30.

144. "Hesse-Cassel Jäger Corps Journal," Burgoyne, *Enemy Views*, 173–74.

145. In describing the cold reception that Lafayette and his party had at Congress in July, Dubuysson commented, "We rightly attributed it to the bad conduct of the Frenchmen who preceded us," and included "the contempt felt

for M. de Borre, also French, by all the officers of his brigade." Lafayette, *Letters and Papers* 1, 77.

146. Letter, "Copy of the Letters Wrote to Congress by the Chl [Chevalier] De Preudhomme DeBorre, Trenton the 17 September 1777," Washington Papers online, ser. 4, General Correspondence, September 1777, images 341–42.

147. Flickinger, "Diary of Heth," 31.

148. Letter, Sullivan to J. Adams, "Camp on Perkiomy [Perkiomen], Sept. 28, 1777," Hammond, *Sullivan*, 471.

149. Ibid., 462–63.

150. Letter, Burke to Caswell, "Philadelphia Sept. 17th, 1777," Smith et. al. *Letters of Delegates* 7, 680.

151. *Annual Register for 1777*, 128. Cynics might be tempted to regard any British praise for Sullivan as gratuitous sarcasm or condescension, since some Americans considered his "incompetence" the reason for British success. The British accounts rightly point to the quality and spirit of their own troops as the reason for success against an American army that was growing stronger and better through hard experience.

152. To Messieurs Powars & Willis Printer in Boston: ". . . I observe in your paper of the 2nd of October you have published Extracts of a Letter from a Gentleman of Distinction in Philadelphia to his Friend in Boston Dated September 15th 1777 Respecting the Battle of Brandywine which is perhaps as Replete with misrepresentation as any yet published." Hammond, *Sullivan*, 472–74.

153. DeBorre, Washington Papers online.

154. Hammond, *Sullivan*, 463–64.

155. Conway's Testimony for Sullivan, "Given under my Hand at Flatland Camp [Fatland Ford] the Twenty day of September 1777," Hammond, *Sullivan*, 555–56.

156. Von Münchhausen, *Diary*, 31.

157. Hammond, *Sullivan*, 464.

158. Ibid., 555–56. "M. de Conway, brigadier general, is detested by the officers of his brigade and envied by all the generals, including Washington, because he makes his brigade work and personally drills and instructs it, instead of leaving it idle in camp." Memoir of Chevalier Dubuysson (who accompanied Lafayette to America), Lafayette, *Letters and Papers* 1, 79.

159. Lafayette, *Letters and Papers* 1, 94.

160. Letter, Col. John Stone to William Paca, "Camp in Philadelphia, County Schuylkill, September 23d, 1777," in Scharf, *Chronicles*, 166–68.

161. Lafayette, *Letters and Papers* 1, 94–95.

162. Stone to Paca, Scharf, *Chronicles*, 166–68.

163. "Papers of Gen. Samuel Smith," 85.

164. DeBorre, Washington Papers online.

165. Stone to Paca, Scharf, *Chronicles*, 166–68.

166. "Papers of Gen. Samuel Smith," 86.

167. DeBorre, Washington Papers online.

168. Stone to Paca, Scharf, *Chronicles*, 166–68.

169. "Journal of Sgt. Maj. John Hawkins," in "Notes and Queries," *Pennsylvania Magazine of History and Biography* 20 (1896): 420–21.

170. "Papers of Gen. Samuel Smith," 86.

171. Robertson Map Key.

172. Osborn Letters 3, 100. In mentioning Maxwell, Osborn was probably referring to the American light troops at Chads's Ford, where the 1st Battalion of Guards ended up. It is also possible that he refers to Maxwell's New Jersey Brigade in Stirling's line.

An extraordinary document in the U.S. National Archives provides documentation about Guards casualties and just how much ammunition each company expended at Brandywine.

"Return of the Number of Cartridges Wanting to Compleat the Brigade of Guards to 60 Rounds Per Man 12th Septemr. 1777.

Grenadiers:	1000	[124]	8 shots per man
Hyde's:	420	[93]	5 shots per man
Wrottesley's:	800	[91]	9 shots per man
Cox's:	840	[90]	9 shots per man
Garth's:	1000	[90]	11 shots per man
1st Battn. total	4060	[488]	8–9 shots per man
Stephen's:	250	[88]	3 shots per man
Murray's:	200	[89]	2 shots per man
O'Hara's:	439	[87]	5 shots per man
Martin's:	470	[91]	5 shots per man
Lt. Infantry:	500	[96]	5 shots per man
2nd Battn. total	1859	[451]	4 shots per man
Brigade total	**5919**	**[939]**	**6–7 shots per man**

Return of Killed, Wounded, Missing: 1 Killed, 5 Wounded, 2 Missing

Orders of British Troops, film 9, reel 1.

173. Cantelupe diary.

174. Hammond, *Sullivan*, 464.

175. "List of Officers Killed Since the Commencement of the War &c.: Compiled by Capt. George Inman, 1784, George Inman's Narrative of the American Revolution," *Pennsylvania Magazine of History and Biography* 7 (1883): 237–48; *Remembrancer of 1777*, 417.

176. Officer B, attached memo.

177. Officer B.

178. Officer B, attached memo.

179. Hammond, *Sullivan*, 464.

180. Futhey and Cope, *Chester County*, 79. McClellan's father was James McClellan, who operated a tavern in Salisbury Township (now Parkesburg). McClellan was one of the chief dignitaries who escorted Lafayette during his return in 1824. The statement that officers were later issued spontoons is correct. The spontoon, or espontoon, was a half-pike, or ornamental spear, usually seven or so feet long. British officers carried them when the war began, but finding that it made them too conspicuous, they changed to fusils. The American forces did the opposite: Finding that officers' loading and firing distracted them from their duty, directives went out in 1778 that officers were not to carry firearms, but spontoons. The spontoon allowed the officer to be seen by his men, provided him with a large pointer or a way to keep his men in alignment, and served as a weapon at close quarters.

181. Officer B.

182. Ibid.

183. Daniel Agnew, "A Biographical Sketch of Governor Richard Howell of New Jersey," *Pennsylvania Magazine of History and Biography* 22 (1898): 224.

184. Smith, *Universal Military Dictionary*, 90.

185. Parker MS. The original text reads, "I visited my friends of the Queens/[Rangers] who had Suffered [wounds?] when I was delighted with the platoons of Genl. Howe on the [rebels'? rig]ht." The words in brackets have been supplied and the brackets removed for clarity in the text.

186. Extract of a Letter, Chambers to Gen. Edward Hand, Hazard, *Pennsylvania Archives* 2, 322–23.

187. John T. Hayes, *A Gentleman of Fortune: The Diary of Baylor Hill, First Continental Light Dragoons, 1777–1781*, vol. I (Fort Lauderdale, FL: The Saddlebag Press, 1995), 70.

188. Letter, Henry Marchant to Rhode Island Governor and Assembly, "Philadelphia Sepr. 17th, 1777," Smith et. al. *Letters of Delegates* 7, 689; Letter, Elbridge Gerry to James Warren, "Philadelphia Sepr 17, 1777," Smith et. al. *Letters of Delegates* 7, 683–84; Letter, Williams to Trumbull, "Philadela. Sepr. 13th, 1777, Saturd. Eveng.," Smith et. al. *Letters of Delegates* 7, 657.

189. Von Münchhausen, *Diary*, 31–32.

190. Robertson Map Key.

191. Montrésor, *Montrésor Journals*, 450.

192. Lushington, *Harris*, 66–67.

193. Lee, *Memoirs*, 90.

194. Lushington, *Harris*, 66–67.

195. Hammond, *Sullivan*, 460–65.

196. Lafayette, *Letters and Papers* I, 94–96.

197. Hammond, *Sullivan*, 460–65.

198. Officer B, attached memo.

199. "Memorial of Capt. Charles Cochrane," written for Lord Germain, *Proceedings of the Massachusetts Historical Society* 6, 2nd ser. (1891): 434–35.

200. Officer B, attached memo.

201. Stuart, *A Prime Minister and His Son*, 108.

202. Ibid., 116–17.

203. Officer B, attached memo.

204. Robertson Map Key.

205. Elmer, "Extracts," 104–5. In the original text, Elmer uses the archaic *ye* for "the" and *ym* for "them": *Ye* is still understood by modern readers, but I have taken the liberty of changing the less-familiar *ym* to 'em for the sake of clarity.

206. "London, December 18: Extract of a letter from an Officer at Philadelphia to his friend at Edinburgh, dated Oct. 27," *Felix Farley's Bristol Journal* 26, no. 1400 (December 26, 1777), British Library.

207. Clark Diary, MS MG 256.

208. Lafayette, *Letters and Papers* I, 83–84.

209. Ibid., 95, 114.

210. Letters, William Dansey to Mrs. Dansey Dansey, "Camp at German Town, Philadelphia Octor 9th 1777"; Dansey to Dansey, October 16, 1777, Historical Society of Delaware.

211. Futhey and Cope, *Chester County*, 78.

212. Agnew, "Howell," 224.

213. Elias Dayton Papers, New Jersey Historical Society, Ryan, *Salute to Courage*, 100.

214. Robertson Map Key.

215. Von Münchhausen, *Diary*, 32.

216. Burgoyne, *Diaries*, 18.

217. Von Wurmb to von Jungkenn, *Schwalm* 6, no. 2 (1998): 10. For clarity, the word *disrupted* has replaced the obscure word *inaccommodated* in the text of the published translation.

218. Jorn Meiners, "Portraits of Hessian Jäger Officers in the Museum of Marburg University," translated by Henry J. Retzer, *Schwalm* 7, no. 4 (2004): 16.

219. Ewald, *Diary*, 86.

220. Von Wurmb to von Jungkenn, *Schwalm* 6, no. 2 (1998): 10.

221. Burgoyne, *Enemy Views*, 173–74. Ewald specifically mentions the use of *Allons! Allons!* at the Battle of Monmouth (136), but it was a favorite and famous shout among German troops, even though it is French. Frederick the Great used French in his court (as did most European monarchs) and introduced the highest military decoration, *Pour la virtue Militaire*, used by Prussian and German military forces for the next two centuries. Ewald, von Wurmb, and von Wreden were all awarded this decoration on June 16, 1777, by the landgraf of Hesse-Cassel. *Schwalm* 7, no. 4 (2004): 18.

Of the word *huzza*, the Oxford English Dictionary etymology notes that it was used in the seventeenth and eighteenth centuries and probably derives from a sailor's shout of greeting. It also says, "German has also '*hussa*' as a cry of hunting and pursuit, and, subsequently, exaltation."

222. Hunter, *Journal*, 29–30.

223. Von Wurmb to von Jungkenn, *Schwalm* 6, no. 2 (1998): 10.

224. Burgoyne, *Diaries*, 18. Casualties are taken from the Journal of the Hessian Jäger Corps. See Ewald, *Diary*, 394, n. 80.

225. Hammond, *Sullivan*, 460–65.

226. Letter, Dr. William Darlington to Dr. A. Elwyn, "West Chester, Nov. 29, 1845," *Proceedings of the Historical Society of Pennsylvania* 1, no. 8 (December, 1846): 57.

227. Von Münchhausen, *Diary*, 32.

228. Letter, Robert H. Harrison to John Hancock, "Chads ford 5 oClock PM 11 Septr 1777," Washington Papers online, ser. 4, General Correspondence, image 136–37. Robert Hanson Harrison was "the best of all the aides at communicating Washington's ideas. The general frequently entrusted Harrison to write to Congress on his behalf." Arthur Lefkowitz, *George Washington's Indispensable Men* (Mechanicsburg, PA: Stackpole Books, 2003), 110. This book is an important resource for understanding the actual functioning of Washington's Headquarters and the roles played by the aides and military secretaries.

229. Grant Papers, October 20, 1777, reel 28.

230. Downman, *Services*, 33.

231. Microfiche #232, Letter FZ, "Short Description of the Journey of the Hon. Hessian Troops," 83–85.

232. Smith Papers, 86.

233. Robertson Map Key.

234. Downman, *Services*, 33.

235. Dann, *Nagle*, 8.

236. Parker Family Papers. The words in brackets followed by a question mark indicate missing words caused by holes and deterioration in the manu-

script. I have cautiously added words to keep the sense of the narrative. The original reads, "The Rebels fired grape & [exploding?] shells. Capt. Steuart who Commanded at our battery kept a [warm?] fire for near a half hour."

237. Clark Diary.

238. Marshall, *Life of Washington* 302–3. Both Marshall and Pickering imply that Washington headed for the right flank as soon as the action began. The letter written to Congress was at 5 P.M., and is headed "Chads's Ford," indicating that it was written from that area or from Headquarters at the Ring House. The letter describes the violent firing in progress. Pinpointing Washington's every movement and location is challenging, for he moved a lot that day. He wrote to Sullivan afterwards, "What happened on your march to the field of battle, your disposition there, and behaviour during the action, I can say nothing about, *no part 'till the retreat commenced having come under my immediate observation.*" Hammond, *Sullivan*, 542.

239. Gordon *Independence*, 225.

240. Letter, Greene to Henry Marchant, "Camp White Plains, July [25?] 1778," Greene, *Papers*, 471. Greene wrote little if anything about Brandywine until this time. His letter indicates frustration on his part with Washington's silence about his role and the role of the Virginia troops: ". . . his Excellency, for fear of being chargeable with partiality, never says anything to the advantage of his friends. In the action of Brandywine last campaign, where I think both the general and the public were as much indebted to me for saving the army from ruin as they have ever been to any one officer in the course of the war; but I was never mentioned upon the occasion. . . . This brigade was commanded by General Weedon, and, unfortunately for their own interests, happened to be all Virginians. They being the general's countrymen, and I thought to be one of his favorites, prevented his ever mentioning a single circumstance of the affair."

241. Greene, *Papers*, 161.

242. Pickering's Criticisms of Judge Johnson's *Life of Greene*, Pickering Papers, reel 52, 184–85. Stone of the 1st Maryland and Elmer of the 3rd New Jersey mention Nash's brigade, or part of it, coming up. Congressman Burke told Richard Caswell, "Greene's Division and Nash's Brigade . . . were ordered to the right to reinforce the Troops on that Wing." Smith et. al. *Letters of Delegates* 7, 679.

243. "Journal of Hawkins," 491.

244. Von Knyphausen to Germain.

245. Wier Letterbook, Historical Society of Pennsylvania.

246. Robertson Map Key.

247. Letter, Adam Hubley to John Hubley, "Camp Lancaster Road, near Sorrel Horse [Radnor Twp.], Sepr. 15. 1777," Peter Force Papers, ser. 9, conts.

21–24, MSS 7, 137, reel 104, Library of Congress. Hubley says that Wayne's Division was "solely stationed" at Chads's Ford. Gordon wrote, "Wayne *and the North-Carolinians*, with the artillery and the light troops, after their defeat by Knyphausen, pass the rear of it [Weedon's Virginia Brigade/Colonel Steven's Regiment] in their retreat. At dark, that also is withdrawn by gen. Greene" [emphasis added]. Gordon, *Independence*, 90.

248. *Journal of Jarvis.*

249. Von Knyphausen to Germain.

250. Robertson Map Key.

251. Von Knyphausen to Germain.

252. Boyle, *Thomas Sullivan Journal*, 134.

253. Parker Journal, Parker Family Papers.

254. *Journal of Jarvis.*

255. Clark Diary.

256. Dann, *Nagle*, 8. Rawdon was wounded, not killed. "Capt. Jones" is probably Capt.-Lt. Gibbs Jones, Independent Pennsylvania Artillery Company. This company lost two men wounded at Brandywine. Hazard, *Pennsylvania Archive*, 5, no. 3, 954.

257. "Note: John Graves Simcoe in his *Remarks on the Travels of the Marquis de Chastellux* (5–6n.) makes the following statement: 'The Marquis is in doubt whether the British troops who passed Chad's Ford, were in one or two columns. Though I have failed in my enquiries relative to this point, I have met with an anecdote that may illustrate his account, and deserves to be made more generally known. The Marquis was informed that the redoubt which Mr. Washington had thrown up to cover Chad's Ford "could not be taken unless turned."'" Howard C. Rice, *Travels in North America by the Marquis de Chastellux*, vol. 1 (Chapel Hill: University of North Carolina Press, 1963), 314, n. 71.]

258. Dann, *Nagle*, 8–9.

259. Chambers, Hazard, *Pennsylvania Archives* 10, 323.

260. Hazard, *Pennsylvania Archives* 3, 1056.

261. Smith, *Universal Military Dictionary*, 31.

262. William Summers, "Obituary Notices of Pennsylvania Soldiers of the Revolution," *Pennsylvania Magazine of History and Biography* 38 (1914): 443–44. Ned has not been entirely forgotten; Hector Street in Conshohocken, Pennsylvania, near where he lived in his last years, is named in his honor. His memory serves as a monument to the other African Americans who served in the Revolution, whose contributions under extremely difficult times have often been overlooked or ignored.

263. Parker Family Papers.

264. Dann, *Nagle*, 9.

265. Boyle, *Thomas Sullivan Journal*, 134.

266. Ibid.

267. *Journal of Jarvis*.

268. Bailey, *British Flintlock Rifles*, 50.

269. Von Knyphausen to Germain.

270. Extract of a letter, Chambers to Gen. Edward Hand, Hazard, *Pennsylvania Archives* 10, 322–23.

271. Letter, Adam Hubley to John Hubley, September 15, 1777, Force Papers.

272. Hazard, *Pennsylvania Archives* 10, 663.

273. Chambers, in Hazard, *Pennsylvania Archives* 10, 323.

274. André, *Journal*, 88.

275. Robertson Map and Map Key.

276. Von Knyphausen to Germain.

277. Patten, Deposition, Pension Papers.

278. Chambers, in Hazard, *Pennsylvania Archives* 10, 323.

279. Von Knyphausen to Germain.

280. Letter, Adam Hubley to John Hubley, September 15, 1777, Force Papers.

281. Clark Diary.

282. Letter, Adam Hubley to John Hubley, September 15, 1777, Force Papers.

283. Letter, Dr. William Darlington to Dr. A. Elwyn, "West Chester, Nov. 29, 1845," *Proceedings of the Historical Society of Pennsylvania* I, no. 8 (December, 1846): 57.

284. Futhey and Cope, *Chester County*, 79.

285. Hammond, *Sullivan*, 454.

286. Pickering Papers, reel 52, 184–85.

287. Ibid.

288. Robertson Map Key.

289. Pickering Papers, reel 52, 184–85.

290. Robertson Map Key.

291. Pickering Papers, reel 52, 184–85.

292. Greene, *Papers*, 471.

293. Officer B.

294. Officer B, attached memo.

295. Burgoyne, *Enemy Views*, 174.

296. [Louis Hue Girardin], *Pulaski Vindicated etc.* (Baltimore: John Toy, 1824), 23–24.

297. Scharf, *Chronicles*, 168.

298. Elmer, 105.

299. Robertson Map Key.

300. Letter, Cliffe to Jack, October 24, 1777.

301. Hammond, *Sullivan*, 557.

302. Dr. Darlington interview with McClellan, Futhey and Cope, *Chester County*, 79.

303. Robertson Map Key.

304. Ewald, *Diary*, 87.

305. Gruber, *Peebles Diary*, 133.

306. Montrésor, *Montrésor Journals*, 449–50.

307. Hammond, *Sullivan*, 474.

308. Ewald, *Diary*, 86.

309. McMichael, "Diary," 150.

310. Letter, Pickering to John Marshall, 1827, Pickering Papers, film 220, reel 16:186A–189A.

311. Ewald, *Diary*, 86. In Tustin's translation, it states that the regiments were the 44th and 64th. The 44th was in the 3rd Brigade and did not engage at Brandywine; the 46th was in the left center of the 4th Brigade, next to the 64th. Ewald may have made the mistake or the handwriting in the German manuscript may have been unclear.

312. "Losses of the Military and Naval Forces Engaged in the War of the American Revolution," *Pennsylvania Magazine of History and Biography* 27 (1903): 176–205; "General Return of the Names, Country, Age and Service of the Officers, &c. of the 64th Regiment of Foot," W.O. 17-184, PRO.

313. Officer B.

314. Robertson Map Key.

315. Ewald, *Diary*, 87.

316. Montrésor, *Montrésor Journals*, 121.

317. Gruber, *Peebles Diary*, 133.

318. Letter, Cliffe to Jack, October 24, 1777.

319. Hunter, *Journal*, 30.

320. Clark, *Diary*, 93.

321. Letter, Pickering to John Marshall, 1827.

322. George Inman, "George Inman's Narrative of the American Revolution," *Pennsylvania Magazine of History and Biography* 7 (1883): 241.

323. "A Memorandum List for 1777," by unidentified officer of the 2nd Battalion of Light Infantry, Washington Papers online, Military papers, reel 118, Library of Congress. Viewable at Washington Papers online, Military Correspondence. The original arcane text actually reads: "The Army being then

Arived at Brandy Wine Crick, they Formd the Lines. Genl. Niphousen the Right[,] Genl. Earl Carnwalls the Lift [left][,] Genl. Sr. Willm. Askin [Erskine] the Flying Army on the Lift [left] of the grad [Grand] Army. The Bragader Genarls Commanding ther Different Bregads in Station . . . they All Gave Way Leving 15 pices of Brass Canon 2 Iron ditto—70 Waggons of Arminishon Bagish and Provishons 150 With Horses Complated at 4 Each for gun and Waggon But Night Came on and Brave Howe not knowing the Cuntery Wass Obliged to halt that night."

324. Futhey and Cope, *Chester County*, 81.

325. Grant to Harvey, October 20, 1777, Grant Papers, reel 28.

CHAPTER 5

1. Letter, Washington to Hancock, Fitzpatrick, *Washington* 9, 207–8.

2. http://www.geocities.com/nadineholder/RevWar.html. Woodward and Allied Families–Revolutionary War, Abraham Woodward home page. "Rye 'n' Injun," a mixture of rye flour and "Injun" ("Indian meal," i.e., cornmeal) was a common daily bread in colonial households. Dutch ovens worked by having glowing coals from the wood fire placed under the pot (which often had "spider legs" on the bottom to raise it a few inches). The contents to be cooked were placed inside, then the lid put on and coals heaped on top. A lip around the top of the lid held the coals in place.

3. Letter, From a Lady near West Chester to Dr. A. L. Elwyn, n.d., "Some Account, Etc.," Townsend Ward, 1846, 62–63.

4. Cope, *Philadelphia Merchant*, 401–2.

5. Futhey and Cope, *Chester County*, 672.

6. Dann, *Nagle*, 9. Much of southeastern Pennsylvania is blessed with a great limestone aquifier, and thousands of springs proliferate. The eighteenth-century wells are typically stone-lined and descend between ten and thirty feet, often having two or three feet of water in them. A combination of a hot, dry summer, together with the sudden crush of hundreds of very thirsty men—biting cartridges full of black gunpowder and inhaling clouds of acrid sulfur smoke dry the mouth considerably, to the point of desperation—no doubt caused numerous wells to go dry temporarily.

7. Woodward home page.

8. Smith, "Memoirs," *Historical Magazine*, 86.

9. Futhey and Cope, *Chester County*, 80.

10. Frazer, *Frazer Memoir*, 155–56.

11. Gruber, *Peebles Diary*, 134.

12. Joseph Townsend.

13. *Remembrancer for 1777* (London: J. Almon, 1778), 415–17.

14. Letter, Fitzpatrick to Lord Ossory, "Philadelphia October 28, 1777," Miscellaneous Manuscripts, Library of Congress.

15. *Remembrancer for 1777*, 415–16; 411.

16. Purdy Diary, entry for September 11.

17. "Memmorandum List for 1777."

18. Letter, Margaret Stedman to Elizabeth Fergusson, "Septembr. Ye 11, 1777," "Excitement in Philadelphia on Hearing of the Defeat at Brandywine," *Pennsylvania Magazine of History and Biography* 14, 66–67.

19. George W. Corner, *The Autobiography of Benjamin Rush* (Princeton, NJ: Princeton University Press for the American Philosophical Society, 1948), 132–33. Washington's letter of September 13 names "Doctors Rush, [possibly Andrew] Leiper and [Henry] Latimer, and Mr. [Elias Willard or] Willet, a Mate in the Hospital. . . . I have thought proper to add Drs. [Nicholas] Way and Coats to the surgeons above mentioned." Dr. Henry Latimer said, "Doctor Rush, Physician General, Doctors Leiper and Coates, hospital physicians and surgeons, Doctor Way (a volunteer) and myself" (132, n. 4).

20. Letter, Fitzpatrick to Ossory, October 28, 1777.

21. Thomas Paine, "The Crisis #4," online at Thomas Paine National Historical Association, www.thomaspaine.org/archives/crisis-4.html.

22. Muhlenberg, *Journals* 3, 74.

23. Letter, John Adams to Abigail, "Philadelphia Monday Septr. 8, 1777," Smith et. al., *Letters of Delegates* 7, 627.

24. Letter, James Hutchinson to James Pemberton, "Philadelphia Septr. 15th 1777," American Philosophical Society, Philadelphia.

25. Eliphalet Dyer to Joseph Trumbull, "Philadelphia Septr. 12, 1777," Smith et. al., *Letters of Delegates* 7, 650.

26. Letter, James Hutchinson to James Pemberton, "Philadelphia Septr. 15th 1777," American Philosophical Society.

27. Letter, Grant to Harvey, "Philadelphia October 20, 1777," Grant Papers.

28. Woodward home page.

29. Cantalupe Diary, entry for September 12.

30. Frazer, *Frazer Memoir*, 159–60.

31. *The Pennsylvania Packet*, December 12, 1778; advertisement by Persifor Frazer for two of his slaves who ran away in March or April 1778 and went to Philadelphia. Accessiblearchives.com.

32. Frazer, *Frazer Memoir*, 157–60.

33. Parker Journal, entry for September 14.

34. Baurmeister, *Letters*, 17–18.

35. Letter, John McKinley to President of Congress Henry Laurens, "20th August, 1778," *Delaware Archives*, 1415.

36. Regiment von Alt Lossberg Journal (Combined Battalion), letter M, fiche # 65, M. 79–80, Lidgerwood Collection.

37. Parker Journal, no date; entry at the end of October.

38. "Memmorandum List for 1777."

39. Gruber, *Peebles Diary*, 134.

40. Futhey and Cope, *Chester County*, 566.

41. Letter, Washington to Armstrong, "Head Qurs., Sunday Morning, 7 O'Clock, September 14, 1777," Fitzpatrick, *Washington* 9, 220–21.

42. Lafayette, *Letters and Papers* 1, 79.

43. Hiltzheimer Diary.

44. Letter, Hancock to Washington, "Philada. Septr. 17th, 1777," Smith et. al., *Letters of Delegates* 7, 687.

45. Rice, *Chastellux*, 312, n. 63.

46. Pickering Journal, entry for September 14.

47. "Journal of Hawkins," entry for September 14.

48. Letter, Wayne to Mifflin, "Radnor, 14th Mile Stone Sepr. 15: 1777," Wayne Papers.

49. Letter, Washington to Smallwood, "Bucks Tavern on the Lancaster Road, September 14, 1777," Fitzpatrick, *Washington* 9, 222.

50. Letter, Smallwood to Washington, "Oxford Meeting House 7 Miles above Nottingham Septr. 15 1777," Washington Papers online. A return was included with the letter: Smallwood had 5 regiments, with 106 officers, 83 sergeants and corporals, 14 drummers and fifers, and 1,210 privates, of whom only 866 had "good guns."

51. Letter, Washington to Hancock, "September 15, 1777," Fitzpatrick, *Washington* 9, 227–28.

52. McMichel, "Diary," 151.

53. George Ewing, *The Military Journal of George Ewing (1754–1824), a Soldier of Valley Forge* (Yonkers, NY: Privately Printed by Thomas Ewing, 1928), 22–23.

54. Montrésor, *Montrésor Journals*, 452.

55. Gruber, *Peebles Diary*, 135.

56. "Sept. 5th—Three Rebels Light Horse deserted to us—all Irishmen—some with the clothing of our 8th Regt. on—with a rifle shirt." Montrésor, 447. Later in the month, Washington chose to use the uniforms for deception: To Comte Pulaski: "You will immediately form a Detachment of at least fifty Horse of which part are to be of Colo. Moylans, in their Red Uniforms, which will serve to deceive both the Enemy and Country people." Washington to Pulaski, "Pennypacker's Mills, Sept. 30, 1777" (Fitzpatrick, *Washington* 9, 288–89).

57. Frazer, *Frazer Memoir*, 161.

58. Henry Stirke, "A British Officer's Revolutionary War Journal, 1776–1778," edited by S. Sydney Bradford, *Maryland Historical Magazine* 56, no. 2 (June, 1961): 170–71. Stirke was a lieutenant in the Light Infantry Company, 10th Regiment of Foot. Interestingly, Frazer's parole, which is pictured opposite 234 of the Frazer book, is dated September 26, 1777, and is signed by Captain Stirke as a witness.

59. Parker, entry for September 16. Unfortunately, the manuscript has many holes in it and is only partially readable.

60. Frazer, *Frazer Memoir*, 161, 167.

61. Letter, Grant to Harvey, "Philadelphia 20th Octor. 1777," Grant Papers.

62. André, *Journal*, 89–90.

63. Futhey and Cope, *Chester County*, 78–79.

64. Kirkwood, Journal and Order Book, 175.

65. Parker Journal, entry for Sept. 16.

66. Stirke, "Journal," 171.

67. Parker Journal, entry for September 16.

68. Ewald, *Diary*, 88–89.

69. Patten Deposition, Pension Files.

70. Letter, Grant to Harvey, "Philadelphia 20th Octor. 1777," Grant Papers.

71. Quoted in Futhey and Cope, *Chester County*, 83.

72. Montrésor, *Montrésor Journals*, 454.

73. Ewald, *Diary*, 89.

74. Dann, *Nagle*, 10.

75. Parker Journal, entry for September 16.

76. Beatty Journal.

77. Dann, *Nagle*, 8.

78. Von Münchhausen, *Diary*, 32.

79. Gruber, *Peebles Diary*, 135.

80. Parker Journal, entry for September 16.

81. Letter, Joseph Reed to Washington, "Swedes Ford, 16th September, 1777," William B. Reed, *Life and Correspondence of Joseph Reed*, vol. I (Philadelphia: Lindsay and Blakiston, 1847), 311.

82. Letter, Thos. Hartley to William Atlee et. al., "Camp Septr 17th 1777," Force Papers.

83. Letter, Henry Knox to Lucy Knox, "Pottsgrove, September 24, 1777," Commager and Morris, *Spirit of Seventy Six* I, 619.

84. Letter, Hartley to Atlee, September 17, 1777.

85. "Prisoners with the Rebels of the Detachmt. from the Brigade of Foot Guards, April 1778," Orders of British Troops.

86. WO 71/84, PRO, 262–66.

87. Montrésor, *Montrésor Journals*, 454.

88. Von Münchhausen, *Diary*, 34.

89. Ibid.

90. Lee, *Memoirs*, 91; Montrésor, *Montrésor Journals*, 455.

91. Syrett and Cooke, *Papers of A. Hamilton*, 326–28.

92. Letter, Hancock to Washington, "Philada., Septr. 18th. 1777 10 O'Clock P. M.," Smith et. al., *Letters of Delegates* 7, 694.

93. Smith, History of 1st City Troop, entry for 19th [*sic*] September.

94. Letter, Joseph Reed to Washington, "Falls of Schuylkill, 18th Sept., 9 o'clock P.M." Reed, *Reed*, 312.

95. Letter, John Hancock to Dorothy Hancock, "York Town in Pennsylvania 90 Miles from Philada., 1st Octor 1777," Smith et. al., *Letters of Delegates* 8, 39–40.

96. Letter, Henry Laurens to John Lewis Gervais, "York October 8, 1777," Smith et. al., *Letters of Delegates* 8, 80–81.

97. John Adams, diary entry, 21st Sept., Smith et. al., *Letters of Delegates* 8, 8–9.

98. Letter, Washington, "Readg. Furnace 6 OClock PM, September 18, 1777, Fitzpatrick, *Washington* 9, 235–36.

99. Letter, Wayne to Washington, "Paoli one-half after 7 OClock AM 19th Sepr 1777," Washington Papers online, ser. 4, reel 44.

100. Letter, Wayne to Washington, Paoli three-quarters After 10 AM 19th Sepr. 1777," ibid.

101. Letter, James Lovell to Robert Treat Paine, "Philada. 24th Sepr. A.M.," Smith et. al., *Letters of Delegates* 8, 15.

102. Parker Journal, entry for Sept. 20.

103. Hartley's Testimony, paper marked "E," Force Papers.

104. Wayne's Defense, version 1, Wayne Papers.

105. Von Münchhausen, *Diary*, 34.

106. Gruber, *Peebles Diary*, entry for Sept. 19.

107. Von Münchhausen, *Diary*, 34.

108. Cantelupe Diary, entry for September 20.

109. Montrésor, *Montrésor Journals*, 455.

110. Robertson, *Diaries*, 148.

111. Cantelupe Diary, entry for September 20.

112. Montrésor, *Montrésor Journals*, 455; Orders of British Troops.

113. Muhlenberg, *Journals* 3, 77–78.

114. Fitzpatrick, *Washington* 9, 243–44.

115. Cliffe, October 24, 1777. Cliffe Papers.

116. Wayne's Testimony, version 1, Wayne Papers.

117. Brodhead's Evidence, Paper marked "I," Force Papers.

118. Letter, James Cox to Mary Cox, "Downing's Town on the Lancaster Road, Sept. 20, 1777," Scharf, *Chronicles*, 165.

119. Hunter, *Journal*, 30.

120. Parker Journal, entry for Sept. 20.

121. Testimony of Colonel Hartley, paper marked "E," Force Papers.

122. Letter, Hartley to Atlee, et. al., "Camp Sepr ye 20th 1777, 6 o'Clock PM," Force Papers.

123. André, *Journal*, 50.

124. Ibid., 49.

125. Hunter, *Journal*, 31.

126. Mentges' Evidence, Paper marked "L," Force Papers.

127. Hunter, *Journal*, 49.

128. Letter, St. George to Imperial, "September 11–October 2," Wayne Papers.

129. André, *Journal*, 50.

130. Letter, Maj. Samuel Hay to Col. Wiliam Irvine, "Camp at the Trap, Sept, 29, 1777," Irvine Papers, vol. I, 94, Historical Society of Pennsylvania, Philadelphia.

131. Hunter, *Journal*, 31.

132. Letter, St. George to Imperial.

133. Letter, A. Wayne to Washington, "Red Lion 21st Septr. 1777: 12 OClock," Wayne Papers, vol. 4.

134. Wayne's Defense, version I, inserted at the end, Wayne Papers.

135. Hunter, *Journal*, 31.

136. Parker Journal, entry for Sept. 21.

137. Hay's Evidence, Paper marked "B," Force Papers.

138. Hunter, *Journal*, 31.

139. Hartley's Evidence, paper marked "E," Force Papers.

140. Letter, Adam Hubley to William Atlee, "Camp at Jones's Tavern Septr. 23, 1777," Force Papers.

141. Lord Cantelupe's copy of *A List of the General and Staff Officers . . . Serving in North America*, published in Philadelphia in early 1778, has a watercolor diagram drawn on the flyleaf and titled, "Sr. Willm. Howe's British Army in Philadelphia. 1778." Cantelupe shows the breakdown of the grenadier and light infantry battalions by company and has two boxes marked "71" in the 2nd Battalion Light Infantry. This would make sense, considering the unusual size of the regiment.

In the 71st, "Short Land Pattern muskets were issued to all enlisted men, while officers and sergeants carried fusils, and each man also carried a Highland broadsword and steel-mounted side pistol. Unlike the 42nd, the 71st resolutely clung to their Highland plaids and weapons, however impractical, long after the senior regiment [the 42nd] had discarded their own for American service. This can be partly explained as a matter of stubborn pride, as Fraser's men were almost entirely Highland-born, while the 42nd had many Lowland Scots in the ranks." Don Troiani, Earl J. Coates, and James L. Kochan, et. al., *Don Troiani's Soldiers in America* (Mechanicsburg, PA: Stackpole Books, 1998), 43.

142. Parker Journal entry for September 21, 1777. Most British accounts of Paoli mention that a sergeant was killed, and investigation of the surviving muster sheets shows Pvt. Daniel Robertson of the 49th as killed September 20. Parker identified the sergeant as being from the 71st Regiment. The muster sheets of the 71st are not in the Public Record Office/National Archives in London. They either have not survived or are in an unknown location. Thus the identity of the sergeant who was killed at Paoli remains unknown.

143. Letter, St. George to Imperial.

144. Hartley's Evidence, Paper marked "E," Force Papers.

145. Letter, Anthony Wayne to Washington, "Camp near White Ma[r]sh 22nd Octr. 1777," Wayne Papers, vol. 4.

146. Hubley's Evidence, Paper marked "N," Force Papers.

147. Boyle, *Thomas Sullivan Journal*, 231.

148. Hunter, *Journal*, 31.

149. Letter, Hartley to Atlee, et. al., "Camp Red Lyon Sepr. Ye 21st 1777," Force Paper.

150. Hazard, *Pennsylvania Archives*, 2nd ser., vol. 10, 548.

151. Benjamin Burd, Pension Narrative, Revolutionary War Pension Papers, film 27, reel 409, National Archives, Washington, DC.

152. Letter, William Smallwood to Go. Thomas Johnson, "Bucks [*sic*; Berks] County Jones Tavern Sept. 23, 1777," MSS 1875, Maryland Historical Society.

153. Letter, St. George to Imperial.

154. Revolutionary War Muster and Payrolls, National Archives.

155. Smallwood to Johnson, September 23, 1777.

156. Hubley to Atlee, September 21, 1777; Letter, Hubley to Atlee, "Camp at Jones's Tavern Septr 23 1777," Force Papers. The British dead are most likely buried at St. Peter's-in-the-Great Valley. See Thomas J. McGuire, *Battle of Paoli* (Mechanicsburg, PA: Stackpole Books, 2000), 133–34.

157. Parker Journal, entry for September 21.

158. George English, Pension Certificate, Revolutionary War State Pension File, RG-4, roll 2, Pennsylvania State Archives, Harrisburg.

159. Hunter, *Journal*, 32.

160. Letter, Abraham Robinson to Anthony Wayne, "East Town Septr. 22nd 1777," Wayne Papers, vol. 4.

161. Osborn Letters, vol. 3, no. 100. "In the campaign of 1760, that excellent general and true genius of a partisan the prince of Brunswick, was situated at some distance from Zerenberg, at that time in possession of the French, and being informed by two Hanoverian officers who had been in the town disguised like peasants, that the garrison were very remiss in their duty, trusting to the vicinity of their army, and the distance of ours. The prince was resolved to surprise them, and after appointing a corps to sustain him, he advanced in the night with Major Maclean of the 88th regiment, and two hundred Highlanders, with bayonets fixed and their arms not loaded, following at a distance. Upon the first centry's challenging, the prince answered in French, and the centry seeing but two persons advancing, (whom he believed to be French), he had no distrust, so that the major getting up to him, stabbed him, and prevented his giving the alarm. The Highlanders immediately rushed in and attacked the guard with their bayonets, and carried the town, having killed or taken the whole garrison of eight hundred men." Roger Stevenson, *Military Instructions for Officers Detached in the Field: Containing a Scheme for Forming a Corps of Partisans, Illustrated with Plans of the Manoeuvres Necessary in Carrying Out the Petite Guerre* (Philadelphia: R. Aitkin, Front Street, 1775), 192–94.

162. Parker Journal, entry for September 21.

163. Montrésor, *Montrésor Journals*, 456.

164. Letter, Grant to Harvey, October 20, 1777.

165. Von Münchhausen, *Diary*, 34–35.

166. Gruber, *Peebles Diary*, entry for September 21, 1777.

167. Ewald, *Diary* 90–91.

168. British Memorandum, entry for September 22.

169. Letter, F. Z., microfiche 45, 112–18, entry for September 22. Hessian Documents, Morristown NHP, Morristown, New Jersey.

170. Osborn Letters, vol. 3, no. 100.

171. Gruber, *Peebles Diary*, 137.

172. Montrésor, *Montrésor Journals*, 457.

173. Parker Journal, entry for September 24.

174. Downman, *Services*, 35.

175. Montrésor, *Montrésor Journals*, 457.

176. Muhlenberg, *Journals*, 79.

177. Reed, *Reed*, 314.

178. James Grant Wilson, "A Memorial of Colonel John Bayard," *Proceedings of the New Jersey Historical Society*, 2nd ser., vol. 5 (1877–79): 150–51. The daugh-

ter is identified only as "Mrs. Kirkpatrick." Christopher Marshall confirmed the details of these stories in his diary a few weeks later: "Oct. 8- In my son's letter [his son lived in Providence Township] are many instances of the wanton cruelty they exercised in his neighborhood, amongst which is *the burning of the house where Col. Reed did live, the house where Thompson kept tavern, with every thing in it, all the hay at Col. Bull's, fifteen hundred bushels of wheat, with other grain, his powder mill and iron works; destroyed all the fences for some miles, with the Indian corn and buckwheat, emptied feather beds, destroyed furniture, cut books to pieces at Col. Bayard's;* at one place emptied some feather beds, and put a cask of yellow ochre, cask of Spanish brown [and] cask of linseed oil, and mixed them all together. So brutal and cruel are all their steps marked, it would be tiresome tracing them with a pen." Marshall, *Remembrancer*, 133–34.

179. Von Münchhausen, *Diary*, 35.

180. Muhlenberg, *Journals*, 79.

181. Parker Journal, entry for September 25.

182. Ewald, *Diary*, 91.

183. Drinker, *Diary*, 234–35.

GLOSSARY
OF EIGHTEENTH-CENTURY MILITARY TERMS

The definitions in italics are taken from Capt. George Smith, *An Universal Military Dictionary* (London: J. Milan, 1779; reprint, Ottawa: Museum Restoration Service, 1969).

Battalion. *"An undetermined body of infantry in regard to number, generally from 500 to 800 men. . . . Sometimes regiments consist of but 1 battalion; but if more numerous are divided into several battalions, according to their strength; so that every one may come within the numbers mentioned . . . each battalion is divided into four divisions, and each division forms two platoons."*

The term *battalion* was confusingly applied to regiments in Pennsylvania in 1776. In the British Army, battalions were units of men put together for battle. The grenadier and light infantry battalions were made up of companies from many different regiments. Sometimes understrength regiments with small numbers of men or missing officers were battalioned together, such as the 40th and 55th Regiments.

Brigade. *"In military affairs, implies a party, or a division of a body of soldiers, whether horse, foot, or artillery, under the command of a brigadier [general]. . . . A brigade of the army is either foot or dragoons, whose exact number is not fixed, but generally consists of three regiments, or six battalions. Brigadier, a military officer, whose rank is the next above that of colonel; appointed to command a corps, consisting of several battalions or regiments, called a brigade."*

The Continental Army brigades in this campaign were generally organized by state and numbers. Most of them seem to have been in the range of 1,500 to 2,000 men, but some brigades were larger and some were smaller. The British brigades mostly consisted of four regiments.

Brigade of Guards. The Brigade of Guards was authorized by the king in February 1776 to consist of 1,000 men drawn by lottery from three regiments of foot guards. A grenadier company was included, and a light company was formed specifically for the American service. The Brigade of Guards functioned as an independent unit, often like light infantry, and unlike the other regiments, it retained its flank companies on campaign. The uniforms and headgear were modified for America, and the men wore round hats in the battalion companies. The flank companies wore light infantry caps.

Chasseur. See *Jäger.*

Company. *"In a military sense, means a small body of foot or artillery, the number of which is never fixed, but generally from 45 to 110, commanded by a captain, a lieutenant, and an ensign, and sometimes by a first and second lieutenant, as in the artillery. A company usually has 2 sergeants, 3 or 4 corporals, and 2 drums [this actually means two musicians, a drummer and a fifer]."*

Most British regiments consisted of ten companies: eight battalion companies and two flank companies—light infantry and grenadiers—so called because they occupied the flanks on parade. The grenadiers were in the "position of honor" on the right of the line.

Most American regiments had eight or nine companies, one of which was light infantry. Some units had rifle companies, and a very few regiments, such as Hartley's Additional Continental Regiment, had a grenadier company.

Corps de Battaille. *"The main body of an army drawn up for battle, whereof the first line is called the van, the second the main body, and the third the body of reserve, or rear-guard."*

Division. *"Of an army, are the number of brigades and squadrons [cavalry] it contains; of a battalion, are the several platoons into which a regiment or battalion is divided."*

Divisions are usually commanded by major generals. In the 1777 campaign, with the derangement of the American officer corps, many officers were brevetted, assigned to command positions but not given the rank permanently. Anthony Wayne was a brigadier general commanding Maj. Gen. Benjamin Lincoln's Division. The two brigades were commanded by colonels. The number of generals was determined by Congress, and the army had to function within the assigned number; promotions were an endless source of contention, especially with foreign professionals regularly arriving.

Dragoon. Dragoons were technically mounted infantry who moved rapidly from place to place on horseback and were also able to fight on foot. Also called *light horse*, they were armed with sabers, horse pistols, and carbines and were used extensively by both sides for scouting, communication, and skirmishing.

Fusilier. A name originally given to men who guarded the artillery train and were armed with fusils, or light muskets. By 1775, the name and headgear—miter caps similar to those of the grenadiers but not as high—distinguished them, but they were armed the same as regular regiments. The Hessian forces had fusilier regiments, and the British had two fusilier regiments in America: the 21st Royal North British (Scots) Fusiliers and the 23rd Royal Welsh Fusiliers.

Grenadier. Grenadiers in the British Army were usually the tallest and strongest men in the regiment, five feet, ten inches or taller, and each regiment had one company of them. The name comes from their original function of throwing hand grenades, which required tall, strong men. Their caps were originally of cloth and miter-shaped to facilitate grenade throwing. By 1750, grenades were no longer used, but the distinction remained. The British grenadiers wore bearskin caps just over a foot tall, and they retained a flaming grenade as a badge. On campaign, the grenadier companies were taken away from their regiments and formed into grenadier battalions.

German (Hessian) grenadiers were modeled on the Prussian Army, chosen for merit rather than height only. They wore metal miter caps of polished brass or tin, depending on the regiment, and were distinguished by mustaches blackened with blackball paste wax and sharpened into points.

Jäger. German sharpshooters who were equipped with short, large-caliber rifles accurate to 200 or more yards. The British often used the French word *chasseur*—both words mean "hunter"—to describe these light troops, who were dressed in green uniforms with red facings.

Light Horse. See *Dragoon.*

Light Infantry. Troops who were lightly equipped and highly mobile. The British Army introduced them during the French and Indian War, when the Howe brothers, George Augustus and William, survivors of Braddock's Defeat, pioneered the concept. In the 1760s, the British Army incorporated a light company in each regiment. They were able to fan out and use partisan tactics or fight in line like regulars. On campaign, they were taken from their regiments and formed into battalions, as were the grenadiers.

Regiment. *"A body of men, either horse, foot, or artillery, commanded by a colonel, lieutenant-colonel, and major: each regiment of foot is divided into companies, but the number of companies differ; though in England our regiments are generally 10 companies, one of which is always grenadiers. . . . Each regiment has a chaplain, quartermaster, adjutant, and surgeon."*

BIBLIOGRAPHY

MANUSCRIPTS AND ARCHIVES

Beatty, William. Journal, 1776–1781. MS 1814. Maryland Historical Society, Baltimore. Beatty was a captain in the 7th Maryland Regiment.

British Depredations Book, Chester County Historical Society, West Chester, PA.

British Journal 1776–1778, Journal of Officer B. Sol Feinstone Collection, David Library of the American Revolution, Washington Crossing, PA.

British Journal 1776–1778, Notes of a Light Infantry Officer of the 17th Regiment of Foot. Sol Feinstone Collection, David Library of the American Revolution.

Burd, Benjamin. Pension Narrative, Revolutionary War Pension Papers. National Archives, Washington, DC.

Cantalupe, William Viscount. Diary. Grey Papers, University of Durham, Durham, UK.

Clark, Joseph. Diary. New Jersey Historical Society, Newark.

Cliff, Loftus. Cliffe Papers, Clements Library.

Cox, James. Papers. Maryland Historical Society, Baltimore.

Dansey, William. Letters. Historical Society of Delaware, Wilmington. Dansey was a captain in the Light Company, 33rd Regiment of Foot.

Dayton, Elias. Papers. New Jersey Historical Society, Newark.

English, George. Pension Certificate. Revolutionary War Pension File. Pennsylvania State Archives, Harrisburg.

Fitzpatrick, Richard. Papers. Miscellaneous Manuscripts 622. Library of Congress, Washington, DC.

Force, Peter. Papers. Library of Congress, Washington, DC.

Gates, Horatio. Papers. Microfilm, David Library.

Glyn, Thomas. "Ensign Glyn's Journal on the American Service with the Detachment of 1000 Men of the Guards. . . ." Princeton University Library, Princeton, New Jersey.

Grant, James. Ballindalloch Papers. National Archives of Scotland, Edinburgh. Microfilm in Library of Congress, Washington, DC.

Hiltzheimer, Jacob. Dairy for 1777. American Philosophical Society, Philadelphia.

Historical Manuscripts Commission. *Report on Manuscripts in Various Collections*. Dublin: His Majesty's Stationery Office, 1909. Reprint, Gregg Press: Boston, 1972.

Hessian Documents of the American Revolution, Lidgerwood Collection, Morristown National Historical Park, Morristown, NJ.

Irvine, William, Papers. Manuscript Division, Library of Congress, Washington, DC.

Journal of the Hessian Grenadier Battalion von Minnegrode. Microfiche 232, Morristown National Historical Park.

Laing Manuscripts. University of Edinburgh, Scotland.

Marshall, Christopher. Remembrancer. Vol. D. Historical Society of Pennsylvania, Philadelphia.

———. Marshall Letterbook. Case 36, Historical Society of Pennsylvania, Philadelphia.

Maryland Historical Society, Manuscript Collection, 1986.

"A Memmorandum List for 1777." By unidentified officer of the 2nd Battalion Light Infantry. George Washington Papers, Military Papers, reel 118. Library of Congress, Washington, DC.

Muhlenberg, Gen. Peter. Orderly Book, 1777–78. Vol. 62, marked "Colledge Camp 1775." Dreer Collection, Historical Society of Pennsylvania, Philadelphia.

Orders, Returns, Morning Reports and Accounts of British Troops, 1776–1781. Film 9, reel 1, M922. National Archives, Washington, DC.

Osborn, Sir George. Letters. Vol. 3, 1771–1782, nos. 98, 100. Private family papers, England.

Parker, James. Parker Family Papers 1760–95 (originals in Liverpool, England). film 45, reel 2, David Library of the American Revolution, Washington's Crossing, PA.

Patten, James. Deposition of Pvt. James Patten, Pennsylvania Militia and Maxwell's Corps of Light Infantry. Revolutionary War Pension Papers, film 27. National Archives, Washington, DC.

Pattison, James. Letter Book. RA 57, 1–4. Royal Artillery Arsenal, Woolwich, London.

———. "Brigade Orders, Royal Artillery, from 28th Sept. 1777 to 21st February 1778, by Brigadier General James Pattison" and "General Orders from 27th Septr. 1777 to 21st February 1778 of the Army under the Command of General Sir William Howe." Papers of General James Pattison, RA. Microfilm 47, reel I, 42–45. David Library of the American Revolution, Washington Crossing, Pennsylvania.

Peebles, John. Journal of Captain-Lieutenant John Peebles, Grenadier Company, 42nd Royal Highland Regiment. Public Records Office, Edinburgh, Scotland. Microfilm in David Library of the American Revolution, Washington's Crossing, Pennsylvania.

Pemberton, Phineas. "Weather Observations." American Philosophical Society, Philadelphia.

Pickering, Timothy. Pickering Papers. Microfilm reels 51 and 52. Massachusetts Historical Society, Boston.

Purdy, Gilbert. Diary. "Memorandum of Lt. Gilbt. Purdy for the Year 1777." Z 20/C21/1975/U2. National Archives of Canada, Ottawa, Ontario. Purdy belonged to the Corps of Guides and Pioneers.

Regiment von Alt Lossberg Journal. Letter M, fiche #65. Lidgerwood Collection, Morristown, NJ.

Reports to General von Ditfurth. Microfiche 334, letter Z. Morristown, NJ.

Revolutionary War Muster and Payrolls, National Archives, Washington, DC.

Richards, ——. Orderly Book of Sergeant Major Richards of the Guards Brigade, September–December 1777. Film 9, reel I, M922. Accounts of British Troops, 1776–1781. David Library of the American Revolution, Washington's Crossing, Pennsylvania; National Archives, Washington, DC.

Robertson, Archibald. Battle of Brandywine. Manuscript map with a 1,200-word text key. RCIN 734026.A. King's Map Collection, Royal Library, Windsor Castle, UK. Map was sent to King George III.

Smith, Capt. J. H. C. History of the 1st City Troop, based largely on the recollections of Trooper John Donnaldson. 1st City Troop Archives, Philadelphia.

Townsend, Joseph. "Some account of the adventures of one day—the memorable September 11, 1777." MS 13292, Julius F. Sachse Collection, Chester County Historical Society, West Chester, PA.

von Donop, Count Carl. Journal of the Hessian Corps in America under General von Heister, 1776–June 1777. Hessian Documents of the American Revolution, Morristown National Historical Park, Morristown, New Jersey.

Wayne, Anthony. Papers. Historical Society of Pennsylvania, Philadelphia.

Wier, Daniel. "Copies of Letters from Danl. Wier, Esq., Commissary to the Army in America, to J. Robinson, Esq., Secretary to the Lords Commissioners of the Treasury; and from John Robinson, Esq., in Answer thereto in the Year 1777." Dreer Collection, Case, 36, Historical Society of Pennsylvania, Philadelphia.

BOOKS

Addison, Joseph. *Cato. A Tragedy.* London: Printed for the booksellers, 1739.

The Annual Register: or, a View of the History, Politics, and Literature for the Year 1776. London: J. Dodsley, 1777.

The Annual Register: or, a View of the History, Politics, and Literature for the Year 1777. 4th ed. London: J. Dodsley, 1794.

André, John. *André's Journal.* Edited by Henry Cabot Lodge. Vol. I. Boston: The Bibliophile Society, 1903.

Archives of Maryland, Muster Rolls, etc., of the Maryland Troops in the American Revolution. Baltimore: Maryland Historical Society, 1900.

Bailey, DeWitt. *British Military Flintlock Rifles.* Lincoln, RI: Andrew Mowbray Publishers, 2002.

Baurmeister, Carl L. *Letters from Major Baurmeister to Colonel von Jungkenn Written during the Philadelphia Campaign, 1777–1778.* Edited by Bernhard A. Uhlendorf and Edna Vosper. Philadelphia: Historical Society of Pennsylvania, 1937.

———. *Revolution in America, Confidential Letters and Journals, 1776–1784, of Adjutant General Major Baurmeister of the Hessian Forces.* Translated and edited by Bernhard A. Uhlendorf. New Brunswick, NJ: Rutgers University Press, 1957.

Bentalou, Paul. *A Reply to Judge Johnson's Remarks . . . Relating to Count Pulaski.* Baltimore: J. D. Toy, 1826.

Biddle, Charles. *Autobiography of Charles Biddle, Vice-President of the Supreme Executive Council of Pennsylvania, 1745–1821.* Philadelphia: E. Claxton and Co., 1883.

Brittingham, Hazel D. "The Fall of the Cape Henlopen Lighthouse." *The Delaware Estuary: Rediscovering a Forgotten Resource.* Edited by Tracey Bryant and Jonathan R. Pennock. Neward, DR: University of Delaware Sea Grant College Program, 1988.

Boatner, Mark M. *Encyclopedia of the American Revolution.* New York: David McKay Company, 1966.

Boyle, Joseph Lee. *From Redcoat to Rebel: The Thomas Sullivan Journal.* Bowie, MD: Heritage Books, 1997. Sullivan was a sergeant in the 49th Regiment of Foot.

Brown, William H. *Archives of Maryland* Vol. 16, *Journal and Correspondence of the Council of Safety/State Council 1777–1778.* Baltimore: Maryland Historical Society, 1897.

Budka, Metchie J. E. *Under Their Vine and Fig Tree: Travels through American in 1797–1799, 1805, with Some Further Account of Life in New Jersey by Julian Ursyn Niemcewicz.* Elizabeth, NJ: Grassmann Publishing Co., 1965.

Burgoyne, Bruce E. *Enemy Views: The American Revolutionary War as Recorded by the Hessian Participants.* Bowie, MD: Heritage Books, 1996.

———. ed. and trans. *Diaries of Two Ansbach Jägers.* Bowie, MD: Heritage Press, 1997. Diaries of Lt. Heinrich von Feilitzsch and Lt. Christian Bartholomai.

Chase, Philander D., et al., eds. *The Papers of George Washington: Revolutionary War Series.* Vols. 9–12. Charlottesville: University Press of Virginia, 1998, 2000, 2001, 2002.

Clark, Elmer T., J. Manning Potts, and Jacob S. Payton, eds. *The Journal and Letters of Francis Asbury.* Vol. 1, *The Journal, 1771–1793.* London: Epworth Press, 1958.

Colonial Records. *Minutes of the Supreme Executive Council of Pennsylvania.* Vol. 9. Harrisburg, PA: Theo Fenn & Co., 1852.

Commager, Henry Steele, and Richard B. Morris, eds. *The Spirit of Seventy Six: The Story of the American Revolution as Told by Participants.* New York: Bonanza Books, 1968.

Cope, Gilbert. *Genealogy of the Baily Family . . . Descendants of Joel Baily.* Lancaster, PA: Wickersham Printing Co., 1912.

Cope, Thomas P. *Philadelphia Merchant: The Diary of Thomas P. Cope, 1800–1851.* Edited by Eliza Cope Harrison. South Bend, IN: Gateway Editions, 1978.

Corner, George W. *The Autobiography of Benjamin Rush. . . .* Princeton, NJ: Princeton University Press for the American Philosophical Society, 1948.

Cresswell, Nicholas. *The Journal of Nicholas Cresswell.* London: Jonathan Cape, 1925.

Dann, John C. *The Nagle Journal.* New York: Weidenfeld and Nicolson, 1988.

———. *The Revolution Remembered.* Chicago: The University of Chicago Press, 1980.

Delaware Archives, Revolutionary War. Vol. 3. Wilmington: Charles Story Co., 1919.

Döhla, Johann Conrad. *A Hessian Diary of the American Revolution by Johann Conrad Döhla.* Translated by Bruce E. Burgoyne. Norman: University of Oklahoma Press, 1990. Döhla was a private in the 4th Company of the Bayreuth Regiment from Anspach-Bayreuth.

Downman, Francis. *The Services of Lieut.-Colonel Francis Downman, R.A. . . . between the Years 1758 and 1784.* Edited by Col. F. A. Whinyates. Woolwich: Royal Artillery Institution, 1898. Microfilm in Harcourt Family Papers, film 424, David Library of the American Revolution, Washington's Crossing, Pennsylvania.

Drinker, Elizabeth. *The Diary of Elizabeth Drinker.* Vol. 1, *1758–1795.* Edited by Elaine F. Crane. Boston: Northeastern University Press, 1991.

Egle, William Henry. *Notes and Queries Historical and Genealogical.* Vol. 2, Harrisburg, PA: Harrisburg Publishing Company, 1895.

Ewald, Johann. *Diary of the American War: A Hessian Journal, Captain Johann Ewald, Field Jager Corps.* Translated and edited by Joseph Tustin. New Haven, CT: Yale University Press, 1979.

———. *Treatise on Partison Warfare.* Translated and edited by Robert A. Selig and David C. Skaggs. New York: Greenwood Press, 1991.

Ewing, George. *The Military Journal of George Ewing, 1754–1824, a Soldier of Valley Forge.* Yonkers, NY: Privately printed by Thomas Ewing, 1928.

Fitzpatrick, John C. *The Writings of George Washington.* Vols. 7–9. Washington, DC: U.S. Government Printing Office, 1932.

Fortescue, Sir John. *The Correspondence of King George the Third.* Vol. 3, *July 1773– December 1777.* London: Macmillan and Co., 1928.

Frazer, Persifor. *General Persifor Frazer: A Memoir Compiled Principally from His Own Papers by His Great-Grandson.* Philadelphia: 1907. Letters of Col. Persifor Frazer of the 5th Pennsylvania Regiment and his wife, Mary "Polly" Worral Frazer, in 1777.

Futhey, J. Smith, and Gilbert Cope. *History of Chester County.* Philadelphia: Louis and Everts, 1881.

Galloway, Joseph. *A Reply to the Observations of Lieut. Gen. Sir William Howe . . .* 1780. Reprint. Boston: Gregg Press, 1972.

[Girardin, Louis Hue.] *Pulaski Vindicated etc.* [Erroneously attributed to Paul Bentalou.] Baltimore: John Toy, 1824.

Gordon, William. *The History of the Rise, Progress, and Establishment of the Independence of the United States of America. . . .* 2nd Amer. ed., vol. 2. New York: Samuel Campbell, 1794.

Graydon, Alexander. *Memoirs of a Life, Chiefly Passed in Pennsylvania, within the Last Sixty Years (1811).* Edinburgh: William Blackwood, 1822.

Greene, Nathanael. *The Papers of General Nathanael Greene.* Vol. 2, *1 January 1777–16 October 1778.* Edited by Richard K. Showman, Robert E. McCarthy, and Margaret Cobb. Chapel Hill: University of North Carolina Press, 1980.

Greenman, Jeremiah. *Diary of a Common Soldier in the American Revolution, 1775– 1783: An Annotated Edition of the Military Journal of Jeremiah Greenman.* Edited by Robert C. Bray and Paul E. Bushnell. DeKalb: Northern Illinois University Press, 1978. Greenman belonged to the 2nd Rhode Island Regiment.

Gruber, Ira D. *John Peebles' American War: The Diary of a Scottish Grenadier, 1776–1782.* Mechanicsburg, PA: Stackpole Books, 1998.

Hammond, Otis G. *Letters and Papers of Major-General John Sullivan.* Vol. 1, *1771– 1777.* Concord, NH: New Hampshire Historical Society, 1930.

Harcourt, Edward William. *The Harcourt Papers.* Vol. 11. Oxford: James Parker and Co., 1880.

Hayes, John T. *A Gentleman of Fortune: The Diary of Baylor Hill, First Continental Light Dragoons, 1777–1781.* Vol. 1. Fort Lauderdale, FL: Saddlebag Press, 1995.

Hazard, Samuel. *Pennsylvania Archives.* Vol. 5. Philadelphia: Joseph Severs & Co., 1853.

Heitman, Francis B. *Historical Register of Officers of the Continental Army during the War of the Revolution.* Baltimore: Genealogical Publishing Co., 1973.

Hiltzheimer, Jacob. *Extracts from the Diary of Jacob Hiltzheimer of Philadelphia, 1765–1798.* Edited by Jacob Cox Parsons. Philadelphia: William Fell, 1893.

Historical Anecdotes Civil and Military in a Series of Letters Written from America in the Years 1777 and 1778, &c. London: Printed for J. Bew, 1779.

Hoffman, Ronald, Sally D. Mason, and Eleanor S. Darcy, eds. *Dear Papa, Dear Charley.* Vol. 2. Chapel Hill: University of North Carolina Press, 2001. Letters of Charles Carroll of Carrollton and his father, Charles Carroll of Annapolis, 1748–82.

Holmes, Richard. *Redcoat.* London: HarperCollins Publishers, 2001.

Hunter, Martin. *The Journal of Gen. Sir Martin Hunter. . . .* Edited by James Hunter, Anne Hunter, and Elizabeth Bell. Edinburgh: Edinburgh Press, 1894.

Huntington Papers: Correspondence of the Brothers Joshua and Jedediah Huntington during the Period of the American Revolution, Collections of the Connecticut Historical Society. Vol. I. Hartford, CT: Connecticut Historical Society, 1923.

James, Arthur E. *Chester County Clocks and Their Makers.* Exton, PA: Schiffler Publishing Co., 1947.

Katcher, Philip. *Uniforms of the Continental Army.* York, PA: George Shumway Publisher, 1981.

Kemble, Stephen. *Journals of Lieut.-Col. Stephen Kemble, 1773–1789. . . .* New introduction and preface by George A. Billias. New York: New York Historical Society, 1883. Reprint. Boston: Gregg Press, 1972.

Ketchum, Richard. "New War Letters of Banastre Tarleton." *Narratives of the Revolution in New York.* New York: New York Historical Society, 1976.

Kirkwood, Robert. *The Journal and Order Book of Captain Robert Kirkwood of the Delaware Regiment of the Continental Line.* Edited by Joseph Brown Turner. Wilmington: Historical Society of Delaware, 1910. Manuscript copy at Historical Society of Delaware.

Lafayette, Le Marquis de. *Lafayette in the Age of the American Revolution: Selected Letters and Papers, 1776–1790.* 5 vols. Edited by Stanley Idzerda, Robert R. Crout, Linda J. Pike, and Mary Ann Quinn. Ithaca, NY: Cornell University Press, 1977.

Lee, Henry. *Memoirs of the War in the Southern Department of the United States.* New York: University Publishing Company, 1869.

Lefkowitz, Arthur. *George Washington's Indispensable Men.* Mechanicsburg, PA: Stackpole Books, 2003.

Linn, John B., and William H. Egle, eds. *Pennsylvania Archives.* 2nd ser. Harrisburg: State Printer of Pennsylvania, 1896.

Linn, John Blair, and William H. Egle, eds. *Pennsylvania in the War of the Revolution, 1775–1783.* Vol. I. Harrisburg, PA: Lane S. Hart, 1880.

A List of the General and Staff Officers . . . Serving in North America. New York and Philadelphia: MacDonald & Cameron, 1777–78.

Livingston, William. *The Papers of William Livingston.* Vol. 1, *June 1774–June 1777.* Edited by Prince, Carl E., Dennis P. Ryan, and Pamela B. Schafler. Trenton: New Jersey Historical Commission, 1979.

Lushington, Stephen R. *The Life and Services of General Lord Harris, GCB, during His Campaigns in America, the West Indies, and India.* 2nd ed. London: John W. Parker, 1845.

Marshall, Christopher. *Extracts from the Diary of Christopher Marshall . . . 1774–1781.* Edited by William Duane. Albany, NY: Joel Munsell, 1877.

Marshall, John. *The Life of George Washington.* Vol. 2. New York: Wm. Wise, 1925.

Martin, Joseph Plumb. *Private Yankee Doodle.* Edited by George F. Scheer. Boston: Little, Brown and Co., 1962.

Mason, A. Hughlette. *The Journal of Charles Mason and Jeremiah Dixon.* Philadelphia: American Philosophical Society, 1969.

McPhee, John. *The Pine Barrens.* New York: Farrar, Straus, Giroux, 1981.

McGuire, Thomas J. *Battle of Paoli.* Mechanicsburg, PA: Stackpole Books, 2000.

Miller, Lillian B., Sidney Hart, and Toby A. Appel, eds. *The Selected Papers of Charles Willson Peale and His Family.* Vol. 1, *Charles Willson Peale: Artist in Revolutionary America, 1735–1791.* New Haven, CT: Yale University Press, 1983.

Montgomery, Charles F., and Patricia Kane. *America Art: 1750–1800, Towards Independence.* New Haven, CT: Yale University Art Gallery, 1976.

Montrésor, John. *The Montrésor Journals.* Edited by G. D. Scull. Collections of the New York Historical Society, vol. 14. New York, 1882.

Morgan, William James, ed. *Naval Documents of the American Revolution.* Vol. 9. Washington, DC: Naval History Division, Department of the Navy, 1980.

Morrison, Alfred J. *Travels in the Confederation 1783–1784.* Philadelphia: William J. Campbell, 1911.

Muhlenberg, Henry Melchior. *The Journals of Henry Melchior Muhlenberg.* Vol. 3, *1777–1787.* Translated and edited by Theodore G. Tappert and John W. Doberstein. Philadelphia: Muhlenberg Press, 1958.

The Musical Miscellany: A Selection of Scots, English, and Irish Songs, set to Music. Perth, Scotland: J. Brown, 1786.

Peterson, Harold L. *The Book of the Continental Soldier.* Harrisburg, PA: Stackpole Books, 1968.

Pickering, Octavius, and Charles W. Upham. *The Life of Timothy Pickering.* 4 vols. Boston: Little, Brown and Company, 1867–73.

Pierce, Arthur D. *Smugglers' Woods.* New Brunswick, NJ: Rutgers University Press, 1960.

Prechtel, Johann Ernst. *A Hessian Officer's Diary of the American Revolution by Johann Ernst Prechtel.* Translated and edited by Bruce E. Burgoyne. Bowie, MD: Heritage Books, 1994. Prechtel was a first sergeant and later a lieutenant in the Anspach Regiment of Anspach-Bayreuth.

Rankin, Hugh F. "An Officer out of His Time: Correspondence of Major Patrick Ferguson, 1779–1780." *Sources of American Independence: Selected Manuscripts from the Collections of the William L. Clements Library.* Edited by Howard Peckham. Vol. 2. Chicago: University of Chicago Press.

Reed, William B. *Life and Correspondence of Joseph Reed.* Vol. I. Philadelphia: Lindsay and Blakiston, 1847.

Remembrancer for 1777. London: J. Almon, 1778.

Robertson, Archibald. *Archibald Robertson, Lieutenant-General Royal Engineers: His Diaries and Sketches in America, 1762–1780.* New York: New York Public Library, 1930.

Robson, Eric, ed. *Letters from America 1773 to 1780: Being the Letters of a Scots Officer, Sir James Murray, to His Home during the War of American Independence.* Manchester, UK: Manchester University Press, 1951.

Rodney, Caesar. *Letters to and from Caesar Rodney, 1756–1784.* Edited by George Herbert Ryden. Philadelphia: University of Pennsylvania Press for the Historical Society of Delaware, 1933.

Ryan, Dennis P., ed. *A Salute to Courage: The American Revolution as Seen through Wartime Writings of Officers of the Continental Army and Navy.* New York: Columbia University Press, 1979.

Saffron, Morris H. *Surgeon to Washington: Dr. John Cochran, 1730–1807.* New York: Columbia University Press, 1977.

Scharf, J. Thomas. *The Chronicles of Baltimore, etc.* Baltimore: Turnbull Brothers, 1874.

Serle, Ambrose. *The American Journal of Ambrose Serle, Secretary to Lord Howe, 1776–1778.* Edited by Edward H. Tatum Jr. San Marino, CA: Huntington Library, 1940. Reprint. New York: Arno Press, 1969.

Simcoe, John Graves. *A Journal of the Operations of the Queen's Rangers . . .* New York: Bartlett & Welford, 1844.

Smith, Paul H., Gerald W. Gawalt, and Ronald M. Gephart, eds. *Letters of Delegates to Congress, 1774–1789.* Vol. 8. Washington, DC: Library of Congress, 1981.

Stephen, Leslie, and Sidney Lee. *The Dictionary of National Biography.* Vol. 7. Oxford, UK: Oxford University Press, 1922.

Stevenson, Roger. *Military Instructions for Officers Detached in the Field: Containing a Scheme for Forming a Corps of Partisans, Illustrated with Plans of the Manoeuvres Necessary in Carrying out the Petite Guerre.* Philadelphia: R. Aitkin, 1775.

Stillé, Charles J. *Major-General Anthony Wayne and the Pennsylvania Line in the Continental Army.* Philadelphia: J. B. Lippincott, 1893.

Stryker, William S., ed. *New Jersey Archives.* 2nd ser., vol. I, *Extracts from American Newspapers, 1776–1777.* Trenton, NJ: John L. Murphy Publishing Co., 1901.

Stuart, Charles. *A Prime Minister and His Son: From the Correspondence of the Third Earl of Bute and Lt. General The Honourable Sir Charles Stuart, KB.* Edited by Mrs. E. Stuart Wortley. London: John Murray, 1925.

———. *New Records of the American Revolution: Letters of Charles Stuart.* Privately printed: n.d.

Syrett, Harold G., and Jacob E. Cooke, eds. *The Papers of Alexander Hamilton.* Vol. I. New York: Columbia University Press, 1961.

Troiani, Don, Earl J. Coates, and James L. Kochan. *Don Troiani's Soldiers in America.* Mechanicsburg, PA: Stackpole Books, 1998.

Trussell, John B. B. *The Pennsylvania Line: Regimental Organization and Operations, 1775–1783.* Harrisburg: Pennsylvania Historical and Museum Commission, 1977.

von Münchhausen, Friedrich. *At General Howe's Side: The Diary of General William Howe's Aide de Camp, Captain Friedrich von Münchhausen.* Translated and edited by Ernst Kipping and Samuel Stelle Smith. Monmouth Beach, NJ: Philip Freneau Press, 1974.

Watson, Winslow C. *Men and Times of the Revolution: or, Memoirs of Elkannah Watson.* New York: Dana and Company, 1856.

Weedon, George. *Valley Forge Orderly Book of General George Weedon . . . 1777–8.* Edited by Samuel Pennypacker. New York: Dodd, Mead and Company, 1902. Manuscript in the American Philosophical Society.

West, Benjamin. *The New-England Almanack, or Lady's and Gentleman's Diary, for the Year of Our Lord Christ 1777.* Providence, RI: Printed and sold by John Carter.

Wheatley, Henry B. *The Historical and the Posthumous Memoirs of Sir Nathaniel William Wraxall, 1772–1784.* Londonn: Bickers and Son, 1884.

Wilkin, Walter Harold. *Some British Soldiers in America.* London: Hugh Rees, 1914.

Wister, Sarah. *Sally Wister's Journal: A True Narrative . . . 1777–1778.* Edited by Albert Myers Cook. Philadelphia: Ferris & Leach, 1902.

JOURNAL ARTICLES

Angew, Daniel. "A Biographical Sketch of Governor Richard Howell of New Jersey." *Pennsylvania Magazine of History and Biography* 22 (1898): 224.

Bruce-Briggs, B. "'The Grenadiers March' in Colonial Massachusetts." *Notes and Documents of Journal of the Society for Army Historical Research* 81, no. 57 (2003): 282.

"Excitement in Philadelphia on Hearing of the Defeat at Brandywine." *Pennsylvania Magazine of History and Biography* 14 (1890): 66.

"Extracts from the Journal of Surgeon Ebenezer Elmer of the New Jersey Continental Line, September 11–19, 1777." *Pennsylvania Magazine of History and Biography* 35 (1911): 104.

Fisher, Sarah Logan. "A Diary of Trifling Occurrences: Philadelphia, 1776–1778." Edited by Nicholas Biddle Wainwright. *Pennsylvania Magazine of History and Biography* 82 (1958): 411–65.

Flickinger, B. Floyd. "The Diary of Lieutenant William Heth while a Prisoner in Quebec," *Annual Papers of Winchester Virginia Historical Society* 1 (1931): 33.

Hale, Capt. William. "Letters Written during the American War of Independence." *Regimental Annual* [1st Nottinghamshire Regiment (Sherwood Foresters), United Kingdom] (1913). Hale was a member of the Grenadier Company, 45th Regiment of Foot.

Hay, Denys. "The Denouement of General Howe's campaign of 1777." *English Historical Review* vol. 74 (1964): 503.

Heyl, John K. "Trout Hall and Its Owner James Allen: Excerpts from Diary of James Allen." *Proceedings of the Lehigh County Historical Society* 24. Allentown, PA: Lehigh County Historical Society, 1962.

Huth, Hans. "Letters from a Hessian Mercenary (Colonel von Donop to the Prince of Prussia)." *Pennsylvania Magazine of History and Biography* 62 (1938): 497.

Inman, George. "George Inman's Narrative of the American Revolution." *Pennsylvania Magazine of History and Biography* 7 (1883): 237–48.

"Journal of Sgt. Maj. John Hawkins." *Pennsylvania Magazine of History and Biography* 20 (1896): 420.

Journal of the Johannes Schwalm Historical Association. [Schwalm].

"List of Officers Killed Since the Commencement of the War &c: Compiled by Capt. George Inman, 1784: George Inman's Narrative of the American Revolution." *Pennsylvania Magazine of History and Biography* 7 (1883): 237–248.

"London, December 18: Extracts of a letter from an Officer at Philadelphia to his friend at Edinburgh, dated Oct. 27." *Felix Farley's Bristol Journal* 26, no. 1400 (1777).

"Lord North's Correspondence," *English Historical Review* 62 (1947): 235.

Magee's Weekly Packet. Dublin, Saturday, August 6, 1777, no. 8.

"Memorial of Capt. Charles Cochrane." *Proceedings of the Massachusetts Historical Society* 6, 2d. ser. (1891): 434–35.

McMichael, James. "Diary of Lieutenant James McMichael, of the Pennsylvania Line, 1776–1778." *Pennsylvania Magazine of History and Biography* 16 (1892): 137–39.

Mordecai, Jacob. "Addenda to Watson's Annals." *Pennsylvania Magazine of History and Biography* 98 (1974).

Morton, Robert. "The Diary of Robert Morton. . . ." *Pennsylvania Magazine of History and Biography* I (1877): 1–39.

"Mr. Joseph Galloway on the American War." *Scots Magazine* 41 (1779): 526.

"Parliament: Commons on Gen. Howe's Conduct." *Scots Magazine* 41 (1779): 644.

Proceedings of the Historical Society of Pennsylvania I, no. 8 (1846).

"Revolutionary Pension Records of Morris Co. NJ." *Preceedings of the New Jersey Historical Society* n. s., vol I (1916).

Smith, Samuel. "The Papers of General Samuel Smith." *Historical Magazine* 7, 2nd. ser., no. 2 (1870): 85.

Stirke, Henry. "A British Officer's Revolutionary War Journal, 1776–1778." Edited by S. Sydney Bradford. *Maryland Historical Magazine* 56, no. 2 (June 1961): 150–75. Lt. Henry Stirke belonged to the Light Infantry Company, 10th Regiment of Foot.

Summers, William. "Obituary Notices of Pennsylvania Soldiers of the Revolution." *Pennsylvania Magazine of History and Biography* 38 (1914): 443.

Wilson, James Grant. "A Memorial of Colonel John Bayard." *Proceedings of the New Jersey Historical Society* 2nd. ser., vol. 5. (1877–79): 150.

WEBSITES

George Washington Papers online at the Library of Congress, http://memory.loc.gov/ammem/gwhtml/.

Ho, Eugene Y. C. "Edward Gibbon, Historian of the Roman Empire." www.his.com/~z/gibho1.html.

Journal of Jarvis. On-Line Institute for Advanced Loyalist Studies. www.royalprovincial.com.

"Sandy Hook Lighthouse." www.njlhs.burlco.org/sandyhk.htm.

Thomas Jefferson Papers online at the Library of Congress, http://loc.gov

Woodward, Abraham. Woodward and Allied-Families-Revolutionary War. http://www.geocities.com/nadineholder/RevWar.html.

INDEX